THE INVENTION OF
GOOD AND EVIL

THE INVENTION OF GOOD AND EVIL

A World History of Morality

HANNO SAUER

Translated by Jo Heinrich

OXFORD
UNIVERSITY PRESS

OXFORD
UNIVERSITY PRESS

Oxford University Press is a department of the University of Oxford. It furthers
the University's objective of excellence in research, scholarship, and education by
publishing worldwide. Oxford is a registered trade mark of Oxford University
Press in the UK and certain other countries.

Published in the United States of America by Oxford University Press
198 Madison Avenue, New York, NY 10016, United States of America.

First published in the United Kingdom by
Profile Books Ltd., London 2024

ISBN 978–0–19–779025–0 (hbk.)

Printed by Sheridan Books, Inc., United States of America

Res nolunt diu male administrari

Contents

Introduction

Let me tell you a story. Will we, once it is done, still feel the same way about ourselves?

It's a long story, and it's about everything that has ever been important to us: our values, our principles, the roots of our identity, the foundations of our coexistence. It's about working with each other and against each other; it's about being on the side judging or the side being judged; and it's about which of these two sides we'll find ourselves on tomorrow.

The story I want to tell is a history of morality. What gives us our bearings? How do we want to live? How can we get along with each other? How did we manage in the past, and how will it be possible in the future? These are all moral questions. Morality can make us think of any number of things: restraint and coercion; restriction and sacrifice; inquisition, confession and guilty conscience; chastity and catechism. For many, it is a concept that feels joyless, claustrophobic, an admonishing finger to shame us into compliance.

And this impression is not necessarily incorrect. But it is most certainly incomplete, just one part of the picture that needs to be filled in. This story will trace humanity's fundamental moral transformations, from our earliest, not-yet-human ancestors in East Africa to the conflicts over identity, inequality and oppression that are all being played out online from today's global metropolises. It explains how our human society has changed through the ages, how new institutions, technologies, knowledge and economic forms have developed in parallel with

I

our values and norms, and delves into the fact that each of these changes has more than one side: anyone who lives in a community excludes others; anyone who understands rules wants to monitor them; anyone who trusts becomes dependent; anyone who generates wealth creates inequality and exploitation.

Every change or welcome development has a hard, dark, cold side and every advancement comes at a cost. Our early evolution millennia ago made us cooperative, but it also made us hostile to anyone who did not belong to our group – once we learned how to say 'us', we also needed to be able to say 'them'. The development of punishment was a form of self-domestication and made us friendly and peaceable, but it also gave us powerful punitive instincts that we would use to monitor compliance with our rules. Culture and learning gave us new knowledge and new skills that we learned from others – and consequently made us dependent on those others. The emergence of inequality and domination brought unprecedented wealth, but, alongside that, hierarchy and oppression surfaced. Modernity set individuals free to bring nature under control with science and technology; in the process, we explained away all the magic and disenchanted our world, as Max Weber put it, and uprooted ourselves from tradition and community, and created the conditions for colonialism and slavery. The twentieth century's aim was to create a peaceful society with the help of global institutions, a society where everyone would enjoy the same moral status, but it brought us some of the most breath-taking crimes in human history and has manoeuvred us to the brink of ecological collapse. Recently we have been trying to finally cast off racism, sexism, homophobia and exclusion. There will be unforeseen aftereffects of this progress too, but it will be worth it.

Our morality is a palimpsest: a parchment that's been written over time after time, often illegible and difficult to decipher. But what is morality? How can we define it? It may be better not to: as Nietzsche wrote, 'It is only that which has no history which can be defined.'[1] However, our morality does have a history, and it is too complex and unwieldy for the sterile formulas we come up with in our armchairs. But the fact that we have difficulty defining what morality is does not mean it's impossible to say what it is with any clarity. It's just that it can't be said *concisely*.

A history of morality is not a history of moral *philosophy*. We have been thinking about our values for a long time, but it's only in recent times that we have been writing down our thoughts. The Code of Hammurabi and the Ten Commandments, the Sermon on the Mount, Kant's categorical imperative and Rawls's veil of ignorance all play a part in this story, but only a comparatively minor one. This is the much bigger history of our values, norms, institutions and practices. Our morality is not in our heads, but in our cities and walls, laws and customs, in our rituals and wars.

As well as helping us understand the past, this long history of morality will also, I hope, contribute to our understanding of the present. Modern societies are currently under moral pressure to reconcile the prospect of their own existence with the most unpleasant truths of their origins. How can we map out the ongoing changes to our moral infrastructure in a way that makes 'light dawn gradually over the whole'?[2] Where did the dynamic of polarisation we are now witnessing come from? What is the relationship between cultural identity and social inequality? To understand the present, we have to turn to the past.

Over the course of this book, we will go on a journey together to chart the evolution of our morality. It made us capable of cooperation, but confined our moral dispositions to those we consider to be from within 'our' group (Chapter 1: 5,000,000 Years). The need for cooperation grew as a result of external environmental changes, which required individuals living together in larger and larger groups. On the one hand, developing and using punishment gave us the self-control and social tolerance essential for this, but on the other hand, it endowed us with a punitive psychology that would be used with the utmost vigilance to monitor compliance with our group's norms (Chapter 2: 500,000 Years). The dual inheritance of genes and culture turned us into beings who would depend on learning from others to be able to best absorb the accumulated cultural capital of information and skills from previous generations. At the same time, it became essential to be able to decide from whom we would like to learn – in other words, whom to trust and believe – and it would be shared values that would bring about this trust (Chapter 3: 50,000 Years).

This species of cooperative, punitive and socially learning beings ultimately managed to build ever larger societies – which threatened to collapse under the pressure of their own headcounts. Strictly hierarchical forms of organisation began to replace our original egalitarianism, in order to contend with this pressure, as a result of which human societies split into groups: socio-economic elites and a majority of politically and materially disadvantaged people. Social inequality grew, as did, conversely, our aversion to it (Chapter 4: 5,000 Years).

It was only a matter of time before the historical evolution of morality produced a cultural situation that replaced kinship and hierarchy with cooperative relationships which were voluntarily entered into between individuals, as structural principles of society. This new stage of social evolution unleashed unprecedented forces of economic growth, scientific progress and political emancipation, which resulted in the modern society in which we live today (Chapter 5: 500 Years). At the same time, tensions have mounted between our psychological aversions to social inequality and the economic advantages made possible by a social structure based on individual liberties. With increasing material abundance, the demand to finally realise the promise of human equality grew more vocal: the socio-political status of disadvantaged minorities became a moral priority (Chapter 6: 50 Years). The fact that this problem could not be solved as quickly as we had hoped characterises our current situation, with the main elements of the history of our morality combining into a toxic mixture: our morally charged group psychology makes us receptive to social division.

The difficulties in overcoming the remaining social inequalities have led to suspicion of anyone who isn't fighting for the same cause with the vehemence we perceive as necessary. This reinforces the division of society into 'us' and 'them', which in turn increases our susceptibility to disinformation as we become increasingly dependent on signals of moral belonging when we make decisions about who to believe. Our punitive psychology is now beginning to scrutinise the symbolic markers of our group membership more and more closely and to penalise any non-compliance with the norms in question more and more excessively. The identity conflicts of the present day – both left- and right-wing – are the result of this dynamic (Chapter 7: 5 Years). Today, our political disagreements may feel like the end of the world, but where will the evolution of morality take us next? It doesn't have to end like this: after all, we all share the same history of morality; our political disagreements are often shallow; underneath them are deep-seated, universal moral values that all people share with each other, and that can be the basis for a new understanding (Conclusion).

This story is a long one which starts aeons ago and ends in the future. Its tempo will increase and intensify. Millions of years pass from the first chapter to the second, while the last three span only a few hundred between them. The chronological arrangement I've chosen shouldn't be taken too literally; after all, many of the developments overlap or aren't clearly attributable to specific times. The sections of time that organise the narrative should be interpreted just as ballpark figures that are intended to bring out the main points and provide an overview.

Other divisions might have been possible, and may even have been more useful. We could tell the story of our morality as the story of growing human societies: from small family alliances with maybe five members to the first clans and tribes of 50 or 500, early cities with 5,000 or 50,000 inhabitants to our modern large societies with 5 billion people or more. The history of morality is also a history of various forms of human evolution. It begins with the mechanisms of biological evolution, with our morality contributing to the kind of creatures we became, and how we are designed as a natural species; it traces the forms of cultural evolution we used to create our own world; and it traces the outline of social and political evolution that shaped our current moment in human history.

Or I could have told a history of the fundamental elements of our moral infrastructure, in which our ability to cooperate, our propensity for punishment, trust in and dependence on others, equality and hierarchy, individuality and autonomy, vulnerability, belonging and identity combine to form our particular human way of life. The segmentation I've chosen here is a map, and a map is intended to provide orientation, not to depict reality. The most accurate map isn't always the most useful.

Each chapter builds on the previous one and continues the inner logic of the narrative. Yet each section is written so it also stands on its own and can be read separately from the others. If you're interested in humankind's biological evolution and how our morality shaped us as a species, you can focus on the first chapters. If you want to learn about humanity's early cultural history and about how the moral infrastructure of the first civilisations shaped this culture, you'll benefit most from the middle chapters. The last chapters are aimed primarily at anyone who wants to have a better understanding of the current moral zeitgeist. And anyone who – like me – believes that the best understanding of the present can be obtained from an understanding of the past should read the book in its entirety.

It is, in many ways, a pessimistic story of progress. Pessimistic because *within* every generation there is too much evil. But it *is* a story of progress because there seem to be mechanisms *between* the generations that have the potential gradually to improve human morality, and because this potential is sometimes drawn upon. Moral progress is always possible and often tangible. But it doesn't happen as a matter of course: every achievement has to be defended from the regressive forces of a stubborn human nature, the irrationalities of the human psyche and the mercilessness of fate.

The idea that we can only understand our morality, with its puzzles and contradictions, if we understand its origin isn't new. Friedrich Nietzsche first referred to this project as 'genealogy', in the style of ancestral research. We can use this approach to ask about the origins of morality. To get there, we must go much further back than Nietzsche himself thought necessary, not just focusing on the shift from the worldly, aristocratic and heroic ethics of antiquity to the Christian early Middle Ages, when the values of compassion and humility, sin, renunciation and the afterlife began to be emphasised. Instead, we need to look at the much more fundamental problem of how our human sense of morality came into being in the first place. Only then can we understand how our values and the social structures that embody these values have been able to change over time.

The history of morality that I have to offer is not a history in the traditional sense, referring to concrete events and developments that may or may not be well documented. It is, instead, a 'deep history' that doesn't use dates or names, sketching out instead a feasible scenario that could have gone along these lines. It will never be possible to fully decipher the precise course of events: deep is the well of the past (and maybe even bottomless). We have to rely on the best possible triangulation of various different disciplines. Genetics, palaeontology, psychology and cognitive sciences, primatology and anthropology, philosophy and evolutionary theory each provide their own perspectives that combine to form a picture.

Will this story bring to light the *pudenda origo* of our values, as Nietzsche believed – their shameful origin? Will we still feel the same way about ourselves when it's over? In the cold light of day, will the uncomfortable truth shatter our confidence in our values? Will it show that our morality can stand up to closer scrutiny? Or will it all end in devastation and hatred and shame?

We have no way of knowing what the future holds, how we will all live together, and how we'd like to. And we don't have to know. Our moral values are like headlights: they don't help us see very far, but if we rely on them, we can go on a long journey. This is the story of that journey.

And it starts like this:

1

Genealogy 2.0

Descent

The trees vanished with the drought, and as cracks emerged, the land formed deep valleys and rugged canyons, giant dark lakes and bogs, tall mountains and low hills. Thorny bushes, shrubs and fine grasses soon appeared in place of the ample forests that had once offered protection among the vines, giant ferns laden with dew and lush succulents, where aromatic mushrooms with caps like bright flowers grew between the roots peeking out of the ground.

After we had left the trees and the trees had left us, only open plains awaited. In this new, boundless world, stones and fire rained from the sky, and there was little to eat. But there were large animals with fierce jaws that were faster than us, and just as hungry.

A shopping trolley half full of fossilised bones[1] is all that remains of our earliest ancestors, or at any rate, all that has ever been found. A few teeth, skull fragments, remnants of eyebrow ridges, sections of lower and upper jaws, splinters from a few thigh bones remain to tell the story of these forebears.

The terminology in this specialised area is confusing. Today researchers distinguish between various *taxa* (from the Ancient Greek *taxis*, 'arrangement'), depending on which branch of the zoological family tree they might be looking at and which differences and evolutionary offshoots they choose to emphasise: the *Hominidae* family includes all anthropoid apes, meaning not only the various species of the *Homo* genus, but also gorillas, orang-utans and panins, whose most recent representatives are chimpanzees and bonobos. The term *Homininae*, on the other hand, does not include the *Ponginae* of Asia (orang-utans) but is reserved for African great apes, which covers, alongside humans, only panins and gorillas. Lastly, the term *Hominini* encompasses all humans in a narrower – though not yet the narrowest – sense. This tribe encompasses the earliest human-like (although admittedly not yet very recognisably human) animals that began to populate parts of southern and eastern Africa about 5 million years ago, a series of australopithecines grouped under various more familiar categories such as *Homo ergaster*, *Homo erectus*, *Homo heidelbergensis* and *Homo neanderthalensis*. Of these *Hominini*, only we, *Homo sapiens*, remain today.

Cooperation

The evolutionary history of the first *Hominini* is the history of our earliest protohuman forebears after splitting off from the ancestor we share with the other anthropoid apes that are still around today. This critical first phase of our evolution can be narrowed down to a time about 5 million years ago.[2]

The surviving fossils – with the exception of *Sahelanthropus tchadensis*, the oldest, whose asymmetrically shaped skull was discovered at the Toros-Menalla excavation site in the arid Djurab Desert in northern Chad – are found mainly in eastern Africa, in present-day Ethiopia, Kenya and Tanzania. Thigh fragments and a thumb bone of *Orrorin tugenensis* were found in the Lukeino Formation in the verdant Tugen hills; the back molars of *Ardipithecus ramidus* and the lower jaw of *Australopithecus afarensis* (the species to which 'Lucy' belongs) on the Awash River in the Afar Triangle. The second main concentration of fossil discoveries from roughly the same time period is in South Africa, where the remains of various human ancestors were found in the caves of Sterkfontein and Gladysvale,

Drimolen and Malapa. It is not unlikely that we owe these discoveries, these evolutionary messages in a bottle, to leopards
and other large predators that lived in caves like these and are
known to have carried their prey back to their dens to eat.

Today, our fossilised remnants are scattered all over the
world in palaeoanthropological research institutes, where they
have been assigned bureaucratic labels, marked down in files,
archived, registered and made distinguishable from each other:
Sahelanthropus tchadensis is known very prosaically as TM 266,
Orrorin tugenensis as BAR 1000'00; other splinters, fragments
and pieces are catalogued as Stw 573, KT-12/H1 or LH4. *Ardipithecus ramidus* is known as 'Ardi' – not very original, but at least
it's a start.[3]

The story of human emergence that these discoveries can
tell us is only tentative. It remains, as philosophers sometimes
say, 'hostage to empirical data', and is at risk of being revised,
corrected or superseded at any moment by new discoveries. And
this is as it should be: only dogmas remain unchanged, and only
in exceptional cases does science have room for ever-lasting
knowledge. Our insight into our most remote past remains
forever speculative, not in the nebulous sense of being unveri-
fiable and far-fetched, but more practically: legions of brilliant
minds, armed with the most sophisticated methods of comparative morphology, molecular genetics, radiocarbon dating,
biochemistry, statistics and geology, attempting to reconstruct
the most plausible version of this story from many heteroge-
neous theories and data sets. This work of reconstruction
remains dependent on which of its secrets the Earth's crust has
decided to reveal to us through random geological chance: we
might often seem like the drunk searching for the keys he's lost
on his way home, who, when asked why he's looking under the
streetlight, replies that the light's better there.

We may have pinpointed the cradle of humanity as being
in East Africa because the geological conditions there revealed
layers of rock that in other places remained buried under dozens

of metres of stone, sand and clay. Added to this, as in all scientific disciplines, is an incentive structure that leads even the most serious researchers to tend to identify their latest finds as belonging to our ancestors and not to what we feel are more mundane species: astonishingly, there are virtually no fossils of chimpanzees or bonobos, although of course, 'no one has been anxious to forgo the chance of being the discoverer of the earliest hominin in favour of being the discoverer of the earliest panin'.[4]

When we talk about our earliest human ancestors, who followed immediately after the evolutionary branching off from the rest of the anthropoid apes, we are talking about animals whose physiognomy and appearance are only very remotely reminiscent of modern humans. Barely over a metre tall, with extra-long arms characteristic of primates, protruding snouts, dilated nostrils and their entire bodies covered with thick brown-black fur, these protohumans resembled today's apes more than they did us. The first signs of culture and intelligent problem solving are not visible until much later: the primitive stone tools that made the Olduvai Gorge in Tanzania famous are at most 2.5 million years old.

It was warm at that point, but not too warm, as our habitat was often at altitudes above 1,000 metres. In these open, loosely wooded grasslands, we spent our days in small groups searching the ground for roots and tubers, bitter shoots and gnarled rhizomes, nuts and termites, and if we were lucky, we found the remains of animals left behind by hyenas or lions – far more talented hunters than we were at that time. Dried remains of meat from their carcasses provided us with protein, as did the marrow from their bones and their brains, which we scooped out of their smashed skulls with nimble fingers.

Two million years ago, the Pleistocene began: one of the crucial geological eras for human evolution. The Earth was populated by bizarre megafauna – mammoths, woolly rhinoceroses, sabre-toothed tigers and giant armadillos roamed the land. They are now all extinct, partly because of us. We lived in a harsh, dangerous world. The open, savannah-like expanses that had formed along the African Great Rift Valley and reshaped the eastern part of the continent made us vulnerable to predators: in this exposed landscape we could no longer protect ourselves by fleeing quickly into the treetops. The mountain ranges that had begun to form in the west cut these plains off from the wind and rain that would otherwise have come in from the Atlantic Ocean and provided water for the Earth.[5]

The Laetoli footprints, preserved and handed down to us almost 4 million years ago by ash from the Sadiman volcano in northern Tanzania, commemorate a family – two adults and a child. They are the oldest tangible evidence of human life walking upright. The new living conditions away from dense forests contributed to this two-legged way of life. Although we remained competent climbers for a long time to come, we were increasingly dependent on the ability to cover longer distances on foot. On these flat, wide plains, it was worthwhile to develop a faster gait and to take in an overview of our surroundings.

Time-budgeting models formulated only very recently give us an insight into the social life of this group of early hominins.[6] In order to survive in our environment, we primates (and other living creatures) ultimately had to do three things: obtain food, pause to rest and maintain social cohesion. Once we have a rough idea of what the archaic environment was like at a given time and we can roughly estimate how many hours of daylight were available to a given species, we can start to gauge the maximum size of the groups, whose cohesion was maintained by what is known as grooming – the reciprocal hair- and skincare that is the key mechanism for establishing social solidarity among primates. If they had to spend this many hours searching for food and that many hours resting, they had a maximum of x hours left to attend to the cohesion of the group. This window of time wasn't enough to maintain groups of over twenty members.

But why was social life so important to our ancestors? Why did our ability to cooperate take on such an important role?

Humanity's first fundamental moral transformation was the discovery of morality in the first place. Most animal species have behavioural norms that enable and facilitate a group's cohesion. Schools of fish, whose movements seem to follow a ghostly, unheard rhythm, cooperate through conformity; social insects such as bees or ants have perfected a division of labour that often demands complete self-sacrifice from the individual for the good of the hive or colony. The special form of cooperation that has shaped human morality consists of putting aside the interests of the individual in favour of a greater common good from which everyone can benefit.

The emergence of human cooperation was the first crucial moral transformation of our species. Why cooperation? The evolution of our unique ability to cooperate can be traced back to climatic and geographical changes that resulted in tropical forests giving way to more open, savannah-like spaces. This also explains why our way of life is so dramatically different from that of chimpanzees and bonobos. Our closest relatives, who were spared climatic upheavals like these, continued to live in densely forested areas around the Congo River in Central Africa, and as a result were exposed to completely different selection pressures. The destabilisation of our environment, and the fact that we were far more drastically exposed to being preyed upon by dangerous predators, increased the pressure to compensate for this new vulnerability with better means of mutual defence. We found support and strength in larger groups with closer cooperation. We humans are what becomes of the most intelligent apes if they're forced to live in large swathes of open grassland for 5 million years.[7]

Adaptation

Evolutionary psychology seeks to find out something about the present from our evolutionary history. It has a bad reputation: to many, it appears to be a clumsily disguised pseudo-scientific attempt to legitimise reactionary prejudices. This accusation is not entirely unfounded, and the study of gender differences, in particular, tempts some theorists to come up with often out-rageous 'just-so stories'. These practically impossible to verify but seemingly plausible versions of our evolutionary prehistory supposedly explain why women like buying shoes and men like watching football: as the gatherer of fruits and berries, the archetypal woman has always been keen to go in search of small, colourful objects to bring home. Conversely, men, who have always been engaged in hunting, naturally have an endless fas-cination for physical competition, having a target, fighting and defeating their opponent. The theory goes that it still follows today for the man to bring the prey home to feed his family, and for the woman in return to ensure she always looks pretty.

Accusing evolutionary psychology of chauvinism is there-fore not entirely unjustified. Nonetheless, the fact that half a discipline is sexist bullshit doesn't necessarily mean the other half is just as untrustworthy. It is undeniable that evolution has shaped our psyches, just as it shaped our bodies. It would be astounding – maybe even disturbing and enigmatic – if natural selection had left its mark only from our necks down. Evolutionary psychology seeks to use evolutionary theory in its approach to psychology. Its aim is to find out whether and to what extent our evolutionary journey has influenced the way we think, feel, perceive and act, to be able to learn from our past for our present.

A significant part of this is understanding the environmen-tal conditions in which this evolution has taken place. It's no coincidence that we fear snakes and spiders, build parks resem-bling savannah landscapes in our cities, appreciate a campfire, spend hours gossiping about other people, have the ability to throw something at a target or run long distances, or become frightened by sudden loud noises. Our visual perception is sensitised to only one part of the electromagnetic spectrum – namely the part that is biologically advantageous to be able to see (we call it 'light'). The assumption is that other traits of our psychology are similar. Our minds still work in line with patterns that were once a competitive advantage for our ancestors. A trait that offers an advantage like this as a result of adaptation is called 'adaptive'. Not all our abilities are necessarily of evolutionary origin, but functionally complex characteristics are very likely to be adaptive – or at least once were adaptive.

One of the most interesting consequences of evolutionary psychology is that it can explain many modern-day malfunctions in our thinking and behaviour. Probably the best-known example of this mismatch between mind and environment is our almost unlimited appetite for sugar. Carbohydrates are an important source of energy for the human body, and in the past energy was usually one thing: scarce. So it made sense for us to have inherited an evolutionary disposition that ensured we would never miss an opportunity to consume sugar. For as long as carbohydrates are scarce, this disposition remains adaptive, as our desire for sugar effectively motivates us to absorb a significant source of energy. But the moment we leave our environment of evolutionary adaptation and have permanent access to unlimited supplies of sugar through supermarkets and petrol stations, our desire becomes a problem: from that moment on, the evolutionary imperative to consume as much energy as possible in preparation for leaner times needs to be consciously reined in.

Unfortunately, modern societies represent an increasingly hostile environment for our psychology, which is endowed with a whole arsenal of atavistic tendencies, and we constantly have to make great efforts to suppress our primeval instincts, patterns of thought and behaviour. This increases the need for self-control and gradually leads to a diffuse 'discontent'[8] in civilisation, because it eliminates our material hardship whilst making greater demands on our cognitive discipline. This perpetuates a paradoxical perception: developed human societies' material prosperity seems to be a promise of happiness that is frustratingly slowly – and never fully – fulfilled, because we pay for every increase in social complexity with an increase in cognitive overload.

For a history of morality, what matters is which attributes of our evolutionary past have shaped the nature and extent of our willingness to cooperate. We know that we have an unusually spontaneous and surprisingly flexible capacity for cooperation. But why?

The crucial phase of our specifically human evolution – the evolutionary prehistory that we do not have in common with amoebae, amphibians or other mammals – took place in a highly volatile environment. That's not to say that the weather at that time was particularly unpredictable, but that our ancestors' populations had to deal with rapid and drastic climate changes over generations: upheavals that would ordinarily have been slower or less extreme, or both. An unstable natural environment puts a premium on increased flexibility and adaptability in terms of food, mobility and settlement. These qualities meant our ancestors could explore new habitats without first having to undergo anatomical changes. Early technological breakthroughs ensured we could cope better with nature's demands and survive new niche conditions. An increasingly volatile environment also meant it made sense to share risks. The knowledge that three out of twenty huts fall victim to storms every year, but not knowing whose hut might be hit this year, made it worthwhile for social structures to have in-built security systems that would provisionally protect a group's members from the vagaries of fate.

The presence of larger mammal species made hunting in groups adaptive, too. Many animals hunt together, but the level of precision and coordination displayed by humanity is unrivalled. At some point, our ancestors became increasingly dependent on being able to get a steady supply of meat from large animals. This made it worthwhile in terms of evolution to develop collective intentions – known as 'we-intentions'[9] – to learn the complex art of hunting and ultimately to carry it out in groups with others. Sophisticated institutions that regulated hunting, as well as the sharing of spoils, began to develop at the same time.

As a result, the cooperative beings that we had become could reap the fruits of the teamwork provided by our natural or social environment. This resulted in economies of scale: the benefits of cooperation actually increased with growing co-operative networks. This phenomenon, which economists call 'increasing returns to scale', means that our achievements do not always develop in a linear way, but can sometimes suddenly explode. If you can only hunt an elephant or a zebra in groups of at least six, choosing between hunting in groups of five and hunting in groups of six doesn't just mean choosing between five and six rabbits, but between five rabbits and one elephant.

The 'stag hunt' is a theoretical model that can be used to demonstrate this form of cooperation. In this assurance game, there are two players (A and B) and two options (stag or hare hunting). The stag can only be killed by the players together; anyone can catch a hare by themselves. It is vital that the players *coordinate* what they do. If A hunts stags and B hunts hares, A goes home hungry and B with a missed opportunity. Only when both decide to hunt stags is the optimum result achieved.

In our environment of evolutionary adaptation, we lived in small groups. A key concept in evolutionary anthropology is 'Dunbar's number'. The British evolutionary psychologist Robin Dunbar was able to prove that there was a correlation between the size of a primate's neocortex and the upper limit to the number of members in their group, as larger groups with correspondingly more complex social structures place increased demands on our ability to process information.[10] We had to decide who to trust and we had to keep our mental records of their social reputations up to date if we were going to be able to gauge who was a good friend, who was a good teacher and who was both, who was best at hunting, cooking or following tracks, or who offended whom, when and how much.

The growing size of a community is destabilising in the long run, because we naturally lack the institutional tools to make cooperative arrangements permanently resilient. Dunbar even stated that for modern human populations, based on their average cerebral volume, their natural group size can be narrowed down relatively precisely to 150 people. This figure can be found in a wide variety of contexts, ranging from tribal societies to the internal structures of military forms of organisation. To put it bluntly, there are 150 people at most you would happily join for a drink in a bar.[11] What makes human societies special is, of course, that they can integrate far more than 150 people. However, this has only been able to happen recently, and it depends on an institutional framework that cooperatively regulates the formation of larger groups. Communities that emerge spontaneously split up as soon as their numerical load-bearing capacity is overstretched.

The small groups in which our evolutionary ancestors were designed to live were in a state of permanent, or at least latent, conflict. For one thing, under the unpredictable environmental conditions in our evolutionary past, there were often fierce conflicts over scarce natural resources. Whether we can describe man as a 'wolf to man' (or, in other words, man as man's own predator), as Thomas Hobbes did, remains a controversial question, but the fact that human groups were usually extremely hostile to each other can clearly be demonstrated by data from forensic archaeology.[12] In some tribes of nomadic hunter-gatherers, it is even said that the concept of a natural death not violently brought about by the members of a neighbouring tribe was more or less unknown.

It's not surprising that ancient groups converging must

usually have led to violent conflict. In terms of evolution, it makes sense to expect territorial warfare and clashes over resources, as group conflicts are ideally suited to increasing the selection pressure on cooperative mechanisms.[13] The more an individual's survival depends on the group's success, the more altruistic actions for the benefit of the collective begin to pay off. Many people are reluctant to cite warfare as an example of altruistic cooperation, but technically speaking, it is the case: anyone who fights along with others gives a common project precedence over their own interest, and in doing so, they choose the cooperative option.[14] Whether the war is won or lost, that individual's own contribution is virtually always negligible. The fruits of victory are also enjoyed by objectors to the conflict itself. As a result, wars are classic collective action problems. Whether or not the acts of war serve a morally good cause is secondary: cooperation is a key element in human morality, even when we're talking about cooperating for the benefit of evil intentions.

Outbreaks of violence probably occurred both through chance encounters and, above all, through strategic raids between hostile groups. The volatile climate mentioned earlier would only have made these more common, as the frequent upheavals caused by migration made previously isolated groups all the more likely to clash. Ethnographic surveys of recent indigenous populations paint the same picture. Inwardly, our ancestors were family-centric pacifists, but outwardly, they were gangs of murderers and plunderers.

The setting for our evolutionary adaptation is not a specific place we can circle on a map of the world, nor a historical period that can be marked on a timeline. Our evolutionary past is a collective term encompassing the range of natural and social conditions that have applied effective selection pressure on our species' development. If we want to understand our morality, we need to understand the history of this selection.

Biological evolution

To gain a better understanding of the mechanisms of human evolution, we first need to get to grips with how evolution works in general. As late as 1790, Kant considered it 'absurd' and therefore simply impossible 'to hope that another Newton will arise in the future, who shall make comprehensible by us the production of a blade of grass'.[15] Charles Darwin's *On the Origin of Species* would appear just sixty-nine years later, once again proving that what may seem impossible one day can be reality the next.

The impression that the living world might be the result of deliberate intervention is irresistible, at first glance. Our eyes are there to see, the heart to pump. Cheetahs are streamlined and fast *so that* they can hunt well. Birds can fly, *so that* ... and so on. The theory of evolution does away with this impression and exposes it as a teleological illusion. Life is only seemingly purpose-driven; it actually follows the haphazard tide of mutation and selection.

In fact, the semblance of intelligent design is due to a gradual process during which the frequency of variants changed over millions and millions of years under external selection pressure (as a result of epidemics or climate change, for example). Evolution always takes place wherever there is 'descent with modification', as Darwin put it. It is based on a combination of several factors such as variation, differing degrees of reproductive success and inheritance. Random mutations provide variation. Differences in the relative reproductive successes of the resulting variants lead to fresh mixes in the next generation through inheritance. This process is called natural selection.

All this happens 'blindly' – in other words it is 'unplanned' in this context. No one is in charge of the process, which progresses 'algorithmically', as the philosopher Daniel Dennett notes.[16] An algorithm is a decision-making procedure that, when applied correctly and repeatedly, mechanically produces a certain result. Evolution produces adaptation – and, in the long run, the emergence of new species (speciation) – by repeatedly applying variation and selection.

Natural selection is not the only mechanism that determines the composition of a population. As well as random genetic drift, sexual selection also plays a part. Whether or not sexual selection is a variety of natural selection is a controversial question, though. In the process of sexual selection, an organism's reproductive success (or more precisely, the success of its genes) doesn't depend on the laws of nature, but on the opposite sex's capricious tastes.

There are probably few scientific concepts that seem as easy to understand and are yet so often misunderstood. The concept of adaptation may prompt the Lamarckian misconception that environmental influences can lead to phenotypic changes in existing organisms. For example, evolution would mean that a giraffe's neck grows longer from trying to reach the leaves from particularly tall treetops. This is contradicted both by the fact that acquired characteristics (apart from a few epigenetic exceptions) are not hereditary and by the fact that certain characteristics cannot be acquired in the first place. An even more fundamental misunderstanding, though, is assuming that evolution is a process that takes place in individuals. In fact, the concept of evolution should be perceived in terms of population statistics, and it refers to the intergenerational variability in a trait's distribution in a population: how a trait's frequency changes from generation to generation. Giraffes with longer necks have more offspring, so the next generation contains more giraffes with longer necks.

The process of 'survival of the fittest', the evolutionary phrase originally coined not by Darwin in his *Origin of Species* but by the English philosopher and sociologist Herbert Spencer five years after its publication, suggests that there are fitness criteria independent of evolution that the evolutionary process, in turn, detects. In fact, the fittest are simply the ones with the most reproductive success. The concept of fitness is virtually circular and tautological: who will ultimately prevail? The fittest. Who are the fittest? The ones who ultimately prevail. *Who* these fittest are, and whether they are big or small, strong or weak, clever or stupid, is irrelevant to evolution, as long as they survive and produce offspring.

A certain trait being adaptive – which always becomes apparent in hindsight and never before the event – doesn't mean it represents the best possible adaptation. Evolution isn't optimisation. Many people wonder, for example, why we humans still develop cancer. Shouldn't this 'emperor of all maladies'[17] have been long defeated? Shouldn't evolution have made us immune? Unfortunately, evolution is indifferent to us individuals and our suffering. The only thing it's concerned with is how a trait affects the reproductive success of our genes. Most people have passed on their genes long before they develop cancer. The fact that it would be *better* not to get cancer in the first place means nothing to evolution: it's only interested in us being *just good enough*. What counts in evolutionary competition is being *comparatively more assertive* than the competition. Optimal quality is irrelevant. In fact, optimisation strategies are even maladaptive, as selective pressure rewards the most efficient use of resources. Perfectionists are always the first to go.

Not every trait is due to a process of adaptation. As well as adaptations, there are also exaptations, where the functional profile of a trait that originally ensured its selection later acquires a different purpose, or even better, a different function. The canonical example of this is the feather, whose original function was controlling the organism's body temperature, and which was only later reinterpreted through evolution as an instrument of flight. Also, changes in the manifestation of traits in a population often don't follow on from the reproductive differences caused by (dys)functional performance, but from random genetic drift. Non-adaptive drift occurs, for example, when a species goes through a population bottleneck: for instance, a flood or storm might eliminate the majority of a group, leaving only the genetic information of those who were randomly spared.

After all, the fact that a trait is adaptive – that it leads to relative reproductive success – has nothing to do with that trait being good or desirable in any other sense. Evolutionary biology and evolutionary psychology are a panopticon of brutalities and obscenities that are often strategically advantageous but are ethically beyond questionable. Depending on the conditions, even murder and manslaughter, rape and theft, xenophobia and jealousy can be considered entirely adaptive. This doesn't make them morally justified.

The significance of the scientific discovery of evolution can hardly be overestimated. The idea that a seemingly deliberate adaptation can be explained by the uncoordinated interplay of mutation and selection is one of the greatest insights in human history, comparable to only three or four other discoveries of a similar magnitude. Nietzsche once predicted that 'when you gaze long into an abyss the abyss also gazes into you'.[18] The 'Darwinian abyss'[19] was to prove deeper than ever imagined. Dennett aptly describes the theory of evolution as a 'universal acid' that eats its way through each of our traditional concepts, ideas and theories.[20] Every ideology that comes into contact with it is fundamentally altered. Many have not survived this contact at all.

The improbability of cooperation

Over the last few millennia, a lot has happened with and to us. The philosopher and neuroscientist Joshua Greene imagines a superior alien civilisation visiting Earth every 10,000 years, hoping to find out if any of the resident species prove promising. When it came to *Homo sapiens* 100,000 years ago, they would have noted: 'hunter-gatherer bands, some primitive tools; population: 10 million';[21] and they would have made the same notes 90,000 years ago, 80,000 years ago and 10,000 years ago. But their notes from their last visit in 2020 would say something very different: 'Global indust. economy, advanced technology w/ nuc. power, telecom., artificial intel., extraterrestrial travel, large-scale social/political institutions, democratic government, advanced scientific inquiry.' We have come a long way, and our capacity for morality has substantially shaped and accelerated this development.

It didn't have to be this way. In fact it's very easy to imagine alternative scenarios. The American anthropologist Sarah Hrdy compares how a flight would play out with chimpanzees or humans as the plane's passengers.[22] I suspect that only very few people actually enjoy flying. But we have to admit that, despite the frustrating obstacles we need to overcome before we can get on board, it's all pretty civilised on the whole. After all, we sit there for several hours, crammed together among strangers, silent and motionless, fed questionable food and entertained by even more questionable media. There's the occasional irritation from a drunk passenger or a crying baby that won't settle, but how many people have ever experienced a serious or violent incident on board a plane?

How would chimpanzees behave under comparable conditions? The experiment would be ill advised: seats would be demolished, windows shattered; there'd be pools of blood on the carpet, torn ears, fingers and penises, countless dead apes throughout the plane, and great howling and gnashing of teeth.

Incidentally, this is not meant to imply that chimpanzees – or non-human animals in general – are entirely bloodthirsty and impulsive monsters incapable of cooperation. On the contrary, the point is that our human ability to cooperate works differently from all other animals': we cooperate more, and more flexibly, more generously, with more discipline and with less suspicion, even with strangers. Something makes it possible for us to see and make use of the benefits of cooperation. A world of new possibilities opens up for species able to recruit their own kind for a range of win-win projects. We are astonishingly good at recognising and embracing this.

Let's play a game

In the twentieth century, a particular scientific discipline emerged that to a large extent deals with the conditions and limits of human cooperation. *Game theory* investigates how rational agents interact with each other, and specifically tries to explain why it is often so difficult to create and stabilise co-operative action.

The term 'game theory' is unfortunate, as it suggests either a scientific preoccupation with playing – chess, poker or basketball, for example – or that human coexistence should be derided as a frivolous pastime. Neither is true. In fact, game theorists are interested in describing human interaction with precise mathematical models – with the aim, first and foremost, of understanding why cooperation so often fails or doesn't even come about. The term 'game theory' refers to the fact that interactions can be regarded as sequences of actions in which the previous move, A, determines what the best return move, B, would be.

Behaviour is described as 'cooperative' at the specific point where it puts immediate self-interest aside in favour of a greater common gain. This has nothing to do with self-sacrifice: everyone benefits from cooperation, which is why it is particularly frustrating when it breaks down as a result of pettiness, impulsiveness or short-sighted thinking.

Cooperative actions are based on norms that limit an individual's maximum rational benefit, but that lead to win-win situations, which in game theory are referred to as games with *positive sums*. Zero-sum games, such as poker, are characterised by the fact that one person's losses are the other's gains – the sum of gains and losses is zero. In negative-sum games, everyone loses. Because no one loses out when cooperative win-win interactions take place, they meet a significant criterion of justice: they can be justified to everyone involved.

There's at least one key concept from game theory that has found its way into popular discourse: the concept of the 'prisoner's dilemma'. The story goes something like this: two criminals have been arrested by the police, who can prove that both have committed a minor crime (such as illegal possession of weapons), but they actually want to charge them with a recent bank robbery, although there isn't enough evidence for this yet. So the two are taken to separate interrogation rooms, and they are offered a deal: if person A blames person B, A gets away with a light prison sentence of one year. Once this has happened and they can prove B has committed both crimes, B will have to serve ten years. But B is offered the same deal. If both remain silent and the police can only charge them with the lesser offence, they both get just three years. If both betray each other, they can each expect five years. Since neither can communicate with the other, they each have to pick the optimal strategy for themselves. A might think, 'If B snitches on me, I should snitch on B as well, otherwise I'll go to prison for ten years as the sole culprit. But what if B keeps his mouth shut? Then I should grass him up anyway, as it'll reduce my sentence to one year.' The problem is that they are both in the same boat. So each will blame the other, and they can both expect five years.

The prisoner's dilemma seems to describe a specific and rare situation that isn't relevant to everyday life. In fact, it is just a dynamic illustration of a more general problem that we can use to accurately model the basic conflict of social interaction. Cooperative behaviour is almost always the best option for everyone involved. The problem is that it's even better *for an individual* if everyone *else* cooperates but if he or she can outsmart all the other people. In other words, uncooperative behaviour is always the best choice for every single person, regardless of whether or not other people cooperate: if I'm going to be lied to, I'm better off lying myself. If the others are honest, I'm still better off lying. Non-cooperation becomes the *dominant strategy*, and so mutual non-cooperation emerges as a stable *Nash equilibrium*: no one person can unilaterally break out of this equilibrium without putting themselves at a disadvantage. The paradox in the prisoner's dilemma is that it shows how individual rationality and collective reasoning can fall apart. When everyone acts rationally on an individual basis, the results are collectively suboptimal. The fruits of cooperation remain unharvested.

Once you get the basic idea, you start to see prisoner's dilemmas everywhere – or more generally speaking, collective action problems. This is mainly due to the fact that in reality, collective action problems are *everywhere*. Perhaps the best-known examples of this can be found in the depletion of natural resources. This problem – anticipated by the Scottish philosopher David Hume as early as the eighteenth century – has been known as the 'tragedy of the commons' since Garrett Hardin wrote about it.[23] The American ecologist observed that natural resources – farmland or fish stocks, for example – tend to be exploited beyond the limits of their capacity if they are not privately owned. Regardless of how others behave – sustainably or exploitatively – the best strategy for every individual is to over-exploit the resource in question. The benefits of this misconduct can be absorbed by every individual; the costs are 'externalised' to the rest of the collective.

Many seemingly trivial everyday phenomena can be analysed as collective action problems. Motorway traffic jams are often caused by the indiscretion of rubberneckers, braking for a quick gawp at a crash and forcing everything to slow down behind them. Trampled footpaths are shortcuts that are beneficial for each individual, but ultimately they leave unsightly furrows in the ground for everyone.

In economics, ever since Thorstein Veblen's *Theory of the Leisure Class* (1899), there has been talk of 'conspicuous consumption', a situation where considerable resources are often spent on status symbols, not for intrinsic pleasure, but for purely *positional* effect: they are only valuable if (and because) other people do not possess these particular items. But as soon as the competition has caught up, they are all worse off: everyone is poorer, but no one is any happier, and it would have been better if the collective 'keeping up with the Joneses' had never begun in the first place.[24]

Politically, game theory has particularly proved its worth in relation to the madness of the arms race during the Cold War.[25] For many intellectuals, the world seemed to have gone crazy, with the two sides' minds poisoned by irreconcilable ideologies that made their opponent seem inferior or evil. But this explanation is also fatally wrong because it relegates the problem to being merely out of the ordinary and insurmountable, instead of seeing the mundane crux of this scenario of reciprocal deterrence. If everyone else gets nuclear armaments, I'm better off having nuclear weapons as well. If I'm the only one, so much the better.

Many social problems can also be described in this way: American gun owners like to point out that they feel safer with a firearm than without; self-defence is recognised by almost everyone as a legitimate aspiration, which is why the US gun lobby explains away the call for more effective regulation, especially of powerful weapons such as assault rifles, either as a symptom of snowflake East Coast decadence or as encroaching control freakery from the Washington elite. Game theory shows that this is nonsense, and in reality, this is also about managing a situation in which the individually rational action of owning a weapon is collectively irrational. Universal possession of weapons immediately eats away at an individual's gain from self-defence: bigger and bigger guns need to be bought until the only way to secure neighbourly peace is with tanks. And even that won't work in the long run.

Today's raging anti-vaccination campaign is a scandal that ultimately also stems from a collective action problem. The alleged risks that exist from vaccination are mainly fictitious, but who wants to sacrifice a morning in the doctor's waiting room, holed up with strangers' sickly children, just to have your own kids kicking and screaming about getting a needle in their arms? If everyone else gets vaccinated, you can enjoy the benefits of herd immunity without having to put your own child through this. It's only when the vaccination rate drops below the level of herd immunity that it becomes rational to opt for individual vaccination again, as the cases start to rise. Anti-vaxxers – apart from the fact that they often believe in outrageous conspiracy theories – don't behave unreasonably, but *immorally*, because they're benefiting from cooperative structures without contributing themselves.

In the biological realm, collective action problems are everywhere. California's sequoias grow over a hundred metres tall just to secure the best spot in the sun. Unfortunately, they are incapable of contractually guaranteeing each other a maximum height of fifty metres, which could put a quick end to this obscenely inefficient competition.[26]

Collective action isn't impossible, but the previous examples and the logic of collective action problems show that massive obstacles, with no universally valid solution, stand in the way of forming an 'us' with the power to act. The problem that cooperative arrangements always remain vulnerable to exploitation is not a problem with a solution. What does this mean for the evolution of our morality? Imagine a small group of fictional humanoid beings. Each fights for itself and is only interested in its own gain. No cooperation takes place at all. And then, through random genetic mutation, an individual emerges that is configured a little more altruistically and cooperatively than the others – but only slightly. This individual has a rudimentary sense of morality and sometimes tends not to exploit others or to put its own self-interest above all the others' interests.

A variant like this could never become established, and it would quickly perish in the struggle for resources and reproduction. Selection pressure would be ruthless for this variant and it would not be able to propagate within the population. The opposite case of a group of cooperative beings helping each other would produce similar results: again, an individual created by chance through mutation, only slightly less willing to cooperate than the others, would benefit from a great competitive advantage. Its genetic material would spread rapidly in the population due to a higher number of offspring. The selection pressure of evolution seemingly always works to the detriment of moral behaviour. This is the enigma of cooperation.

Cooperation in the lab

The fact that cooperative structures have a tendency to collapse and even get caught up in cycles of destructive violence has been substantiated empirically over and over again. Experimental games in behavioural economics prove that although people tend to be conditionally willing to cooperate, this willingness is usually exploited by freeloaders to the extent that an individual's average contribution to the common good quickly decreases dramatically and eventually drops to almost zero.

To be able to study human cooperation precisely, we first need to put it into operation scientifically. In the 'public goods game', collective action problems are modelled as decision-making situations in which four or five players are given a certain amount of tokens that they can all either keep for themselves or donate to a public pot.[27] After each round, the amount in the public pot is multiplied (usually doubled) and paid out in equal parts to all the players – regardless of what they contributed themselves. It immediately becomes clear that freeloading, also known as 'defection', is the dominant strategy. Individually, everyone benefits from the others' contributions, and everyone can pocket their share that they didn't donate to the pot in each round.

This effect is amplified over several rounds, and as it goes on, the players taking part are aware of the number of turns in this iteration of the prisoner's dilemma. It is possible to work out the best strategy in each round from the previous round's optimal strategy, using backward induction. If it is clear to the players that ten rounds are being played, it is also clear that their own behaviour in the tenth and final round will have no consequence for the results in an eleventh round (because it won't take place). In the final round, therefore, we can expect the players to behave uncooperatively – which by definition makes the ninth round the last round, so non-cooperation can be expected in this round as well. So the whole chain collapses, and non-cooperation is already impossible to resist as early on as the first round. This theoretical result has been empirically substantiated: although many players are willing to cooperate in the first few rounds of the public goods game, this quickly breaks down after the first players have begun to benefit from others' contributions, without making any contribution of their own. After a few rounds, donations to the public pot reduce to virtually zero.

Of course, the real-world significance (in technical terms, 'ecological validity') of experimental studies always remains suspect, since the implications of carefully instructed test subjects' behaviour in highly artificial laboratory situations are limited for real people in the maze of daily life. Nonetheless, this phenomenon is well known to anyone who has ever had a bad camping trip with a group of friends: it always results when all the campers' willingness to cooperate gradually decreases after the first members of the group fail to contribute to the smooth running of the whole. Even a new understanding of humanity won't change this. The notion that collective action problems only arise if we assume humankind is *Homo economicus*, sworn to the ideological premisses of economics, is a popular fairy tale that has long since been debunked. Cooperation is fragile, and, like glass, china and reputation, it should belong on Benjamin Franklin's list of things that are easily cracked but never well mended.

At the beginning of this chapter, I mentioned that it's very hard to cooperate, and even more difficult to maintain good, established cooperation. The world's die is cast for effective cooperation. Cooperation requires explanation, and non-cooperation is the normal state of affairs. The sociologist Niklas Luhmann might have said that cooperation is 'improbable', in comparison to its failure. Whenever two – or more – people meet, there is a 'double contingency':[28] there are countless things that could happen. They could ignore each other, attack each other, behave absurdly in some way, or they could at least try to cooperate, but then fail. *Ego* and *alter* managing to 'join up' their actions is only one of many possibilities – and therefore improbable.

People and apes

Wouldn't you keep your mouth shut and refuse to snitch on your accomplice? Isn't it a matter of honour? Even thieves know honour, as Cicero is said to have once declared, and students, too, almost always refuse to acknowledge the logic of instrumental action; it takes training to see the benefits of non-cooperative behaviour.

If you feel like this too, it shows that your moral compass is working. It also confirms the theory that cooperative instincts are probably innate. The fact that you might find collective action innately attractive and might even feel anger and indignation towards freeloaders shows that evolution has instilled social preferences in us humans over the course of many millions of years of learning, making cooperation seem intrinsically essential.[29] We don't need to learn how cooperation works.

The notion that our ability to cooperate is innate remains a controversial claim that cannot be proven with mathematical certainty. Nonetheless, there is robust evidence to show that a pattern of behaviour is innate or, technically more accurately, is significantly 'canalised' in evolutionary terms. Whenever a skill a) develops very early on, b) occurs in every culture and c) is difficult or impossible to change, it is highly likely to be a 'hardwired' disposition.

This is precisely the case with our sense of morality. The fact that proto-moral tendencies emerge surprisingly early in life can be particularly well demonstrated. With the help of 'looking-time studies',[30] it can be proven that children under twelve months of age prefer to watch figures and shapes that look helpful rather than ones that seem to hinder or harm others. Even small children are 'allergic' to unfairness; punishing wrongdoers for their offences is a spontaneous reaction that does not need to be learned.

Hypotheses about us humans, like medicines, are often tested on primates. But this approach remains very limited. The fact that certain skills are found in one primate or other can actually just as much be seen as evidence that these skills *do not* explain our human morality. Primates and humans are very different and do very different things (cast your mind back to the thought experiment of chimpanzees on a plane). Just because a trait is found in primates doesn't mean that it serves as an explanation for specifically human behaviour: if monkeys could build ships, get married or write books, why don't they?

The Dutch primatologist Frans de Waal repeatedly falls into this trap. Most notably in his prestigious Tanner Lectures on Human Values, given at Princeton University in 2003 and later published as *Primates and Philosophers*, de Waal attempts to reject the veneer theory of morality by showing that our morality has profound evolutionary origins. 'Scratch an altruist and see a hypocrite bleed' is the slogan of the veneer theorists; according to them, hiding behind our civilised facades are amoral cut-throats who abide by the rules reluctantly at best, only conditionally and for our own benefit. But as soon as a golden opportunity appears, even the seemingly most innocent little angel is ready to murder and pillage at any moment.[31]

According to de Waal, this cannot be true because basic moral faculties are evident in our closest relatives, who would not be able to disguise themselves so strategically. Human morality therefore has to be more authentic and go deeper than assumed by cynics who consider our values to be Potemkin villages – mere facades with little behind them. Chimpanzees, in particular, clearly show social instincts such as empathy or care, and seem to have a similar aversion to social inequality to ours as humans.[32] The study in which one chimpanzee rejects a cucumber simply because another is offered a grape is now legendary (although its interpretation remains controversial).

The problem is that empathy and reciprocity *must* fall short in explaining human morality for precisely this reason: human beings who can build groups with millions of members and find cooperative solutions for these groups must have fundamentally different psychological tools at their disposal. If a little compassion and grooming were enough to build gigantic, highly complex chains of cooperation, why is it that chimpanzees live in groups that are extremely hierarchical and never have more than a few dozen members? It is precisely this phenomenon of human *hypersociality* whose origin is still unclear. Primates can be extremely helpful when it comes to solving this mystery, but only by showing us which of our qualities to rule out as a defining feature of our human morality – namely, those we share with our closest relatives.

A modern, scientifically based genealogy of morality therefore has to explain one thing above all: how did we humans manage to develop cooperative dispositions even though this is unstable in terms of evolution? To answer this question, we need to take a closer look at the conditions in which we had to overcome this evolutionary challenge.

Godless virtues

Our morality is a psychosocial mechanism that makes cooperation possible. We have now found out about some of the scientific tools essential for understanding this mechanism.

Against this theoretical background, the problem of moral development can be formulated more precisely: as our morality isn't a catalogue of norms that is divinely inspired or known from experience, but instead has a history, moral philosophy is genealogical.[33] A sound history of morality relies on the latest findings from evolutionary theory, moral psychology and anthropology. Using these, it can avoid both Nietzsche's accusation of naivety in contemporary speculation on the origin of morality, and the hyperbolic polemics that are part of Nietzsche's own entertaining, but bad, habits.

Our morality has developed under certain conditions, against our backdrop of evolutionary conformity. We lived in small, conflicting groups that had to ensure their survival by hunting large mammals in a climatically volatile environment. This made us flexible, intelligent and cooperative, but also tribalistic and violent.

Our morality is a *specifically human* morality. Primates can show us – by ruling things out – which abilities do *not* explain the root of our morality. If monkeys have a certain characteristic, it automatically fails to explain human cooperation, precisely because monkeys fail to cooperate in the ways that humans do.

Cooperation and altruism have to overcome some formidable obstacles in order to emerge at all. These obstacles persist and have a permanently destabilising effect on our moral tendencies, so that successful cooperation, once achieved, remains fragile. The main problem is that non-cooperation, the route to our own individual maximum benefit, is almost always the best choice. Unfortunately, this applies to everyone, repeatedly throwing moral norms out of balance.

The fact that cooperation is unlikely can be formulated as an explanatory problem in evolutionary theory: how did evolution manage to create altruistic or cooperative tendencies, even though – apparently, at any rate – these tendencies inevitably *reduce our reproductive fitness?* How could it ever be beneficial *for me* to help *someone else?* How could it ever be worth subordinating my self-interest for the well-being of the community?

For a long time, the fact that the theory of evolution cannot explain our altruistic morality was one of the most popular talking points for God-fearing evolutionary sceptics, who clung to morality as the last straw of human nature, believing it *had to* have a divine origin. The theory of evolution, especially when trivialised as 'survival of the fittest', seemed to predict that everyone had to be looking out for their own gain. But don't neighbours help each other, and don't we make sacrifices for our children? Is there no friendship, no community, no solidarity? Can we not love our neighbour? From a godless perspective, our morality seems to be at the very least a huge mistake, or at worst an inexplicable mystery, a scientific anomaly that atheists can only acknowledge as mere fact with a shrug of the shoulders.

The theory, still popular with religious apologists, that the origin of altruism and selflessness cannot be evolutionary, can now be called what it is: a myth that has been definitively debunked. Nonetheless, we shouldn't overshoot the mark here: sometimes atheistic evolutionary biologists or philosophers tend to exaggerate the scope of naturalistic explanations just to avoid giving God one iota of credit. This temptation ought to be resisted. In fact, scientific modesty dictates that evolutionary research's considerable successes mustn't conceal its gaps. We don't – yet – know what has made us cooperative beings and how cooperation actually works.

In reality, it is not the fact that we have definitively explained the emergence and spread of morality that undermines the theistic perspective, but the gradual acceptance of naturalistic moral explanations over time: at the end of the nineteenth century, there was no choice but to regard cooperation and morality as complete mysteries in evolutionary theory. Since then, many aspects of our morality have been deciphered satisfactorily, so we have good reason to hope that the remaining problems can also ultimately be solved: as Wittgenstein eloquently put it, 'Light dawns gradually over the whole.'[34]

Two brothers (or eight cousins)

Basic moral behavioural patterns can be explained in evolutionary terms. Acting altruistically can cost us dearly – that much is true. Nonetheless, it is possible to identify mechanisms that enable cooperative behaviour to stay the course long term in the battle with strategically shrewd competitors for scarce resources.

The theory of evolution seems to paint a gloomy, inexorable picture of life. All living organisms are in a ruthless, never-ending struggle for better or worse, with the weak falling by the wayside. Only the strong come through, and only they succeed in producing offspring with good prospects, passing on their copies of their genes to the next generation. It's a cold, pitiless world where winners are rewarded and there is no room for losers. This all sounds relentless enough, but the truth is much, much darker. To be able to see this, we have to recognise who is actually being favoured or weeded out by the selection pressure of evolutionary events. Is it individual organisms that try to come out on top? Is it entire species that carve up the Earth among themselves? In fact, it's neither. The fundamental unit of selection, whose fate is being decided in the evolutionary process, is the *gene*.

What we call the 'gene-centred view' was popularised in the second half of the twentieth century by Richard Dawkins, the British evolutionary biologist who has a legitimate claim to have written the book with the most misunderstood title of all time, his milestone *The Selfish Gene*.[35] To many readers, *The Selfish Gene* seemed to want to point out that the struggle for survival outlined above had naturally and without any hope of reform turned all living beings, including us humans, into cold-blooded sociopaths who were constantly out for their own gain, tempted by moral niceties at most temporarily, and then through calculation or hypocrisy. Dawkins's book actually shows that the complete opposite is true. We are altruistic because *our genes* are selfish. And it is precisely because they are indifferent to the state of our affairs that we became moral beings. In fact, we humans (and all other organisms) are almost selfless slaves whose entire purpose is to serve our molecular masters. To sum up this Copernican turn in evolutionary biology, Dawkins came up with the distinction between *replicators* and *vehicles*. A replicator is an entity that makes copies of itself. A vehicle is the means through which replicators achieve this. *We* are these vehicles.

Chickens don't lay eggs to make new chickens. Eggs produce chickens to make new eggs. It becomes immediately clear that evolution has to be primarily about genes. Evolution is sometimes even defined simply as changes in the relative frequency of genes (or more precisely, alleles) between generations. But without wanting to settle this question by conceptual decree, it doesn't take much to realise that ultimately it cannot be individual organisms that are subject to the blind play of selection and mutation. Only entities that can create copies of themselves, whose varying reproductive success over time leads to the accumulation of certain variants, are able to evolve. Trees create new trees, rather than copies of old trees. Strictly speaking, only genes are capable of replication.

If you found the story of evolution as a relentless struggle for survival sobering, you'll find even less solace here. If the gene-centred view is correct, then evolution is nothing at all to do with 'us'. We are nothing more than sophisticated robots, constructed over 3.5 billion years of mutation and selection to protect self-replicating genes from an inhospitable environment.[36] This is supported by the fact that a major part of our DNA doesn't fulfil any function, but only acts as a placeholder. Why is this seemingly worthless 'junk DNA' even there? From the perspective of our genes, this question makes no sense at all. It is only if we assume that our genes exist for our sake that genetic material with no useful encoded information seems enigmatic. But if *we* exist *for the sake of our genes*, we can immediately recognise that for us as their vehicles to fulfil their mission, we replicator carriers only need the instructions that enable us to ensure our survival and reproduction. All the other genes are copied automatically, which makes no difference to them – whether they are useless or not doesn't matter to genes at all. And anyway: useless for whom?

At this point, I should reiterate how difficult it is for morally commendable patterns of behaviour to remain evolutionary, and why altruism and cooperation have seemed absurd, in evolutionary terms, for so long. Even if the process of indiscriminate mutation might have managed to create a cooperatively inclined individual by chance, selection would immediately work against them. Nor is the integrity of a group of cooperative elements safe from being corrupted from within by exploiters and freeloaders: statistically speaking, long-term gene recombination can produce organisms that are both more and less cooperative, with the less cooperative ones always performing better and, as a result, gradually increasing in frequency. Cooperative altruists, it seems, are weeded out *by necessity*. It seems inevitable that non-cooperative strategies will bring about an invasion.

A first indication of how altruistic dispositions can be evolutionarily stable can be found in William D. Hamilton's concept of 'inclusive fitness'.[37] Probably the best-known equation in evolutionary biology is called Hamilton's rule. It states that we can count on altruistic actions in certain conditions, although they are disadvantageous for the helper, namely if a) the altruistic action comes at a small enough cost and b) the altruistic individual and the individual who gains from the altruistic action are related closely enough that the helpful organism helps *its own genes*, in a manner of speaking. Formally expressed, Hamilton's rule is $rB > C$. The recipient must derive a greater benefit from the altruistic act than the 'actor', i.e. $B > C$ (B = benefit, C = cost). However, the magnitude of the benefit received decreases with the degree of relatedness (r = relatedness) and must therefore be multiplied by a coefficient. I share 100 per cent of my genes with myself, but only – on average – half this amount with my parents or biological siblings. Even cousins only share 12.5 per cent of their genetic make-up. To justify a fitness-reducing cost that I would have to incur for doing a good deed for my brother, the benefit for my brother must be at least twice as great as my cost: B is multiplied by r, which is now 0.5. The British biologist John Haldane is alleged to have got to the heart of this insight a few years before his compatriot Hamilton: 'Would I give my life to save my brother? No, but I would gladly lay down my life for two brothers or eight cousins.'

Someone who helps their relatives helps their own genes – in other words, their copies. This is what makes altruism adaptive. Dawkins's anthropomorphic metaphor of the selfish gene suggests that egotistical genes can give rise to altruistic vehicles – namely, us. While my genes might well have been completely indifferent to *my* welfare as long as their copies were being looked after, qualities such as helpfulness and caring could come about, provided they had a positive impact on the fitness of my family's gene copies. This insight can have a disturbing effect that might temporarily alienate you, or distance you from your key values and relationships. Could it be true that we don't love our children for their own sakes, but because, forever benefiting the replicators that inhabit us and our off-spring, we are genetically programmed to put our own interests at the service of mindless and unfeeling molecules whose alien agendas haunt our motives without us even realising it? And could it be that we love our partners because deep romantic attachment acts as a commitment device that is adaptive for a species that relies on extensive periods of child-rearing for their highly dependent offspring?

Tit for tat

The evolution of cooperative attitudes between family members can be explained by combining Hamilton's rule with a gene-centred view. This mechanism is also called 'kin selection'.

There is a second mechanism that enables moral dispositions to evolve; it is visible in reciprocal relationships of mutual benefit. Reciprocity ('you scratch my back, I'll scratch yours') also works between genetically unrelated or only very distantly related relatives. Technically, this isn't a form of altruism because mutual support doesn't incur a net cost for the helper. This is why we sometimes talk of 'mutualism'. Both sides benefit, while in genuinely altruistic cases only the recipient gains.

The adaptivity of mutualistic cooperation has a stability problem similar to the evolution of altruism. Much like inclusive fitness, the benefits of reciprocal cooperation must be offset against a coefficient (such as the previously mentioned r) that can drastically dilute its benefits. Hamilton showed that kin selection fosters moral action the more closely the interaction partners are related, so that unrequited assistance between distant relatives or unrelated people very quickly ceases to pay off. In the context of reciprocal altruism, on the other hand, it all depends on the probability of two interaction partners meeting again in the future if the benefits of mutual support are to be ultimately realised. As the American evolutionary biologist Robert Trivers noted, reciprocal altruism only pays off if the probability of meeting again is high enough.[38]

In many cases, it pays to form alliances that can be beneficial in the long run by pledging mutual support. But which cooperation strategy has the best chance of success? How can reciprocity be practically implemented? To answer this question, the American political scientist Robert Axelrod set up one of the twentieth century's most famous experiments in the early 1980s.[39] The basic idea was to have different strategies compete against each other in a simulated computer tournament to find out which form of cooperation would prove particularly successful. Axelrod invited psychologists, mathematicians, economists and social scientists to propose strategies that he could pit against each other in an iterated prisoner's dilemma. Each course of action would compete against all the others (and against itself), over 200 rounds. At the end, it would become apparent which strategy had collected the most points.

The fourteen participants in Axelrod's tournament submitted a wide variety of strategies. One possibility was 'permanent retaliation', meaning cooperation, but in the case of one-off exploitation, responding with everlasting non-cooperation. Another strategy was acting randomly and unpredictably; another was always cooperating; and another again, never.

It was impossible to foresee which strategy would be the best. Would it be the stronger, more ruthless participants, always seeking their own gain, who would come out on top? Or the meek and considerate ones who invariably cooperated, even when they were being exploited? Or maybe the unpredictable ones with haphazard behaviour that couldn't be anticipated? Or the vindictive ones who just wanted to see the world burn after pulling off a one-off deceit?

Various strategies with cryptic names such as LOOK AHEAD, DOWNING or TIDEMAN AND CHIERUZZI were submitted. The winning strategy came from the American mathematician Anatol Rapoport, a professor at the University of Toronto. It was also the simplest of all the entrants. Its name was TIT FOR TAT. TIT FOR TAT always chose cooperation in the first move and then copied its opponent's last move. If the latter cooperated, TIT FOR TAT cooperated too. If the opponent defected, in other words chose non-cooperation, TIT FOR TAT responded accordingly.

TIT FOR TAT was amazingly intuitive, and on the whole it corresponds to our own moral sense of how cooperative we should be with others and where the limits of our goodwill lie. Intuitively, it seems right to offer cooperation first, but not to let ourselves be exploited. And we should always be prepared to start cooperating again after a corresponding offer of reconciliation from the other party. The fact that this strategy seems emotionally reasonable to us is an indication that through

43

evolution we are equipped with a formula for cooperation that roughly corresponds to TIT FOR TAT.

Many people were surprised by the results of Axelrod's experiment, so it was immediately repeated. All the participants in the second round were told which strategy had been most successful the first time around. TIT FOR TAT was still unbeatable in the second round, although many applicants submitted more complex, seemingly improved versions of the same rules. The simple original strategy once again outperformed all the rest. The top eight strategies also shared a characteristic: they were all 'nice'. A 'nice' strategy never defected first, whatever other characteristics it may have had.

Axelrod was therefore able to show that moral psychology tailored to cooperation can become established in evolutionary terms, under certain conditions. Actors who are willing to cooperate on the one hand, but won't let themselves be exploited on the other, benefit from each other and at the same time deprive uncooperative actors of opportunities both to form win-win alliances themselves and to be taken advantage of, like hyper-cooperative victims. This approach, also known as 'conditional cooperation', is potentially stable from an evolutionary perspective.

Imagine a population consisting of three different types of people: suckers, cheaters and grudgers. These types personify three different strategies.[40] Cheaters never cooperate; suckers always cooperate, even if they end up being exploited. Grudgers only cooperate with other cooperators, in other words with suckers and other grudgers, and with cheaters they only cooperate once, and never again after that. Everything goes wonderfully for the uncooperative cheaters to begin with. In the first dealings with them, they exploit the grudgers and, in particular, the suckers. But the suckers soon begin to die out because they have nothing to counter the cheaters' relentless exploitation. As the grudgers refuse to be exploited by the cheaters, and the last sucker is soon extinct, at some point there will only be cheaters who exploit each other, and grudgers who cooperate with each other. Even the cheaters eventually die out. Now all that remains is grudgers, who have found their niche in a positive feedback loop – what we call a 'virtuous circle' – of cooperating with each other.

Costly signals and green beards

For reciprocal cooperation to work, we have to be able to identify appropriate cooperation partners. This requires information about who will reciprocate our own offers of cooperation and who will take advantage of our willingness to help. Social signals are therefore paramount for the evolution of mutual cooperation, because it is difficult to make an individual's reputation as a reliable cooperation partner transparent in any other way. To give us the crucial information we need to initiate reciprocal cooperation, it would be helpful if there were conspicuous external features so we could identify appropriate cooperation partners as such.

Evolutionary biologists like to speculate about whether signals of this kind exist and how they might work. A famous example is the 'green beard'.[41] It would be so simple if potential cooperation partners had an unmistakable physical feature – such as a long green beard – so everyone could immediately recognise them as good-natured counterparts. But green beards are probably extremely rare in nature. The genetic code for green beards would have to satisfy three conditions at once: a) produce the green beard, b) develop the ability to reliably recognise other green beards, and c) create the disposition to act altruistically towards other green beards (and only towards them). But while genetic information was being repeatedly recombined, random mutations would inevitably produce pseudo-green beards that carried the external signal but lacked the costly altruistic motivation, having been separated from the other two conditions by the genes' random recombination.

45

These 'false beards' would always perform better in the process of natural selection, and would therefore ultimately dominate.

If reliable signals exist, unreliable signals also exist. And if unreliable signals exist, this creates evolutionary incentives to perfect the credible faking of false signals.[42] This, in turn, led us to become better and better at guessing other people's genuine intentions. Let's take the following sentence: 'Paul has forgotten that Charlotte knows that Fatih does not believe that Julia is jealous of Johan.' We are dealing with a tricky interpersonal situation here, but semantically we have no problem understanding this sentence, although it describes several levels of nested mental attitudes. There is no other animal whose ability to understand other people's beliefs, intentions and feelings – often called mind-reading – comes close to ours. Evolution has clearly equipped us with a module that intuitively gives us access to other people's minds.

This dialectic of more subtle mind-reading, a more sophisticated ability to deceive and the resulting mind-reading that was even further refined, served to deepen our minds. The best way to hide our true intentions from others is to hide them *from ourselves*. Most people who claim to collect expensive paintings just for art's sake or to have school buildings named after them as a result of philanthropic donations are probably sincere: they aren't consciously liars. Nonetheless, we don't need to be great experts in human nature to understand that placebo reasons like this primarily fulfil the function of morally dressing up what are in fact egotistical motives and the flaunting of status symbols. However, our true motives often remain hidden from ourselves precisely because this is the best way to credibly deceive the people around us.

Fortunately, we don't have to rely on green beards. A better way to solve the problem of false signals is to ensure authentic signals are *costly*, so it takes great sacrifice – or is impossible – to simulate them. According to Amotz Zahavi's *handicap principle*, the best signals are those whose possession is detrimental to the bearer.[43] The Israeli evolutionary biologist's idea follows a perverse logic, because disadvantageous signals indirectly show that their bearer can tolerate them. Only the strongest and most assertive peacocks can cope with extravagant tail feathers, which would be too much of a hindrance for less impressive species of that kind. Luxurious plumage is a costly signal that cannot be 'faked' because genetically less fit individuals simply couldn't manage this signal physically.

Some religious practices that are difficult to explain to outsiders can be interpreted as being costly and are therefore reliable signals of willingness to cooperate within a group. Monotheistic religions, in particular, seem to compete to outdo each other in demanding a commitment to the more outlandish dogmas and absurd ideas from their followers. Whether it's a promise that only by fasting can someone truly be satisfied, the concept of being able to turn wine into blood by reciting a few set phrases (which still looks and tastes like wine, and gets you just as drunk), or the admirably audacious claim to have copied a clearly self-written book from conveniently untraceable gold plates printed with strange hieroglyphics, their location revealed by an angel and made legible by a magic stone, the doctrines of most religions consist predominantly of such obvious falsehoods that no sensible person would ever give the slightest credence to them. How do people come not only to accept them, but even to express them publicly? Looking on from the perspective of the theory of costly signals, the bizarre nature of religious denominations is precisely their point: we can recognise true believers precisely from the fact that they are willing to publicly incriminate themselves as spiritually unhinged.

The fact that scientific treatises are often written in hermetic jargon can also be explained in this way. Why do scientists often write so awkwardly and obscurely, even though it could be clear and simple? And most notably, how can it be that some intellectuals are taken especially seriously precisely because

47

they express themselves so incomprehensibly, even though sometimes there is little or nothing hidden behind their long sentences? Originally, it made sense to develop a stilted scientific language to be able to talk about processes with technical precision in a way that is free of everyday language's flamboyant semantic connotations. As a result, artificially esoteric language became a signal of integrity and erudition. After a while, though, the first people began to copy the 'complex jargon' signal without having the requisite underlying properties – they were false beards. This is the fundamental problem in the evolution of morality: every supposed solution to the problem of how cooperation could arise only ever creates a new status quo that remains vulnerable to new non-cooperative strategies, created by random mutation, taking over and undermining the problem's solution.

Altruists sticking together

The basic building blocks of morality – altruism and cooperation – can be accounted for in evolutionary terms because there are plausible mechanisms that make these patterns of behaviour adaptive. However, it is now also known that kin selection and reciprocity are not 'scalable' enough to give an adequate explanation of the human ability to cooperate.

We humans are hypersocial animals that cooperate in large groups. It is easy to see why inclusive fitness and TIT FOR TAT are not robust enough to support the scope of coexistence we can see in our human communities. If altruistic dispositions can only become established among close relatives, the extent of genetic connectedness decreases so much with just a few hundred group members that the costs of helpful behaviour are no longer worthwhile. At the same time, chains of reciprocal interaction become so confusing beyond a certain number of members that social give-and-take is not ideal for integrating larger communities.

The mystery of the shift from one state of affairs to another remains: some species live in large swarms, some in loose-knit networks consisting of a few individuals – but which animal species used to live in small groups 100,000 years ago, but now forms a global civilisation that dominates the Earth? None, besides ourselves.

To explain how the remarkable extent of human cooperation became possible, an increasing number of scientists are resorting to the notion of *group selection*.[44] The idea behind this is that we humans have developed the capacity for extensive cooperation because, in the competition for scarce resources in our environment of evolutionary adaptation, only groups with hyper-cooperative members could assert themselves against other groups.

Darwin himself had already speculated that a mechanism of this kind could exist: 'A tribe including many members who, from possessing in a high degree the spirit of patriotism, fidelity, obedience, courage, and sympathy, were always ready to give aid to one another and to sacrifice themselves for the common good, would be victorious over most other tribes; and this would be natural selection.'[45]

The consensus now is that this kind of theory about group selection – sometimes referred to as *naive* group selection theory – is untenable. The main reason for this is that by and large, a vaguely defined competitive advantage – cooperation is 'good for the group' – is not enough to counterbalance selection *in favour of* freeloaders *within* the group. Of course, it would be 'good for the group' if everyone behaved altruistically. And it is also true that although egoistic individuals come out on top of altruistic individuals, groups of altruists outclass groups of egoists.[46] But it remains the case, too, that every individual is better off acting uncooperatively themselves. The positive effect of individual cooperation on the group is not substantial enough to neutralise the freeloader problem's subversive force. The fact that it would be beneficial for the whole group if all members had character trait x is not automatically sufficient to make character trait x evolutionarily adaptive.[47]

On the other hand, the theory of group selection also has obvious advantages, for example in that it offers an elegant and empirically substantiated explanation for various characteristics in our psychology. We are inwardly highly group-oriented and often surprisingly willing to help and make sacrifices for individuals who belong to 'us'. At the same time, we are often hostile to other groups and their members.[48] An evolutionary past in which small tribal units had to fight each other for scarce resources could actually be responsible for this moral psychological profile. Groups that were peaceful among themselves and warlike towards others had the greatest chance of success.

Conversely, for group selection to work, the selection pressure against cooperative dispositions *within* a group must be weaker than the selection pressure in favour of the same trait *between* groups. It can also only happen if the carriers of the corresponding cooperation genes come together in some way. Both kin and group selection are based on an equivalent sorting mechanism: altruism can be evolutionarily stable if – and only if – the altruists remain among themselves.

Natural selection can only unleash its power if the differences between the units that are competing in evolutionary terms are great enough. The more similar two groups are, the smaller the competitive advantage of one over the other, by definition. However, genetic studies suggest that the migration flow – and therefore the exchange of genetic material – between human groups was usually significant. This could occur either through migration in and out of groups, or through enslavement and marriage. All these genetic 'flow' mechanisms undermine the group's coherence, weakening selection.

Even if the genetic integrity of various groups could be ensured in some way, selection in favour of groups of cooperative individuals could only work if there was also a mechanism that gathered altruists into groups with other altruists. It is unclear, though, how this kind of sorting filter would have worked. In the case of kin selection, we can immediately see that family structures and emotional relationships between parents and their children will ensure that they remain close to each other. But what if family ties were missing?

The best candidate for an alternative mechanism of this kind is probably the hypothesis that individuals willing to cooperate preferred to live with other cooperative people, so altruistically minded people stayed together by choice. Of course, this suggestion also has to contend with the problem of false signals, which would make scrupulous altruists vulnerable to uncooperative wolves in sheep's clothing. Another option is that for purely statistical reasons, through 'fission' – in other words, splitting up – groups above a certain number of members could at some point (or even several times) have formed new groups that happened to consist largely of cooperating individuals. From then on, these groups would have been superior to all the others and would have become established in the selection process.[49]

Five million years ago, we discovered the benefits of co-operation. But cooperation is always costly, and uncooperative behaviour remains profitable. To become stable in evolutionary terms, we had to limit our cooperative efforts to a small group of people: we became altruistic and helpful, but only in combination with a psychology that divided people into 'us' and 'them'. Our morality became group-oriented. But how did we succeed in enforcing cooperative structures in larger groups so that we could build on the advantages of cooperative behaviour? What moral transformations were necessary to make antisocial behaviour even more costly, and to make us more helpful, peaceable and social?

2

500,000 YEARS

Crime and Punishment

The Cave of Addaura

Not far from Palermo's Old Town – a short walk through the Quartiere Arenella with its small port, past the Cimitero di Santa Maria dei Rotoli and through a suburb named, like so many in Sicily, after the Virgin Mary, is a path that leads you along the base of Monte Pellegrino to the small town of Addaura. From here it's an easy climb to a set of caves, which are now a reminder to us that the history of humankind has always been a history of cruelty.[1]

From 1943 onwards, these three *grotti* were used by the Allies as ammunition dumps when they adopted the occupied island as a base during the invasion of fascist Europe. When the end of the war was almost in sight, the explosives stored there combusted, causing the limestone walls to collapse. The explosion revealed a rock face behind, on which strange scenes could be seen: someone had apparently committed them to the stone a very long time ago. Along with bulls and wild horses, it was possible to make out figures cheering and dancing as if in a frenzy with their arms in the air, gathered around two unnaturally contorted people lying on the ground. One thing is certain: the two figures aren't primeval athletes performing feats of strength. Nor do they seem to give us any insight into prehistoric desire, and in fact it is neither lust nor willpower holding the pair in their painful poses. A closer look reveals a rope binding their necks to their feet, running behind each of their backs and stretched so tightly that they won't be able to hold out much longer. Their exhausted bodies will inevitably tighten the noose. We are witnessing an execution.

The death penalty is much, much older than the graffiti carved into the Sicilian rock 20,000 years ago.[2] This may come as a surprise to some people who imagine the natural state of man as a harmonious camp in which peaceable, scarcely clad beings, warmed by the campfire and high on exotic herbs, slowly drift off to sleep as they listen to rhythmic chants about the heroic deeds of their ancestors and whisper tales of benevolent spirits' high jinks to their children. Scenes like this may well have taken place too, but they are only half the story. The other half is about blood and guts, screaming and gnashing of teeth, dismemberment and death.

Today, the death penalty – or, in more abstract terms, the planned killing of one person by several others as a normative sanction – is on the wane worldwide.[3] In most countries it has been entirely abolished. In places where it still exists in legislation, it is rarely carried out – barring a few particularly draconian regimes – and usually only for the most serious crimes. It was abolished in Germany in 1949, Australia in 1985 and the United Kingdom in 1998.

The death penalty occupies a special place in Western thought. The history of Western philosophy itself even begins with the execution of its founder. In 399 BCE, Socrates was sentenced by an Athenian court to drink a cup of poisonous hemlock tea – not without reason, you might think: after all, he had backed the 'Thirty Tyrants' who destroyed Athenian democracy and had ordered the mass murder of its representatives during their eight months of rule. Or was he actually innocent?

From a historical point of view, societies in which there was *no* ritualised and legally sanctioned murder of undesirable elements were very much the exception. What is often underestimated, though, is the key role punishment has played in the evolution of humankind and, above all, in the evolution of good and evil.

The first important step in the history of our morality was the emergence of cooperation: we discovered that the wisest strategy in the long term is to cultivate altruistic dispositions and direct our immediate self-interest towards the common good. At the same time, it turned out that the evolutionary mechanisms that stabilise simple forms of cooperative action quickly reach their limits. The binding force of inclusive fitness and direct reciprocity is not enough to guarantee cooperative behaviour in groups of more than a few dozen members (or, in exceptional circumstances, a few hundred at most). Beyond core family groups, genetic relationships become so watered down, and chains of mutual support so fragile and hard to keep track of, that a better set of tools was needed to ensure larger groups could come into being, and survive in harmony in this close proximity. And that is precisely what was necessary: living together with people outside the ties of family love and friendship required people who were able to keep their most aggressive impulses largely in check.

The institutions of punishment and domestication made this possible. Around 500,000 years ago, we learned to use social sanctions to make uncooperative behaviour relatively unprofitable. In the most extreme case, a person's tendency to tyrannise, subjugate, bully, attack or even just exploit others led to this person simply being murdered, often in a deliberate act by those who had finally had enough. A species that kills its most belligerent, aggressive and ruthless members over hundreds of generations creates a strong selection pressure in favour of peacefulness, tolerance and impulse control. We are the descendants of the friendliest.

The fact that the murder of undesirable elements made sense at some point in our evolutionary past, and the fact that today, with the benefit of hindsight, we can see the welcome long-term benefits it has brought us, doesn't mean that behaviour like this is still justified. On the contrary, the history of morality shows that our punitive instincts had their heyday, but that this has long been a thing of the past. In the modern world, there is often no place for them.

Exodus

Genetic data shows that between 750,000 and 250,000 years ago, our lineage split away from the line that eventually gave rise to Neanderthals.[4] The characteristic traits that we can identify as changes associated with domestication are collected under the umbrella term of 'domestication syndrome'. The domestication syndrome characteristic of modern humans was scarcely noticeable at all in *Homo neanderthalensis*. Modern man, by contrast, has become more peaceable, compliant, controlled and cooperative. This suggests that the punitive mechanisms that caused this domestication syndrome in *Homo sapiens* must have gained influence around this time. Robin Dunbar also pinpointed the evolution of *Homo heidelbergensis*, which he classifies as the first archaic human, to 500,000 years ago.[5] The end of this development, which turned us into social beings through punishment, marks the arrival of anatomically and behaviourally modern man – the human being we have no hesitation in classing as our equal. To start with, there were a number of archaic hominins that lived at different times and in different places: *Homo antecessor* is typically associated with Europe, *Homo ergaster* was located in Africa, and *Homo erectus* was well established in Asia. *Homo heidelbergensis*, considered to be the last common ancestor of Neanderthals and humans, gradually replaced and superseded these earlier species before becoming today's humans.

The better we learned to cooperate with each other, to protect each other from dangerous predators, to hunt together and to safeguard each other from the hardships of a barren environment, the better we became at surviving. Our enhanced ability to cooperate and survive led to continuous population growth, so we had to learn to live in larger and larger groups. A higher population density brings not only opportunities but also risks: being surrounded by more members of your species offers the advantages of cooperation, but simultaneously leads to a greater need for coordination and, as a result, more potential for miscoordination and conflict. To avoid the collapse of social cohesion, the resulting potential for friction made it essential to have more self-control and to moderate our aggression. We managed to initiate the taming of our species by developing punitive practices – a combination of brutal punishment and 'softer' social sanctions.

Unlike the australopithecines – those very early prehuman ancestors that emerged around 5 million years ago – our early contemporaries already looked very human. One of the best and most complete early human fossils ever discovered is 'Turkana Boy', a prepubescent *Homo ergaster* who was found in Kenya by the lake of the same name. A reconstruction by the French palaeoartist Élisabeth Daynès reveals a nine-year-old, with tired, sad eyes above a round nose, his bare skin covered with pale patches of dried mud. *Homo naledi*, a similarly complete skeleton discovered only a few years ago in South Africa's Rising Star Cave, was depicted by American palaeoartist John Gurche as a grown man with a grim look and a bristly beard who seems to be observing something with the corners of his mouth twisted down disapprovingly.

There is now a consensus that humankind originated in Africa. Today, we can pinpoint two distinct phases of the exodus from this continent – 'Out of Africa I' and 'Out of Africa II' – when the first, various archaic human species, and later *Homo sapiens*, managed to leave Africa and colonise large areas of the Eurasian continent. From there we finally reached America and Australia. Initially limited to eastern Africa, our habitat progressively expanded into North Africa as part of the first Out of Africa phase. Our path led us eventually to the Caucasus via the Sinai Peninsula (the oldest human fossils outside Africa were found in Dmanisi, in Georgia), and from there across what is now Turkish territory to Europe. In the opposite direction, we also eventually spread to southern and eastern Asia. So, by 500,000 years ago, we had already come quite far.

In the 1990s in Boxgrove Quarry in southern England, a gravel pit between Brighton and Portsmouth was excavated. The shinbone of a *heidelbergensis* was found whose height was estimated to be 1.8 metres; the bone was dated to roughly 500,000 years ago. We had managed to reach that area – now surrounded by water – because the gigantic glaciers covering the northern hemisphere at that time were so large that today's England could be reached on foot from mainland Europe. The tools and animal bones found there indicate that there must have been a kind of slaughterhouse where our ancestors harvested the meat of hunted wolves, beavers, red deer, bison and small rhinos from their bones with hand axes that had been painstakingly, very crudely sharpened.

In modern-day Italy, fifty-six footprints, known locally as the 'Devil's Trails', tell the story of an escape in which a group of *heidelbergensis* and animals, apparently stumbling, sliding, slipping and panicking, tried to escape a volcanic eruption near Roccamonfina in Campania.

In the South of France, at the Terra Amata site by the old port of Nice, archaeologists found remains of huts made of interwoven sticks and branches braced against each other. These dwellings had an oval layout and were supported by two central pillars; they provided protection from wind and weather for a fire, and could accommodate up to two dozen people, once again *heidelbergensis*. There they would prepare food, sleep, breastfeed their children, hang up skins to dry and sharpen their spears.

All these findings, scattered across much of the world, point to larger civilisations who hunted, travelled and slept together – all of which requires not just cooperation but, increasingly, mechanisms for keeping everyone in check, too.

Free to make promises

Nietzsche was one of the first to suspect that it was impossible to write a history of morality without also writing a history of punishment. In the second treatise of his *Genealogy of Morality*, he tried to prove that a bad conscience – in other words, the awareness of having fallen short of our own moral claims, or of others' – was due to an internalisation of instinctive aggression, which had to find new outlets with humankind's increasing socialisation: 'All instincts that cannot be given external expression, *turn inwards* – this is what I mean by the *internalization* of man, and with this we have the first appearance in man of what subsequently was called his "soul".'[6]

This idea was based on a now-outdated 'hydraulic' model of our psychology, in which the pressure of urges that are not acted upon must accumulate and eventually be channelled somehow and somewhere:

> Enmity, cruelty, the delight in persecution, in attack, destruction, pillage – the turning of all those instincts *against* their own owners is the origin of the 'bad conscience'. It was man who, lacking external enemies and obstacles, and imprisoned as he was in the oppressive confines and monotony of custom, in his own impatience, frustration and rage, lacerated, persecuted, gnawed, frightened and abused himself; it was this animal, which is supposed to be 'tamed', which beat itself against the bars of its cage.[7]

This hydraulic model, whereby pressure builds up within our psyche and at some point virtually erupts and comes into its own, has turned out to be incorrect. Nonetheless, Nietzsche was right in how he saw the problem: what part did punishment play in the evolution of our morality? What function did it fulfil at the time? And what function does it fulfil now? Or is punishment an evolutionary 'hangover', something that no longer has a place in modern society, an atavistic relic that we should abandon? 'Breeding an animal which is free to make promises'[8] was the task nature set itself with the creation of humanity. When did this animal come into being, and what made it so docile and disciplined, so far-sighted and malleable? How and by what means did it come about? And in particular, what skills do we need to be able to make a promise?

Making a promise is giving a commitment to another person: we say we'll do x at time t, and at the same time we mean the other person can legitimately expect this to happen. To promise something, we first need to have an understanding of the future. Above all, however, we have to trust that we can have enough control of ourselves not to manoeuvre ourselves into a position that makes it impossible for us to do x, and that when t has come, we'll have the discipline to keep the promise – regardless of whether or not we feel like it. Consequently, only people with sufficient control over themselves, who can therefore guarantee they have the necessary self-discipline, should 'be free to' make promises. If I promise a friend I'll pick her up from her home on Monday morning and accompany her to a doctor's appointment, I'm making a commitment to myself not to party so hard on the Sunday that I can't get out of bed the next day. I'm also signalling that I'll turn up for her even if I don't really feel like it. How extraordinary is the ability to make plans like this far into the future? How special is this human privilege? For Nietzsche, being able to make promises – or even 'being free' to – becomes a cipher for the more general problem of the emergence of a being who has human forms of self-control, foresight, discipline and willingness to cooperate.

We now know that punishment was one of the crucial factors in the history of our morality, and we have it to thank for these qualities. Of course, this was completely different from what Nietzsche had imagined. It isn't the internalisation of aggressive impulses to which we owe our self-control and foresight, but an evolutionary selection against impulsivity and aggression that made it possible for us to make promises.

A tamed monkey

Often in academic moral philosophy, the argument goes that punishment is generally regarded as a necessary evil, as a burden and an annoying duty that we'd at best like to carry out reluctantly and that we'd rather see done discreetly outside the city walls. Nietzsche also saw this differently: 'To witness suffering does one good, to *inflict* suffering does one even more good.' This sounds harsh to modern ears, and would have even to many of Nietzsche's contemporaries, but it is an old, potent and very human sentiment that even other primates might endorse: we know they foreshadow humankind impressively in thinking up bizarre cruelties. 'Without cruelty, no feast: this is what the most ancient and greatest part of human history teaches – and in punishment too is there so much of the *festive!*'[9]

A quick glance at the history of punishment confirms the suggestion that we are endowed with powerful punitive instincts. The French social theorist Michel Foucault opens his *Discipline and Punish* with the following gruesome description of the execution of Robert-François Damiens on the Place de Grève in central Paris:

> On March 2, 1757, Damiens had been condemned 'to make the *amende honorable* before the main door of the Church of Paris', where he was 'to be taken and conveyed in a cart, wearing nothing but a shirt, holding a torch of burning wax weighing two pounds'; then, 'in the said cart, to the Place de Grève, where, on a scaffold that will be erected there, the flesh will be torn from his breasts, arms, thighs and calves with red-hot pincers, his right hand, holding the knife with which he committed the said parricide, burnt with sulphur, and, on those places where the flesh will be torn away, poured molten lead, boiling oil, burning resin, wax and sulphur melted together'.[10]

The saturnalian lust with which the unfortunate Damiens was

to be put to death is particularly striking. The accusation of regicide was, strictly speaking, unfounded, as his assassination attempt on Louis XV had been unsuccessful: he only inflicted a small wound and gave the king a fright. This was not just dispassionate and bureaucratic compliance with the law: a spectacle was staged, a theatrical show was performed, which, as lithographs from the time testify, was attended by thousands of onlookers. It was, in short, an event intended for maximum impact for the spectators.

Whereas just thirty years later the 1791 Eighth Amendment to the US Constitution explicitly forbade 'cruel and unusual' punishments, it seems the French executioner Nicolas-Charles-Gabriel Sanson could not have been cruel and unusual enough when he did away with Damiens:

> 'Finally, he was quartered,' recounts the *Gazette d'Amsterdam* ... 'This last operation was very long, because the horses used were not accustomed to drawing; consequently, instead of four, six were needed; and when that did not suffice, they were forced, in order to cut off the wretch's thighs, to sever the sinews and hack at the joints.'[11]

Most people today regard the public torture of criminals as grotesque barbarism, only fit to feature in the kind of horror story we use to assure ourselves of the superiority of our own civilisation. But this aversion to violence and displays of cruelty is actually a very late result of the selection process that began a very long time ago.

Self-domestication

If we compare humanity with its closest non-human relatives, the chimpanzees, we can immediately see how thoroughly harmless humankind is. We are feeble and skinny in stature, naked, subdued and lacklustre, completely inoffensive and pitiful (most of us, at any rate). This is no coincidence, because the evolutionary history of modern humanity is to a considerable extent a story of 'survival of the friendliest'.[12] This isn't meant as an alternative to Herbert Spencer's 'survival of the fittest'. Our compliance was the reason for our adaptability.

One of the most significant differences between humans and chimpanzees is their capacity for 'reactive aggression' in response to a threat or provocation.[13] In contrast to this is 'proactive aggression', which has a planned, calculated nature. Chimpanzees are extremely *reactively* aggressive and often resolve conflicts violently, for example by biting off their opponent's genitals or tearing at their faces. Humans have also been victims of this, such as Charla Nash, who was mauled by the chimpanzee Travis in 2009.

When groups of chimpanzees meet by chance in their natural habitat, violent clashes almost always occur, often ending in the death of some members of the warring groups. Humans, on the other hand, are to chimpanzees as golden retrievers are to wolves. This analogy is, of course, only half-serious, but the fundamental idea that man is strangely reminiscent of a domesticated animal is not a new one. Darwin entertained this suggestion, but ultimately rejected it because he could not think of a candidate that could be responsible for our domestication in the way that we are responsible for the domestication of dogs. The theistic explanation, which presumed divine intervention was responsible, seemed scientifically worthless to him, and the idea that a higher *non*-human species could have domesticated humans sounded too dubious. The suggestion that we humans could have domesticated *ourselves* was clearly too unlikely for him. So he dropped the hypothesis.

Originally, the concept of human domestication came from the German anthropologist Johann Friedrich Blumenbach, who pointed out in his 1775 book *On the Natural Varieties of Mankind* and in later writings that human trait patterns resemble those of domesticated animals in many respects. Of course, the idea of human domestication was also misused, as almost always happens with evolutionary speculations, to justify racial discrimination, purporting that white people had allegedly become superior to all others because of their greater degree of domestication. This theory has long been proven untenable and was indeed rejected by Blumenbach himself.

Domestication syndrome was systematically examined, notably in the twentieth century, and we now have a good understanding of what the syndrome consists of, how it manifests itself, what the genetic processes that cause it physiologically are, and what specific evolutionary mechanisms have led to selection in favour of greater peacefulness in humans.

Domesticated animals almost always have a configuration of specific and, to a great extent, conspicuous traits distinguishing them from their wild relatives.[14] They are usually more docile, receptive to training, playful and less aggressive than their wild counterparts. These traits are key to this phenomenon. Along the same lines, there is also usually pronounced neoteny, which means the retention of juvenile traits into adulthood. In many dogs and other species, we can see these played out to varying degrees in features including a smaller body and a greater need for physical closeness and cuddling. Most domesticated species also have slightly reduced brains and skulls, accompanied by smaller teeth and ears as well as a shorter snout or muzzle. At the same time, there are a number of features that intuitively correspond to the appearance of tamer, more peaceable animals, but it is not immediately clear why they are so often found in domesticated animals: for example, curled tails, floppy ears and noticeable depigmentation, which manifests itself, for example, in white markings, often on the forehead or between the eyes.

The Belyayev brothers were early pioneers in the discovery and definition of the domestication syndrome. A human geneticist seen as politically suspect in the Soviet Union, Nikolai Belyayev was shot by the Stalinist secret police in 1937. From the early 1950s, his brother Dmitry and his colleague Lyudmila

Trut carried on with his studies and made ground-breaking contributions to the understanding of the processes that lead to the domestication of wild animals. It has long been known that the traits mentioned above are frequently found in domesticated animals. These characteristics, or similar ones, can be seen in horses, dogs, guinea pigs, camels, cows, mice, pigs, cats and even llamas. Belyayev and Trut's interest, however, was in the deeper evolutionary question of whether the same change in characteristics could be recreated through specific selection in favour of prosocial behaviour. What happens when you systematically breed an animal species for friendliness?

To investigate this question, Belyayev and Trut devoted themselves over decades to an experiment with the Siberian silver fox.[15] Although it took thousands of years to turn wolves into dogs, this process could be compressed to a few decades by artificially selecting the most trusting foxes. After Belyayev and Trut started granting reproductive success to only the tamest specimens from their population, after ten, twenty and ultimately fifty generations – in the process the foxes began to develop not one but several mating phases a year, another typical effect of domestication – the solitary woodland animals had become affable playmates, not only in terms of behaviour but also in terms of the more common traits we see in other domesticated species like dogs.

The domestication syndrome's genetic basis was only decoded a decade ago.[16] For a long time, how and why selection in favour of friendliness and willingness to cooperate – whether natural or through breeding – simultaneously produces this domestication syndrome was simply a mystery. What does diminished aggression have to do with floppy ears and white markings? There is now very clear evidence to show that the solution to this mystery lies in a special type of stem cell known as neural crest cells. During early embryonic development, these stem cells eventually form the adrenal glands, which play an important part in producing and regulating stress and anxiety hormones. Domestication is ultimately a process that indirectly results in underactive adrenal glands. In the early developmental stages of vertebrate embryos, these neural crest cells are located in a specific position, at the dorsal end (towards the back) of the neural tube, which later forms the central nervous system. As the embryo develops, this cell type migrates both to the adrenal glands and to the skull and extremities. Since neural crest cells are coincidentally involved in forming the skull and teeth and also influence pigmentation, they can result in white markings and shorter snouts with smaller teeth. Domestication syndrome is therefore due to a selection in favour of a certain form of adrenal deficiency. This deficiency affects both the hormones regulating fear and aggression and the cell type, leading, as a by-product, to less pigmentation and reduced skull growth.

Human self-domestication not only had ethological – in other words, behavioural – consequences, but also profoundly reshaped humans' cognitive capacity. Only then were increased tolerance, reduced aggression and consequently a more developed social life possible. The fragile harmony of the group was put to the test less and less by violent outbreaks. This, in turn, created a new niche where improved communication skills and social cognition – consideration of what other people think or want – could thrive particularly well. Incidentally, the phenomenon of depigmentation is also found in our eyeballs: their light colour means we can quickly and accurately see where people are looking and what they are focusing on. This makes our intentions and thoughts more transparent to others. Great apes' eyeballs, on the other hand, are almost black, making it much harder to guess where they are directing their attention.

The physical basis of these cognitive abilities is the frontal lobe of the neocortex, which is responsible for controlling and directing actions. Injuries to this part of our brain behind the forehead, caused by accidents, tumours or strokes, for example, typically lead to limitations in the ability to act and plan, as well as difficulties in carrying out intentions. Increased impulsiveness, reduced self-control and problems complying with norms and rules are the result.[17] This phenomenon is called acquired sociopathy.

It is plain to see that domestication syndrome – extensive neoteny, a scaled-down skull, smaller teeth, friendly and cooperative behaviour – is also found in humans. But while with silver foxes it is obvious where the selection pressure came from that made wild predators into pets with wagging tails, we do not know with absolute certainty who or what tamed man. The most likely assumption right now is that we domesticated ourselves by simply killing the most aggressive and violent members of our groups. This was often the result of small-scale conspiracies between group members, who put to death the most blatant disturbers of the peace in ambushes by night. The fact that these prehistoric tyrants were deprived of any further reproductive success by their violent demise meant that aggression, poor impulse control and violent behaviour gradually tailed off. Man became domesticated just as the silver fox and (in earlier times) the wolf had.

Our evolutionary history made us simultaneously more and less brutal. Although, from this stage on, we have by and large been peaceable, cooperative and fond of harmony, we have been all the more sensitive to other people's deviations from the norm, and we monitor them meticulously and punish them mercilessly. Much later on, we directed our aversion to violence against punishment itself. But we'll come to that in time.

It is, of course, difficult to find direct evidence of the prevalence of archaic forms of the death penalty. We do know, though, that the murder of unpopular group members and troublemakers was carried out in modern-day hunter-gatherer societies. For example, for the !Kung San, native to southern Africa, who maintained their traditional lifestyle until well into the twentieth century, planned executions were the last resort in conflict resolution. Richard Borshay Lee, the world's leading expert on the life of the !Kung, reports:

> The Ju/'hoansi [an alternative name for the !Kung] do have one method of last resort, a trump card, for bringing a string of homicides to an end. The only word to describe it is an execution ... In the most dramatic case on record, a man named /Twi had killed three other people, when the community, in a rare move of unanimity, ambushed and fatally wounded him in full daylight. As he lay dying, all the men fired at him with poisoned arrows until, in the words of one informant, 'he looked like a porcupine'. Then, after he was dead, all the women as well as the men approached his body and stabbed him with spears, symbolically sharing the responsibility for his death.[18]

Everyone was allowed to take part: another indication that human societies are organised in an egalitarian way. Unlike chimpanzees, who live in strict hierarchies with an alpha male at the top who has food, resources and sex under largely monopolistic control, until the Neolithic revolution humans lived in more fluid structures without a stable leadership caste or distinct material inequality. It goes without saying that this equilibrium is not self-sustaining, and the execution of rebellious would-be tyrants probably goes some way to explaining how people managed to maintain their egalitarian way of life in the long run.

It was essential, of course, to ensure social cohesion in small groups of people in some way. So the absence of a monopoly on violence – a central government or penal system, for example – does not necessarily entail the absence of violence. Even if our prehistoric statelessness is often presented as idyllic by palaeo-anarchists and libertarians sceptical of authority, it is wrong to assume that leaderless hunter-gatherer units did not have to keep their coexistence under control to some extent. Often this must have led to an atmosphere bordering on paranoia, with virtually all the adult members constantly feeling they had to meticulously adhere to the norms of social interaction that applied in their group, to avoid putting themselves forward as the next candidate for execution.

The cultural processes that began reshaping the human mind and body at that time paved the way for the death penalty to come into force in practical terms. Killing a human being has always represented a technical problem associated with risks: in most cases, the person in question would certainly have other ideas, and would not be willing to go on their final journey without a fight. A number of anatomical findings suggest that humans may have acquired the ability to throw projectiles around 500,000 years ago. Their brains' increasing volume meant their energy requirements grew so much that they could only have been met by a rise in meat consumption. However, obtaining this meat was probably only possible for anyone who was able to hunt cooperatively with spears. On the other hand, the strength and precision necessary in spear throwing required a specific anatomical capacity to coordinate the shoulder, arm, hip and upper body to work together harmoniously to fatally injure a large mammal – such as another human, for example – from a distance. Fossil findings show that these anatomical changes may have already happened by that time.[19] The taming of humanity was facilitated not least by technical achievements that made it easier and *safer* to murder each other.

Punishment and cooperation

When they were found by the two British divers John Volanthen and Richard Stanton on an elevated rock, the twelve Thai players of the Wild Boars youth football team had been trapped more than two kilometres inside the Tham Luang cave for ten days.[20] Without food and light, but in good health, they had lost all sense of time.

In the cave, the boys discussed who should be rescued first.

Together they decided that the ones who had the furthest to travel home would be the first to take the dive. The boys thought they would have to bike home. And why wouldn't they? After all, they had cycled there, and they didn't realise that their fate had been captivating the entire world's attention for weeks, and that more than 10,000 people were involved in the rescue operation outside the cave's entrance, including more than a hundred professional divers, 2,000 soldiers, government agency representatives from a hundred countries, journalists, doctors, onlookers – and, of course, their parents. Hundreds of volunteers cooked food, helped pump water out of the flooded cave and took care of the camps.

None of the participants really believed the rescue operation would work. And justifiably so: it simply seemed too unlikely that a young man and twelve children could be rescued from one of the deepest and most dangerous cave systems in the world during heavy monsoon rains. None of the boys had any diving experience, and many of them couldn't even swim. To ensure they didn't panic under water, the boys had to be heavily sedated and equipped with breathing masks that covered their entire faces. Only then were they manoeuvred through the rocky cave in adverse currents and poor visibility for hours by the experienced divers from England, the US and Australia as well as Thai Navy SEALs. One of the divers lost his life. But the rescue was ultimately successful, and eighteen days after their disappearance, the last boy to be recovered, Mongkhon Bunpiam, reached the cave entrance.

Our morality makes it possible for us to cooperate on a global scale and make amazing sacrifices to come to the aid of strangers in need. But how does it do that? We share over 99 per cent of our genetic material with chimpanzees and bonobos who have lived in small groups for millions of years and who have never progressed beyond cracking nuts with stones the size of fists.

Part of the answer, as we have seen, lies in humans'

self-domestication. The systematic selection against the most violent and aggressive members of our species made us unusually peaceable and disciplined. The death penalty's formative power has literally been etched into – or *we* have literally etched it into – our DNA. But punishment didn't just affect our morality by creating the most compliant primate of all time. Punishment is also an institution that creates incentives discouraging uncooperative behaviour through social sanctions.

The problem, after all, that the evolution of cooperation had to solve was (and is) its instability. In any form of interaction between individuals, there is the question of whether or not to behave cooperatively towards the other. Cooperative behaviour is initially always costly: helping another person or not exploiting them presents a disadvantage. It is, as evolutionary theorists say, 'maladaptive'.

Hamilton's notion of inclusive fitness – that altruism is adaptive if certain conditions are met (the action is low-cost to the altruist or that the individuals involved are closely related) – and Trivers's concept of reciprocal altruism – which only pays off if the probability of meeting again is high enough – explain how simple forms of cooperation can spread in evolutionary terms. It pays to help genetically related individuals or potential future cooperation partners if a close enough relationship is at stake or if the probability of meeting again is high enough. However, neither of these conditions is usually met in larger groups, and so cooperative arrangements require extra reinforcement in these circumstances.

A tension quickly emerges, however: the bigger a group becomes, the more difficult it is to share the benefits of cooperation just with other members of this group, even if most of them are cooperative. This has paradoxical consequences, because in the end, non-cooperators inevitably fare better in a large group and they gradually become more and more widespread, because they benefit both from the advantages of their non-cooperation and from other members' cooperation.[21] Over time, uncooperative strategies ('defection') would take over. For a small number of cooperators to grow and ultimately dominate, it is essential for the number of non-cooperators not to be too large, or the entire structure will soon collapse.

Punishment can solve this problem because it makes non-cooperative behaviour costly in the long run.[22] Initially, robbing others is an excellent strategy, especially if you are surrounded by people who aren't constantly robbing you back. But that quickly changes if you are punished for your behaviour. The haul from your last three bank robberies is of little consolation if you get caught and go to prison for years.

Sanctioning uncooperative behaviour isn't unique to humans, of course; animals can sanction such behaviour by defending themselves against an attack or retaliating at a later date. What is special about our human punitive system is the fact that we are familiar with the concept of *altruistic punishment*. The idea that an individual C can be very deeply motivated to punish B for what he did to A – without C himself being one of B's victims – is virtually unique.

Punishment contributes to the establishment of human cooperation in larger groups and therefore promotes the common good. But there are two key omissions in this explanation: first, the practice of punishment cannot provide a fundamental answer to the question of how cooperation could arise in evolutionary terms, because altruistic punishment is itself a form of cooperation that is costly for individuals. (This is a *second-order* collective action problem: we clearly cannot explain the possibility of cooperation by simply presupposing another form of cooperation.) Second, social sanctions can stabilise *any* behaviour, not just beneficial types of behaviour. Sharing what you have hunted also means sharing risks: anyone can be unlucky on a hunt, so it pays for everyone to be covered against streaks of bad luck by conventions about sharing meat. Anyone who wants a share of other people's meat but doesn't want to share themselves is therefore punished.

In some cases, however, conventions emerge in human societies that are in nobody's interest, or only serve powerful minorities. Foot binding in China or genital mutilation in various cultures are striking examples of how objectively harmful, painful and bizarre types of behaviour can spread throughout a social group. Once the conventions in question are established, they are enforced with the same punitive mechanisms that make violating any other (perhaps much more useful) behavioural expectations unattractive. As disregarding conventions that may exist or refusing to monitor compliance with them is often associated with extensive reputational damage, deviant and misanthropic conventions can result from this – and can be further cemented by altruistic punishment.

Group selection may have played a significant part here. Perhaps we ought to imagine the evolution of punishment in terms of an institution that some groups happened to discover, while others did not. The groups that did discover and adopt the institution of punishment would have performed better than those that didn't because of the cooperation benefits achieved through punishment. If the selection pressure between those competing groups is stronger than the selection pressure between individuals within groups, punitive communities could have dominated in the long run, and non-punitive communities, we can assume, would have disappeared.

We know punishment can maintain cooperative arrangements, and the mechanics of how it works have been investigated through experiments. The economists Ernst Fehr and Simon Gächter have shown that punishment can be surprisingly effective in keeping the degree of social cooperation at a desirable level.[23] We've already seen that cooperative conventions rapidly collapse in problem situations because the incentive structure of freeloading makes uncooperative behaviour the dominant strategy: no matter what anyone else does, not cooperating is always more worthwhile. The public goods game shows that contributions to the public pot go down sharply after just a few rounds and ultimately tend towards zero.

To determine the influence of punitive sanctions on a group's social stability, we have to simulate a situation in which it would be advantageous for all participants if everyone did x, but in which it would always remain advantageous for each individual participant to do y. This control group is then compared to a group that has an extra option: namely, to punish uncooperative behaviour. Which of the two groups will be more willing to work for the common good?

This is precisely the question Fehr and Gächter asked. They set up an experiment putting together several groups of four participants, each equipped with a certain amount of money (in this case, twenty Swiss francs or 'monetary units'). For several rounds, the participants were able to decide how much should be contributed to the public pot. The payment options were regulated so that it was most worthwhile for the individual to make no contribution at all, or only a very small one. For the whole group, however, it was better if everyone always put in the maximum.

Six rounds were played, with the following results: the participants' willingness to cooperate – represented as the average contribution thrown into the public pot per round – started weak and soon fell sharply. By the end of the sixth round, the players kept most for themselves. Only when they played the game a second time were the participants given the opportunity to 'punish' the meanest players. For every monetary unit spent by one player on punishing another uncooperative player, three monetary units were deducted from the player who was punished. The effect on the overall willingness to cooperate was spectacular: by the end of these six rounds, the level of cooperation had reached almost the maximum possible (the maximum being the result if everybody behaved cooperatively all of the time). Punishing individuals who refuse to cooperate therefore solves the problem of freeloading, at least in an experimental setting.

The real situations our ancestors had to deal with 500,000 years ago were structured in a very similar way. Whether in violent clashes between hostile groups, hunting large wildlife or building shelters, it was crucial for everyone to contribute to a larger project that would not have been possible without the group's efforts. But even at that time, it did not depend on literally every individual contributing. Even members who did not fight or hunt, such as the sick, elderly or children, would benefit from a safe village or a sizeable haul. This possibility of benefiting from social cooperation without participating in it could be contained through altruistic punishment, but even today it can persist at any given time.

The psychology of retribution

To counteract potential freeloading, we had to acquire a taste for punishment. The selection processes we faced didn't just create punitive norms and practices that could be passed on to the generations that followed as cultural institutions; they also instilled a preference for sanctioning rule-breakers deep into our psyche.

This can still be seen today in the grammar of our punitive psychology.[24] To a considerable extent this is innate: it may be different depending on our culture, but it also has universal patterns which we are often not even aware of. We cannot observe them by merely thinking about ourselves; we have to conduct cunning experiments to be able to detect them at all.

In our day-to-day lives, our need for retribution and the justifications we give for specific punitive acts often differ significantly.[25] When we are explicitly asked why we want to punish someone, we consider the sanctions' deterrent effect to be relevant. We put rules in place to punish, say, theft, in the hope that the punishment is steep enough to deter anybody from committing theft in the first place. But if the possibility of deterrence is expressly ruled out, it turns out that little changes in our judgements about how harshly a perpetrator should be punished. In an interesting study, the behavioural scientist Eyal Aharoni and the social psychologist Alan Fridlund clearly identified that punishing a rapist who had become completely paralysed (as the result of an illness since his crime), along with the private nature of the trial, would not be expected to have any effect – that is, the perpetrator is, regardless of punishment, unable to reoffend. This did not prevent participants from continuing to consider deterrence as the main reason for punishing the rapist, even if its futility had been expressly pointed out to them. Our official justifications for imposing punishments remain committed to the disciplinary force of social sanctions, even if a deterrent effect is unequivocally ruled out by the case in question. We do not, in other words, want to admit to ourselves that we simply wish to punish regardless of deterrence.

If someone violates a norm, we seek retribution or revenge. We find it difficult to include the probable consequences of our punishment in our calculations. If we ask study participants to evaluate a case in which a pharmaceutical company manufactures a flu vaccine that in general saves lives, but still kills some children, the majority of participants will be largely indifferent to what effect punishing the company might have.[26] Regardless of whether the penalty was made public or was behind closed doors, whether it caused the company to stop producing the vaccine altogether (and many more children ultimately dying), and whether the company was insured against lawsuits of this kind (so that it did not suffer any consequences), the study participants suggested the same penalty amount. Even the risk of repeating a misdemeanour does not seem to have much influence on how, and how harshly, we think someone should be punished.[27]

Our psychology of retribution seems oddly contradictory: punishment's function is actually to produce a certain effect, namely compliance with the norms of cooperative coexistence. But at the same time, our conscious judgements about whether and how to punish someone seem strangely unaffected by how successful the suggested punishment is at producing that effect. How can this be?

This sounds paradoxical but is easily explained. It often happens that the evolutionary function and the actual content of a cognitive state are at odds with each other. Why, for example, do we have sex? The *distal* explanation (related to the distant past) for our preoccupation with sex is evolutionary and relates to the function of biological reproduction in our species' past: we want sex because we are the descendants of individuals who were interested in reproducing sexually. People with ancestors who were more indifferent to this concept obviously left a weaker genetic stamp on subsequent generations. This is the *function* of sex. When we feel like having sex, however, its reproductive function rarely plays a part *at that specific moment*: the *proximal* explanation (related to the present) for acts like these (or others) is almost always different. We are simply attracted to each other – physically or emotionally, or both. This is the *content* of the feeling, regardless of its function. Making the distal function of sex its proximal motive can often in fact create quite an unfavourable atmosphere: many couples keen to start a family can confirm that results-oriented pragmatism and spontaneous passion are often incompatible.

It is a similar case with our punitive psychology. The distal function of punishment is to prevent large groups from falling apart. In technical jargon, a function of this kind is therefore called *consequentialist* – its aim is to achieve a certain result. From a proximal point of view, though, our need for punishment is not consequentialist and results-oriented, but *retributive* – in other words, we want offenders to get what they deserve. Whether or not this will help us or our group is completely irrelevant at that moment in time.

Liars and cheaters

If punishment is adaptive, it makes sense to be equipped with the cognitive apparatus required to carry it out. We have cognitive modules specifically dedicated to the task of detecting uncooperative individuals who break norms. As Konrad Lorenz put it, the *a priori* of our thinking (what we don't need to learn through our own experience) is the *a posteriori* (what we only know from experience) of our evolutionary history.[28] Or, more succinctly, our ancestors' experiences have been embedded into our mental faculties over generations of adaptive trial and error.[29] Some of these hardwired thought patterns are specifically dedicated to the task of enabling and maintaining cooperative structures, and the detection of social fraudsters (cheater detection) is a well-known example.

The fact that we are naturally attuned to social norms being transgressed can be shown by studies based on what is known as the 'Wason selection task'. There are two different versions of this test: one is a purely mental task, while the other adds social norms to this task. Although it is the same test, most people fail the first version, but pass the second without any problems. Thinking about social norms is intuitively easy for us because it is part of our social being.

In its original version, this test aims to assess our capacity for conditional cognition – in other words, thinking about 'if–then' relationships. Four cards are presented to study participants. One card depicts an ace (A), one a king (K) and the other two are a 4 and a 7 respectively. The task is to test if the following 'if–then' rule applies to these four cards: if there is a consonant on one side of a card, then there will be an odd number on the other side. The aim is to reveal as few cards as possible until the rule is clearly confirmed or disproved. Most participants choose to flip the K and the 7. But this is the incorrect solution: K and 4 would be correct, as only a consonant on the back of an even number can indicate whether the established rule is true or not (by proving it untrue). Whether there is a consonant on the back of the 7 or not is irrelevant to how true the rule is (because it does *not* prove an odd number is *only* on the front if a consonant is on the reverse).

Almost everyone makes this mistake because we all fall victim to our tendency towards confirmation bias, and in general we are not very good at thinking about abstract conditional sentences with no relevance to us in real life. For the genealogy of morality, it becomes interesting when the card test's content is varied so that it relates to the violation of social rules. When consonants and numbers are replaced by norms and human actions, we suddenly become astute logicians. When the rule becomes 'If a person drinks alcohol, they must be over eighteen years old' and the cards show a) drinks alcohol, b) does not drink alcohol, c) is over eighteen, d) is under eighteen, we automatically reveal the correct cards a) and d), although this test is structurally identical to the abstract variant discussed above.[30]

Why is conditional cognition suddenly so easy for us when stark numbers and letters are replaced by social content? Evolutionary psychology suggests that we are equipped, hardwired even, with an intuitive aptitude that helps us to detect rule violations accurately and quickly. This makes evolutionary sense if only because it means we do not have to consciously waste our efforts constantly thinking about recurring problems to come to a result. If human groups depend on cooperative success, routinely dealing with uncooperative freeloaders has top priority – if we were unable to manage them, humanity would have (completely) sunk into chaos long ago.

Social sanctions

Punishment helped domesticate us because it taught us important skills such as self-control, compliance, foresight and peacefulness that made life in burgeoning groups possible. The fact that the early hominids might have coped without state structures and a centralised monopoly on the use of force could well inspire anarchist fantasies these days. But the seemingly limitless freedom from official authority came at an expensive price: it was still essential to exert force and discipline, but this was offset by a softer, but omnipresent, collective control of social norms.

Not all social sanctions were as harsh and definitive as the death penalty. Our human morality is held together at least as much by more subtle practices of informal norm surveillance. A community uses these very artfully to keep records of its members' social reputations. For cooperative beings like us, a damaged reputation can be catastrophic. The method used to log and archive a community member's trustworthiness and prestige was (and still is) gossip. The exchange of gossip and rumours has played an important part in our evolutionary history, especially for the evolution of language, whose original function may primarily have been social communication about other people's behaviour.[31] Gossiping could have been a kind of extension of monkeys' mutual grooming and sitting around, which until then had primarily ensured social cohesion. Here, too, as the size of the group increased, it was crucial to shift to new forms of social cooperation: as grooming requires direct physical contact and is very time-consuming, it was not a suitable means for humans to strengthen cohesion beyond the limits of the closest family members. Language, on the other hand, has the advantage that it can send signals to a larger number of contemporaries at the same time. Networks of trust are developed in this way, information about other group members' characters is exchanged, alliances are formed and behavioural norms are determined, refined and abandoned.

A ruined reputation has always had devastating consequences, and many people who suffered this fate would never recover. But why? Who cares, you might assume, what others think about you? As long as no one has suffered any harm to life, limb or property, you could be quite indifferent to what the other tribe members, ageing relatives or a horde of unfavourable strangers on social media think of you. Though we can rationally dispel worries about what strangers think of us, in reality we very much *are* concerned with what everyone else thinks: 'A man will be mortified, if you tell him he has a stinking breath; tho' 'tis evidently no annoyance to himself,'[32] David Hume laconically and aptly stated, and Immanuel Kant – not usually known for his sensitivity and powers of observation – couldn't help but notice the importance to us of how we are perceived by others, and how much rumours and gossip matter in collective coexistence:

> Now, of all arguments there are none that more excite the participation of persons who are otherwise soon bored with subtle reasoning and that bring a certain liveliness into the company than arguments about the moral worth of this or that action by which the character of some person is to be made out. Those for whom anything subtle and refined in theoretical questions is dry and irksome soon join in when it is a question of how to make out the moral import of a good or evil action that has been related, and to an extent one does not otherwise expect of them on any object of speculation they are precise, refined, and subtle in thinking out everything that could lessen or even just make suspect the purity of purpose and consequently the degree of virtue in it.[33]

Incidentally, Kant had much less understanding of the darker forms of gossip, which he denounced as 'defamation', 'spying on the morals of others' and 'ridicule'.[34]

It is certainly true that loss of social acceptance often has very tangible consequences. For the inhabitants of Yasawa, a tiny archipelago in the South Pacific, a person's social reputation also marks their legal status. The more severely a person's reputation is damaged, the more he or she becomes the legitimate victim of ostracism, ridicule, violence, theft and destruction.

While people who are socially excluded in this way may be out busy fishing, their homes are set on fire or their tools stolen, and their tormentors get away scot-free. This also has a domesticating effect: 'Individuals who fail to learn the correct local norms, can't control themselves, or repeatedly make mistaken violations are eventually driven from the village after having been relentlessly targeted for exploitation.'[35]

The proverbial loss of face is, in no small measure, a frequent motive for suicide. Among the Ghanaian Ashanti, for example, at the beginning of the twentieth century:

'If it be a choice between disgrace and death, then death is preferable.' This is best illustrated by a story about a village elder who bent down in obeisance to a visiting dignitary but 'inadvertently broke wind'; within an hour he had gone home and hanged himself. His tribal brothers, when queried about his drastic reaction, were of one mind, [and] agreed he had done the appropriate thing under the circumstances.[36]

In some groups, the loss of social reputation is not seen as a milder alternative to execution, but as the worse evil.

The dawn of crime and punishment

One of humanity's greatest moral developments was delighting in cruelty. It was all the more difficult to unlearn this lust for cruelty after it had fulfilled its purpose.

If we look back in time, we might be forgiven for thinking that most of our ingenuity and craftsmanship went into developing ever more sophisticated methods of inflicting pain on other people. House number 449 on the Singel in Amsterdam's canal belt hosts a torture museum where you can see some of the most original of these methods for just 7.50 euros (or 4 euros for under twelves). You can find chains and cages here, along with blades and chests, thumbscrews, racks, scalding tongs, scaffolds, pillories, gallows and iron maidens. The museum's website invites visitors to 'Discover the painful past' (contrary to what you might think, it's not the advertising slogan of the psychotherapist next door). Medieval engineers were probably particularly fascinated by the connection between pain and sitting, as torture chairs with the seat and back covered with iron spikes seemed to be very popular. The repertoire also included devices seemingly like gym equipment, but with a pyramid-shaped top for the tortured to sit on. People were imprisoned in the belly of the 'Sicilian bull', a hollow bronze sculpture in the shape of a bull, and roasted alive over a fire while a system of funnels and pipes would transform the cries of pain from the condemned into bull-like bellowing.

Our evolutionary history has evidently given us a tendency towards excess. For a long time, we preferred to err on the side of penalties that were too harsh rather than too lenient, based on the assumption that ever harsher, more cruel and merciless sanctions were particularly effective. Punishing a wrongdoer too leniently is emotionally unacceptable to us. Even curbing our bloodlust in small amounts will therefore have spelled out enormous progress. The *lex talionis*, the law of retribution found in most cultures stating that like should be rewarded with like, is often seen today as an example of the most primitive barbarism. In fact, we should compare the commandment 'an eye for an eye, a tooth for a tooth' with the alternatives that were popular back then. In a society where never-ending cycles of destructive bloody revenge ensue, a call for proportionality, as in this *talionis* principle, can mean a massive improvement.

At the same time, the simplicity of the principle was its undoing, because simple rules are intuitively plausible and easy to teach and learn, but can break down as a result of all sorts of specific cases and the hurdles of technical implementation. In some societies, for example, the rape or murder of a man's daughter was atoned for by raping or murdering the perpetrator's daughter.[37] But what if the perpetrator had no daughter?

The Babylonian Code of Hammurabi decrees that the punishment for destroying an eye is the destruction of an eye, the penalty for the loss of a tooth is the loss of a tooth, but for hearing loss it suddenly becomes 'one mina of silver'. Maybe they weren't quite sure how to destroy a person's hearing and had to come up with an alternative compensation?

In any case, crime and punishment were never fairly distributed. The social inequalities within a society are always evident when norms are violated and this misdemeanour is subsequently punished. There is one group that has always made up the overwhelming majority of perpetrators and victims of violent crime: young men. Typically, just over 80 per cent of all murder victims are male. Men are even more glaringly over-represented among murderers, at well over 90 per cent.[38] Male criminals were always punished much more severely, not least because they were seen as a greater danger. Hanging, evisceration and quartering, for example, was reserved as the punishment for high treason in England from the reign of Henry III in the thirteenth century, but it was never administered to a woman.

Differences in the socio-economic status of different groups are also reflected in penal practice. Some legal codes, such as the Indian Manusmriti written about 2,000 years ago, explicitly differentiate according to social caste.[39] In general, the higher the caste, the milder the punishment. In particular, corporal punishments were harshest for the low-ranking Shudra and only applied to the highest-ranking Brahmins in rare exceptional cases; financial compensation for property damage, on the other hand, was structured the other way round, so that higher social prestige required greater reparation.

Aside from archaic and curious methods of punishment, above all history can give us examples of how our punitive practice became more and more individualised. While in most societies the family has almost always been regarded as a fundamental social unit, developing societies also gradually began to recognise the rights and duties of individuals. In medieval China, the criminality of an act was still measured by the family relationship between the accused and the victim. Crimes against close relatives were punished more severely than crimes against more distant relatives, and these in turn were punished more harshly than offences against non-relatives.[40] The structure within the family also played a role: older people generally had more legal elbow room; a father could kill his son and get away with just a warning, while a son would fear far more drastic consequences for patricide.

Entire families could be held liable for the shameful deeds of individual members. It was only in the European High Middle Ages that 'clan liability' principles like this gradually softened. In the twelfth century, for the first time, the Magdeburg Rights formulated the idea that a father could not be held accountable for a murder that was actually committed by his son – if six independent male witnesses with impeccable reputations could confirm this, at any rate.[41]

This structural shift in punishment away from the principle of blood relationships towards the punishment of individuals by anonymous third parties can still be seen today in punitive methods among different cultures.[42] People seem to intuitively want to punish uncooperative behaviour in most societies, as experimental games show; however, in Eastern European cultures or the Middle East, participants who have been punished in one round are more likely to take revenge on the players they suspect of sanctioning them in the next. This mainly happens in societies with a weak rule of law and low 'social capital' – in other words, informal forms of social trust. In Western societies, behaviour like this almost never occurs.

This change, and the partial abolition of kinship-based legal norms, was accompanied by the idea of *mens rea*, 'culpable intent', as a basic principle in attributing violations of the law. Medieval legal canonists began to distinguish guilt as an act (*actus reus*) from guilt as a mental state (*mens rea*). To be able to replace the erosion of clan liability with corresponding principles of individual responsibility, it was now necessary to spell out the extent to which knowledge, intent, predictability and causation were relevant to the assessment of a crime:

> Consider this case: a blacksmith throws a hammer at his assistant and kills him. Medieval lawyers began asking not only if the smith *wanted* to kill his assistant (motive: the dead man had flirted with the blacksmith's wife) but also whether the smith *intended* to kill his assistant and *believed* the hammer would do the job. Does it matter if the black-smith had intended to kill his assistant next week (using poison) but accidentally killed him early with the hammer, thinking he was an intruder breaking in? They decided that the smith's culpability varied depending on which of several distinct mental states existed.[43]

From this point, it was not much of a leap to get to the concession that extenuating circumstances can compromise a person's guilt: an immature, drunk, emotional, mentally confused or ill person no longer had to expect the same punishment as a perpetrator who acted with full awareness of their wrongdoing.

The abolition of the death penalty, on the other hand, remained unthinkable for a long time. Here, in the rationalisation of violence, is where one of the questionable strengths of German philosophy is revealed. Immanuel Kant, widely known and celebrated as a fearless defender of human dignity, had a clear opinion on how to deal with criminals and he allowed himself to be carried away by one of the darkest and most obscene passages of Enlightenment philosophy:

> If, however, he has committed murder he must *die*. Here there is no substitute that will satisfy justice. There is no similarity between life, however wretched it may be, and death, hence no likeness between the crime and the retribution unless death is judicially carried out upon the

wrongdoer, although it must still be freed from any mistreatment that could make the humanity in the person suffering it into something abominable. Even if a civil society were to be dissolved by the consent of all its members (e.g., if a people inhabiting an island decided to separate and disperse throughout the world), the last murderer remaining in prison would first have to be executed, so that each has done to him what his deeds deserve.[44]

Georg Wilhelm Friedrich Hegel even went so far in his philosophical system that he rejected the abandonment of execution as disrespect for the convict. A murderer has a right to recognition, which is implicit in the death penalty, as it does not reduce man to an animal at the mercy of his urges and instincts:

> In so far as the punishment which this entails is seen as embodying *the criminal's own right*, the criminal is *honoured* as a rational being. He is denied this honour if the concept and criterion of his punishment are not derived from his own act; and he is also denied it if he is regarded simply as a harmful animal which must be rendered harmless, or punished with a view to deterring or reforming him.[45]

The overdue humanisation of punishment was then called for by *utilitarian* thinkers. Utilitarianism is the philosophical movement that sees morality's purpose as maximising human well-being. Utilitarians were (and still are) of the opinion that social sanctions should ultimately be judged using the criterion of social usefulness – the 'greatest happiness of the greatest number'. The Italian legal philosopher Cesare Beccaria gained particular influence when he first systematically argued for the abolition of the death penalty and a general modernisation of state punishments in his short treatise *On Crimes and Punishments* in 1764. He believed the death penalty could not be part of the social contract, as no one would voluntarily give the state the right to kill him. As Beccaria also suspected that the threat of a quick death was less of a deterrent than the prospect of long-term misery in prison, and executions brutalised rather than civilised a society, he flatly rejected capital punishment.

Utilitarian moral philosophy leads to a certain bean-counting mentality when it comes to socio-political questions (for better or for worse). The first utilitarians often allowed themselves to be carried away by reform proposals that ranged anywhere between touching naivety and dystopian planning hubris. Jeremy Bentham's design of a new kind of prison architecture, with honeycomb-like cells arranged in a circle around a central tower, has become particularly famous. Bentham himself described his design as a 'panopticon' – an all-seeing eye. This layout meant that as many occupants as possible could be monitored by as few personnel as possible: as each cell should be visible from the central tower, but the prisoners wouldn't be able to tell whether the guard was looking at them or someone else. The prisoners monitored themselves, for all intents and purposes, and were forced to visit their assigned punishment upon themselves.

The trial

In most societies, before a wrongdoer's punishment there is some kind of procedure in which formally established rules are used to determine whether and how they should be punished. Here, too, we often look at the history of trials and hearings with a view to uncritically assuring ourselves of our own progressiveness and depicting the protagonists back then either as unscrupulous executioners or as delusional zealots who, from cynicism or ideological delusion, abused their legal authority to organise savage mercilessness. In reality, even the most outdated practices follow an internal logic that can only be deciphered by looking more precisely at the historical circumstances at that time.

The Invention of Good and Evil

As children of the modern age, we like to throw up our hands and poke fun at the naivety of the medieval judgement of God, whereby a defendant's guilt was established by creating an opportunity for the Lord God to reveal the truth about the course of events. In fact, the judgement of God was surprisingly rational and not at all deluded.[46] First of all, we should emphasise that the *iudicium dei* was only considered for the most serious and therefore least common crimes, and even then only if there was no confession, if no alibi could be given by reliable witnesses and no other circumstantial evidence or proof could be found that would have made a decision possible. It is also little known that the judgement of God led to acquittal in most cases. According to the Hungarian *Regestrum Varadinense*, for example, a kind of document of trials from the early thirteenth century, what was known as the hot water test, in which a ring or other object had to be fished out of a cauldron of boiling water, acquitted over 60 per cent of all accused. How could that have happened?

Apparently, the threat of the hot water test alone was enough to persuade many devout perpetrators to admit their guilt. Nowadays we often overlook how fervently the accused themselves believed in the effectiveness of these divine judgements. However, most of the innocent people, also convinced that divine verdicts were reliable, would agree to them, and as a result it was generally the innocent ones who were subjected to the test. But how could it be that masses of innocent people were prevented from being declared guilty by the inevitable scalding? According to official regulations, the preparation of the cauldron had to take place in secret, and at this point the cleric responsible had the opportunity to adjust the water's temperature to a tolerable level so that the pre-screened subjects could survive the ritual largely unscathed. The prosecutors also had a vested interest in not convicting an innocent person. Occasionally it is said to have happened that someone would be convicted of murder, and soon afterwards the alleged murder

victim would resurface alive. The resulting invalidity of allegedly infallible judgements could permanently shake the faith of
even the most devout flock in the community, which was something to be avoided at all costs. The worldly influence on divine
judgements was much greater than many people assumed at
the time.

Even animals, dead people and inanimate objects could not
always depend on remaining safe from the long arm of the law.
World history is full of creatures that have been judged with the
greatest aplomb and in all seriousness, so their misdemeanours
might be made known before God and the world and they might
be appropriately disciplined.[47] In the French Alpine village
of Saint-Julien, in 1545, there were proceedings against some
weevils that had eaten the year's harvest; at Lake Geneva in 1451
an injunction was imposed on lampreys that were damaging
the salmon; some time later, a cockerel accused of laying an egg
was beheaded in Basel; unfortunate mules, dogs and donkeys
that had become the object of overly fond human attention
were whipped, exiled or burned to death. Pigs, cows, rats and
horses were regularly accused of murder – and convicted. In
Madagascar, it was reported by early twentieth-century anthropologists that crocodiles captured randomly were interrogated
when one of their kind had committed murder. The Cadaver
Synod (*Synodus Horrenda*) in 897 was the trial of Pope Formo-
sus for irregularities in his election; although he was present in
the courtroom for all intents and purposes, he had died months
earlier and first had to be exhumed. Even swords, wells and
carts would be put on trial if they were suspected of 'murder'.
Church bells, a deadly danger unknown today but not to be
underestimated at the time, were imprisoned in the seven-
teenth century; and when Anthony Wylde was suffocated by a
haystack in Nottinghamshire in 1535, the astute jury managed
to identify a particular tuft of hay as the main culprit.[48]

The future of punishment

Punishment's role in the history of morality can also give us clues as to how modern societies ought to penalise our accused. The future of punishment lies in milder sanctions, and in turning away from and largely restraining our most merciless instincts.

The history of punishment proves that harsher penalties are not necessarily better at having a deterrent effect. The evolution of morality shows that some social sanctions do play an indispensable part in keeping social cooperation at an acceptable level. However, the key variable is not the punishment's severity but its expected benefit (or for the person being punished, the damage or loss). And this clearly depends both on how unpleasant the punishment is, and on the likelihood of its occurrence. Even the death penalty will only intimidate me to a certain extent if I can assume I will never be caught. Having to endure ten lashes can have a far greater effect if there is enough certainty that I'll get them one day.

The existence of excellent reasons for curbing our need for punishment is particularly evident when we make political decisions simply because we want to see our desire for retribution satisfied, for example. The American philosopher Neil Sinhababu has calculated that for the cost of the Iraq War, every single one of the 3,000 or so pandas alive in the wild could have been given their own stealth plane (the price of one is more than US$700 million).[49] Even if we may have thought the 'war on terror' was justified at first, we have to ask ourselves whether the murder of 3,000 innocent Americans on 11 September 2001 was appropriately compensated by sending more than 6,000 further Americans to their deaths, not to mention the hundreds of thousands who died on the Afghan and Iraqi sides, only to agree a peace treaty with the original enemy twenty years after the war started. An approach like this does not stand up to a cost–benefit analysis.

Even the so-called 'war on drugs', which has barely stopped

being vehemently waged ever since the spread of crack cocaine in America in the 1990s, can now confidently be described as lost: it is based on the same principles of crime and punishment inherited through evolution, claiming we can allegedly only succeed in combating socially unwanted behaviour with ever harsher penalties. This leads both to over-criminalising acts that should not be classified as crimes at all and to excessively punishing acts such as drug use, which harm either no one or the perpetrator alone.[50] At the same time, there is a worldwide trend shifting from physical punishment to prisons and from there on to financial sanctions or compensation, a trend that ought to be pursued or, better still, accelerated.[51]

Punitive over-reactions are unjustified because the circumstances a person is born into are often pure chance through genetic lottery, as are the resulting socially problematic opportunities and incentives for criminal behaviour.[52] Increasingly harsh prison sentences only exacerbate these problems, as a long prison term makes returning to a more socially appropriate path harder rather than easier. Punishment is most effective when it is carried out quickly and with a high degree of probability. Harsh penalties seldom meet these criteria. Sentencing and carrying out the death penalty, for example, is usually extremely protracted because the process takes a lot of time – nobody wants to accidentally execute innocent people – and because it is rarely enforced.

In many cases, carrots are preferable to sticks: incentives for non-criminal behaviour often have even more impact than the deterrent effect of punishment.[53] Measures like this are often denounced moralistically as 'rewards' for a criminal career. More than anything, this shows how difficult it is for us to choose better policies over worse ones – even when the data is at our fingertips. As soon as a penal sanction runs counter to our deep-seated emotional structures, in our doubt we tend to opt for the alternative that will not benefit anyone over one that could really make a difference.

But despite many deplorable exceptions, modern societies are slowly but unmistakably moving towards a humanisation of their penal practices. The Wolvenplein Penitentiary is a prison in Utrecht in the Netherlands. Built from clinker bricks and located in a prime location in the city centre's canal ring, it has been empty since 2014. There are fewer and fewer crimes in the Netherlands, not only because fewer and fewer crimes are being committed, but also because fewer and fewer acts are illegal and fewer and fewer of the remaining illegal acts are punished with imprisonment. Many people in Utrecht are hoping the former prison will help the overstretched housing market to ease a little after its conversion into redeveloped loft apartments with macabre historical surroundings.

Creeping death

Qianlong is ill. He is suffering from an allergic reaction to Tibetan fungal spores, and as he, the emperor of China, believes that a disease of Tibetan origin is best treated by Tibetan doctors, two shamans from Lhasa are consulted to bring the 'Lord of Ten Thousand Years' back to his feet. Meanwhile in the Forbidden City, rumours are spreading that the emperor is dying – a lie, probably put around by two court physicians who feel duped and have had their pride injured.

They probably did not expect what happened next:

The court tribunal had deliberated for only three hours before reaching a verdict and a sentence: the day after the Great Snow Festival, the liars were to endure *ling chi* – *Creeping Death*. Shackled to posts and facing each other, one would be forced to follow the torture inflicted on the other, step by step, in the knowledge that it would be his own fate the next moment. The executioner would first use scissors to slice off their left nipple, then the right; next, he would hack through their chest with a knife, then the bunched muscles of the legs, starting on their thighs and continuing on their shanks, removing thin strips with each incision until the bones glinted through streams of blood. Next, the flesh of the upper and lower arms was to fall into the blood-soaked sawdust until the liars resembled dripping, screaming skeletons – reduced to ghosts not by the executioner but by their lies alone.[54]

Ling chi, a method of killing that was occasionally carried out for a thousand years in China – at least two dozen cases from the Ming and Qing dynasties are known of – and that was only discontinued at the beginning of the twentieth century, has long preoccupied European intellectuals and writers. A fascination with the macabre and exotic has certainly led to some descriptions being exaggerated and embellished; not infrequently, the convicts would have been sedated with opium before their dismemberment began. The French philosopher Georges Bataille, on seeing contemporary photographs of the procedure, even indulged in the sentimental folly of believing he could detect the signs of ecstatic and blissful devotion in a dying man's absent gaze.[55]

The 'death by a thousand cuts' once again illustrates the passion with which we humans have always responded to crime: liars, fraudsters, adulterers, murderers and thieves must be brought to justice. Although evolution made us peaceable, far-sighted and self-controlled, it also equipped us with powerful punitive instincts that often want to see the violation of the norms of coexistence punished with relentless severity.[56]

Human self-domestication, which this made possible, made us more docile and capable of cooperation than any other human species we shared the Earth with at that time. But it was not only this domestication that ultimately made us superior to other human species, but also the degree of cultural complexity – the development of techniques for producing clothing, housing, weapons, food and knowledge – that gave us an advantage. The co-evolution of culture and morality allowed us to increase the size of human societies again; this made us socially adaptive beings who could act according to moral norms and social rules. Our culture gave us flexibility and diversity. So we became the curse of our fellow species, and the destiny of the world.

3

Deficient Beings

The lives of others

We often wonder if we are alone in the universe. But we have just forgotten that, for most of our time on Earth, we weren't. Is there intelligent life out there besides us? Perhaps far out among the stars. But here on Earth, we haven't been among other intelligent beings – beings like ourselves – for quite some time.

The fact that we underestimate the Neanderthals is often criticised: their sturdy, muscular physique, a bulky physiognomy framed by matted hair, awkward hands culminating in chunky fingers with splintered nails, combined with our own tendency to narrow-mindedness, meant that we dismissed our human relatives for too long as dim-witted savages and violent cretins – so much so that the term 'Neanderthal' eventually evolved from a biological taxon to a derogatory term for our fellow humans when we wanted to describe them as uncultivated brutes.

The actual existence of Neanderthals was hard to deny, once evidence of these not-too-distant relatives of ours was discovered, and so it was categorically all the more crucial to somehow keep them at a distance, separating 'them' from 'us'. We were so unwilling to admit the possibility that another long-extinct species of humanity might have been living in the heart of Europe alongside us that even a scientist as eminent as Rudolf Virchow, upon inspecting the peculiar fragments of a skull he was presented with in 1872, suspected they were the remains of an ordinary human deformed by arthritis, various fractures and softened bones: a lonely Russian Cossack, maybe, who had somehow ended up in the Kleine Feldhofer Grotte cave near Düsseldorf a long – admittedly surprisingly long – time ago.

It was in those same caves that Johann Carl Fuhlrott, visiting as the founding chairman of the local natural history association, had the intellectual audacity to misidentify the remarkable bone findings, which he had travelled to investigate out of curiosity in the late summer of 1856, as human. Fuhlrott would soon show the bones to the Bonn anatomist Hermann Schaaff-hausen, and the two of them went on to present the shocking discovery at a conference of the Natural History Society of the Prussian Rhineland and Westphalia a year later. The workers in that momentous limestone quarry in the Neander valley had meanwhile confirmed that the bones had been hidden half a metre deep in untouched sandstone. So they had to be old – very old, surprisingly old, maybe even unfathomably old.[1]

One of the classic ways to judge how developed a culture is can be found in how that culture buries their dead – and indeed, whether they bury them at all. Until relatively recently, the subjective sophistication associated with this was considered our inviolable privilege, unique to our species. Yet by this measure, we must credit the inner workings of the Neanderthals with a level of intricacy that matches our own. In 1960, the American archaeologist Ralph Solecki discovered the grave of an adult Neanderthal man in the Shanidar Cave in the Kurdish Zagros mountains. His undertakers had clearly wanted to make the corpse entrusted to them comfortable: this father, friend and brother-in-arms had been handed over to eternity laid down in a childlike position on his side and tenderly and delicately covered with sheaves of grain and bunches of medicinal flowers. Until this discovery, such levels of attentiveness towards the dead were thought to be reserved exclusively for *Homo sapiens*.

The mysterious stone circles of Bruniquel, in the Aveyron

Gorges in southern France, which were discovered by student Bruno Kowalczewski in the early 1990s, reveal a similar taste for the transcendental. No one knows what function the super-structures, found hundreds of metres deep in a stalactite cave, might have had at that time, but who could rule out the possibility that the stacked arrangements of broken stalagmites might have been places for ritual dance, song and inebriation, where our relatives were beginning to articulate their awakening sense of a world beyond what was sensually tangible?

Neanderthals were human through and through. The use of toothpicks, treating animal skins and ropemaking all combined to wear down their teeth. Their brains were larger than ours, and they managed to colonise the entirety of Europe for hundreds of thousands of years in an inhospitable environment that experienced rapid cycles of climate change, sometimes cooling down drastically, becoming increasingly covered in glaciers, and then rapidly warming up. Europe's oak and lime woodlands were populated not only by ibexes and aurochs, still native today, but also by giant forest elephants, hippos and Barbary macaques.

Faced with such fauna, the Neanderthals made double-edged flint wedge tools that they kept sharp and in shape with other smaller tools. They wore jewellery made from eagle feathers and scallop shells,[2] as well as pearl necklaces intertwined in elaborate geometric patterns. The holes arranged in straight lines in some animal bones suggest that these may have served as wind instruments. They built incredible houses from the largest mammoth bones covered with animal skins, their entrances held open by enormous tusks. The anatomy of their throats and palates facilitated the production of human speech, and the construction of their ears aided its understanding.

About 50,000 years ago, Neanderthals began to disappear. It is often suspected that it could have been us, *Homo sapiens*, who, having migrated to Europe, then exterminated our benign cousins. Then again, it is not unusual for any species to simply die out at some point; we lived in parallel in different regions of Eurasia for many tens of thousands of years without annihilating each other. There are probably several factors that eventually led to the demise of these first Europeans: the climatic upheavals of the last cold period, which buried large areas of northern Europe under hundreds of metres of desolate ice; the subsequent dearth of large mammals suitable for hunting; new diseases; and volcanic eruptions that darkened the skies. Their last traces, found in Gorham's Cave in Gibraltar, are 30,000 years old. At last, our time had come.

Who we are

We, the last survivors, think we are absolutely fabulous. But for many other species, our arrival was for the most part a nightmarish scourge: when we first arrived with our 'projectile weapons to hunt and gather in Eurasia [roughly] 50,000 years ago, we wiped out nearly every predator of the Ice Age'.[3] There were reasons behind our appalling superiority: during this period from about 50,000 years ago, there was a 'veritable sea change in the quality and quantity of weapons, tools, jewellery and artwork of a kind and quality never seen before, not to mention tents, lamps and a host of more substantial gear, including boats'.[4] The change was a fairly sudden one, a relative boom in innovation, ambition and human supremacy. So where did all this gear come from?

This period coincides with the spread of *Homo sapiens* along the 'southern route' from East Africa via the Arabian peninsula to Europe and Asia, the route now known as 'Out of Africa II'. By that time, we already possessed a unique combination of characteristics and abilities that made us – now anatomically modern humans – superior to all other large mammals and especially to all other human species we still shared the Earth with at that point. As well as advanced cognitive faculties, which included a grammatically structured language, our hypersociality and our capacity for social learning are of particular interest when it comes to the evolution of morality.[5] Our ultra-cooperative dispositions, evolved millennia earlier, made it possible for us to live in larger and larger groups; at the same time, these groups created the conditions for a burgeoning reservoir of cultural knowhow, which we learned to absorb meticulously. Anthropologists refer to this as 'high-fidelity learning'.

Most animals are far superior to us in speed, strength and skill (in relation to the challenges they have to face, at any rate). And yet we have managed to establish an unprecedented level of global ecological dominance, prompting many scientists to refer to the current geological era simply as the Anthropocene: the 'age of humans'. Our strength, in the face of relative physical weakness, lies in our ability to compensate for our physical shortcomings with the help of external structures. Moral norms, values and practices are all part of this. In many ways, our morality is the niche we constructed for ourselves, and is what enabled us to achieve all that we have.

These external structures or 'scaffolding'[6] provided by our self-constructed environment – our language, cities, inventions and institutions – are made possible by our hypersociality. The dominance of humankind, deficient as we are, depends essentially on our ability to cooperate in large groups. Without morality, this level of successful cooperation would be unthinkable. Moral norms and values are the way that otherwise deficient beings with poor resources like us manage to achieve a level of cooperation that is nowhere to be found in non-human wildlife – except in some social insect species, the difference being that these follow rigid genetic programmes, whereas we can establish flexible cooperative structures. This makes morality a crucial factor in the evolution of our human nature and the culture in which it is embedded. Humans in general, and philosophers more specifically, have made numerous attempts across history to identify what it is that makes us unique, and to reduce the essence of humanity to the formula 'animal + x'.[7]

But all new attempts to find this elusive *x* that we humans, and only we humans, possess have turned out to be misleading or incomplete.

Is humanity *Homo faber*: the only animal that can use tools? Nut-cracking chimpanzees and ravens fishing for insects with twigs have long since debunked this idea. Or are we *Homo ludens*: the playing animal? Anyone who has ever observed a cat with a ball of wool or a litter of young foxes will find it hard to see playing as humankind's exclusive privilege. Or should we stay with *Homo sapiens*, the rational animal, the animal that can think and possesses intelligence?[8] This definition too is inadequate, and falls short upon closer inspection; I am not sure how you would normally go about separating wheat from the chaff, but what the Japanese macaques do, washing the grains in seawater so they can skim off the lighter, edible part from the water's surface, seems quite clever to me. Even intelligent problem-solving is ruled out as a unique selling point for the most status-obsessed of all animal species.

Another problem is that a definition of the concept of humanity does not merely have to be, as philosophers like to say, 'extensionally adequate': it doesn't just have to find characteristics that are unique to humans alone. When asked what man is, the ancient philosopher Plato is said to have replied that man is a featherless biped – a definition that deserves every iota of ridicule it has been given over the past 2,500 years. Being unique is also a trite cliché: every creature is unique in its own way, without necessarily being particularly interesting.

The 'anthropological difference' we are looking for that supposedly distinguishes humanity from all other species must pick out something that explains our (alleged) special position, and on top of that, it must help us understand ourselves. People who believe that no living being except humankind is both bipedal and featherless have learned nothing about the mystery of humanity – or about themselves.

A little later, Aristotle dared to give it another try, and

he developed the most famous and influential definition of the concept of humankind of all time: the human is a being capable of language, the *zoon logon echon*, eventually translated by Latin scholars as *animal rationale*. This proposal also needed later revision, because although our talkativeness may be unrivalled, human language and the chirping and singing, calling and gesticulating of many animal species seem to lie on the same continuum of symbolic communication. Immanuel Kant, making an attempt at the definition himself, called for a little more modesty by degrading us to mere animals *endowed* with a capacity for reason (*animal rationabile*).[9] Reason is a potential inherent in all human beings; however, it is only tapped into by some, and even then, only occasionally and imperfectly, an observation that will resonate with anyone who has ever made an impulse purchase, or experienced road rage.

The quest for what makes us unique was eventually declared futile. Humans are the animals that seek their own essence – and never find it.

The telephone and its inventor's four deaths

For the inventor of the telephone, it must have been a breathtaking moment when he first managed to transmit sounds from one place to another using electrical signals. It's easy to imagine how he would have been overcome by a sublime thrill. In 1854 he presented his invention to the public for the first time, still as a mere idea at that point; from 1860 he knew how sounds could be transformed into voltage pulses; in 1861 he gave his invention the name 'telephone', which would be adopted from then on; in 1871 the United States Patent and Trademark Office approved a provisional patent under the number 3335 for an apparatus called the 'Sound Telegraph', which had first made a dialogue between two people over a distance possible; after the first public demonstration at the World's Fair in Philadelphia in 1876, the success of his breakthrough was unstoppable.

The inventor of the telephone died his first, second, third and fourth deaths in Nova Scotia in Canada, Friedrichsdorf im Taunus in Germany, Saint-Céré in France and Staten Island, New York – sometimes near and sometimes far from his birthplaces in Florence, Edinburgh, Brussels and Gelnhausen.

The history of the telephone on French Wikipedia goes like this: 'En France, Charles Bourseul, agent de l'administration des télégraphes, posa le principe du téléphone.' The Italian version of the online encyclopedia, on the other hand, stated until recently: 'L'invenzione del telefono elettrico è ufficialmente attribuita al fiorentino Antonio Meucci.' Philipp Reis and Heinrich von Stephan are the first two names mentioned on the website's German counterpart. In the Anglophone world, of course, the Scotsman Alexander Graham Bell is known as the inventor.

But, in fact, no one invented the telephone at all – at any rate, no *one* human being. The notion that a great invention has to be traced back to a single inventor – a lone genius in his study, modestly coaxing out its deepest secrets – is largely a fiction upheld by patriotic historians. The fact that we can communicate directly with each other over long distances is not due to one person, but to a process that largely took place without our knowledge: a process in which a large number of individuals, through minor and minute scientific, conceptual and technical improvements, managed to find a solution to a problem that probably would not even have occurred to anyone as being a problem just a few decades earlier. This process is called 'cumulative cultural evolution' – the process by which beneficial innovations are culturally transmitted, and accumulate over time. How does cultural evolution work, though? And why did it play such a crucial part in the evolution of our morality?

The emergence of cultural expertise enabled us to produce an entire range of profound developments that made the transition to modern humanity possible. For one thing, these developments gave us the ability to provide material support for larger and larger social groups through improved technology and more efficient economic activity. For another, they also made it possible for us to live according to rules entirely constructed by ourselves – rules that set out how to participate in rituals or games, for example – which created a plurality of different roles a human could assume, which in turn freed us from the imperatives and limitations of a single human body. Culture generates diversity and can reinforce our tendency to gravitate towards group membership – our hypersociality – by giving us the opportunity to symbolically mark community boundaries. We have done this for tens of thousands of years through things such as fashion, language, flags and rituals.

These developments also made us into beings who depend on social learning and whose skills and knowledge must be acquired from others. This created a momentous fusion of knowledge and morality: we became even more group-oriented than we already were, because successful learning relied largely on discerning who to trust by identifying shared values and norms. Culture means diversity, flexibility and community, but it also means dependence and being at the mercy of others. After a certain time, these qualities eventually allowed us to make the shift to large hierarchical societies.

Over the past ten to twenty years there has been a growing recognition in the academic world that understanding what drives cultural evolution will help us solve one of the most persistent mysteries of human history: how we came to global dominance. Without cultural evolution there would be no reading or writing, no dancing or painting, no cities, bridges or walls. And without cultural evolution there would be no morality. It's essential to recognise that this is a relationship that goes both ways, too: the context-specific moral norms that regulate and enable our coexistence can only be passed on as cultural heritage. It is only by understanding and following these norms that we can live in communities large and extensive enough to maintain complex information and techniques that were not inherited genetically.

The course of cultural evolution has radically transformed us humans as *biological* beings – our genes, anatomy and physiology. The concept of the 'deficient being' alludes to the fact that we humans can scarcely compete with many non-human animals in terms of physical strength or innate instincts. This is no mere coincidence, but owes itself to the process of cultural evolution, over the course of which we have had more and more of our bodies' functions taken over by a self-constructed environment. Pots and pans replaced large proportions of our digestion process. Spears and arrows made physical strength superfluous. Norms of sharing and helping replaced the rule of a dominant alpha male.

Cumulative culture

So now we know what makes humans unique *and* special: we are the only animals that have *cumulative culture*.

'Culture' needs to be understood in its broadest sense; it does not just include Beethoven and Proust, but the entire multitude of information, skills, practices, rituals, institutions, rules, values, technologies and artefacts that are passed on from one generation to the next through teaching and learning. This transfer happens *horizontally*: the transmission of cultural objects – be they ideas or tools – is not bound to the glacial pace of genetic mutation and selection because cultural knowledge is passed on directly from one person to the next through *social learning*. Adapting better to our external living conditions doesn't have to mean being subject to the merciless trial and error of birth and death. Instead, social learning allows us to have the flexibility to be able to try out new variants without always having to produce a new creature with a new genetic make-up.

Some, though very few, animals have rudimentary cultural

practices. The Japanese macaques mentioned previously wash sweet potatoes as well as wheat. They learned these techniques from Imo, a female of the species on the island of Kōjima, who spontaneously began to do it in 1953 at the age of eighteen months.[10] Soon, most of the other monkeys in Imo's circle had adopted the technique, apart from the oldest. As these elders died, the skill was mastered by all of them. It's not just primates, either: among sparrows too, songs often develop differently from area to area, and are passed on within each group through learning processes.[11]

The difference with us is that we did not just start by creating cultural products and passing them on. Crucially, each successive generation did not merely absorb those products passively, but gradually made improvements to their cultural heritage. Changes like this, considered individually, often seem trivial, unspectacular and only incremental; with enough time, however, groups of people managed to develop practices of astonishing complexity in this way. At a certain point, the reservoir of knowledge and skills created like this became so sophisticated that it could no longer be explained by individual innovation or, once lost, be recreated. Our culture took on a life of its own.

The fact that we have a cumulative culture is not just the key that makes us unique. It is also important enough as a feature to largely solve the mystery that we are to ourselves. The capacity for cumulative culture explains why we have language, why we feel, how we feel and how we live as we do. Its explanatory potential can hardly be overestimated: according to the Canadian scientist and evolutionary expert Joseph Henrich, cultural processes have been the dominant driving force of our evolution over the past 50,000 years – the crucial phase of recent human development.[12] Cumulative culture, amazingly, explains why some people have blue eyes and are lactose tolerant; it explains walking upright, and our ability to walk long distances and to throw objects with startling accuracy; it explains our seemingly endless childhood, extended dependence and extreme vulnerability in the first years of our lives, and it explains why female humans, unlike most other animals, experience pain when they give birth. All these developments have come about due to cultural processes that we, cumulatively, dreamed up.

Cumulative culture also explains our shortcomings. Perhaps our most striking feature is how little innate knowledge or skill we have as individuals. The observation that we humans are poorly equipped in comparison to non-human animals is not a new one. After all, the contrast with the relatively self-contained nature of other mammals is striking: newborn foals stand up immediately after they are born; their development seems more or less complete. The rest is just growth.

We humans, on the other hand, are radically vulnerable: no fur, claws or wings but a slender, naked body bearing a hypertrophied skull with a diminished jaw. And without instincts, innate knowledge or even the most basic abilities needed to survive, for the first few years of our lives we are totally reliant on a network of parents, grandparents, teachers and mentors whose main task seems to be to protect us from involuntary suicide. We remain relatively dependent on this network until adulthood.

In the first section of his 1772 *Treatise on the Origin of Language*, the Prussian philosopher Johann Gottfried Herder observed this same quirk of humanity and remarked that the human being was 'the most orphaned child of nature, naked and exposed, weak and necessitous, timid and unarmed, and what constitutes the sum of misery, devoid of any guide through life'.[13] The same motif of human instinct and being at the mercy of others returned over a century later in Nietzsche's *Beyond Good and Evil*. According to Nietzsche, a human is a 'sublime abortion' and the 'animal *whose nature has not yet been fixed*'.[14]

The very things that make us unique and special – that make us human – our openness to new sensations and experiences, flexibility in the choice of habitat and creativity in dealing with the ever-changing challenges that the environment imposes on us – all come at a high price: that of complete, utter helplessness for a significant chunk of our infancy and adolescence. For all our qualities, we are also uniquely flawed.

In philosophical anthropology, which emerged in the German-speaking world in the first half of the twentieth century, the theory of humanity being 'deficient' is systematically taken to extremes. Max Scheler saw humanity as being characterised by our 'world-openness'.[15] Other animals are *in* the world; humanity *has* a world. This differentiation in the relationship between human organism and environment means we can look at nature and at ourselves in it from the outside, to all intents and purposes, instead of remaining directly rooted in it. Helmuth Plessner's concept of humanity's 'eccentric positionality' suggests a similar distance.[16] All living beings are characterised by establishing a boundary between organism and environment. Human beings manage to do this reflexively by not merely surviving, but also consciously negotiating their relationship with the world through intelligent behaviour and deliberate manipulation of their environment. Arnold Gehlen developed the concept of deficient beings with a political and sociological focus, by attributing a relieving function to social institutions to make up for humanity's inadequate abilities. In other words, entrenched and traditional social practices, on which we remain existentially dependent, compensate for the fact that humankind is not yet fixed.[17] Our culture compensates for our defects.

At around the same time, the Swiss biologist Adolf Portmann coined the phrase 'physiological prematurity' for the human being. The increasing complexity of human coexistence made it necessary for the neocortex to grow so it could cognitively meet the gradually escalating demands of information processing. As well as more and more energy, this largest section of the human brain needs one thing more than anything else:

space. Our skulls, which soon swelled to a ridiculous size, dictated that we needed to be born earlier and earlier, and this was only just manageable for our female ancestors' anatomies. So human birth became an unusually risky business. An extremely high mortality rate among mothers was one consequence, and the almost complete lack of development in human children at birth was another.

Catching fire

You and forty-nine of your colleagues are parachuted over the tropical rainforest. On the plane with you are fifty capuchin monkeys that you have to compete against in a fight for survival. No equipment is allowed, except clothing (for the humans). After two years, the survivors are counted. Whoever survives the longest wins. Joseph Henrich asks:

> Who would you bet on, the monkeys or you and your colleagues? Well, do you know how to make arrows, nets, and shelters? Do you know which plants and insects are toxic (many are) or how to detoxify them? Can you start a fire without matches or cook without a pot? Can you manufacture a fish hook? Do you know how to make natural adhesives? Which snakes are venomous? How will you protect yourself from predators at night? How will you get water? What is your knowledge of animal tracking?[18]

The monkeys will cope – at least, no worse than they would be able to normally. We humans, on the other hand, are 'addicted' to culture. On our own and without the support of tools, regionally specific knowledge or practices that help us navigate a familiar environment, we are little more than a snack for more competent predators.

Scenarios like these are not mere thought experiments, either. HMS *Erebus* and HMS *Terror* were two British warships led by Captain John Franklin that set out in 1845 to complete an expedition to discover the Northwest Passage to the Pacific. In the second winter, the ships were trapped in pack ice, as they had been in the first. None of the men were ever seen again. In 2014, the two ships were rediscovered on the seabed a short distance from each other. What had happened? A major problem was that the crew had increasingly been suffering from lead poisoning because the cans they had packed as provisions – which should have been enough to last them five years – were not properly sealed. And obtaining food in the Arctic seems a hopeless task. Or does it?

In fact, the area around King William Island has been inhabited for 30,000 years by the Netsilik, who manage just fine there. The environment is harsh but rich in resources. The problem was never that there was no food for the two ships' 105 crew members, but that the highly trained and unknowingly doomed crew could not benefit from millennia of cultural evolution that enables the native Inuit populations to build safe shelters and hunt seals using harpoons constructed from reindeer and polar bear bones. Highly specific knowledge – preserved, passed on and refined over generations – is crucial for spotting the seals' holes, detecting their presence at just the right moment and using skill and strength to kill the animals. It is essential to know how to light a fire and make frozen seawater safe to drink.

After all, could you have managed to build an igloo? I doubt it.[19] The knowledge required for this is so complex and precise, and the necessary instructions have to be followed so pedantically, that it would be impossible to start from scratch within a generation – once lost, this knowledge would be largely irretrievable (for the time being). The house made of snow has no designer, and no inventor. It was designed by cultural evolution.

We will never know exactly how we became a cultural species. The exact sequence of events is lost in the depths of the past. Nonetheless, we can say with some confidence that of all the myths we humans tell ourselves about our origins, the Promethean version, with the anthropogenic force of fire, comes closest to the truth. Probably the most momentous cultural innovation of all was the taming of fire.[20] With this development, we embarked on a path of escalating feedback loops that irreversibly accelerated the co-evolution of a culturally enriched environment and adaptive primates that benefit from this environment.

Nowhere is it more evident that we are deficient than in the organs we use to absorb and digest our food. Our mouths are far too small, our jaw muscles are not worth mentioning and our teeth are mostly useless; tiny stomachs and a short intestine complete the tragedy of our digestion. The ability to control, create and use fire for cooking explains better than anything else why and how we became such deficient beings. Cooked food is both higher in energy and easier to digest; therefore it allows us to 'externalise' ever greater aspects of our digestion and food processing. We started chopping, grinding, pounding, grating, curing and fermenting, the result of which was food that was largely pre-digested, for one thing, and higher in energy than raw food, for another. These key things meant we could save resources that would otherwise have had to be invested in maintaining bloated internal organs and bulky jaw muscles. The energy saved could instead be channelled into developing our brains, which our atrophied chewing equipment and bloated skulls had left more than enough space for.

This feedback process put us on a path to learning and, with it, culture: primates that cook live longer, are healthier and as a result leave a legacy of more offspring, which makes a disposition to cook more and more established. Smaller organs and larger brains eventually lay the foundation for most of the adaptations in our anatomy we have seen. Meanwhile, we have become addicted to cooked food – largely unable to subsist without it. Plus there is the fact that if you change your diet to raw meat, you need to eat more. Soon you find you are still hungry after every meal, despite larger and larger helpings. After two weeks, protein poisoning and diarrhoea set in; after a few weeks death is inevitable.[21]

Probably the most significant consequence of the co-evolution of genes and culture is the premium that a culturally enriched environment places on individuals' learning capacity. The knowledge, and especially the expertise, held in a cultural environment offers many survival benefits. The individuals who are best placed to tap into the cultural reservoir offered to them and draw on – or in modern terms, download – the information available to them have a distinct and crucial edge. The ones most capable of learning have the greatest reproductive success, so the entire population becomes more and more capable of learning from generation to generation. This continues to enrich the cultural memory, which in turn becomes more and more receptive, like a sponge that is becoming both larger and denser. And the more content available to download, the more worthwhile it is to invest in the cognitive apparatus that makes that content accessible.

This dynamic accelerates rapidly not only at the moment when cultural learning takes place incidentally, but also when it is actively structured by teachers and learners together. From a certain point in human history, we began to consciously set up the learning environment for adolescents so it would foster and facilitate learning itself. According to the Australian philosopher Kim Sterelny, this has turned us into 'evolved apprentices'.[22]

The skills needed to cook, make tools, tell stories or hunt are easier to acquire the more the learning environment is designed to make teaching and learning as easy as possible. The culmination of this development is the establishment of nurseries, schools and universities, so that in most societies today a large part of the first half of our lives is spent in institutions that disseminate social knowledge. Anyone who has completed secondary school and passed their exams nowadays would have been by far the greatest mathematician of their time 500 years ago and would have gone down in history as a superhuman genius with their encyclopedic knowledge. Yesterday's geniuses – on whose shoulders, of course, we stand – became today's average, through cultural evolution.

Most animals eke out an existence in a narrowly defined ecological niche. Frogs live on the edge of shallow waters rich in food; storks often settle in an environment close to humans. There is a high degree of adaptation between these species and their niches, which means a species has no alternative but to stick close to a certain niche for its survival. Some animals, on the other hand, are genetically equipped to construct their own niches. Beavers are experts in building dams; many birds are competent nest builders. These inherited prescribed actions play such a key role in various species' lives that Richard Dawkins coined the term 'extended phenotype' for them.[23] And yet beavers still depend on a set of environmental provisions, as do birds.

We humans are unique in that we can flexibly adapt our niche construction to our environment.[24] This ability has made us the only large mammal that can successfully survive and thrive in virtually any environment, from the hostile icy wastes of the Arctic to the tropical rainforests in Indonesia and on to the busy streets of London. In Arizona and Dubai, air conditioning helps us manage the hot climate. In crowded cities, it is our ability to cooperate peacefully with a large number of strangers that ensures we survive.

The co-evolution of genes and culture

The interplay of biological and cultural evolution is crucial for the emergence of the deficient being that is humanity. These two processes do not just run in parallel, but are connected by complex feedback loops that influence and reinforce one another. Biological changes made cultural advances possible. The cultural innovations then began at an exponentially increasing pace, giving our genetic evolution a specifically human form. This amalgamation is known as 'gene–culture co-evolution', and it is largely 'autocatalytic': it produces its own fuel.[25] Selection pressure, to which the vast majority of organisms are subjected in an uncontrollable natural environment, is now applied by a self-made environment. The better our ancestors adapted to a thoroughly cultural way of life, the better their genes were represented in the next generation.

The list of co-evolutionary effects of this kind is extensive; our entire bodies are shaped by culture, from head to toe. Thermoregulatory adaptations are maybe the most intriguing example of how cultural innovations have determined our genetic trajectory. Two techniques in particular have made us a 'sweating species': tracking prey, and our curious ability to run and walk long distances. Our long limbs, specially designed muscle fibres, powerful back muscles and a separate torso-to-head rotation that helps us keep our balance all combined to make us perfect long-distance runners. At the same time, our fluid requirements increased, but meanwhile there had been other co-evolutionary processes that caused our internal organs to shrink, which set sensitive upper limits on the body's ability to transport water internally. Cultural evolution then solved this problem: human hunters quickly figured out how to carry water in external reservoirs and began using ostrich eggs, animal skins or large shells as water containers. The co-evolutionary combination – the sets of developments that went hand in hand – of tracking our prey, long-distance running and transporting water eventually made us the naked, sweating monkeys we are today.

Lactose tolerance is another famous example of the genetic consequences of cumulative culture,[26] and it is all down to a mutation in one single genetic location. Virtually all newborn humans are lactose tolerant, an aptitude that typically disappears during childhood. The moment our sedentary ancestors started keeping dairy cattle, conditions were created that drastically increased selection pressure in favour of lactose tolerance in adulthood. It is not just a random mutation that enabled some groups to metabolise lactose, but the combination of this mutation with the *cultural* innovations in animal husbandry (that we ourselves brought about) which we have to thank for our *genetically* inherited lactose tolerance. The cultural innovation, in other words, reinforced the random mutation to bring about a genetic predisposition that is now present in over a third of the global population.

In cities, people live closer to each other, and there is closer contact between humans and animals than there would otherwise be. Urban life has therefore always been the ideal breeding ground for epidemics and plagues. As a result, increased disease resistance and higher immunity rates are found in populations whose history of urbanisation goes further back. City living reinforced a genetic ability to better resist disease.

Blue eyes, it may surprise you to learn, are also a product of the co-evolution of genes and culture. Historically, blue eyes suggest a Baltic and northern European origin and are a by-product of reduced melanin production. Darker skin tones caused by increased melanin production offer important protection against the risks of UVA and UVB rays in the regions of the Earth closer to the equator. The emergence of agriculture made it possible for us humans to colonise northern regions with fewer food resources. Weaker sunlight in these areas reduced the need for melanin in the skin; at the same time, melanin makes it more difficult to synthesise vitamin D, which is essential for survival, so having lighter skin in regions with less sun is evolutionarily advantageous. The less melanin the body produces, the brighter a person's eyes become. So the cultural evolution of agricultural practices created a new kind of selection pressure that made the skin of northern European populations pale and their eyes blue.

Using tools shaped our hands, whose dexterity is unsurpassed in the animal kingdom, in another spectacular feat of co-evolution. Our hands became ideal teaching and learning tools predestined to produce and use complex artefacts. At the same time, we became the only species with ballistic skills: we could aim and throw accurately. All these innovations made us artificially strong and physically weak, because there came a point when investment in muscle power was no longer worthwhile. A cooperatively harmonious group of primates that can use bows and arrows as well as spears and blowpipes is seldom exposed to any danger when hunting. As a result, it becomes the stuff of nightmares for the local megafauna, whose extinction has often been a consequence of our arrival.

Apart from specific examples of the traces a cumulative culture has left in our genes, a stock of knowledge and skills that is not genetically encoded but is only culturally available creates an increased need for cognitive powers. It pays to have a greater learning capacity wherever there is more useful information to learn. This ability to learn calls for larger brains with denser neural structures. Cultural evolution gave us over-sized brains, risky births and an extremely prolonged period of childhood development with a heightened capacity to learn, and to absorb and be shaped by what we learn. Our cumulative culture even made our brain so large that our two cranial hemispheres ultimately only grow together after birth, so a foetus can survive its head being compressed in a birth canal that is actually too narrow for it.

Cultural evolution

No one alive today knows how to build an aeroplane.[27] All the aircraft in use today are direct descendants of the first working design made by the Wright brothers in 1903. Hundreds of designs that did not work had preceded it. When the first one remained in the air, it became the forebear of every design that followed it. Of course, 'we' know how to build an aeroplane – cultural evolution never goes back to the drawing board but instead works on the basis of gradual improvement and experimental modification of our cultural heritage. If every plane and blueprint disappeared overnight, humanity would have literally forgotten how to fly. Cultural knowledge can get so lost that for all intents and purposes it becomes impossible, or at least exceedingly difficult, to retrieve it from scratch with sheer intelligence and strenuous thought.

This has happened a number of times throughout human history: concrete, for example, played a key role in architecture and urban planning in ancient Rome. After the collapse of the Roman Empire, the technology for making concrete fell into oblivion.[28] For centuries, humankind had to dispense with the use of concrete because the cultural expertise had been lost. It was not until the beginning of modern times that the necessary knowledge was rediscovered.

A shrinking pool of cultural knowledge does not necessarily have to spell disaster. In 2007, during a routine inspection of its W76 nuclear warheads, the US government found that it had forgotten how to build nuclear weapons.[29] A crucial component by the name of 'Fogbank' (its exact purpose is subject to secrecy) could no longer be produced because there was no one left who knew how. Cultural knowledge needs to be *nurtured*. When the people or generation responsible for it die out, it dies out with them.

Cultural products are subject to the same mechanisms of change and selection that apply in biological evolution: modifications as they are passed down, and varying reproductive success. Evolutionary mechanisms can therefore be found everywhere in nature; biological and cultural evolution are both merely specific cases of a more general principle.

Anyone who has spent just a few hours on the internet will already be familiar with the vocabulary of cultural theories of evolution, probably without even knowing it. Nowadays we call almost any form of content that circulates on internet forums for more than half a day a 'meme'. The term was originally coined by Richard Dawkins, who wanted to describe the spread of cultural products with an analogy to the effect of mutation, selection and transmission on genes.[30] He realised that ideas, information, concepts, rumours or theories are subject to the same mechanisms as biological organisms. Memes are copied and imitated; as this happens with varying degrees of success, some become established, while others die out. Many memes develop a life of their own, and some, such as believing in witchcraft or anti-Semitic conspiracy theories, cause great damage.

Particularly successful memes 'go viral'. We have the French anthropologist Dan Sperber's 'epidemiological' cultural theory to thank for this eloquent phrase.[31] According to two Americans, biologist Peter Richerson and anthropologist Robert Boyd, culture is any 'information capable of affecting individuals' behavior that they acquire from other members of their species through teaching, imitation, and other forms of social transmission'.[32] It stands to reason that not all these pieces of information are equally successful during the process of social transmission. The more successful ones, just as with genetic mutations, become established and begin to populate the cultural memory in ever greater numbers. The less successful ones die out.

Ideas, concepts, practices and technologies are reproduced in social interaction between individuals. Some ideas become established because they are particularly simple, some for their elegance or memorability, others because they appeal to particularly strong feelings or resonate in our basic instincts. An evolutionary approach also explains why cultures are never done and dusted in one go. Cultures are not monolithic but fragmented, so that their content is fuelled by different eras, traditions and the context of their origins: 'Nothing about culture makes sense except in the light of evolution.'[33]

Paris or California?

Cultural evolution is based on Darwin's principle of descent with modification – that is, that species change over time. But what is more important: the self-perpetuating aspect of descent or the constructive aspect of change? In the debate over this fundamental question, two 'schools' of cultural evolutionary theory have developed, sometimes referred to as the Paris and California programmes.[34] For proponents of the California school, the social transmission of units of cultural information is essentially *copying*. Only by conscientiously, even pedantically, imitating tried and tested practices is the cumulative success that characterises our human culture possible. To be able to improve an inherited technique and ultimately pass it on to the next generation, we must first be able to imitate it exactly.

The Paris programme, on the other hand, lays the emphasis on change rather than passing down. While genes literally create copies of themselves, memes and other cultural products are constantly undergoing changes during the process of teaching and learning. This process of transmission is regulated by what are known as 'cultural attractors', through which the reproduction process is biased in favour of certain variants. My complete edition of *Grimms' Fairy Tales* has three volumes and contains hundreds of stories. I am familiar with ten, at most. I could tell two or three, and even then, only since I brushed up my knowledge of them as a father. I am sure you don't know many more either, and I would bet that the ones you know are the same as the ones I know. *Little Red Riding Hood, Hansel and Gretel* and *The Frog Prince* obviously appeal to our archetypal feelings and cognitive patterns that make them 'fitter' in the competition to be told and remembered than the little-known fairy tale *Fitcher's Bird*. Even the apparent absurdity of a tale can act as a cultural attractor. For example, the story of the omnipotent and omniscient God who then became a man and had himself executed to erase the sins of all humankind, only to rise from the dead three days later, is quite clearly outlandish – ridiculous, even. But it could be precisely that blatant implausibility, and even the contradictions in this story, that have led to it being shared, told and interpreted over and over again. Contemporary rival religions, which may have made more apparent sense, may simply not have been able to become established in the face of the baffling catchiness of this bizarre fable.

Paris or California? The truth probably lies somewhere in the middle. Some forms of cultural production are best modelled on accurate copying: if you reprint a book or cook a recipe for the first time, you strive for the most accurate reproduction of the content. Of course, this process is never perfect. Imperfections in the copying process play a major part in medieval studies, for example, when the origin of a manuscript's copy can be ascertained according to certain 'evidential errors'. Other forms of cultural transmission tend to follow the creative Parisian model. If you cover a song, or cook a recipe for the second time, you usually strive for a creation with a character all of its own. Along these same lines, cultural evolution can consist of a blend of careful imitation and constructive modification that perpetuates and preserves its essence while experimentally improving it.

Cognitive gadgets

There is some evidence to show that the thought structures enabling us to learn culturally are themselves acquired culturally. The British evolutionary biologist Cecilia Heyes argues that we have cultural evolution to thank both for the 'water' of our thinking and for the 'mills' that harness this water. She refers to these mills as 'cognitive gadgets'.[35]

To build a cultural reservoir of knowledge and skills, we need one thing above all else: the ability to learn from others. This *social learning* is often contrasted with *individual learning*: social learning is learning from others – for example, when an older member of our tribe shows us how to make a poison arrow or when a YouTube video shows us how to change a tyre – whereas individual learning is not taught directly by other people – for example, when we're alone at a traffic light and notice that it's gone green.

Evolutionary psychology seeks to understand how the human mind – our feelings, thinking and perception – works by studying its evolutionary origins. In its classic form, it tries to identify what are known as cognitive 'modules'.[36] These are hardwired, in other words not 'learned', thought patterns that perform a very specific function and are often carried out by neural structures dedicated specifically to this function. A significant indication of the presence of a cognitive module is that it can be damaged very specifically – for example by tumours, injuries or developmental anomalies – without other thought functions being affected as well. People with prosopagnosia, for example, have difficulty recognising faces. Facial recognition is very probably a perceptual ability mostly channelled through our genes and shaped by evolution – a skill that does not need to be learned. *Cultural* evolutionary psychology now claims that there are cognitive modules exactly like this that are not genetically hardwired, but are in turn shaped and passed on by cultural processes. To be successful, social learning, for example, relies on various filtering mechanisms that tell a learner who to learn from: social learning has to be *selective*, not indiscriminate. However, these selection strategies – 'Do what most people do', 'Do what the most prestigious individuals do', 'Do what our elders do', 'Do what the most successful people do' or 'Do what the experts do' – are themselves often culturally transmitted strategies.

According to Heyes, there is also a kind of 'starter kit' of perceptual processes that are fundamental to enabling social learning, including the natural tendency to pay more attention to human voices than to other sounds. (Obviously, this innate bias in favour of one of the most important means of human information transmission has a beneficial effect on social learning.) However, many selective social learning strategies are not plausibly determined genetically. 'Do what digital natives do' is a rule that is used with great success by older people when they are dealing with modern communication technologies and media. It is precisely what we call 'metacognitive rules' like this that are learned culturally and passed on socially without having a genetic basis.

Hyperimitators

As well as selective social learning, copying other people's behaviour is crucial for building a cumulative culture. Imitating established behaviour is almost always effective because it is the only way to learn useful expertise without having to invest in time-consuming and costly trial and error.

Both chimpanzees and human children learn from others. In many cases, social learning optimises an action's outcome – we achieve our goals better if we focus on what others do. It is characteristic of us humans to adopt even seemingly super-fluous components of a complex behaviour pattern. Humans are hyperimitators. For example, a study comparing two-year-old children's learning with chimpanzees showed that human children adopted a technique even when it was actually less efficient than an alternative.[37] The task was to use a rake-like tool to reach a desired object (such as a sweet). The rake was presented to the test subjects – the chimpanzees or the children – with its teeth pointing downwards. When the rake was handed to them like this, it was hard to reach the object, which often slipped through the teeth due to its size. Human children performed the task as an adult demonstrator had done – with the rake facing downwards, making it more difficult. Many of the chimpanzees spotted this disadvantage and simply turned the rake over. Slavish imitation of others' actions – often misleadingly derided by us as 'aping' – is typical of humans.

The human tendency to hyperimitate pays off all the more

when it comes to learning complex courses of action that are goal-oriented, but whose operating principles are not immediately comprehensible. The documentary *Jiro Dreams of Sushi* (2011) strikingly shows how long a phase of practice and imitation can last: Yoshikazu Ono's years of apprenticeship with his father, the eighty-five-year-old sushi master Jiro, are not yet over, even though he is now in his sixties himself. Perhaps the most astounding implication of cultural evolution is the fact that it can produce objects and processes that are wholly or partially beyond the comprehension of the users involved, teachers and learners alike. Only human hyperimitators, who adopt activities demonstrated to them even if their meaning is not immediately apparent, can learn processes like this and gradually improve them over generations.

The preparation and, in particular, detoxification of food among indigenous peoples impressively demonstrates how the mechanisms of cultural evolution can generate knowledge and skills that far exceed the insight of the humans who know these techniques. Nardoo is a fern native to eastern Australia. It is shaped a little like clover, and its fruits produce spores that were processed into an edible flour by some Aborigines such as the Yandruwandha.[38] If left unprocessed, nardoo is toxic and can cause beriberi – a disease that causes nerve inflammation and heart failure – through thiamine deficiency. To make nardoo safe to eat, the Aborigines developed a processing technique with several stages: once harvested, the nardoo was ground and rinsed; ash was added to cakes made from it during baking to reduce their pH; very specific seashells completed the detoxification process.

It was not clear to those involved why each of these steps is necessary, nor was it necessary for those involved to understand the complex chemical processes at play during each step of the process. Robert Burke and William Wills, in their 1860 expedition in Yandruwandha lands, did not take them so seriously when they resorted to baking with nardoo after their provisions were used up. They only roughly copied the preparation of the nardoo cakes and found they were dying of starvation after a few weeks despite having enough food. Their failure to imitate accurately came at a lethal cost.

The preparation of cassava roots is even trickier than that of nardoo. Cassava, which looks like a cross between salsify and potato, is very nutritious and especially widespread in South America.[39] The Colombian Tucano have developed a breathtakingly complex procedure to make cassava edible. The roots are scraped, ground, washed and boiled, and then the fibres must remain untouched for two days. Prussic acid poisoning, which this process prevents, is particularly insidious: it manifests itself only after years of consumption, which makes it almost impossible to accurately attribute the disease to cassava without the appropriate medical knowledge. Each stage is essential, but the women responsible for processing cassava cannot explain why; they simply know that it is.

Culture is cleverer than the individuals who hold it and pass it on. One last example can be found in the manufacture of poison arrows for hunting: it is often so complex that even botanists have difficulty deciphering the exact purpose of various stages of the procedure. Amazonian tribes such as the Yagua often require dozens of components to make their arrows. The poison (often curare) needs to be mixed with other substances, heated and cooled before it can be used for hunting. Here, too, the necessary expertise was acquired and passed on over generations of cultural evolution.[40]

Cultural artefacts' lack of transparency is also evident in social institutions as well as traditions. The functioning of democratic societies, for example, depends on the complex interplay of institutions, traditions, rules, values, behaviours and thought patterns, and even after decades of systematic research, it is not definitively clear what keeps them stable. Division of power, party systems, elections, political campaigns, robust civil societies and corresponding media systems all work together in a way that is unique to each democratic system and that cannot be replicated at will. This is one of the reasons why it is notoriously difficult to export democratic institutions to countries where they are not already ingrained through centuries of cultural traditions. There is often no shortcut for cultural evolution. It has to first be worked through before a network of institutions can function in the long term.

Our dependence on a culturally inherited environment can hardly be overestimated. Among other things, this can be seen in the phenomenon of the 'shallows' of our causal knowledge.[41] We can all *use* a toilet and *operate* our phones. But do you have the slightest idea – apart from a few extremely vague ideas that may have something to do with pipes and data signals – how these everyday objects work? Could you fix your phone? Or build one? If you were to travel a hundred years back in time with a time machine, could you explain how it works to your great-grandparents? What about an induction hob? A car engine? A ballpoint pen? You might know something about one of these devices, but you'll have absolutely no understanding of the overwhelming majority of artefacts you use every day as a matter of course.

In most cases, the causal opacity of cultural products – the inability to know what each step or facet of the product does and how it works – is merely a side effect of their complexity. In some cases, though, this opacity is a key aspect of what makes it work in the first place. The Naskapi in the Canadian province of Labrador are excellent hunters.[42] Unfortunately, the caribou they hunt are at least as excellent at not being hunted. As these North American reindeer avoid places where they have previously come across hunters, the Naskapi have to try to anticipate to the best of their ability where the animals are, and choose their hunting grounds accordingly. They do this by charring the shoulder bone of a dead reindeer over a fire until the patterns of cracks, fractures and burn marks reveal a map that will supposedly indicate the animals' whereabouts.

Of course, this does not work – or at any rate, not as expected. This ritual's actual function is to make the Naskapi's hunting behaviour unpredictable for the animals. The fact that the fire's patterns on the caribou bones have no real significance *is* their significance: they make it possible to randomly determine where to hunt. For the Naskapi themselves, this ritual of divination may have a deeper significance that could easily be undermined by the truth about the ritual.

Randomisation also helps resolve interpersonal conflicts. The culture of the Azande living in northern Central Africa is characterised by a strong belief in witchcraft. At the same time, witchcraft is regarded there as something trivial that has nothing to do with the scandalous metaphysical affront that Europeans used to see in this alleged pact with Satan. For the Azande, much of their everyday misfortune can be explained by the influence of witchcraft from begrudging neighbours. This can be set in motion unintentionally, even while they are unconscious or asleep.[43] To determine whether a neighbour suspected of witchcraft is really guilty, the Azande consult an oracle called the *benge*. For the ritual, a poison is mixed together and administered to a chicken. The prosecutor appeals to the oracle to kill the chicken if the defendant is guilty (and to spare it if he or she is innocent). What makes the *benge* special is that for a final judgement, the ritual must be held *twice*. The poison is administered to another chicken, which is asked the same questions, but with opposite indications. So if the poison has killed the chicken the first time, giving a guilty verdict, another poor animal must now survive the ritual. It is only when guilt is confirmed by the poison having an opposite effect that it is considered proven beyond doubt. In the case of a 'conviction', a ritualised apology from the suspected perpetrator is usually enough to restore social peace.

Why twice? The answer is that it guarantees a random result: a 50:50 probability of a guilty verdict, which represents acceptable chances of winning for both sides. For a typical chicken to survive the ritual half of the time but not the other half, the poison must be neither too strong – which would kill both chickens – nor too weak. The *benge* probably also relies on the participants not seeing through the actual mechanism of the ritual. Who wants to leave things to chance when you're expecting a wise judgement from the gods?

The fourth humiliation

Cultural evolution works without us being aware of it. What does this mean for our self-image? Ever since Freud, we have been hearing the theory that scientific and technical modernity has not passed us by without leaving traces: with the dawn of modern times, an increasingly decentralised worldview has inflicted three 'blows' to our metaphysical narcissism, gradually downgrading us from an omnipotent creator's favourite child to a cosmic triviality.[44] The first humiliation was Copernicus's discovery of the heliocentric worldview, which banished the Earth from the centre of the universe to the periphery of a solar system that is only one among many. Darwin's second blow then dispelled the idea of humanity's privileged position among living beings; instead of being the pinnacle of creation with a tailor-made immortal soul, we became a run-of-the-mill commodity from the assembly line of evolution, in principle no longer set far apart from excrement-slinging apes or even the most primitive jellyfish and amoebae; the fact that our conscious thinking is only the tip of our cognitive structure, and that the majority of our spiritual life takes place in an underbelly of repressed feelings and inaccessible urges, was the third blow that Freud claimed to have taught us. Similar stocktaking exercises had already been done by Schopenhauer and Nietzsche, who, despite all their philosophical differences of opinion, at least agreed that humankind's insignificance is only surpassed by our overestimation of ourselves. When it came to the 'human place in the cosmos', Schopenhauer took no prisoners: 'In endless space countless luminous spheres, round each of which some dozen smaller illuminated ones revolve, hot at the core and covered over with a hard cold crust; on this crust a mouldy film has produced living and knowing beings.'[45]

And Nietzsche put it very similarly:

In some remote corner of the sprawling universe, twinkling among the countless solar systems, there was once a star on which some clever animals invented knowledge. It was the most arrogant, most mendacious minute in 'world history', but it was only a minute. After nature caught its breath a little, the star froze, and the clever animals had to die. – One could invent a fable like this and still not have illustrated sufficiently how miserable, how shadowy and fleeting, how aimless and arbitrary the human intellect appears in nature. There were eternities in which it did not exist, and when it has vanished once again, it will have left nothing in its wake.[46]

The theory of cultural evolution adds a fourth blow to these analyses, joining the genre of 'displacement narratives' that increasingly drive human beings out of the centre of the universe and fundamentally deny them any control over, and even understanding of, their world.[47] Cultural evolution theories suggest that every human being is just a small and entirely replaceable part of a process that we cannot fathom, that preceded us and that will long outlast us. This leads to the erosion of the comforting idea that we humans occupy a prominent position in nature, and that the universe is our *home* where we are welcome. The fact that insights like this are uncomfortable is not necessarily an argument against them. After all, if a theory is hard to swallow, that does not necessarily mean that it is wrong. On the contrary: the likelihood of a theory increases the more it contradicts long-held illusions.

The individualist prejudice

Another theory that has been challenged in the light of cultural evolution might be described as an *individualist prejudice*. 'Have courage to use your own understanding,' said Kant, who made 'Sapere aude' ('dare to know') the Enlightenment's motto.[48] And who would contradict it? Who likes to see themselves as part of a cognitive herd that parrots other people's opinions uncritically without forming their own views? And hasn't the twentieth century demonstrated the pitfalls of conforming, going along with the crowd and peer pressure – in the most spectacular and terrifying way possible?

If cultural evolution theories are correct, this individualistic bias must also be revised. Humans, deficient as we are, remain dependent on a cumulative culture that compensates for our physical deficiencies through culturally transmitted knowledge refined over generations. The question of whether we should live with and through a cumulative culture does not even arise: we are cultural beings by nature, which means there is absolutely no alternative for us except life in a culturally constructed niche. And we would never actually wish for this alternative: both our survival and specifically human commodities such as art, spirituality or play cannot exist without culture.

It is this insight that makes individualistic bias flounder. Our cultural reservoir consists of information and skills that can only be created through a multi-generational process of passing down and gradually improving knowledge and expertise. This reservoir cannot be recreated within one generation, as the complexity of cultural knowledge radically exceeds the innovative power of individuals. This process depends on two factors: with a view to passing on information, experienced people strive to structure the educational environment so that the next generation of human learners can absorb the culturally stored body of information as easily and safely as possible. With a view to receiving information, human learners are concerned with absorbing the available knowledge through imitation and tentative trial and error.

The possibility, as well as the success, of human existence – and coexistence – is linked extremely closely with behavioural dispositions that directly contradict the individualist maxim that it is better to think for ourselves, form our own opinions and cultivate an attitude of critical scepticism towards knowledge bases passed down to us and towards traditions. All our cognition and cooperation is based on the notion of us adopting the previous generation's opinions and behaviours more or less uncritically. To build a cumulative culture, imitation and conformity are paramount.[49] Questioning, reviewing and reflecting always remain secondary to the avalanche of cultural evolution. The saying should really go 'Have courage to use *others'* understanding,' or to put it more precisely, 'My understanding *is others'* understanding, without which it cannot exist.'

Same but different

An anti-individualistic focus on the importance of proven knowledge and tried and tested behavioural patterns in our human lives seems to push theories of cumulative cultural evolution in a conservative direction politically. And it is not difficult to see where this impression comes from. The tradition of conservative political thought has always had its roots in combining the gravity of proven traditions with scepticism towards the prospect of radically restructuring social institutions. Edmund Burke, probably the most important conservative critic of the French Revolution, expressed doubts about its chances of success, which related directly to the process of cumulative cultural evolution: 'The work itself requires the aid of more minds than one age can furnish.'[50] Stable social institutions are always easier to destroy than to build. Radical proposals to fundamentally reshape society should be viewed with great caution.

Rationalist utopias therefore often make more sense on paper than in real life. Philosophers have often tended towards the grand design of the single and ultimate utopian society in which all divisions are dissolved, all injustices abolished and all conflicts reconciled, once and for all. The institution of the family usually appeared particularly scandalous in the light of this vision. To achieve a truly fair society, this nucleus of kinship and partisanship first had to be reformed. Utopian experiments – from the American Brook Farm to the Shakers and on to the Israeli kibbutzim and the 1968 communes[51] – often started at precisely that point and tried to put the exalted designs of philosophers and social reformers into practice. These experiments almost always ended in disaster, and where it did not, the collapse of the experiment in question was usually avoided by reproducing step by step those very structures – family and partnership, division of labour, exchange of goods, social sanctions – that they had actually wanted to abolish with the experiment. We cannot go back into dry dock to rebuild our social institutions from scratch. Instead, we remain dependent on proven ways of life.

Nonetheless, it is possible to resist this conservative interpretation of cultural evolution. First, there is the question of whether the reality of cumulative cultural change actually recommends precisely the social institutions and ways of life that conservative people would most like to return to. What was the life they had in mind? When was that golden age that we would be better off inhabiting? The 1950s? In fact, these structures – the traditional family consisting of a man, a woman and two children, an economic system dominated by a few nationally established industrial families, a political regime that offers law and order in exchange for the majority's loyalty, a social community that gathers around a canon of shared values – have long since crumbled or already completely disappeared. Going back *from today's reality* to the society that most conservatives envisage as an ideal would be exactly the kind of radical social transformation conservatives have always warned against. The rational core of conservative thinking is about not abolishing tried and tested values and institutions without very good reason; this needs, though, to be combined with a benevolent acceptance of moderate change.

Second, the conservative implications of cultural evolution theories are overestimated. The sometimes apocalyptic predictions of society's impending decay, which was supposed to come about through the legalisation of same-sex marriage or what the women's movement had achieved, for example, turned out to be completely unfounded in hindsight. It remains true that proven knowledge and tried and tested forms of social cooperation should only be eliminated with caution and not without compelling reasons. At the same time, cumulative evolution's track record promotes openness to experimentation, constantly renegotiating our inherited cultural reservoir with the potential for innovation and change.

Culture and morality

Morality and culture are intrinsically linked. For one thing, moral norms and values are essential for enabling the complex forms of social cooperation that allow a cumulative culture to be built in the first place. The feedback loops that arise from the dynamics of a more advanced learning ability and a growing reservoir of cultural knowledge are strongly dependent on a certain group size. The more members a group has, the better and faster a niche can be filled with cultural content for the next generation to absorb and improve on. Morality makes this easier: human groups cannot achieve the size required for this dynamic without moral norms. Morality makes human coexistence 'scalable', which, in turn, creates the conditions for cumulative cultural evolution to gain momentum.

In other words, morality makes it possible for deficient humankind to compensate for its physical deficits by organising a cooperative coexistence that prepares the ground for a cumulative culture to emerge. A group's size correlates directly with the level of cultural complexity it can maintain because certain technical and intellectual developments rely on a critical mass of teachers and learners.[52] This can be seen, for example, in a comparison of the levels of cultural complexity in indigenous groups in Australia and New Zealand: at some point, the much smaller, geographically isolated populations in New Zealand were no longer able to reproduce certain artefacts and social structures or to sustain a certain level of technological development.

The concrete moral norms and values that different groups of people use to organise their coexistence are themselves products of cultural evolution. Beings with cumulative culture – you and I, in other words – are moral beings. Our advanced learning capacities equipped us with a strong norm-oriented psychology that makes it possible for us to learn and follow complex social rules. At the same time, cultural evolution allows a certain degree of variation in the norms and rules a group uses to structure its cooperation. Evolution allows us to cooperate, on the basis of moral norms and social institutions. How these norms and institutions are specifically designed, though, depends on various factors. Our human nature dictates certain lines that the process of cultural evolution draws in various ways. As a result, compensating for our deficiencies with a culture made possible by cooperation creates new problems – new deficiencies – which in turn require appropriate solutions.

The repeatedly increased size of human societies was driven by the technological advances enabling social learners to produce an economic surplus in the right conditions. Once a small group of individuals had managed to appropriate this surplus, cementing their own power in an increasingly hierarchical society, we found that social inequality was a new basis for the construction of human groupings. Material inequality and social stratification led to the emergence of the first large-scale human societies, early imperial civilisations and an initial wave of urbanisation that paid for the finery of hallowed god-kings with oppression and human slavery. How did it feel to live in societies like these?

4

The Origins of Inequality

The moon god

Come and see, everyone! Hurry, put down your day's work and make your way there, or you will have missed it!

For today he's coming to the ziggurat of Nanna, the Nameless One who bears all names, the Mighty, the Never-before-Seen, the Longbeard, the Radiant One.

And don't we owe everything to him? We have dates and nuts, juicy snakes and fresh bread, olives, honey, brightly coloured fish, goat meat and spicy soups. Fragrant billowing purple smoke announces his arrival; the path of his procession is lined with majestic drummers; horns ring out in the distance, from the palace, to ensure no one forgets to throw themselves down into the dust when Ur-Nammu comes to dream with the moon god in the High House.

They have travelled here from afar: from Larsa, where they lock their doors twice; from Nippur, where the falcon lives; even from Eshnunna, where they say the fire never goes out. Here there are strangers who speak in strange tongues and warn of the end of time, women gone mad and clutching their lifeless children in their arms, who beg the lesser gods for solace, lepers in rags trying to conceal their smallpox; here there are girls with dark eyes waiting in the alleys, conjurers who relieve rich men of their boredom and a few shekels; here there is bitter potion that makes men tired and yet wakeful, and the wind is so hot that a man could drink the well dry.

There it lies, beneath the sacred roof: the great red stone that tells us what pleases God. Few can bear the sight of it, and even fewer have ever seen it, but it is there; this everyone knows, this we all know. And today that day has come again when the Great Man asks it for guidance, so there may be justice within the walls of Ur. He's coming from the Royal House, the place we call Echursanga, and the procession announces his coming. Servants lead the cows festooned with rattling chains. Eunuchs bear the litters with women reposing in them, women who belong only to him. The wise priests and advisers follow them on goats; Šulgi, the Sweet One, the Light of our Future, sits high above them on the elephant, bearing the great bell around its neck.

But alas, our lives are often hard. We must thank the Tiamat, from whose eyes the Buranun and the Idigina, which nourish our soil, once sprang forth, and we must also thank the Meskalamdug, the Greatest of the Great, who has lain below us for so long and who gave us the dams. Be still, then you can hear them whispering, the women and the men and the poor children down below, laid there with him so long before their time.

And yet we would be nothing without the red stone of the laws. It tells us how things must be in the world, where glory lies and where sacrilege, and who the evil men are. Do I strike down the man who takes my wife as his own? The man who steals from my brother? May he who lets his farmland go to waste be permitted to keep it? What do I owe to the one who heals me? And to whom does the water belong?

He is here. He is here at last. There are many steps that lead to the Forbidden Place, and even the Barely Mortal takes a long time to master the stairs. He's coming in now. The New Year begins! May it grant us as great a bounty as the last and – Nanna willing – a greater one still!

The golden age

Almost every culture is familiar with the idea of a golden age. People who talk about a golden, bygone era tend to look upon the present day as a time of decay – a deplorable but surmountable transitional state where humanity has temporarily lost its former way of life of exquisite simplicity and serene splendour. In the past, the thinking goes, we lived at peace with nature, which we now exploit and defile; where now there is discord, mistrust and competition, our life together was once marked by harmony, decency and virtue; today we strain under the burden of hard labour, whereas back then we drew what little we needed from the Earth's abundant cornucopia.

The bad thing about golden ages is how fleeting they are. They are beyond our grasp, and no matter how far back we go, this state of harmony and bliss always lies in the past for every generation. It is almost as if it never really existed.

The Judeo-Christian myth of the Garden of Eden, the Greco-Roman concept of Arcadia, the Nordic Gullaldr, the Dreamtime of the Australian Aborigines or the Indian Satya Yuga – none of these are based on any historically identifiable era, but they express a cross-cultural yearning for an unspecified carefree past. And the return to the promised land, where milk and honey flow and the lion lies down with the lamb, must be put off, time after time. In his 1516 publication, Thomas More was quite right when he set his version of an ideal future society on a 'new island' which he called *Utopia* – in other words 'no place', nowhere. The promise of one day being able to leave misery, death and hardship behind us has yet to be fulfilled.

Myths are always untrue, but they often have a grain of truth. And it has become increasingly apparent that humankind's original way of life might have been remarkably bearable. Although no penicillin, no dentistry and no taxis existed, hardly anyone was bothered by infectious diseases, periodontitis or annoying appointments. More than anything else, the era between the separation of humanity from our closest relatives the primates (a few million years ago) and the emergence of the first complex societies (a few thousand years ago) seems to have been characterised by an astonishing degree of *political, material* and *social equality*.

5,000 Years

It was only about 5,000 years ago that the first civilisations emerged, and with them the first cities, which, in turn, banded together to form empires. Around that time, the same technological developments and social evolutionary processes became established in several places all at once: people began systematic agriculture, they started baking earth to form clay vessels, and they learned to build dams and divert rivers to irrigate their fields. Gradually, new forms of labour division emerged, and specialised artisans and merchants appeared. Economy and trade developed, and for the first time it was possible to produce a surplus. A ruling class emerged and attempted to carve its own authority in stone with imposing, monumental buildings. At the same time, the new cultural techniques of writing, arithmetic and planning flourished. Trade networks that went beyond the village market and that relied on complex logistical processes began to thrive. And finally, the arts also came into their own as a need for the skills of painters, sculptors or mosaicists grew. All these developments, seemingly advanced by some invisible force simultaneously all over the globe, have come to be known as 'Childe's criteria', after the twentieth-century archaeologist Vere Gordon Childe.[1]

Five millennia ago, in Mesopotamia's 'Fertile Crescent' between the Euphrates (Buranun in Sumerian) and Tigris (Idigina) rivers, Sumerian culture flourished, with its metropolises Uruk, Lagash, Kish and later Babylon ruled by the Ur dynasties and the kings Sargon and Gilgamesh. In Mehrgarh and Harappa in South Asia, the culture of the Indus Valley developed in parallel; in China, the emperors of the Xia dynasty assumed power around this time as well. A short time later in Central America, the Olmecs stepped onto the historical stage: the little-known oldest civilisation in what is now the Gulf of Mexico; we are mainly aware of them from the giant helmeted heads they fashioned from basalt boulders to commemorate their dead rulers.

In all these places there are traces of pottery, architecture and the construction of cities, the manufacture of decorative objects and jewellery, the cultivation of plants, the use of animals in agriculture and the ritual acknowledgement of a (proto-) state. It is as if humanity were following a global rhythm. This rhythm produced the first advanced civilisations, but it brought with it the concept of rule and an unprecedented level of social inequality.[2]

Ever since the early twentieth century, the phase that spans roughly the 800 to 200 years before the beginning of the Western calendar has been called the Axial Age. This term was coined by the psychiatrist and philosopher Karl Jaspers, who singled out this period as a time of radical transformation and epochal progress, a time when our fundamental vocabulary and humanistic self-understanding became established, and which ultimately formed the basis for the Enlightenment and modernity, albeit much later.[3] Jaspers, rather self-servingly, singles out *philosophers* as the decisive driving force in history.

A number of intellectually influential people did live and work during this period: from Homer and Plato to Jesus of Nazareth and from Zarathustra to Siddhartha Gautama, Confucius or Laozi. However, to describe this global period as a defining 'Axial Age' is to confuse the cultural superstructure of a social formation with its material basis. In other words: it assumes that products of the human intellect such as philosophical theories or religious ideologies are the cause, rather than the effect, of social changes. The Axial Age is overrated and, upon closer inspection, it's clear that these scholars changed little about the morality at that time in those societies: after the Axial Age, it took another 2,000 years before the foundations of feudal societies built on extreme forms of hierarchy and material inequality could be renegotiated – a process that is still ongoing today.

Inter pares

What led to the dawn of inequality 5,000 years ago? As we have become used to accepting social inequality as a natural and immutable fact, it might seem reasonable to assume that we humans have always lived in communities where the distribution of prestige, power, influence and wealth depended on our individual positions in a framework of more or less arbitrary status markers. This assumption seems plausible at first glance: under more advanced conditions, we might think, natural differences between people and social groups could possibly be balanced out by the fact that a given individual might not be beautiful, clever or strong, but may at least be rich; another might be poor, but good-looking and intelligent. In developed societies there are all sorts of skills, talents or qualities that can potentially set a person apart. As no one possesses all these positive or useful qualities, or at least only very few people do, everyone should be able to find their place within the group on the basis of their individual strengths. But as long as a person's social position is dependent on little more than the qualities they are naturally endowed with, it seems likely that the strongest or most unscrupulous member of a group can dominate all the others. By this logic, the natural state of humanity would always have been a state of inequality.

The same is true of our closest relatives: groups of chimpanzees and other anthropoid apes are structured according to a strict hierarchy. The life of the entire group revolves around an alpha male who determines the power structure, oversees the distribution of resources and monopolises access to sex and reproduction.[4] His dictatorial grip on power ends only with his death or the onset of unmistakable signs of physical weakness.

Even the human societies that left behind noteworthy historical traces also invariably had an extremely unequal structure. Written records and other symbolic artefacts left to posterity document the trappings of previously unheard-of wealth and elevated social status.[5] Tombs are especially revealing in this

regard, showing us that only a small number of our rich ancestors were equipped for the journey to the afterlife with a bizarre
excess of jewels, sacrificial animals and other ritual objects. And
yet, by contrast, there is almost universal agreement that simple,
often nomadic groups of hunter-gatherers were almost always
organised in a surprisingly egalitarian manner. This pattern is
confirmed by observations of present-day tribal societies from
the Arctic to the Kalahari and the Brazilian plains, where significant differences in status and wealth, as well as political
centralisation, are largely unknown, or at the very least much
less pronounced.[6]

When it came to gender equality, hunter-gatherer communities also performed commendably compared to the modern
and pre-modern societies of the last 5,000 years. Although there
was a division of labour – the theory we hear so often about
Stone Age men devoting themselves primarily to hunting,
while Stone Age women were busy collecting fruit and raising
the children, is largely true[7] – the female members of such
an extended family often had considerable (proto-)political
influence: in other words, they were just as involved in the decision-making processes about their coexistence as the men. The
first instances of rigidly structured, sedentary societies with a
complex division of labour appeared after we had abandoned
our nomadic lifestyle.[8] Why we ever left our golden age of
equality is puzzling, but leave it we did.

The greatest mistake of all time

One of the main factors in the transition away from egalitarianism and equality and towards hierarchy and inequality seems
to have been the development of an increasingly sedentary way
of life, as well as agriculture. With the end of the last Ice Age
about 10,000 years ago – after a phase of instability lasting many
hundreds of thousands of years, which made us intelligent and
capable of learning – the climatic conditions for successful

farming, animal husbandry and plant cultivation came about for the first time. This made an agricultural way of life possible which gave us security and stability both within our group and externally, as well as a regular supply of food, and protection from all the injustices of nature.

But were we merely swapping one injustice for another? The geographer and historian Jared Diamond refers to the invention of agriculture as 'the worst mistake in human history'.[9] The question of whether humankind's natural state was a curse or a blessing has long held a key role in political philosophy. If you are trying to investigate whether state-organised coexistence with a central monopoly on the use of force and the wielding of political authority is at all justifiable, it stands to reason that you would compare this with the anarchic alternative. Have we humans been better off since we left our original stateless condition? Or is the shift from tribe to state really the root of all evil?

In one of the most-quoted passages in the history of philosophy, Thomas Hobbes wrote:

> In such condition there is no place for industry, because the fruit thereof is uncertain, and consequently no culture of the earth; no navigation, nor use of the commodities that may be imported by sea; no commodious building; no instruments of moving and removing such things as require much force; no knowledge of the face of the earth; no account of time; no arts; no letters; no society; and, which is worst of all, continual fear and danger of violent death; and the life of man, solitary, poor, nasty, brutish, and short.[10]

Unless some kind of coercive authority reins them in, Hobbes thought, humans are doomed to live in a state of never-ending conflict.

Jean-Jacques Rousseau's 1755 *Discourse on the Origin and Basis of Inequality among Men* – probably *the* founding text for the modern critique of culture and civilisation – on the other hand, makes a strong case for the corrupting influence of human culture.[11] By living in larger and longer-term communities, man's wholesome and healthy self-love (*amour de soi*) is replaced by a corrupted self-love (*amour propre*) that transforms his natural simplicity and virtue into resentment and rivalry for status.

Who was right? Nowadays we no longer have to settle for largely unfounded speculations with Rousseau's concept of the noble savage (*sauvage noble*) being played off against Hobbes's conflicting vision of humanity, in which man is wolf to man (*homo homini lupus*). In actual fact, both were wrong: Rousseau because he described humankind as peaceful loners – we humans have always been social beings who, while inwardly peaceful, egalitarian and cooperative, behaved outwardly like bloodthirsty gangs of robbers, rapists and murderers; and Hobbes because he saw us merely as cold-hearted, strategic egoists whose pledges of allegiance are worthless without the sword of the state; we are cooperative beings who only need a central authority when we are in large groups.

Nonetheless, Hobbes correctly described the problem that our evolution first had to solve: cooperation can only emerge when uncooperative behaviour ceases to be the dominant strategy. There must be some solution to the prisoner's dilemma – the problem that individually rational behaviour often produces collectively devastating results. Hobbes was clearly unable to imagine that there might be a solution to this problem other than state force.

The emergence of (pre-)modern states and early civilisations would not have been possible without the shift to agriculture as the primary source of food, because the needs of a growing number of people living together in smaller and smaller areas can only be provided for through the controlled cultivation of nutrient-rich crops. The price of this development was a more monotonous way of eating, of course, and a diet consisting largely of rice or potatoes did not offer the same variety as the dozens of plants, fruits and animals regularly consumed by hunter-gatherers. Concentrating on just a few foods also gave rise to the risk of extreme famine if bad weather or pests targeting a specific crop destroyed the entire harvest. A sedentary, agricultural life increased the risk, too, of zoonotic (transmissible from animals to humans) diseases and epidemics, which have been constantly plaguing human civilisations ever since, the consequences of which have often been disastrous: many of the deadliest pandemics of all time, for instance the Black Plague, tuberculosis, Spanish flu, AIDS and malaria, can be directly or indirectly traced back to mass-scale animal husbandry, and were only made possible by increased population density.

We might assume, though, that the mind-blowing increase in material comfort and security offered by this sedentary life balanced out these obvious disadvantages. Except that doesn't seem to have been the case, either. Our pre-civilisational ancestors worked less, slept more and had more free time than us. Some estimates suggest that the working week of a hunter-gatherer was well below the forty hours we're accustomed to today, and they suffered dramatically less from the never-ending drudgery that has defined daily life for the vast majority of people over the last few thousand years. Civilisational ailments such as depression, back pain, acne, cardiovascular diseases and even cancer were much less common, perhaps even virtually unknown to our earliest ancestors.[12] True, average life expectancy was low, but this was mainly due to the fact that without recourse to advanced medicines, human infant mortality was almost always comparatively high. Only just over half of all people lived beyond their first five years, but those who had overcome this hurdle could enjoy a largely healthy, relaxed life that was by no means short: they could easily live to sixty, sometimes even significantly older.

It depends enormously on what we are comparing, of course.

Whether hunter-gatherers were *on average* happier than *some* modern humans is a controversial question. Still, an incredibly large number of people have undeniably suffered catastrophic consequences as a result of exchanging the original way of life for a life bordering on modernity. Millions of child labourers would undoubtedly have been much better off under pre-Neolithic conditions.

Insulting the meat

So it seems that social equality is the 'natural' way of life for humankind. Nonetheless, even the original tribal societies had to go to considerable effort to maintain this state. There are various forces – from social coalitions to superior skills, individual unscrupulousness or sheer coincidence – that repeatedly challenge the egalitarian status quo and threaten to throw it off balance.

To keep the centrifugal forces of social inequality at bay, our ancestors developed various techniques that established a 'reverse dominance hierarchy'.[13] A proven method for our forebears was to remind power-hungry upstarts through rumours, gossip and ridicule that even the strongest self-declared leader is only mortal. If that didn't help, all that remained was tyrannicide. For the group, it was a permanent challenge to level out burgeoning inequalities in prosperity or status socially. Equality may be the 'more natural' state, but it did not come naturally. By learning to cooperate, we also learned how to conspire against other individuals as a small group.

Before the Neolithic revolution changed everything, egalitarian property ownership structures prevented individual group members from raising their profile socially through excessive wealth. Rudimentary forms of private property – or more precisely, privileged rights of use – did exist, but as the use of tools, resources, meat or shelter was regulated by communal access norms that excluded no one, a gross imbalance never arose. Tools could be used by anyone who needed them. Child-care was shouldered by everyone. A person only had to starve if *everyone* was starving. As a result, it was almost impossible for one individual or nuclear family to manage to accumulate enough property to rise above the rest of the group. Since there was virtually no long-term ownership, there was also little to inherit, so passing down wealth intergenerationally was also ruled out as a source of inequality.

As we have already seen, a tried and tested, if drastic, way to restore the egalitarian balance was simply to assassinate the would-be despot who was claiming control of the group. To counter particularly intolerable 'big shots', a coalition of oppressed people – or even just people threatened by oppression – would often form to get rid of their tormentor for good through public execution or a secret ambush.

A particularly original way of nipping social differences in the bud in early human societies was the systematic mini-misation of individual achievements: an individual was not supposed to be able to rise above the rest of the group through exceptional achievements, for example in hunting. Among the !Kung San, who still inhabit the Kalahari savannah today, it is customary to acknowledge outstanding hunting fortunes with ritual modesty. If a man manages to bring home an unusually large bag, he is expected to downplay his performance as much as possible. One member of the !Kung San describes this process as follows:

> Say that a man has been hunting. He must not come home and announce like a braggart, 'I have killed a big one in the bush!' He must first sit down in silence until I or someone else comes up to his fire and asks, 'What did you see today?' He replies quietly. 'Ah, I'm no good for hunting. I saw nothing at all ... maybe just a tiny one.' Then I smile to myself because I now know he has killed something big.[14]

When the other men finally see the hunter's haul, they react accordingly:

> 'You mean to say you have dragged us all the way out here to make us cart home your pile of bones? Oh, if I had known it was this thin I wouldn't have come.' 'People, to think I gave up a nice day in the shade for this. At home we may be hungry but at least we have nice cool water to drink.'[15]

By 'insulting the meat', social communication practices make it clear that any form of excessive pride will not be tolerated. In some cultures, clever taboos also determine how the haul is shared: certain parts of an animal may only be eaten by certain people, depending on gender, age or social role, so a fair division is more or less guaranteed.

A species' way of life is also the niche in which the selection pressures relevant to that species manifest themselves. As a result, our ancestors' de facto way of life became the socio-cultural context that shaped our continuing history of adaptation. Gradually, we developed an egalitarian predisposition that makes us fundamentally sceptical of social inequalities. An aversion to too great, or obviously arbitrary, social differences has been permanently etched into our minds.

Against the grain

Aversions aside, for the overwhelming majority of people, the shift from the 'golden age' of their hunter-gatherer existence to a life of hard work and servitude was a drastic change for the worse, and smaller communities often put up fierce resistance to being absorbed by the earliest large-scale societies. It may be the case that now, albeit very recently and in very few regions worldwide, we have finally begun to catch up with our prehistoric levels of satisfaction and well-being. If so, the tragedy of the last 5,000 years is the price our ancestors had to pay for our modern-day quality of life. A diversion through despotic rule, exploitation and war over several millennia eventually created the conditions for modern societies to emerge. Was it worth it?

The inequality, slavery, foreign rule and misery that the first civilisations imposed on humankind were an ideal breeding ground for religions based on salvation and afterlife, which, rather than rolling over and accepting death as a mere banality in the inevitable generational ups and downs, began to see it as a redemption from the worldly valley of tears which was imposed on us poor sinners as a punishment. 'There are no atheists in foxholes' is said to have been an aphorism widespread among US soldiers during the Second World War, and Marx was also correct in his diagnosis when he described religions as the 'sigh of the oppressed creature' and suspected their function to be a primarily palliative comfort.[16]

Inequality and domination are forms of 'social stratification'. It is difficult to imagine the extent of the stratification that would have been present in the first larger societies of thousands or tens of thousands of members that we know of from Mesopotamia or North Africa. Even today's societies do not come close to those early forms of domination and servitude that required subjects to literally throw themselves in the dust before the mostly extravagantly crowned god-kings overloaded with jewellery, shells, bones or precious metals.

Still, for organisational reasons, there would increasingly be no alternative to this level of inequality, and few ways of balancing it back out again. Pre-Neolithic social structures of sharing and informally monitoring norms of community life are not enough to hold together a grouping of humans above a certain number of members. A form of society that is stabilised by relationships based on kinship and reciprocity cannot be scaled up arbitrarily. This model approaches its limits with just a few hundred members. We can only start to solve this organisational problem in a hierarchically structured society with centralised bureaucracy and the power to make decisions – and this is costly.

The method of choice for financing the new hierarchies has always been taxation. Primitive human societies predominantly lived within a subsistence economy, in other words from hand to mouth. State-building, therefore, was only possible when a surplus was generated, allowing some members of a society to devote themselves to nobler business. The ceremonies with which monarchs were honoured, the rituals perfected by priests and the enlightened, and the requisite calculating, monitoring, recording, planning and writing down all meant a profession-alised administration was essential, and sentencing criminals required a caste of legal experts. These are challenging tasks that hunters and gatherers have neither the time nor resources for.

Besides slavery, almost all early civilisations were based on the cultivation of grain.[17] Before a formal means of exchange such as coins was established, taxation had to resort to some-thing else that could be stored, transported and, above all, counted. Root vegetables such as parsnips, carrots or Jerusalem artichokes grow under ground and are therefore easy to hide from the grasp of the tax authorities; other plants are usually delicate and perishable; cows and sheep are difficult to trans-port and soon worthless once they are dead. All these goods also vary in size and weight, making reliable and comparable taxation difficult. Grain, on the other hand, is outstanding in every respect: it is difficult to hide, and can be stored for long periods of time, bunched or packaged in precisely comparable quantities and transported easily. The earliest states were there-fore always dependent on cereal cultivation.

The exploitative mechanism that came with taxation, however, placed new demands on the rulers – namely, to give something back. The notion that hunter-gatherer communi-ties would have been only too happy to give up their existence overshadowed by a merciless natural environment with preda-tors and other dangers to life and limb, in exchange for a safe, stable existence as arable and livestock farmers, is a myth conjured up by precisely the exploitative elites who profited from this development. The emergence of glaring inequality in tribal chiefdoms and early empires created a growing need for legitimacy over time: if you are going to be tortured, exploited, oppressed and worn down, you at least want to hear some good reasons for it. This niche was soon filled by castes of priests, whose task it was to explain why it was right that only a few were allowed to decide who should build the temples, cultivate the fields and be sacrificed to the gods – and that these few were allowed a life of luxury while the rest remained condemned to serfdom from cradle to grave.

But if the disadvantages of a sedentary society built on agriculture are so drastic and obvious, how did it become so firmly established in the first place? How did tribal chiefdoms and the first states manage to keep their members in line when most of them seemed to have nothing to gain from it?

The answer to both questions is with coercion and force. In most cases, people did not voluntarily give up their lives in small groups among (more or less) equals. Instead, they resisted, by either fighting, refusing or fleeing. Even the (relatively recent) wars between the Roman Empire and Germanic tribes about 2,000 years ago can be explained with this model, as can most historical scenarios where an expansive empire met recalcitrant 'barbarians' who did not want to submit to the giant imperial enemy and its form of government without a fight. This process can also be seen as a form of evolutionary group selection: even before those vast empires could emerge, there must have been some collectives that managed to eradicate or absorb competing groups through larger numbers, stricter cooperation structures and superior warfare.[18]

With few exceptions, any resistance was futile in the long run, so in general the first empires eliminated the much smaller tribal societies that crossed their paths, subjugated their members, or both. This is one of the main reasons why the highly inegalitarian and oppressive social model of early civilisations eventually became established: the model of small, scattered groups, which is far more attractive to most people, had little ability to counter the sheer military power and imperial ambitions of self-proclaimed god-kings.

The archaeologist Ian Morris claims that a society's moral value system reflects its social structure and main method of energy production. This would mean that when humans shifted from hunting and gathering to agriculture and then to fossil fuels (social structure and energy production), each shift directly impacted how much social inequality and physical violence a community using these techniques was willing to tolerate (the value system).[19] As a result, gatherer societies prefer equality and an (inwardly) peaceful coexistence. The societies that marked the beginning of the shift to agriculture, on the other hand, were blatantly organised unequally and were extremely prepared to use violence, both within the group and outwardly. A society that relies on fossil fuels as its primary source of energy, while accepting material inequalities, increasingly develops an aversion to inward-facing and ultimately also outward violence – in other words, war. Every age works with the values it needs.

Despite their military successes, imperial structures tend to collapse, in many cases by becoming victims of their own success. For the first civilisations, as their economies grew, they gradually began, perhaps due to scarce natural resources or land, to overload their environment, without being able to make up for this in time with more advanced technology.[20] At some point, territorial expansion was also no longer able to absorb the population growth that had been set in motion by new forms of economy and cooperation. The material reproduction of society became fragile, leading to famine and political instability. One particularly famous example of this happening can be found in the history of Easter Island in Polynesia, whose early inhabitants (c.700–800 CE) paid tribute to their chiefs and ancestors with gigantic stone sculptures – the *moai*.[21] Apparently, this form of sculptural recognition took on so much importance that the society carrying it out at some point deforested the island, and neglected fishing to such an extent that it had to return to a more primitive form of organisation, inevitably falling into cannibalism.

The limits of bureaucratic organisation and information processing also meant that most promising empires eventually disintegrated. A society that is growing has a greater degree of social complexity, which in turn increases the need for complex administration. But even this complexity is subject to the law of diminishing marginal utility: at a certain point, the investments necessary to cope with the next increase in complexity rise.[22] When this moment is reached, there is stagnation, frustration and an inability to act. Internal conflicts like this force an empire to reorganise itself at a 'lower' level of development. Through growth, it goes downhill.

Why we are stuck

Inequality is frustrating, and as we've seen, it often puts a strain on the very stability of society. So why don't we just get rid of it?

Tereoboo, the king of Hawai'i and dynastic ancestor of the *ali'i*, the traditional nobility of the islands, was worshipped as a god: contemporary paintings depict him with a grim and dignified expression, his black hair covered by a royal feather headdress which seems to cascade over his forehead like an ocean wave, and he is draped in a regal cloak decorated with a red and yellow rhomboid pattern that was deemed to give him warmth and spiritual protection.

When James Cook reached the islands he named after the Earl of Sandwich on HMS *Resolution* in 1778, even he and his entourage were surprised by the extent of social inequality they found there. Eighteenth-century Englishmen were familiar with the reality of differences in social status,[23] but the humble obedience accorded to Kalani'ōpu'u, the supreme ruler of the island of Hawai'i, was remarkable even to the class-obsessed British at that point. The common people had to submit body and soul to the members of the ruling class and especially to the king himself. Human sacrifice was practised with cruel indifference, and the death penalty was imposed for transgressing even seemingly insignificant prohibitions. The chiefs and the royal family owned the land, which was farmed by slaves, whose worthless status of exclusion was often inscribed on their faces with tattoos.

The shift from prehistoric small groups to pre-modern large-scale civilisations has almost always been a shift from communities with an egalitarian structure to social inequality and despotic rule.[24] The fact that we still live with extreme social inequalities in wealth, power and status seems to have been the inevitable price to pay for social evolution towards complex large societies. But was it truly inevitable? There are growing doubts about the oversimplified narrative that humans throughout the Pleistocene lived in scattered small groups organised in an egalitarian way.[25]

The anthropologist David Graeber and the archaeologist David Wengrow have warned against falling for the allure of these kinds of simplifications,[26] and recent research shows that even back then, tens of thousands of years ago, there was a plethora of social structures that were more entrenched, larger and politically more unequal than previously assumed. The popular narrative of the shift from egalitarian tribal societies to large inegalitarian societies prepares us to accept that this shift – and the forms of social inequality and political domination that came with it – was inevitable and had no alternative. What appears to be a sober description of the historical course of events is actually an ideologically charged narrative designed to suffocate our political imagination.

In fact, according to Graeber and Wengrow, we humans have always lived in all kinds of conditions and, regardless of climate and group size, in all kinds of socio-political arrangements. We have always been conscious political actors who would not allow ourselves to be put in an 'evolutionary straitjacket';[27] some micro-societies were familiar with strict hierarchies and despotic exploitation; and the inhabitants of some impressively large indigenous communities of North America with tens of thousands of members made fun of the lack of self-respect shown by the French and English who had just arrived in the New World, cowering in front of their social superiors and kissing their boots. Some societies were familiar with leaders or chiefs, but they were understood to have a serving role; other groups moved effortlessly – depending on the season – between radically divergent political structures, and were free masters of their own destinies during the summer months of abundance, but in the barren winter months would at any given time temporarily subject themselves to the necessary evil of a political sovereign.

The existence of different varieties of socialisation over the course of social evolution is not surprising. The real question is why we are *stuck* today: why do material inequality and political hierarchy seem to have no alternative, and feel non-negotiable to us? Graeber and Wengrow rightly point out that thinking about political alternatives is always worthwhile; what would we miss out on if we agreed with Francis Fukuyama that the liberal-democratic-capitalist compromise was the end of history, and the only remaining serious candidate in the competition of political systems?[28]

Yet even if we manage to throw a spanner in the works when it comes to simple stories of progression from small and equal to big and unequal, and show that human history has always been a history of intense political plasticity and social variability, in which we largely shaped our coexistence ourselves, could *modern large societies* really exist without inequality and domination? Perhaps this is precisely the reason why it seems as though we are stuck now: *we really are stuck,* and beyond returning to radically simpler forms of living – with their own particular blend of romance and harshness – it is very unlikely that developed societies can be organised without considerable socio-political stratification. How did we get to this?

Big gods

The first large imperial societies began to write down the rules of their coexistence around 5,000 years ago. The most famous example of these is the Babylonian Code of Hammurabi, which dates from around the eighteenth century BCE. The black stone stele that now stands in the Louvre regulated how homicide, property or contractual offences and other cultural and situational issues were dealt with (much like the Code of Ur-Nammu, inscribed in red stone, from around the twenty-first century BCE did): are the children a man had with his slave recognised as legitimate after his death? What is the penalty for killing a citizen? What is it for killing a court dignitary?

The Sumerian Code of Lipit-Ishtar (from around the nineteenth century BCE) established rules like this, too. It was stated, for example, that he who had cut down a tree in another man's garden owed him a mina of silver, and he who had injured the flesh around the nose ring of an ox was to pay a third of the estimated price for the animal.[29]

These codices almost always begin by establishing the divine legitimacy of the ruler, or the entire ruling dynasty: before getting bogged down in legal details, it has to be made clear that the legislation's validity is not due to the privilege of the strongest, of course, but to divine blessing. This is no coincidence, because belief in the authority of moralising gods – in other words, gods who monitor compliance with rules – played a key role in the emergence of early advanced civilisations.

The cast of spirits found in smaller tribal societies consisted mostly of mischievous, amoral embodiments of various forces of nature who had their own agenda and could be bribed with sacrificial gifts or appeased with threats. The first civilisations, on the other hand, almost always went through a paradigm shift towards so-called 'big gods'[30] – a few mega-deities increasingly imagined as abstract and otherworldly, which, after several waves of mergers among the theological dramatis personae, ultimately led to the monotheistic notion of an eternal, omnipotent and omniscient God completely removed from the earthly world, who sees all and is therefore able to punish every shameful deed.

With a group's increasing size and extreme material inequalities, it becomes increasingly difficult to stabilise social cooperation through reciprocity, family ties or simple social sanctions. Penal institutions increase our willingness to cooperate, but do not solve the problem completely: what about the crimes that remain uncovered or unpunished? This is the point where it gets easier for societies that come up with the idea of an omniscient and omnipresent punishing God who registers and prosecutes every violation of the rules.

It is only through this development that the concept of an immortal soul becomes crucial. The notion that individuals will always be given their just punishment in the event of misconduct contradicts our experience of life – that there is no actual connection between praiseworthy behaviour and earthly success. On the contrary: the baddies often do surprisingly well, while many good people come off rather badly. So a concept had to be thought up that would be sure to serve justice, punish sinners and balance moral value and welfare. As the English philosopher John Locke put it, the idea of an immortal soul has a forensic origin, and is therefore all about making the otherworldly sanctioning of this worldly misconduct metaphysically comprehensible: in simple terms, people who can be held responsible for their misconduct beyond death in their afterlife are more willing to abide by the rules in this world.

As hyper-cooperative beings, we are capable of advanced forms of social cognition that mean we can intuitively and very reliably guess the mental states of the people around us. This ability also means we can assume we are not merely walking piles of bones and flesh, but also endowed with something else: a separate vessel – a spirit or a soul – to hold our intentions, desires, beliefs, desires and opinions. The moment we began to categorically detach a spirit like this from its physical substrate – an individual's mortal body – to gain a better understanding of other people's psyches, it was only a small step to the notion that there could also be wholly immaterial, purely spiritual beings. All that remained after that was for this basic idea to be inflated to the size of a superhuman God.

Was it only the societies with big gods that could become civilisations? Or was it the growing, increasingly civilised societies that invented big gods?[31] We cannot know which came first, but one thing is certain: big gods encourage cooperation.[32] In economic game theory, participants make higher contributions if they are unobtrusively made aware of the possibility of divine supervision. In an experiment known as the dictator game, a person is free to decide how they want to divide a certain amount of money between themselves and another participant. Test subjects gave away around a quarter of this amount, but subjects who had previously completed a task that contained references to God shared around half. These unconscious stimuli – known in psychology as 'primes' – had a particularly powerful effect on people of faith: their willingness to cooperate increased significantly when they were first asked to take part in a game to put a number of words containing the terms 'divine' or 'spiritual', for example, in the grammatically correct order (one instance was 'dessert divine was the').[33]

Nonetheless, it is not entirely clear exactly which mechanism is at work here: do big gods motivate through fear of punishment, so we do not often give in to our impulses to commit moral misconduct because we are afraid of hellfire? Or does the idea of a punishing God simply make it easier for us to make decisions, because it reminds us of our moral norms that already exist?

The psychology of inequality

We spent one of the most crucial phases of our human evolution in egalitarian small groups, and that shaped our psyche. Even now, people try to create an environment of equality as often as possible. We want to deal with each other 'on an equal footing', which is why we feel as comfortable in groups, social gatherings and Facebook communities as we do in clubs, bars, concerts or around the campfire. Anonymous large societies, where strangers trade with each other or develop political solutions to global problems through formal procedures, always remain a little scary, alien and suspect to us. This evolutionary 'hangover' also explains why every generation rediscovers socialism for itself. The vision of a society based on spontaneous solidarity and informal sharing remains emotionally irresistible. And it also remains the preferable concept – for families as well as for campsites.[34]

We find it psychologically incomprehensible that modern, anonymous, large societies can seldom be organised in this way and instead have the annoying tendency of degenerating into ultra-hierarchical dystopias after a short time. Unfortunately, our cultural evolution has not yet found a way to organise large societies in a truly egalitarian way. There is some fascinating research that reveals that test subjects who are shown pie charts depicting various wealth distribution patterns with no further information prefer the more egalitarian Swedish variant to the US variant, in which the top 20 per cent own more than 80 per cent of the wealth.[35]

Our evolutionary past has made us sceptical of dominance and hierarchy while also being allergic to social – and above all economic – inequality. A significant reason for this could be that we tend to judge inequality from the perspective of evolutionarily inherited zero-sum thinking.[36] As hunter-gatherer communities all had a very small economy, everyone received a share of what was killed or foraged. So if one person got more than another, that extra amount had ultimately to be taken away from another person. One person's advantages had to come at the expense of others, and this trade-off was highly visible. The fact that there can be inequalities that are not based on cheating, theft or exploitation is intuitively alien to us. And the fact that there can even be inequalities whose creation could have been beneficial for all involved sounds almost absurd. We find it hard to accept inequalities because the prosperity of some always seems to be at the expense of others.

Levelling down

Our aversion to hierarchy and dominance is activated by social inequalities, but in fact our indignation, deep down, is not about inequality as such – the mathematical fact that some have more and some have less – but about injustice, in other words unjustified inequality.[37] It is clear that an unequal distribution of goods or benefits can be seen as just, and equal distribution can be seen as unjust: equality is neither necessary nor enough on its own for there to be justice. A professor who gives every student the same top marks, regardless of their performance, is acting unfairly; a wealthy good-for-nothing who's wielding Daddy's wallet violates our understanding of fairness and merit. Yet most people agree that inequality is evil, and there is much less of a consensus over why this is so.

If we delve a little deeper and insist on there being an intimate connection between justice and equality, we arrive at egalitarianism. One of the most unwelcome implications of egalitarianism is that it seems to legitimise actions that help no one and harm some. Would it be in the spirit of justice to gouge out the eyes of everyone who could see, just to achieve equality with the visually impaired? This argument has become known as the 'levelling down objection', and seen in this light, it becomes easier for us to appreciate where justice and equality diverge.[38]

Philosophical anti-egalitarians take these objections very

seriously and from the outset, they tailor their political designs to show that comparative considerations are morally irrelevant. For a just society, therefore, whether one person has more than someone else or less is irrelevant – what is relevant is whether they have *enough*.[39] Of course, there are plenty of cases where a person is richer than they deserve to be, or poorer. But according to anti-egalitarians, whether this is the case does not depend on how much a person possesses in relation to others. Distributive justice does not need these comparisons. A just society ensures that everyone has enough to live on and has their dignity – whether or not some have more than enough does not matter.

Even anti-egalitarians can easily argue that virtually all inequalities, both current and historical, are or have been unjust. Anti-egalitarians are not necessarily *in*egalitarianists who consider *in*equality intrinsically desirable: equality and inequality simply have no moral significance of their own. European feudalism, South Asian caste systems, apartheid, segregation, slavery and discrimination can be classified as injustices even without pondering comparative equality. The fact that people are exploited, mistreated or excluded because of their skin colour, gender or social class can be condemned even without seeing equality as an end in itself.

Regardless of where one stands in terms of egalitarianism, anti-egalitarianism or inegalitarianism, it is clear that societies do not automatically remain in a state of social equality; equality needs to be defended. As an equal distribution of resources and status does not happen on its own, constant intervention is needed to bring the status quo (which is invariably out of balance) to the desired ideal. To make this happen, a Faustian pact needs to be made: the necessary redistribution can only happen if a central authority – in most cases, a form of government – is given the power to intervene in the personal destinies of its subjects. But in defending equality, we are unable really to get rid of the problem of inequality. Instead, we simply end up constantly exchanging one form of inequality for another. The price of replacing economic inequality with political inequality may be justified, but hoping that social inequalities can be *eliminated* through political intervention is futile; effective political action itself is only made possible by social asymmetries of power, which constitute their own form of inequality.

In twentieth-century political philosophy, a similar point was emphasised by libertarian thinkers such as the American Robert Nozick, who wanted to show in a famous thought experiment that we can go from a state of perfect material equality – let's call this Z_1 – to a state of blatant inequality – Z_2 – without the need for any injustice along the way. But, Nozick asked, how could Z_2 be unjust at all if it had arisen from a perfect initial state through unobjectionable intermediate steps? We might be forgiven for thinking that a just state of affairs cannot become unjust through a series of just exchanges.[40]

Nozick used Wilt Chamberlain, the world's greatest basketball player at the time, for his thought experiment, which goes as follows: we live in a perfectly equal society. One day, shortly before the start of his game, Wilt Chamberlain announces that from then on, he will only play if every stadium visitor throws ten extra cents into a money box at the entrance, which would go directly to Wilt. As most people have come to see him play anyway, all 10,000 spectators happily accept the deal, and Wilt goes home after the game with $1,000 more than his teammates.

The resulting situation is clearly one of financial inequality, but at what point did an injustice happen? Moreover, it quickly becomes clear that Z_1 – perfect equality – could only be maintained permanently if completely harmless transactions of this kind, gladly and voluntarily undertaken by all participants, were prevented in full. Not only does this intervention feel despotic, but it also seems extremely unfair to prevent adults from being free to decide what to do with their ten cents.

Some philosophers now believe that it is no longer possible to defend the concept of the fundamental moral equality of all human beings under secular conditions.[41] This was Nietzsche's idea, at any rate: only as recipients of God's unconditional love are we equal. After God's demise, we have to come to terms with the harsh truth that a theistic foundation for equality was a dead end. What should our fundamental equality be based on instead, though?

It is hard to deny that it needs to be based on something: no one believes that stones and grasshoppers have the same moral value as a human being. Of course, this is because humans possess certain qualities that inanimate objects or simpler creatures lack. But as soon as we try to identify a quality that makes us morally equal subjects – is it our ability to reason? Our consciousness? Our ability to suffer? – we soon realise it is impossible to pick a quality that a) seems to be morally relevant in some way and b) is actually shared by every human. Babies have no ability to reason, brain-dead people have no consciousness, and even if we managed to find a quality that could create equality, there would be countless other characteristics that distinguish people from one another. The metaphysical foundation of our supposed moral equality remains a mystery.[42]

Everyone is equal (after war)

Even if inegalitarians were wrong and socio-economic equality were an intrinsically valuable asset, the question of whether this asset could be easily implemented – and if so, how – would still remain. The road to hell is paved with good intentions, and politically speaking, it is no good demanding something if you cannot also suggest how realistically to achieve it.

The rise of inequality can be seen as a development in which early elites appropriated the extra yield generated by population growth and agricultural innovations. The ideological legitimisation of these status hierarchies was achieved, as we have seen, through the emergence of a religious and intellectual tier of professional ideologists.[43] The resulting military power of the first civilisations led to the elimination or absorption of the small egalitarian groups coexisting until then: their way of life was initially displaced and ultimately almost completely killed off.

For many millennia, there seemed to be no alternative to a few people usurping resources that had previously been managed communally. All over the world, the most unscrupulous warlords and robber barons became feudal lords, whose primary concern from that point on was consolidating and expanding their privileges. So social inequality became our second nature, and the notion of there actually being no first-, second- or third-class people could only be politically revived in the early modern period, and later more insistently by the Enlightenment; still today we have not completely achieved this goal.

Over the intervening years, phases of escalating social equality usually came at a high price. Historically, there seem to be four key mechanisms for effectively eradicating social inequalities: war, revolution, state collapse and plagues.[44] The second half of the twentieth century is inscribed in many countries' collective memory as an epoch of particular harmony and prosperity – in France, for example, as the *Trente Glorieuses*, the 'thirty glorious years', or as the *Wirtschaftswunder*, the 'economic miracle', in Germany. But you don't have to be an economist to understand that equality and growth are only easy to come by if you're prepared to throw everything out first. Even the *zaibatsu* model, which had placed Japan's economic power in the hands of a few gigantic family businesses, could not be saved after 1945. The pattern of wars having an equalising effect can be seen again and again: in the American South, the richest upper class's share of the society's total wealth fell by over 10 per cent in the mid-nineteenth century as a result of the Civil War.

In the Russian Revolution and during the Chinese Great Leap Forward, in North Korea and Cambodia, and of course during the French Revolution over 150 years earlier, social equality was preferably achieved by murdering or, at the very least, starving and dispossessing the bourgeois kulak powers, the counter-revolutionary landowners and the *ancien régime*. The number of victims reached tens of millions in these instances.

Victims were also claimed by the Black Death, which reached Sicily in 1347 and whose devastating effect was perhaps best summed up by Agnolo di Tura, the chronicler of Siena, around a year later:

And so they died. And none could be found to bury the dead for money or friendship. Members of a household brought their dead to a ditch as best they could, without priest, without divine offices. Nor did the death bell sound. And in many places in Siena great pits were dug and piled deep with the multitude of dead. And they died by the hundreds, both day and night, and all were thrown in those ditches and covered with earth. And as soon as those ditches were filled, more were dug. And I, Agnolo di Tura ... buried my five children with my own hands ... And so many died that all believed it was the end of the world.[45]

By the end, the plague had gone a considerable way towards levelling out every social difference, but at the same time it halved the populations of Europe and North Africa. The new levels of equality came at a terrible cost.

Inequality today

There are few topics today that engage the minds and keyboards of political commentators more than the problem of social inequality.

Social inequality can be measured in different ways, but the best-known tool for determining the inequality of wealth is the 'Gini coefficient'. This is always a figure between 0 and 1 which reflects distributive inequalities at a national level – in other words it relates to entire countries. A Gini score of 1 would mean that one single person has all of one nation's wealth, while everyone else has nothing. A value of 0 means every person has exactly the same amount of wealth or income. Broadly speaking, the most inegalitarian nations in the world, such as South Africa, have a Gini coefficient of about 0.6. Sitting in the middle – between 0.4 and 0.5 – are countries such as the United States and Russia, where there are also pronounced inequalities. Comparatively egalitarian countries such as Germany or the Netherlands are at 0.3 or just below.

In order to measure inequalities between smaller groups or even individuals, socio-economic status (SES) is often used. This value paints a rather more complex picture, and with its help, we can draw conclusions about the distribution of income and wealth, about educational levels, lifestyle aspects, mental and physical health or even professional prestige.[46] A culturally aware editor-in-chief or a doctor with above-average income and/or inherited wealth has a high SES, whereas an unemployed person without any education would have a correspondingly low SES.

With increasing access to data and various methods of measuring inequality, theories abound as to what the causes – and consequences – of inequality actually are. In his bestselling book *Capital in the Twenty-First Century*, the French economist Thomas Piketty argues that the period of relative equality that we saw in the second half of the twentieth century was an exceptional phase that came at the price of war and destruction; equality with a heavy cost indeed.[47]

Other commentators, such as Simon Kuznets, regard the historical development of distributive imbalances as a curve: an egalitarian starting point is followed by a period of expanding inequality for the benefit of a few profiteers, which declines again as an ever-increasing number of people gain access to the fruits of economic growth made possible by technology.[48] In this model, societies will typically experience a shift from equality to inequality and back again; historically, however, profit from assets has almost always outweighed economic growth.[49] As long as this remains the case, socio-economic inequalities are bound to grow and stabilise in the long term without aggressive redistribution – resulting in what is known as the Matthew effect: to everyone who has will more be given.

Several times a year, the problem of social inequality at a worldwide level is succinctly summed up by non-governmental organisations such as Oxfam. In 2020, the imbalance of global prosperity was roughly summarised as follows: the twenty-two richest men in the world are more wealthy than *all the women in Africa combined* (whose number is estimated at 325 million).[50] These claims rarely come without contradictions – for example, by focusing on a person's net worth, i.e. their assets minus their liabilities, a London resident with a mortgage of over £1 million would have to be poorer than someone from Zimbabwe who owns nothing but at least has no debts. Nonetheless, they show that the accumulation of wealth and the rapid rise in income in a few regions in a handful of countries have created levels of material inequality that for a long time were largely unknown in this form.

Inheriting inequality

Socio-economic inequalities are only one dimension of injustice. Whether an unequal distribution of resources such as power or wealth is unjust depends both on how pronounced the social upheavals are in a society and on how much movement between existing milieus is possible. Are power, wealth and status open to everyone, or are they locked in insurmountable divides?

Clearly social differences are only part of the picture, and we must also consider social mobility. Once established, inequalities are amazingly persistent. This is not surprising, as today's elite decides who will belong to tomorrow's elite, of course.

As a rule, these are their own children, who are (or should be) prepared for their future role in the upper class by parents concerned with status, often at astonishing expense, through piano and riding lessons, museum visits, language tuition and the prospect of inheriting the family fortune.

To better understand the degree to which these kinds of things impacted and persisted in society at large, the Scottish economist Gregory Clark took it upon himself to examine the permeability of modern societies by tracking the social position of families with rare surnames over generations.[51] The first known Pepys, for example, appears in 1496 as a student at the University of Cambridge. Since then, more than fifty Pepyses have attended the same educational institution, over twenty times as many as would have been expected statistically. Four of the eighteen Pepyses still alive today are doctors. The Pepyses who have died in recent times each left an average fortune of over £400,000.

It is particularly astonishing that this level of social mobility has remained almost untouchable politically. Neither a state education system with compulsory schooling, nor far-reaching economic growth, nor the demographic expansion of voting and civil rights, nor tax redistribution have made modern societies appreciably more permeable. Softer forms of social inequality, too, such as status hierarchies – who belongs to the upper class, and who to the lower class? – are also practically impossible to eradicate, particularly as they are not explicitly codified. If status differences are laid down in law, they can be abolished officially, or at least toned down by changing the laws in question. Kurt von Kleefeld, a brother-in-law of Chancellor Gustav Stresemann, was the last German to be given an aristocratic title in 1918. Article 109 of the Weimar Constitution, adopted shortly afterwards, stated: 'Public legal privileges or disadvantages of birth or of rank are abolished. Titles of nobility shall be regarded merely as part of the name and may no longer be bestowed.' As a result, one major source of social inequality in

Germany became a thing of the past, though of course many others remained.

Beyond titles, there are plenty of more subtle factors that denote which socio-economic class people belong to. Pierre Bourdieu's fascinating landmark text on distinction notably showed how social differences are embodied in an individual habitus – a person's lifestyle choices, manner of speaking or taste that make up their cultural capital – so that membership of a social group manifests itself in external signals and behavioural traits.[52] In particular, a person's cultural capital directly contributes to how they are perceived socially. How we hold our cutlery, whether we are familiar with classical music or have heard of the more obscure museums in Paris, how we speak and what accent or dialect we have, how and where we live, how we dress and how easily we can keep up with dinner party conversations about Riesling vineyards, vintage watches, Bauhaus architecture, Impressionist painting, family offices and Latin American magical realism all go to determine how much cultural capital someone has.

As this kind of 'knowledge as a power base' must be acquired at a young age to appear authentic, anyone who has grown up in an appropriately studious household will often enjoy an almost unassailable advantage. This head start is difficult to neutralise, because the codes of conduct that define a person's lifestyle and habitus are only implicitly cultivated and passed on, making it impossible to simply redistribute them. Even a society that could guarantee perfect material equality would ultimately be powerless against these mechanisms to transfer social privileges intergenerationally. Greater economic equality would probably exacerbate the problem of smaller differences in status, because elites hungry for distinction and no longer able to distance themselves pecuniarily from the unwashed masses would focus all their energy into perfecting subtle status symbols such as the use of the word 'pecuniarily'.

Gender trouble

As well as economic class differences, there are other forms of social inequality in most societies that make people's positions in the social fabric dependent on their membership of various groups. The best-known case of this is gender inequality.

For a long time, the story of the origins of gender inequality has gone something like this: once upon a time, there was a society where men and women had equal rights. One day, as a result of a mixture of base motives such as jealousy and misogyny, the men managed to seize control. Since then, patriarchy has prevailed everywhere, wielding the political, economic and cultural power and establishing social structures that systematically exclude women, discriminate against them, disenfranchise them and condemn them to a life of 'the little woman at home'.

In fact, there are now much more sophisticated explanatory models that portray inequalities between the sexes not as a quasi-conspiratorial subjugation of women by the patriarchy (and its female accomplices), but as the result of a social and evolutionary process over the course of which gender categories were introduced to pragmatically coordinate activities, which later became the foundation for social disadvantage.

Human societies consist of a web of coordination problems. Sometimes coordination is *correlative*: in these cases, it is important for everyone to do the same thing. It is irrelevant which side of the road you are driving on; the only thing that matters is that everyone drives on the same side. Other coordination problems are *complementary*: it is immaterial who leads the waltz; the only thing that counts is that half of the dancers lead, while the other half let themselves be led. Social division of labour is effective. It makes sense for people to do different things, and a society where everyone was a teacher or a policeman would not be very appealing. But how does a society decide who takes on which task? This requires a characteristic that makes it possible for tasks to be allocated. As a result, division of labour becomes a complementary coordination problem.

To be able to deal with complementary coordination problems as smoothly as possible, it can help to agree on a distribution of roles that associates the alternative activities in question – leading or being led, ploughing or cooking – to different social categories. All known human societies solve a significant proportion of their coordination problems by resorting to social categories and 'tags'. In principle, there is a great deal of scope as to which categories are assigned social significance; mostly, though, the choice comes down to classification features that can be easily, quickly and unambiguously recognised by anyone with functioning eyes. For this reason, there are differences in the social roles and functions carried out by the sexes in every society. These functional gender differences are not 'natural' or innate in the sense that evolution might have hardwired which sex would hunt and which would bring up the children. It's just that for the most part men and women are easily distinguished, and this fact provides characteristics that can be helpful for the purposes of coordination, when it comes to allocating social roles.

This allocation is broadly, but not entirely, arbitrary. In all traditional societies, for example, hunting large animals and metalworking are de facto done by men.[53] Washing and spinning, on the other hand, are almost exclusively done by women. Other activities, such as manufacturing ropes, building houses or sowing crops, are sometimes assigned to one sex and sometimes to the other. Even in modern societies, it is statistically fairly atypical for women (in heterosexual relationships) to spend their time mowing the lawn or shovelling snow while men are taking care of the laundry and domestic chores, although the roles could easily be distributed in this way.

As long as no differences in power, status or income result from this task structure, there is little reason to object to a division of labour of this kind. Yet it can be demonstrated that almost every society moves towards a state of social inequality on its own, even without a group of sinister puppeteers rigging the cards in their favour. Social inequality is a 'population equilibrium'. The reason for this is that social coordination problems are usually best solved by one easily recognisable group (for example 'women') taking over task A and the other easily recognisable group (for example 'men') taking over task B. As luck would have it, there are situations where not every task is equally lucrative, so the group that happens to be assigned the more desirable or fruitful of the two tasks ends up better off.

It can still make sense for everyone involved to agree to an asymmetrical equilibrium of this kind, because the benefits of efficiency reaped through successful coordination are still more attractive than the prospect of the attempt at coordination completely running aground. If there are some forms of division of labour that are more advantageous for one social category than for the other, it is ultimately inevitable that at some point task distributions will arise that systematically favour one group. As long as there are complementary coordination processes with this kind of asymmetrical equilibrium, social inequalities will arise almost spontaneously. And as human coexistence is subject to the forces of cultural evolution, social disparities, once established, are passed on and perpetuated as a matter of course. This is not a justification of inequality, but it does show how difficult it is to get rid of it completely.

The price of inequality

Social inequalities arise spontaneously, are reproduced over generations and are difficult to eliminate. In short, the problem of socio-economic inequality is here to stay. It is what we call a 'wicked problem': nobody is exactly sure what the problem is, and the best solutions for it have been debated for quite some time. A completely egalitarian society is not on the horizon for the time being. It is also misleading to argue between unfettered inequality and radical equality: even if full socio-economic equalisation might neither be possible nor desirable, a comparatively more equal society could still be beneficial to all.

One of the biggest drawbacks of growing inequality is that inegalitarian structures destroy a society's social capital: the informal web of universally accepted social norms that enables smooth cooperation between all members of society.[54] More than anything else this means the resource of *social trust* erodes: only if people fundamentally trust each other can the social fabric that paves the way for successful and peaceful coexistence be maintained. The symptoms of a loss of trust created by social inequality range from an erosion of elementary forms of community to a deterioration in public health, to an increase in mental health problems, or an increasing propensity for violence and resignation, because large sections of society rightly suspect that their chances of success are not fair. A situation like this can lead to a rise in deaths of despair, often resulting from suicide or drug abuse.[55]

Modern societies must be able to tolerate a certain degree of inequality, but only if the institutions enabling that inequality have other benefits that adequately compensate for its psychological and emotional costs. Even markets that function well generate socio-economic asymmetries because they make economic success dependent on lucky coincidences, a favourable start in life and individual talent. Nonetheless, the gains in efficiency and prosperity that this kind of arrangement produces can be beneficial to all. Humanity does not yet know how to build large societies that are not characterised by gross inequality, even though these social arrangements contradict our moral intuitions. Only a few people find the return to 'more primitive' forms of coexistence truly attractive, and usually only because these lifestyles are romanticised.

Inequality becomes a problem when no one becomes better off as a result of it. What we call 'positional goods' are items whose value is primarily determined by the fact that other people do *not* have them. Not everyone can buy a luxury watch from F. P. Journe, and the number of apartments on Central Park West is limited. Acquiring limited or positional goods like these is a zero-sum game for society as a whole, because one person's gain must be the other's loss. As a result, the social inequality created by status competition for positional goods does not make society happier on average because it creates complementary winners and losers.

In developed societies, material inequality mainly becomes a problem when it undermines the social basis of individual self-respect. The concept of relative poverty, which is used in statistics on the state of a country's society, does not primarily measure economic deprivation, but instead a lack of the resources necessary to actively participate in society. You do not have to be hungry or cold to suffer from the social stigma that comes from not being able to go to a restaurant or not having the money to buy a ticket to the cinema. As far back as the eighteenth century, the Scottish economist and Enlightenment philosopher Adam Smith formulated a benchmark for an acceptable society that everyone in it must have the means to be seen in public 'without shame':

> A linen shirt . . . is, strictly speaking, not a necessary of life. The Greeks and Romans lived, I suppose, very comfortably though they had no linen. But in the present times, through the greater part of Europe, a creditable day-labourer would be ashamed to appear in public without a linen shirt, the want of which would be supposed to denote that disgraceful degree of poverty which, it is presumed, nobody can well fall into without extreme bad conduct.[56]

Admittedly, even this standard only indicates an *adequate* level of social participation, which could be ensured primarily by guaranteeing that everyone at the lower end of income distribution was given a minimum. Of course, Smith's criterion does not rule out billionaires whose existence is, by definition, in keeping with the self-respect of every member of society.

A particular strength of decentralised societies lies in the fact that, under the conditions of modern pluralism with its diversity of values, an unlimited number of status hierarchies can be created in principle, each operating with its own standards of prestige and success. Provided there is no need to be a billionaire to gain social recognition, if we can distinguish ourselves as competent pigeon fanciers, accomplished rowers or gifted choral singers, there is enough status to go round for everyone.[57] Given certain parameters, some degree of inequality is justifiable.

Of course, there have been countless extremely successful examples of attempts to create equality that we would in no way want to abandon: the past 300 years have brought about the abolition of the aristocracy's formal social privileges, the end of slavery (in most places), the introduction of civil rights for the Black population of the United States after the end of the Jim Crow era, the introduction of women's suffrage, the end of apartheid, the erosion of caste systems, greater civil rights for minorities (same-sex marriage, for example) and more inclusive treatment for physically or mentally disabled people. These developments, though still a work in progress, reflect a moral standard that it would now be unthinkable to fall below.[58]

By now, we can see that even dismantling politically enforced discrimination and abolishing aristocratic sinecures does not lead directly to the egalitarian paradise of a classless society. The meritocratic transformation of modern societies comes at its own (often considerable) social price:[59] it is true that children from previously disadvantaged groups now manage to compete in the contest for status and income through intelligence, hard work and talent. Using standardised tests, Harvard now admits more Jewish and Japanese students, who were still extensively discriminated against in the twentieth century. Then again, a society that links self-respect to success and success to performance promotes toxic competitions, so even toddlers, encouraged and guided by status-sensitive parents, have to take violin and Mandarin lessons to compete for a place in the best nursery. At the same time, it creates a narrative where anyone who has not 'made it' has no one but themselves to blame for their failure – at least under feudal conditions it was clear to everyone that the connection between wealth and an individual's personal qualities was only very fragile. A society that rewards an elite of highly qualified 'knowledge workers', flocking together in the same superstar cities from San Francisco to Singapore, finds it hard to give the minority that is left behind the recognition it deserves.

The idea of meritocracy – that social inequalities can be justified when social positions are fundamentally accessible to everyone on the basis of a person's performance – is often met with a surprisingly high degree of scepticism. But given what we know now, do we have a problem with this idea in itself, or is it simply that we take issue with its poor implementation? In his critique of meritocratic performance societies, the American philosopher Michael J. Sandel wrote: 'There is nothing wrong with hiring people based on merit.'[60] And: 'Having well-educated people run the government is generally desirable' as well as 'An aristocracy is unjust, because it consigns people to the class of their birth. It does not let them rise.'[61] So where exactly is the tyranny in meritocracy? What alternative could there be? And is the problem simply that we have never been able to achieve a true meritocracy?

The problem of social inequality is one that persists to this day – and we don't seem to be much closer to 'solving it' than our ancestors, when it arose in the early civilisations of the ancient world. Over the past 5,000 years, it has always been indisputable that a few hold the power and wealth, while the overwhelming majority remain poor and disenfranchised. Only recently has the question of the basic principles of a just society been renegotiated with unprecedented urgency.

What does a society that recognises the dignity of the individual look like?

How do we manage to reconcile freedom of the individual with a desire for earthly happiness?

And what does it mean to live among equals?

These questions are the spectres that have haunted the world for the past 500 years.

5

The Discovery of WEIRDness

Downfall

Many years ago – I can't remember exactly how long – I met a man who had just returned from a journey to a faraway land. He was much older than me, and as we dined together, I asked him for advice, telling him of my hopes and plans and of everything I still wanted to achieve in life. He listened to me patiently, and when I finally paused for a moment, he smiled with the good-natured scepticism of those who have put most of life's ambitions behind them, and he answered me most mysteriously. It was only much later that the meaning of his words became clear to me.

He told me he had just travelled across a desert. There, one day, after a long journey, he came across two enormous stone legs pointing up to the sky; next to them, half-buried in the sand, lay a giant face, cracked, its wrinkled lips and scornfully furrowed brow giving it a serious expression. It was clear that the sculptor must have been personally familiar with the emotions written on that face. The work of art whose remains had appeared before my acquaintance was clearly ancient; it had long outlived its creator, who had entrusted his vision to the stone with a mocking hand. And on the plinth were the following words which, strangely, my acquaintance could remember in full: 'My name is Ramses, son of Sethos and Tuja, heir of Ra, bearer of the Atef crown, king of kings. Look on my works, ye Mighty, and despair!'

No more remained of him than this, the man assured me. And around the ruins of that decaying giant he could see only desert, bare and desolate, its sands stretching endlessly into the horizon.

A genealogy of the modern age

The great empires and the first urban centres of the ancient world are long gone. The remains of their former glory are now admired by tourists who archive the lost splendour of their ruins and the remains of their walls on Instagram.

It can be hard to imagine how this world, our world, emerged from that one. But by retracing the genealogy of the modern age, we can begin to see a development in which the demand for human autonomy and individuality was made with unprecedented urgency. Weirdness, uniqueness, individuality; whatever you want to call it, this development forced a complete transformation of our values, institutions and infrastructures, and in doing so, it redefined the rules of our coexistence. It unleashed new economic, scientific and technological energies that challenged traditional hierarchies and asserted the rights of the individual. This development was an entirely new one.

To understand this paradigm shift, we must look further back, and remind ourselves how we humans have lived over the previous 5,000 years, since the dawn of inequality in the first large-scale human societies: a short life of poverty and filth, misery and serfdom, harassed by murderous despots, plagued by disease, wiped out in senseless wars, terrorised by religious superstition and anxiously dreading (or hoping for) death; children with backs deformed from carrying water, and women endlessly chained to the cycle of pregnancy and childbirth until their untimely end.

The essential trajectory of life was predetermined by the random accident of birth: barely anyone was able to leave their eternally unchanging village, where their grandfathers and great-grandfathers before them had been blacksmiths, carpenters or shepherds, and if they did leave, it was only at great risk, on foot or shaken about on rickety carts, through dark forests or across endless steppes inhabited by dangerous animals and lawless tribes, or in the belly of wooden ships over stormy seas to the ends of an unknown world.

Once this paradigm ended, and another came to predominate, we entered a new age, one where globally connected cosmopolitans have to demonstrate their capacity for inventiveness to be able to give any meaning to their lives, the average length of which has now doubled. This is a time when many are freed from the yoke of hard labour, and can decide who they want to be and where they want to live. It is an age when the sweet fruits from distant lands, once so rare and unattainable that even the rich knew them only from paintings in the salons of the even richer, are at hand at any time, when the dream of flying has come true and when the hearts of strangers can beat in the chests of those once destined to die.

The genealogy of the modern age explains how the two-pronged promise of happiness and freedom could emerge from misery and oppression – a promise that, of course, is still far from being fulfilled in equal measure for everyone. Nonetheless, modernity created a new human being: it created people who see themselves as individuals, surrounded by other individuals with whom they live freely and voluntarily, and who – according to their degree of entitlement, at any rate – have the sole and ultimate authority over the conditions in which they would like to live their lives. This is a radical break with the previous millennia, when humans had learned to see themselves primarily as family members and part of a natural hierarchy, as mere nodes in a network of familial relationships, and as underlings.

The story of this new human being is an origin story of the roots of individualism, of political freedom and of dignity for the individual. The quest to solve the puzzle of our origin has long preoccupied intellectuals, cultural theorists, philosophers and sociologists. How did the change from traditional 'community' to modern 'society' come about, replacing inherited customs with mutual agreement?[1] What brought about the transition from 'mechanical' to 'organic' solidarity, replacing simple structures with a functional division of labour?[2] Where did Max Weber's 'occidental rationalism' come from: the desire to systematically comprehend the whole world and turn it into something that can be calculated and predicted?[3]

The shift to modern times marks the end of a development that was 'largely complete 500 years ago',[4] and with it, a shift in our moral thinking. How exactly did our values need to adapt to usher in this transformation to modernity? And why did it come about 500 years ago?

The weirdest people in the world, part one

In the summer of 2010, I was working as a PhD student in a research project at Leiden University in the Netherlands. In our reading group, which met about twice a month, we would discuss the latest developments in research literature that could potentially be relevant to our project's overarching theme: the psychological foundations of moral thought and action. We concentrated on the (often overly technical and unexciting) philosophical debates that attempted to analyse the cognitive foundations of moral judgement, the possibility of human free will or the influence of general personality traits and character traits on our behaviour. One of my colleagues suggested we read a recent publication with the cryptic title 'The WEIRDest people in the world?' in preparation for the next meeting. This text by a team of Canadian psychologists, led by Joseph Henrich, has been cited almost 9,000 times since it was published just over ten years ago and it was immediately recognised as a modern classic.

The purpose of psychologists is to try to understand the human mind: how does our perception work? How do memories come about? How are feelings processed? How are our thoughts formed? What shapes our identity? What is the cause of differences in intelligence? How do we make decisions? To be able to answer these questions, they design studies that will shed light on human behaviour and investigate the mechanisms that govern the human psyche. For over a century, psychologists have been using these studies to investigate every facet of human behaviour, from willpower to risk aversion. The problem Henrich and his colleagues noticed is that the insights into the *universal* human nature that psychology is supposedly searching for are almost always obtained on the basis of very *non-universal* data.

The gold standard of psychological research is the randomised trial: by haphazardly selecting study participants from the overall population and then, again haphazardly, assigning them to a control group or experimental conditions, psychologists hope to find out whether their experimental manipulation has an effect or not, and if so, how great this effect is. However, for largely pragmatic reasons – to save costs and time – they almost always use their own students for these kinds of studies, often in exchange for credit points.

So general statements about the universal nature of the human psyche are made on the basis of thought patterns and behaviour gathered from a highly specific group: almost all the participants in psychological studies come from wealthy, Western, industrialised, democratic regions with a high level of education.[5] Henrich and his colleagues coined what is probably the best acronym of all time for this group: WEIRD people. These initials stand for *Western, educated, industrialised, rich* and *democratic*.

It would not be a problem if the people in this group were representative of the rest of humanity, in other words if there were no systematic and robust differences between WEIRD humans and everyone else. The fact that this is not particularly likely should be clear from the start: it would be very surprising if a selection of highly intelligent adolescents from the world's richest countries studying at a handful of ultra-selective elite universities had the same cognitive intuitions, perceptual patterns, preferences and behavioural dispositions as an individual randomly selected from the rest of the human population.

But even Henrich and his team didn't seem prepared for

how 'weird' their subjects would turn out to be. If we look at this question systematically, it becomes apparent that WEIRD populations are almost always the exception statistically. The most impressive example of them being outliers can be found in visual perception: WEIRD people see things in a weird way. In many cases, there is a lot to learn about how people access the world visually by exploring misconceptions. Optical illusions provide an insight into how visual perception normally works.

Perhaps the best-known of all sensory illusions is the Müller-Lyer illusion, in which two lines, objectively of equal length, appear subjectively to have different lengths when they have arrow-like tips at each end pointing either inwards or outwards. This illusion has long been thought to be a universally occurring misconception in all human beings, related to how our sensory system works. But in fact, there are many cultures worldwide where the Müller-Lyer illusion is simply *not* an illusion. For the Kalahari San, for example, the lines look the same length, as well as for the Nigerian Ijaw and the Songye from the Congo. In Henrich and his colleagues' study, North American students' scores showed that they were much more susceptible to illusion than all other groups.

One possible explanation for this is that some people grow up in a 'carpentered' environment from the earliest stages of their childhood development, so that their visual information processing adapts to the frequent presence of right angles, but whatever the reason, the fact that there is a difference – though it seems blindingly obvious in retrospect – was like an atom bomb for the field of psychology.

When Henrich and his team looked further, they found a similar pattern emerging with almost every other psychological trait, and this is apparent when comparing developed countries with simpler societies, Western with non-Western societies, and even within Western societies where university students with certain cognitive abilities and socio-economic backgrounds deviate significantly from the average. WEIRD people – people from modern Western industrial nations – think differently, feel differently, live differently, have different values and are consistently the statistical outliers. When asked to name objects, they say 'tree' and 'bird' instead of 'birch' and 'robin', going first for the general category before moving on to the concrete example. When asked who they are, they give their profession, personal achievements, age and idiosyncrasies, only later mentioning whose daughter or son they are and what community they feel they belong to.

How did these WEIRD people come about, and why? When did they come into being, and what makes them who they are? By now, it has become apparent that it was *moral* and *institutional* changes that radically reshaped the perception, thinking and feelings of modern man – and this is the story of how that happened.

The weirdest people in the world, part two

WEIRD humans exhibit a complex plethora of cognitive and moral traits. They are typically, but not exclusively, represented in modern Western democracies: Denmark and Germany, Norway and Switzerland, the UK, Australia, Canada and the United States, Spain and Argentina. WEIRD people are, though, a statistical anomaly, globally speaking. First of all we need to find out what defines these people *morally* before we can consider how they became that way in the first place.

One of the most significant aspects of WEIRD morality is a pronounced tendency towards moral *universalism*. A universalist morality differs from what is known as a particularist morality, mostly in the fact that it is based on universally valid moral rules that apply equally to every human being. The special values of social communities or personal relationships between friends or relatives do not affect the validity of these rules.

To fully appreciate the difference, imagine you were involved in an accident where a pedestrian had been hit.[6] You were a passenger in the car, which was travelling at almost 60 miles per hour in a 30 mph zone, and one of your close friends was driving. Should you testify against your friend in court, and does your friend have a right to expect you not to? This is what is known as the passenger's dilemma. Most people, universalists and particularists alike, think it is fundamentally appropriate for the truth to be told in court. There is, however, a crucial question that distinguishes a universalist viewpoint from a particularist one: whether the fact that it is *your* friend whose liability is at stake plays a *moral* role. In WEIRD places, the overwhelming majority of people find it unacceptable to treat their friend differently from any other person they are not personally connected to. This is moral universalism.

'Weird people are bad friends,' concludes Henrich,[7] but this social aloofness has a welcome flipside, which is referred to in technical jargon as 'impersonal prosociality'. This factor relates to the extent to which a person is willing to trust people they do not know and cooperate with strangers. As we have already seen, our willingness to cooperate remains largely group-oriented for evolutionary reasons, so impersonal prosociality goes against the evolutionary grain.

If we ask study participants whether and to what extent they trust other people or whether they need to take more care when they are dealing with strangers, there is once again a big difference between WEIRD and non-WEIRD popula-tions. Seventy per cent of all Norwegians indicated that they do trust strangers, while only about 5 per cent of all people from Trinidad and Tobago said the same. Even within Europe, different levels of WEIRDness are evident: northern Italians score significantly higher than Sicilians in terms of 'impersonal trust' (trust of strangers). Unlike most of the global popula-tion, WEIRD people give comparatively lower moral priority to members of their own group – family, friends or nation – in favour of strangers.

Of course, WEIRD people also prefer relatives and friends

to strangers, treating them with more friendliness and less hostility, but it is noteworthy that this tendency is on average much weaker in this group. A similar pattern can be seen when it comes to dealing with a person's own *future self*. In psychology, the importance attributed to one's own future is often described in terms of 'time discounting' and 'delayed gratification'. Time discounting relates to how a person's preference for an item or event changes depending on how far in advance the event is or whether the person receives the item now or at a later date. Many people would rather have a smaller amount of money now than a larger one later. The ability to assess the value of things regardless of their temporal distance from the present moment is the capacity for delayed gratification or, put more simply, patience.

All people tend towards time discounting and value the present more highly than the future. And this is not fundamentally irrational: as long as there is no guarantee that I will even live to see next year, or that rampant inflation is on the horizon, 100 euros today are not equivalent to 100 euros next summer. But there are also significant differences in the amounts we have to offer (on average) a Norwegian to give up the 100 euros now in favour of waiting (namely 144 euros) and someone from Rwanda, who is only willing to wait for 212 euros, on average. This effect is reinforced by the fact that thinking in the long term sometimes pays off more and sometimes less, depending on the political environment: under conditions of socio-economic stability, it is easier to plan ahead.

WEIRD people are also nonconformists. In social psychology, conformist patterns of behaviour – the tendency to base our own behaviour closely on the actual or supposed behaviour of others – are traditionally examined in the 'Asch paradigm'.[8] In this experiment, developed in the 1950s by the Polish-American Gestalt psychologist Solomon Asch and one of the most famous studies in psychology ever since, test subjects are asked to select, from three straight lines, the one whose length is identical to a template. The test itself is extremely easy: under normal conditions, almost 100 per cent of all people find the correct solution. In Asch's experimental set-up, though, the participants are unwittingly surrounded by a group of 'insiders' who are instructed to give the wrong answer. Faced with this form of peer pressure, a significant number of people agree to an obviously incorrect opinion. It does not necessarily matter whether the test subjects really believe the wrong answer; the effect of the pressure to conform makes them publicly agree to the wrong answer. WEIRD people are the least susceptible to this pressure compared to all other populations – whether from Kuwait, Hong Kong or Zimbabwe – and this effect is even more pronounced in today's generations than in older ones. Consequently, young WEIRD people are least likely to conform to others' behaviour.

The moral feelings of WEIRD populations are also generally exceptional. In many traditional societies there is a 'culture of honour': an important currency in social intercourse is the individual's reputation as a woman or man, mother or father, businessperson, craftsperson or member of a community. This honour can depend on various factors such as someone's professional success, reliability or sexual behaviour. People react to violations of honour with *shame*: they feel degraded, humiliated and publicly exposed, and want to escape the gaze of others, crawl under a rock and hide their faces. Shame is the register of a degradation in others' social judgement of us.

WEIRD people, on the other hand, are shameless. Instead, they tend to feel guilty. Most people find these reactions very unpleasant and try to avoid guilty and shameful feelings: guilt and shame are moral emotions whose motivational power allows us to regulate our behaviour. However, they do this in different ways. Whereas feelings of shame depend largely on the judgement of others – the same action can cause intense shame or no shame at all, depending whether it is observed or in private – feelings of guilt are particularly triggered when a person falls short of their own moral standards. A person who intends to be vegetarian can feel extremely guilty after a moment of carnivorous weak will, even if they are surrounded exclusively by non-vegetarian friends who can fully understand why they just devoured a steak. WEIRD people are far more susceptible to these feelings of guilt that are not transmitted socially.

This also has an impact on how the violation of social norms is sanctioned. WEIRD people are less likely to react to the violation of their honour (or that of a family member or confidant) with revenge, but are more likely to enforce social rules with third parties.[9] In traditional societies, it is of prime importance to defend the socio-economic status of our own group against possible threats. What other people or communities do, what disputes they have and what rules they break is none of my business as long as it does not affect me or my nearest and dearest. WEIRD people, on the other hand, are less inclined to take revenge, but are more prepared to sanction the violation of general social norms.

One reason for these differences in the thoughts and actions of WEIRD populations is that their members have a different perception of themselves and the sources of their identity. WEIRD people see their identity as impersonal and abstract, while most other people have a concrete self-conception shaped by complex social relationships and roles.[10] If we ask WEIRD people to use sentences starting with 'I am ...', they name a range of personal attributes, achievements, accomplishments or ambitions. WEIRD people perceive the question of their identity as a question of what makes them unique and what defines them, and them only. This identity is determined by whether they are a movie buff or foodie, Manchester United fan or philatelist, entrepreneur or extreme athlete, doctor or chess player, and it depends largely on the particular interests and abilities of the person in question. For non-WEIRD people, belonging to a tight network of social roles and relationships is more important. In WEIRD environments, there is a *dispositionalist* expectation which requires individuals to build a stable personality that is consistent across different social contexts.[11] In non-WEIRD societies, it is normal to be quiet, shy and respectful towards a friend's grandparents, but to be loud, extroverted and self-confident in other situations. A clear majority of non-WEIRD people see themselves primarily as members of a family and religious community, as heirs, carers and guardians of a network of relationships and habits.

Does it make a moral difference whether someone has done something intentionally or unintentionally? The focus on the individual as a key ethical unit is also reflected in how this question is answered. The relevance of how intentional an action is to its culpability and criminality can be tested by asking people from different forms of society – urban populations from Los Angeles, livestock breeders such as the Angolan Himba people, hunters and farmers like the Tsimané in present-day Bolivia, or the Yasawa from Fiji, who are mainly fishermen – whether they see a morally relevant difference between actions which have the same consequences (and therefore cause the same amount of damage, for example) but were carried out for different reasons.[12] WEIRD people think it is much more forgivable to accidentally 'steal' someone's shopping bag because you have mistaken it for your own than to take it intentionally (although in general all people can see this difference). Did I want to steal the bag? Was it compulsion, greed or malice that made me want it? These things matter to WEIRD people. In non-WEIRD societies, though intention does matter, an action's consequences are far more relevant to moral judgements than the attitude behind it.

One final difference affects our abstract thinking. WEIRD populations are more inclined (as always: on average) towards *analytical* thinking, while non-WEIRD groups tend to do more *holistic* thinking. People who think analytically try to understand the world as a collection of isolated entities with certain characteristics that distinguish them from others. A holistic way of thinking emphasises the relationships between things and attempts to detect kinship relations and similarities instead. Holistic thinkers see 'the whole'; analytical thinkers see its parts. A simple and very intuitive way of testing the two styles of thinking in an experiment is by presenting test subjects with what are known as triad tasks, where they need to choose one of two objects to go with a third. Let's assume that the 'target' object is a rabbit, and the other two objects are a carrot and a cat. The task is to decide which of the two objects 'belongs' with the rabbit. WEIRD people put the rabbit and cat together because both belong to the category of mammal. People from Thailand or Bulgaria, in contrast, usually see a closer correlation between the rabbit and the carrot, because they have a certain relationship with each other. And when non-WEIRD people give answers that correspond to the more analytical response, they often turn out to be holistic in hindsight: Henrich reports on a case where a member of the South American Mapuche people matched 'dog' with 'pig' rather than 'maize' – not because dogs and pigs belong to the same category, but because dogs 'protect' pigs.[13]

The ten countries with the highest scores for analytical thinking were the Netherlands, Finland, Sweden, Ireland, New Zealand, Germany, the United States, the UK, Canada and Australia. It is easy to see how an analytical mindset and an individualistic morality complement each other: the tendency to view the world as a collection of isolated entities is more compatible with a moral perspective that compares individuals with individual rights, duties and intentions than to socially embedded family members whose role in the community gives their lives an ethical structure.

The differences between these styles of thinking do not correlate exactly with the difference between better and worse thinking, or right and wrong, when it comes to any of the traits I have mentioned. A more analytical style of thinking, a greater emphasis on the role of intentions or a keener focus on the future can be appropriate depending on the cultural or natural environment we inhabit. In some societies it is more important to know that rabbits and cats are mammals, in others the fact that rabbits eat carrots is more relevant. However, living in a society that tends to consist of more WEIRD and analytical people, or of more non-WEIRD ones who think holistically, can make a big difference culturally.

WEIRD people have an atypical moral psychology: they are moral universalists who cooperate with strangers, regardless of personal relationships, comparatively speaking. They consider the individual as the key moral unit that willingly enters into cooperative relationships with others, and they judge a person's actions according to their intentions. They associate a person's identity with their personal achievements and character traits rather than family, clan or tribe, and are more patient when it comes to deferred rewards. Although the combination of these traits may seem familiar to those who are WEIRD, it is actually technically unusual, an exception worldwide and historically a very new phenomenon.

Probably the most momentous change brought about by the cultural evolution of WEIRD people was of an economic and political nature: for one thing, the institutions that made the shift to modern large-scale societies possible were extensive trade and exchange networks organised through decentralised price signals, also known as *markets*; for another, it necessitated a greater focus on protecting the individual rights of an ever-expanding group of citizens demanding freedom and involvement, also known as *democracy*. At the same time, though, this shift could only thrive in a certain socio-cultural environment where the structures of kinship and power that had previously provided society's key organisational framework gradually became weaker.

The weirdest people in the world, part three

From a global perspective, the inhabitants of rich Western industrial nations are a cognitively moral exception. WEIRD people think differently and have different values. But why? How did this 'individualism complex'[14] come about?

Joseph Henrich and his research team, while noting that there are people with a WEIRD psychological profile, did not offer an explanation of where these cognitive and moral patterns, which ultimately led to the rise of modernity, came from. It also remained unclear what factors were responsible for this transformation happening in the precise areas where we see it today.

A few years after the publication of these now legendary research findings, the first indications began to leak out that Henrich, now a professor at Harvard, and his team were working on a general theory of the origin of WEIRD values and thought patterns. In 2020 his monumental book *The WEIRDest People in the World* was published, offering a comprehensive and deeply intriguing explanation of the emergence of modern WEIRD-ness. Henrich argues that WEIRD populations' universalist morality and analytical thinking are the result of more than a thousand years of development, over the course of which the Catholic Church destroyed the traditional family structures of Europe. The demolition of kinship networks as a core organisational principle of economy, politics, law, religion and private life set in motion a process of cultural evolution that led to modernity about 500 years ago.

The theory that it was the Catholic Church's family policy that produced the characteristics of Western morality and cognition may seem surprising at first glance. But Henrich supports this theory with data-obsessed detail that is disarming, and even breath-taking. *The WEIRDest People in the World* is probably the most significant social science publication of the twenty-first century to date.

A key element in Henrich's theory is the concept of the

Western Church's marriage and family programme, or MFP. In the thousand-odd years between the Synod of Elvira near Granada, Spain in around the year 300 and the Fourth Lateran Council held in Rome in November 1215, the Roman Catholic Church enforced a complete transformation of European marriage and inheritance structures, which gradually dissolved the intense kinship and family relationships of Western society that had prevailed until then.[15] Kinship and family provide the basic structure of social coexistence in all societies. This is not a normative statement decreeing that 'the family' should take this role, but a descriptive statement: this is the way it is. The essential characteristics of traditional kinship ties in most societies, but especially in pre-Christian Europe, were as follows:[16]

- Human life largely took place in kin-based groups, which were in turn embedded in larger groups or networks (clans, tribes, etc.).
- Families were organised 'patrilineally': the paternal line held sway on inheritance, assets and where they lived. (This is not always the case. In some societies, it is not the wife who moves in with her husband but, conversely, the husband who lives in his mother-in-law's household after marriage.)
- These kinship units exercised collective control over land and property.
- People's individual identities depended on the social roles they assumed in their kinship networks.
- Conflicts and questions of liability or responsibility were dealt with and, if possible, settled according to the customs within a family community.
- Family relationships functioned as social safety nets, caring for members suffering from illness, poverty or the misfortunes of fate.
- Arranged marriages were widespread. The decision

about who married whom was often made in the interests of the whole family and its assets.

- Polygamous marriages were widespread, or more precisely polygynous marriages – in which a man has several wives (polyandry does exist, but is extremely rare) – at least for powerful and/or wealthy men.

In traditional, non-WEIRD societies, kinship relationships dominated the individual's entire life, with their abode, spouse, occupation and life path all defined by their social role in family-based networks. But how could the Western Church's marriage and family programme have gradually diluted these structures? The Synod of Elvira, mentioned earlier, gives us some insight: during this assembly in Spain, clerics drew up decrees that are now some of the oldest surviving written testimonies of the Catholic Church. The focus was on a moral way of life, marriage and other everyday issues that called for Christian orientation. The decrees therefore paint a picture of European church history at that time as well as showing how significantly family-organised social structures changed: at the Councils of Neocaesarea and Nicaea, levirate marriage (the marriage of a childless widow to her dead husband's brother) was forbidden; in September 506, the Council of Agde in southern France declared marriage between first and second cousins to be intolerable, as well as marriage between a man and his brother's widow, marriage to a wife's sister and marriage to an uncle's, or any other relative's, stepmother, widow or daughter. All this was classified as incest from then on and was often punishable by death. The Church also introduced godparenthood, where unrelated people can assume a kind of spiritual fatherhood or motherhood for a child, which reduced the emphasis on orphaned children being adopted by their own blood relatives; marriage between godparents and their godchildren was also forbidden, further reducing the power of family ties.

In the centuries that followed, the Church surpassed itself

with stricter and stricter regulations and prohibitions about who was allowed to marry whom: the ban on marriage between cousins played a particularly important role in the MFP,[17] and this was to become a significant distinguishing feature between the Western and Eastern Orthodox churches. The MFP's key points were as follows:

- prohibition of marriage between blood relatives (up to sixth cousins),
- prohibition of polygynous marriage,
- introduction of spiritual kinship (godparenthood),
- public verbal consent at the marriage ceremony, to discourage arranged marriages,
- neolocal residence (both newlyweds had to move out of the parental home),
- individual ownership and inheritance through personal wills.

This development's culmination marked the dawn of the proto-bourgeois nuclear family, which replaced the patriarchal structures of extended clans, in which everyone was related to everyone, with a loose association of fundamentally separate households. This trend was also reflected in the vocabulary for various kinship and legal relationships, with specific terms for family members – many societies distinguishing mothers' brothers from fathers' brothers – being replaced by terms that emphasised the incestuous nature of sexual relations. So the mother of your wife became his mother-in-law, for example, and your brother's wife became your sister-in-law.

There are no physical barriers that could prevent genetic relatives from having sex with each other. So most societies had to find a solution to the de facto possibility of incestuous reproduction. Part of the problem is solved biologically: children who have grown up in very close proximity to each other are automatically very unlikely to feel sexually attracted to each other later on, regardless of whether they are actually related (this is known as the Westermarck effect). This also explains why almost everyone intuitively has a very intense aversion to sex between siblings, for biological, rather than simply cultural, reasons. Beyond this, the cultural evolution of norms also needs to spell out the intricacies of the incest taboo. There is great cultural variation with this, with the measures taken by the early European Church at an extreme end of the spectrum.

Henrich summarises what these measures meant: 'The Church's MFP reshaped the European family in a process that was largely complete 500 years ago. But, does this really influence psychology today? Does growing up in less intensive kin-based institutions influence our motivations, perceptions, emotions, thinking-styles and self-concepts in significant ways? Is there a way to trace contemporary psychological variation back to the Church?'[18]

The cultural evolution of the modern soul

Although it did not happen overnight, the Catholic Church's marriage and family programme gradually brought about the destruction of previous Western European family and clan structures. Close kinship networks were replaced as the principle of social organisation: from this point on, politics and business increasingly had to be handled without recourse to genetic loyalties. This nurtured the cultural evolution of an analytical style of thinking and, more importantly for a history of morality, the emergence of impersonal prosociality and moral individualism that enabled strangers to cooperate on a voluntary basis and for mutual benefit.

The result was an even greater expansion of relational structures and unprecedented levels of economic growth, technological development, political emancipation and scientific progress, because these key elements of modern societies require precisely the analytical style of thinking and the more fluid forms of cooperation that the MFP initiated. The global hegemony of WEIRD societies was set in motion.

But why did the Western Church do this in the first place? There cannot have been any foresight behind it, and the developments it caused were so original, unpredictable and lengthy that they could not possibly have been brought about intentionally. The clerical decision-makers saw themselves as trustees of divine plans. They had no idea what institutional changes they would spawn or what their long-term consequences would be for the cultural, economic, political and military dominance of the West. It is in many cases unclear what goals this development's architects were pursuing and what reasons they believed they had for doing so.

The concept of cultural evolution has shown that mutation and selection processes can generate complex artefacts such as tools or institutions, which are not necessarily intentional and do not necessarily involve conscious design (recall how adult lactose tolerance was selected for in early agricultural societies). Here, too, we are probably dealing with a process of cultural evolution where the forces of natural selection were exerting their pressure on more or less randomly generated cultural packages. At the time when the foundations of the Western Church's MFP were being set out, there was an entire range of other religious currents that had – probably just as coincidentally – fixated on completely different moral norms and taboos. There were no restrictions in Islam, Judaism, the Eastern Orthodox Church or Persian Zoroastrianism whose stringency came close to the mercilessness of the Western Church's marriage norms. In those societies, polygyny, levirate marriage and marriage between cousins largely continued. Traditional family structures could continue to flourish without ever having the functional need to switch to new forms of social cooperation.

Ultimately, no one would have been able to plan or predict it, but the WEIRD model turned out to be the one that, in the process of aimless cultural evolution, had discovered a variant that enabled the transition to modernity with its institutions of market-style economy, participatory and egalitarian politics, impersonal bureaucracy and the pursuit of science free from religious dogmas. This path to modernity was not a predetermined goal, as if all societies were in a global race to be the one to first discover the psychological and institutional profile that held the key to success. As with the emergence of the first hierarchically organised large societies, the WEIRD model was the one that proved to be the most relatively assertive *in hindsight*.

Innovative rules of ownership and inheritance that meant more and more assets could fall into the hands of the Western Church contributed significantly to this model's success. Individual prosperity has always been considered morally suspect in Christian ethics. The New Testament repeatedly makes it clear that a camel is more likely to pass through the eye of a needle than a rich man go to heaven. For wealthy individuals, at first glance this is bleak news, tying any hope of earthly happiness in with the prospect of eternal damnation. This makes the Church's moral code seem extremely unattractive. The clever way out of this dilemma that the Church quickly had to offer was to promise rich people access to paradise if they kept their wealth in the here and now and enjoyed it, as long as they were willing to bequeath it to the Church after their deaths. Arrangements of this kind consolidated the Church's power in this world as well as the next, while further contributing to the weakening of existing family structures by ethically blocking the transfer of wealth within families.

Thicker than water

To be able to causally prove the Western Church's marriage and family programme's influence, Henrich and his team developed their own original methodology that correlated the closeness of kinship networks with the extent of Church influence a cultural region had been exposed to over the centuries. These two factors – 'how important is kinship?' and 'how great was the MFP's influence?' – can then be compared with the psychological profiles characteristic of WEIRD thinking and WEIRD morality.

Are societies WEIRDer, the greater the 'dose' of the Catholic Church's MFP they had received since 300 in Western Europe? The short answer is yes, and it can be clearly demonstrated. Henrich and his colleagues managed to develop numerical scales (known as a kinship intensity index) that reflect both a society's contact with clerical family policy and the relative intensity of existing kinship relationships. Comparing these values with each other, we can see that the psychological characteristics discussed in detail earlier are invariably very closely correlated with those indices. The greater the 'dose' of the MFP, the lower a population's value on the kinship intensity index, and the WEIRDer the population in question. Individualism, intentionality, analytical thinking, guilt rather than shame, nonconformism and impersonal prosociality or trust of strangers are all closely related to both values.

The 'new' Catholic family morality's influence was so strong that even today, 500 years after the entire transformation process was complete, it can be traced precisely to the municipal boundaries of ninety-three Italian provinces. Depending on how strong the contact with the Western Church's MFP was under papal leadership, there are still sometimes drastic differences in thought and behaviour even in today's Italy (as well as in other countries) – often from one village to the next. The frequency of marriages between cousins 500 years ago can still be seen in how many people donate blood anonymously, for example, how many people prefer cash to other forms of saving, and how high the level of corruption is in a region.[19]

Ultimately, these examples also show the key function of social cooperation for our coexistence: a morality that enables more inclusive forms of cooperation with a greater number of people has almost always led to improved scientific and technological performance, increased economic prosperity and greater military dominance throughout human history.

Dialectic of WEIRDness

The greatest feat the Devil ever accomplished was to win the Catholic Church over to values that would eventually lead to its own demise.

Every beginning has to have an end. The flipside of traditional family structures being destroyed is the endorsement of non-traditional forms of socialisation, as the dissolution of the (extended) family did not lead to the dissolution of society at all, of course. Instead, it forced the European world to find other forms of coexistence and to channel its energies into new methods of economic activity and cooperation. A community that cannot be organised on the basis of genetic kinship must find other ways of interacting and must develop new ways to exchange goods, information and values. This led to the consolidation of social institutions based not on blood ties but on voluntary participation; the first universities were founded in Bologna, Oxford and Heidelberg in the eleventh, twelfth and fourteenth centuries respectively, free imperial cities such as Frankfurt am Main and Cologne were formed and extensive trade networks sprung up, like the cities of Lübeck, Bremen and Danzig being amalgamated into the Hanseatic League. Monasteries, associations and corporations also first came about during this period. In all these cases, new forms of sociality were invented and institutionalised, paving the way for cooperation between individuals on the basis of voluntary membership, contractual arrangements and explicitly codified regulations, rather than kinship. This meant that the production of goods, access to knowledge and decisions gradually changed from patriarchal clan structures to individualist agreements.

Political communities were also subjected to the new moral logic of individualism and voluntary consent. Whereas especially in the early and high Middle Ages the state was considered as the holy kingdom of God which had to administer, promote and perfect humankind's morality, the state became increasingly seen as a service provider whose legitimacy consisted of guaranteeing the security and rights of the individual. Society was no longer focused on carrying out the Lord's plans, but on providing people with the legal and institutional conditions for a life of freedom and prosperity. Not least through the political theories of Thomas Hobbes, John Locke, Jean-Jacques Rousseau and Immanuel Kant, the state went from being an instrument of God to something contractual whose secular logic increasingly broke down the intimacy of the bond between church and state.

The religious realm itself wasn't even immune to the logic of individualism. In fact Henrich describes Protestantism, which grew from the sixteenth century onwards, as the WEIRDest of all religions because it detached faith, virtue and the fear of God from intervention by hierarchical authorities and clerical dignitaries in brocade slippers, and made them an issue for the individual. It is no coincidence that Martin Luther belonged to three organisations that had radically ruled out the principle of kinship as a criterion of affiliation: as a monk, university employee and citizen of a free city, he was the epitome of WEIRDness.[20]

So, the Catholic Church's marriage and family programme ushered in its own decline by creating the cognitive and moral dispositions that would eventually undermine Rome's authority, based on tradition and revelation, from within. Proto-Protestant currents had occurred over and over again – orders such as the Cistercians and medieval theologians including John Wycliffe had anticipated the basic idea of *sola scriptura* even before Luther and Calvin. Faith and piety were essentially dependent on the individual's doctrinal understanding. The grace of God, according to this line of thinking, is not granted by secular officeholders, but is instead received through the believer's individual conscience. It was no longer of prime importance to be a member of a certain organisation whose dogmas and rules must be accepted unquestioningly. People now had to enter into a personal relationship with God, whose revealed word they must understand and intellectually absorb, to be able to believe it authentically.

The new pressure on authority to justify itself soon took over the political order of the Middle Ages – not least in the form of various revolutions. In the German Peasants' War between 1524 and 1526, a rebellion that examined traditional structures and found them to be inadequate, these demands were already clearly formulated (even if they were still dressed up in theological terms): as God created all men free, the peasants no longer wanted to be serfs; their livelihood should not be hampered by excessive taxes and servitude; their access to land, forest and game should not be restricted by the greed of the nobility; and punishments should not depend on their whim. New sources of authority were needed: what would they comprise?

The disenchantment of the world

The modernisation of morality did not advance just politics and religion, but our entire way of thinking. A new morality does not come without profound epistemological consequences. In 1919 this was described by Max Weber as the 'disenchantment of the world': not in the sense of having discovered every truth and solved every mystery of the universe, but instead as a recognition that there are no magical, supernatural or unrecognisable powers that could escape the complete grasp of the laws of nature.[21]

The worldview that had set the tone until the dawn of modernity, roughly 500 years ago, had been thoroughly teleological – purposeful – in that nature was understood as a cosmos, as an order of purposes and means established by a wise hand, in which things have a natural place and state to aspire to. This idea is found both in Aristotle's concept of the *final cause*[22] and in Christian metaphysics, which sees the natural environment as a 'book of nature' that just needs to be read for its meaning to be understood.

Writings on natural history such as the late antique *Physiologus* were widespread in the sixteenth century. These texts described living nature as a collection of parables and allusions in physical form, with the behaviour of (often mythical) animals serving as a catechism from which a virtuous code of exemplary behaviour could be gleaned.[23] The unicorn's innocence, the lion's courage, the phoenix's resurrection, the hoopoe's helpfulness or the villainy of the hyena and the serpent all refer in some way to David, Job or Jesus of Nazareth, who are held up as examples to be imitated for their good qualities.

The disenchantment of the world, therefore, came with the expulsion of morality from nature. Before that, it was generally accepted that the universe consisted of two distinct realms: the *sublunary* sphere was the realm of becoming and decaying, of movement and variability, whereas the *supralunary* sphere ('above the moon': the moon, not yet being recognised as a mere celestial body, did *not* belong to nature) was populated by eternally unchanging objects of mathematical perfection, consisting of *quinta essentia*, an unearthly fifth element along with fire, water, earth and air. The real revolution brought about by the discoveries of Copernicus, and later Galileo Galilei, Tycho Brahe and Johannes Kepler, was not merely the realisation that the earth revolves around the sun – Aristarchus of Samos had already put forward an idea like this in 300 BCE and it did not shock anyone 500 years ago – but the insight that the entire universe, small and large, on earth and in the heavens, belongs to one and the same nature, which knows no goals but obeys the same rules.

The better we learned to understand nature, the less scope was left for the ethereal objects of ancient metaphysics. The universe became a huge, forbidding, desolate and mostly empty vessel. On the smallest scale, we came to understand that the world is made up of mysterious particles so tiny that no human eye will ever be able to see them. In both the vast and the minuscule scales of the universe, humanity searched for a benevolent creator, but this search was in vain.

WEIRD people's analytical impetus did not stop with the dissection of the universe and the matter that made it up; the human body began to be dissected and mapped out with increasing dedication and vigour. Just as there seemed to be no place for God in the universe, there also seemed to be no place for the soul in the body. It went from a life-giving *pneuma*, which permeates a breathing, bleeding, raging, dancing human body, to an abstract substance of pure thought – a *res cogitans* – banished into the non-sensual exile of a dualistic worldview to make room for unconscious matter. Man's image of God became more and more vague and ultimately turned into a negative theology, not daring to make any tangible statements about the nature of God, instead only capable of stating what God was not.

The individualistic way of life and analytical thinking enforced socially by the Western Church's marriage and family programme led to a new scientific methodology that liberated the creation of knowledge from ancient authorities such as the Bible, the pope and ancient philosophers, and subjected it to the uncoercive coercion of the better experiment. The highly moralistic medieval understanding of nature turned out to be increasingly untenable. Suspicions were quickly confirmed, for example, that it was not sin and sacrilege that caused diseases and strokes of fate – as if they could be prevented by impeccable behaviour – but in most cases, simply the random mercilessness of contagion and infection.

In 1755, the city of Lisbon was almost completely destroyed by an earthquake. The moral arbitrariness of the devastation, which spared many brothels but reduced places of worship to rubble, was immediately apparent.[24] The Thirty Years' War had long since proven that the subtleties of theology are barely able to make the ultimate truths about God and the world tangible, but that disagreements about these subtleties can lead to much more tangible decades of murder and rape:

> It was a good year later before the war came to us after all. One night we heard whinnying, and then there were many voices laughing outside, and soon we heard the crash of doors being smashed in, and before we were even on the street, armed with useless pitchforks or knives, the flames were flickering. The soldiers were hungrier than usual, and deeper in their cups. It had been a long time since they entered a town that offered them so much. Old Luise, who had been fast asleep and this time had no presentiment, died in her bed. The priest died standing protectively in front of the church portal. Lise Schoch died trying to conceal a stash of gold coins. The baker and the smith and old Lembke and Moritz Blatt and most of the other men died trying to protect their women. And the women died as women do in war.[25]

As there was no end to the deaths, and the disputes over celibacy or transubstantiation (the transformation of bread and wine into the body and blood of Christ) or other problems of confessional orthodoxy could not be settled scientifically, a truce of ideological liberalism – a thoroughly WEIRD way of life never attempted before – became increasingly attractive as a pragmatic solution.

This dynamic, in which a morally charged interpretation of nature and society was gradually being replaced by the cold, hard currency of dispassionate facts, is still ongoing. It became increasingly clear that most of the facts of nature supposedly proving there was no alternative to the existing social hierarchies and inequalities were based on prejudices and half-truths. Sexist discrimination against women and racist exploitation of other countries had always been sold as an inevitable consequence of the natural inferiority of the weaker sex and uncivilised savages. But as the factual basis of these forms of abuse and social disadvantage became more and more fragile, the fundamental natural equality of people could be less easily denied, regardless of gender or ethnicity.

Handwritten accounts of the horrors of the transatlantic slave trade, like the one written by Ayuba Suleiman Diallo, a highly educated Fulani prince from Senegal who was kidnapped and sold in 1731 and could only return to his homeland years later, conveyed shockingly to an ignorant audience convinced of the superiority of Europe that the idea of the weak-willed, simple-minded and primitive peoples of Africa was a myth intended to legitimise the unscrupulous acquisition of cheap labour for the 'New World'.

In 1792 Mary Wollstonecraft's *A Vindication of the Rights of Woman* had a similar effect, by refusing to acknowledge the socio-political differences between men and women as a result of natural gender disparities that divided the world into intellectually underdeveloped females, always bordering a little on hysteria, and no-nonsense males, instead describing them as a culturally constructed – and therefore politically optional – outcome of education. And as it seemed too far-fetched for even the status quo's most audacious apologists to attribute an interest in human values to mindless micro-organisms, the medical germ theory finally (but only much later) cleared up the idea that illness and infirmity were due to an immoral lifestyle.

In philosophy, the discovery of WEIRDness triggered an intellectual revolution that sought the origins of moral action and political legitimacy in individuals' or communities' capacities for *self-legislation*.[26] Natural law, enacted by God and ratified by the Church, became obsolete, and instead, from now on, the individual was to liberate himself from the authority of traditionally grown family and power structures and live only according to rules reasonable for a free citizen.

The culmination of all these developments was twofold: first, David Hume's insight into the – now unbridgeable – gap between 'is' and 'ought'.[27] Humanity has nothing to do with nature, which has been reduced to the embodiment of morally indifferent facts with no normative form. Facts are value-neutral: nature and its laws do not follow ethical principles and make no moral recommendations. And second, if all concrete, interpersonal, evolved relationships of love and affection, friendship and kinship, community and belonging are eliminated in order to prescribe our moral laws for human behaviour, then only pure lawfulness itself remains, exercising moral authority over our choices. This is, in essence, Kant's main argument for his universalist moral principle: 'Act according to maxims that can at the same time have as their object themselves as universal laws of nature.'[28]

Both the fundamental distinction between facts and values and the most consistent formulation of an individualistic ethic of autonomy, Kant's categorical imperative, are the cognitive end products of the medieval Catholic Church's family policy.

No more heroes

In the twenty-first book of the *Iliad*, Achilles makes it clear to Lykaon – whom he will slaughter shortly afterwards – what is important:

> So, my friend, you die too. Why are you sad? Patroklos died, he who was much better than you. Don't you see how I am more handsome than you, and taller? I come from a good father, and my mother was a goddess. But dread fate and death hangs on me too, whether it will beat dawn, at dusk, or at noon, when someone will give my spirit to Ares by a cast of the spear or an arrow us flying from the string.[29]

This talk of greatness and power underscores an ethic of putting oneself to the test and of overpowering, of rage and deathly courage, that has no place in the burgeoning world of credit and capital. From Gilgamesh to the German epics of the High Middle Ages, bold warriors such as Parzival and Lohengrin, Siegfried and Hagen had to prove their noble honour in more and more adventurous tales – but what good is a handsome body, skilful sword wielding and cold courage that defiantly looks enemy and death in the eye in a world where we trade and barter flowers and spices?

These assets of courage and strength did not lose their worth completely, of course, but the bourgeoisie's discreet virtues now replaced the heroic ethics that had previously shaped the ruling classes' Western canon of values. The emergence of WEIRD people ousted the martial ideals of a society dominated by aristocratic nobility and replaced them with a reformed catalogue of bourgeois virtues tailored to functioning in a modernising economy. The American economist Deirdre McCloskey considers a catalogue of Christian and pagan, typically 'male' and typically 'female' virtues to be the mixture of ethical value orientations that helped set the 'commercial age' in motion.[30] This new catalogue also included virtues such as prudence, moderation, justice and love.

The heroic ethics of the previous 5,000 years had had no time for things like feminine long-suffering. Of course, the heroic ethos propagated in the ancient and medieval epics had always been considerably more about ideology than reality, and a privilege of the noble upper classes anyway, playing no part in the day-to-day life of the plebs. Nonetheless, it is remarkable how quickly the ideological superstructure of pre-modern feudal society could go from chivalrous machismo to discreet refinement and restraint of emotions.

The great escape

In the eleventh century, the Venetian doge married a Byzantine princess with some remarkable habits.[31] At any rate, she did not eat like respectable people; instead, it was said, she took her food to her mouth with a strange tool, a small golden wand with two prongs. The courtiers were furious. Never before had they heard of a more excessive sophistication, never before had they been so belittled, and so snobbishly and arrogantly insulted. Some time later, the princess was afflicted by a terrible disease. The clergy hailed the fate of poor Argillo – this was her name – as a just punishment for her finicky manners. This was all to change. Soon – just a few centuries later – it was considered crude and uncouth to blow your nose on the tablecloth, spit on the floor or eat without a fork. This trend, described by Norbert Elias as a 'civilizing process', unleashed a new wave of domestication that established the refined behavioural norms of the ruling class and made greater control of our impulses a distinguishing feature socially, replacing belligerence with gallantry and propagating values and behavioural patterns better suited to dinner parties than to sword fighting.

The discovery of WEIRDness was the discovery of new forms of belief, domination and research. Its most dramatic consequences, however, concerned the economy: humankind had always tried in vain to escape the 'Malthusian trap' – the theory that as populations grow, so too does the pressure on environmental resources, which constrains further population growth. Our inability to escape this trap ensured that humankind's standard of living had barely changed for millennia.[32] WEIRDness, however, was about to change all that.

Contrary to popular belief, poverty has no causes. *Wealth* has causes, while poverty is the undisturbed normal state. (This does not mean, of course, that people who have been prosperous cannot become poor through war, mismanagement or natural disasters, but that the existence of social prosperity itself was an achievement and not a given.) Ensnared in the Malthusian trap, as humanity had been until that point, there was no sustainable economic growth, because any improvement in living standards was always eaten up immediately by the population growth that produced it.

Only once modern forms of economic activity not based on idle robber barons expropriating a toiling peasantry had emerged did modernity's cultural evolution reveal the possibility of real economic growth. Prosperity was no longer a matter of robbing Peter to pay Paul – or more precisely, going from the bottom up – but became a genuine surplus that (in theory) everyone could benefit from. This economic revolution would not have been possible without a moral revolution. We had to learn to widen the net of our cooperation more than ever before, and this could only be achieved with the help of new moral structures that went beyond a small trustworthy group that we called family or friends.

Economists often refer to long-term economic growth in WEIRD societies, which began a few centuries ago, as the 'great divergence' or the 'great escape'.[33] The gross world product – the total value of all goods and services produced worldwide in a year, if this can be estimated realistically – had only seen stagnation until then, and had not changed significantly over millennia.[34] People lived at subsistence level – in other words, from hand to mouth. With the advent of modern times roughly 500 years ago, a few regions of the world managed to decipher the secret of economic productivity, which, through technical innovations, astute division of labour, accelerated logistics, new forms of bartering, trade and negotiation, as well as allocating resources efficiently, not only carved up the economic pie here, there and everywhere, but also made it possible to produce a pie that grew larger and larger.

WEIRD people's impersonal prosociality, which they had had to practise and get better at as traditional family structures were being destroyed while all this was going on, was the condition essential for this development to take hold. A surprising and – for many people used to the legend of the egotistically minded *Homo economicus* – counterintuitive result from Henrich's studies is that the behaviour of people from more commercialised societies differs most from the behaviour that would have the maximum rational benefit. Henrich found that WEIRD people from market-based societies tend to have the fairest, most cooperative, most trustworthy and least selfish behaviour of all, acting less purely in their own self-interest than one might expect. The more a society became structured towards a market economy – this is determined by the percentage of goods that a person has bought, rather than producing or hunting them themselves or receiving them through family or simple exchange – the more generous the offers that people made, on average, in behavioural economic experiments.

Perhaps counterintuitively, modern market-based societies do not produce cool and calculating cut-throats only ever concerned with their own gain, but the exact opposite: Henrich found that WEIRD people were comparatively less loyal to family and community, but behaved more altruistically and cooperatively towards strangers than the global average. Non-WEIRD people may be extremely cooperative when it comes to close friends, clan members and blood relatives, but they are just as dismissive, suspicious and egotistic towards everyone else as *Homo economicus* was always assumed to be. So it is exactly the opposite of what oversimplified forms of social critique claim, when they reflexively attribute every social evil to the corrupting influence of capitalist competition.

Only the move towards market norms of fair trade between individuals, with buyers and sellers having to convince each other that the exchange of goods and services can create an advantage for both, made the great escape possible. The enormous geopolitical disparities between nations that we see today are a result of regions having developed so very differently in this way.

The Anna Karenina principle

Humanity's WEIRDness is not solely responsible for all these developments. It complements existing explanatory models for global inequality, which since 1997, as a result of Jared Diamond's *Guns, Germs, and Steel,* have primarily emphasised the advantage enjoyed by some regions of the world due to a certain geographical alignment or particularly favourable flora and fauna.

Diamond refers to this as the Anna Karenina principle,[35] alluding to the famous first sentence in Tolstoy's novel: 'All happy families are alike; each unhappy family is unhappy in its own way.'[36] According to Diamond, this is because there is only one way to be happy, namely by *not* having a single one of *all* the possible problems that could cause unhappiness – such as jealousy, illness, financial hardship, quarrels or an unfulfilled desire to have children. Unhappiness, on the other hand, has many faces, depending on which problem or combination of problems is bothering a family.

According to Diamond, you can see this same principle as it applies to cereals or livestock: to be domesticable, a large mammal must have several characteristics, none of which must be missing. Elephants are so big that they take over ten years to become adult. Until then, they generate more costs than benefits. Zebras tend to run away. Big cats are extremely dangerous carnivores and do not provide products such as milk or wool. Suitable candidates for domestication as farm animals must be the right size and have the right temperament and eating habits. Around the world there are 148 species of large, herbivorous land mammals that could be considered candidates for domestication, but only fourteen of these candidates are able to be domesticated; thirteen of these fourteen, from cattle to rabbits, are native to the Eurasian continent. In Africa or Australia there is not a single species of mammal that meets the necessary criteria.

Crops also need to have a number of characteristics in order to be agriculturally productive. Lentils, wheat, barley and rice are native to Eurasia; they are resilient and nutritious as well as easy to store and sow. The horizontal axis of the Eurasian continent also ensured that both the necessary agricultural techniques and the plants themselves could spread east and west under similar climatic conditions. The land masses of Africa as well as North and South America are oriented from north to south, making the reproduction and cultivation of already sparse plants and animals even more complicated.

The story of the WEIRD person, however, begins where the Anna Karenina principle reaches its limits: while a number of characteristics needed to be in place to ensure humanity's 'success' – random geographical and biological factors may explain why the first empires and early civilisations had to emerge in a comparatively narrow but unusually fertile corridor on the Eurasian continent – Henrich's WEIRDness shows that the next wave of socio-cultural evolution could only begin where kinship as a basic principle of social organisation was replaced by a more individualistic moral outlook.

Plundered bodies

Are the differences in the levels of technical, scientific and economic development between various world regions due to the plundering of one by the other? 'Rich man and his poorer brother / Stood and looked at one another / Till the poor one softly swore / You'd not be rich if I weren't poor,'[37] Bertolt Brecht once wrote, demonstrating his talent for snappy formulations and cluelessness about economics.

The basic idea behind the theory of plundering is that the prosperity in a few regions of the world, which began to grow so rapidly a few hundred years ago, cannot be explained without mention of the imperial exploitation and colonial oppression of other regions. Around the year 1000 CE, all countries were roughly as rich as each other – or, to put it more precisely, equally poor. Today, some regions of the world, especially in Western Europe and its postcolonial offshoots the United States, Canada and Australia, are about fifty times as rich as the poorest nations. How, if not through theft and looting, is this possible?[38]

After all, it does look suspicious that some getting rich coincides with the others being plundered. In recent years, a group of historians have been writing a 'new history of capitalism', which sees slavery and colonial exploitation as a prerequisite for the emergence of modern economies.[39]

The slave trade and colonialism were, and are, episodes of unimaginable atrocities, deeply immoral methods of exploitation and subjugation, abuse and genocide. The Spaniard Bartolomé de las Casas, who as a Dominican missionary witnessed the atrocities initiated by Christopher Columbus in the West Indies, described them as a never-ending series of habitual cruelties and murderous arrogance:

> A Spaniard . . . suddenly drew his sword. Then the whole hundred drew theirs and began to rip open the bellies, to cut and kill those lambs – men, women, children, and old folk, all of whom were seated, off guard, and frightened . . . The Spaniards enter the large house nearby, for this was happening at its door, and in the same way, with cuts and stabs, begin to kill as many as they found there, so that a stream of blood was running, as if a great number of cows had perished.[40]

At the end of the nineteenth century, almost all European states, but also the Ottoman Empire, China, Japan and the United States, had colonies or protectorates in South America, South-East Asia or Africa, which often functioned as administrative structures in parallel with internationally operating trading enterprises such as the Dutch West and East India Companies. Colonial regimes are always a form of imperial political oppression, and in most cases around this time they were accompanied by staggering atrocities aimed at whipping the indigenous population into political subservience, forced labour or (usually) both. A particularly startling photograph taken by Alice Seeley Harris in May 1904 shows a Congolese father propping his head up, staring absent-mindedly at his five-year-old daughter Boali's hand and foot, which lie, cut off, in front of him. Boali had just been murdered by the *Force Publique* set up by King Leopold II of Belgium because she had not been able to extract the quota of valuable rubber demanded by the *Compagnie du Congo Belge*.[41] But colonial empires do not merely tell the story of the exploitation of one country by another. In most cases, it is the story of the exploitation of the poorer classes *in both countries* by the elites *in both countries*.

Imperial colonialism is not solely responsible for global inequality between countries, although it is easy and therefore tempting to label it the only cause. The truth is, in the long run, colonialism, slavery, oppression, as well as being morally abhorrent, are all economically bad propositions. This may seem counterintuitive, but the countries with the greatest empires were, and are, by no means always the richest, and the richest were not, and are not, always the ones who built and maintained their empires with the greatest fervour. If you were to look at a list of countries ranked by GDP per capita today, most of the top contenders are not the usual suspects responsible for colonising other countries. And obviously colonialism cannot explain how some countries became colonial powers, while others became colonies, in the first place. Examining the ways in which nations and empires exploited their own populations can point us towards other convincing reasons for global inequalities between countries that paint a more complex picture.

With the advent of modern times, the *global* economic product grew – this is something that cannot be explained by plundering alone. Plundering merely moves wealth from one pocket into another, it doesn't create any. Colonialism, conquest, slavery and oppression have, as we've seen, been around for millennia without automatically leading to longer-term economic growth. This is a subtle point: while colonialism has sometimes contributed to locking countries into poverty by destroying their infrastructure and institutions, it didn't make anyone rich. What it has, undoubtedly, done, is make many people poor, because its socio-political consequences could remain detrimental to the institutional fabric of former colonies in the long term.

In recent years, the new historians of capitalism have attempted to resolve these contradictions with concrete calculations driven, it seems, by the desire to show that the economic impact of such dreadful institutions as slavery must somehow be proportionate to its moral horrendousness. One set of authors tried to claim that the slave trade and cotton production accounted for almost half of US economic output by inflating the cotton industry's 5 per cent share of the US economy in the time before the Civil War, to 50 per cent by adding logistics, labour, management, agriculture, land acquisition and every expense in the entire value chain in general to the end product's final value. But you cannot simply retrofit an economy in this way in order to achieve the interpretation you wish to find.

Similarly, the *New York Times*'s 1619 Project tries to replace the year 1776 with the year 1619 as the true founding of the United States: the year the first slave ship arrived on the shores of the new world. The hope seems to be that one can develop a radical critique of contemporary society by indicting its origins. But when it comes to the question of whether racist exploitation is baked into its *contemporary* institutions, pointing towards its ugly – or noble – genealogy is neither here nor there. The debate around when the United States were 'truly' founded is a red herring that doesn't help us at all in understanding or tackling systemic disadvantage today. Paradoxically, the idea that slavery and oppression play a key role in explaining modern prosperity sometimes veers close to inadvertently defending them: in some sense, what these attempts end up saying is that economically speaking, slavery is a *really, really good idea.*

And they're not. Slavery and colonialism are not sound economic concepts at all.

In reality, subjugation and forced labour are doubly bad; they are not only morally catastrophic, but also economically inadvisable. Economic growth – the only long-term effective means of combating poverty and deprivation that we know of – depends to a large extent on 'inclusive' institutions:[42] a functioning rule of law, sufficiently free markets, robust property rights, minimal corruption, a solid public infrastructure with adequate safety nets and social mobility all combine to create the institutional situation that makes escaping from the Malthusian trap possible. *Extractive* institutions that define the rules of the game in favour of a small group of exploitative elites allow them to appropriate an excessive share of the available resources through political coercion without themselves producing anything that would raise the standard of living for the rest of society. *Inclusive* institutions are precisely those that could only gradually gain a foothold in some parts of the world as WEIRDness emerged.

Western triumphalism?

There are not two 'types' of people – WEIRD and non-WEIRD. Instead, there is a continuum of WEIRDness with vague trends; different people in different cultures can always be located somewhere along it. Differences in individual self-control, analytical thinking and universal prosociality are not genetically hardwired, but are due to a co-evolution of psychological traits and institutional frameworks in which these traits emerge and are encouraged.

Differences in social, technological and political development in individual regions are not related to genetic and ethnic differences, but to the forces of cultural evolution. Above all, factors such as a society's size, which depends on the integrative powers of its institutions of learning and cooperation, determine which psychological characteristics are socially represented, and to what extent. One of cultural evolution's key lessons has been that a society's complexity almost never depends on the characteristics of the individuals living in it, but on the framework of cultural customs and institutions a society has inherited.

When European explorers first came across Tasmanian Aborigines about 400 years ago, their level of technological development was even lower than that of Stone Age populations. At the same time, not far away, Australian Aborigines had hundreds of complex tools, from boats, spears and cooking utensils to medicines and transport vessels. For many people, it is tempting to suspect genetic racial differences behind such dramatic differences.[43] But in fact, until 12,000 years ago, Bass Strait, which now separates Australia from Tasmania, was a bridge of land passable on foot. With the end of the last Ice Age, rising water physically separated the inhabitants from each other; the group of people isolated in Tasmania, though genetically the same as the groups in mainland Australia, was simply too small to keep a sophisticated level of technology culturally alive.

Henrich's ambition is to show why the Western world became psychologically WEIRD and what impact this has had on the West's values and prosperity. The historical developments he outlines, according to one of his main theories, not only gave the West the notions of individual freedom and human dignity, but also made it rich. It is understandable that this theory may make many people nervous, because it seems to serve the ethnocentric prejudices of Western Europe's intellectual superiority, which were not infrequently used to legitimise colonial oppression and are now rightly considered unacceptable. The irony of being accused of triumphalism, which suspects sheer intellectually negligent ethnocentric bigotry of being behind every social and scientific explanation of Western de facto hegemony, is that concern about an ethnocentric view is itself one of the main symptoms of psychological WEIRDness. The universalist perspective, which seeks to free itself from the prejudices of a contingent culture and regards its own values and norms merely as one worldview among many, is a profoundly Western perspective. Almost everywhere else in the world, an ethnocentric attitude is a given; the majority have no doubt that their own values, traditions and customs are the only correct ones.

The current convergence in various world societal development trends towards a market-based economy, democratically structured political institutions and 'consumer culture' is sometimes described as a 'softer variant of colonialism'. Western nations may have stopped extolling their institutions and values to other countries with muskets and bloodhounds, as was common just a few generations ago, but the expansionist dynamic is still ongoing. The aggressors now know better and are using more subtle but also more perfidious means of cultural assimilation. It is said that the West no longer spreads its culture by force but with the superficial temptations of a modern lifestyle, while failing to mention that, despite all the conveniences, you can't get rid of its downsides once you've invited it into your home.

The significance of Westernisation is grossly overestimated; Westernisation undoubtedly does exist, but strictly speaking it is only accurately described as such if non-Western countries adopt cultural practices that are institutionally optional. The Chinese Communist Party's leaders wear the same dark suits and plain ties as the governing bodies of the FTSE-100 companies. This is true Westernisation, because this style of dress originated on Western soil, and apart from its symbolic effect of inspiring a sense of solidity and trustworthiness, there is no deeper reason to make political decisions in these clothes rather than in a *hanfu*, a traditional Chinese silk robe.

On the flipside are examples such as when Japan began dismantling its clan structures in the late nineteenth century. This was done not to copy the West, but because an amalgamation of certain kinship systems (such as polygynous marriage or pronounced patrilineality) was objectively incompatible with the modernisation push that Japan experienced under the Meiji emperor after 1880. Organising a modern economy with freer and freer markets creates a range of functional imperatives that require a social shift from family relationships (at least officially) to impartial bureaucratic and legal administration, individual property rights and a free choice of profession and place of residence.[44]

China, similarly, made this transition in the mid-twentieth century, banning polygamy, marriage between close blood relatives and the exclusion of daughters from family inheritance, although in this case, it was the shift to a communist workers' and peasants' state and not the transition to a capitalist market economy that led to the weakening of kinship relations. Nevertheless, the principle is the same: a modernising society cannot coexist with arbitrarily intense family structures.

The example of China shows particularly clearly that psychological WEIRDness is not something specifically Western, but dependent on a society's institutional framework. Although the data situation in this instance is much more patchy, the evidence to hand shows the pattern we already know: the intensity of kinship systems has a negative correlation with an individualistic value profile and analytical thinking. Historically, of course, it was the cultivation of rice fields, rather than the Catholic Church's family policy, that was responsible for these differences. The construction of the dykes, irrigation canals and terraces essential for rice growing required organisational capacities that under pre-modern conditions were only possible through extensive clan structures. This form of agriculture was for centuries (and is still today) particularly strongly represented in the south of China; initial studies now show that residents of northern China, which relied more heavily on wheat than rice, are psychologically just as WEIRD as US students.

*

Does this mean that modern individualism, technological rationalisation and scientification of the living environment will eventually – maybe with a few exceptions – reach every region of the Earth? We don't know. An optimistic scenario would suggest that sharing in the blessings and curses of a scientific and technical civilisation leads to thoughts and actions that inevitably undermine despotic ideologies and religious superstitions from within. A society that does not want to do without modern medicine and comfortable air travel will have to train some of its members as doctors and engineers, who will soon become aware that their thirst for knowledge does not fit with fundamentalist dogmas. But there is also a pessimistic scenario: it could be that the fact that the Enlightenment and the scientific revolution have already taken place in some regions means that other regions can avoid moving in the same direction. One part of the world can import the comforts of modern civilisation, such as aeroplanes or vaccines, from other countries without needing to have gone through the same cultural and institutional revolutions itself.

Many regions of the world are now on the same path to modernisation that was first taken in Europe. Europe was the first for the coincidental reasons detailed above, but the apparent Eurocentrism of the story I am telling here is only an illusion created by historical proximity. In reality, we are currently in the midst of a new Axial Age, in which the lives of large numbers of the world's population are being swept along by the same wave of modernisation that has lasted for a few centuries – it's just that we are too close to it to see it.

6

The Moral of the Story

Harsh lessons

The twentieth century is not difficult to understand once we know that Ronald Ridenhour was not in Princeton at the time, but a man with the same name was.

On 16 March 1968 in My Lai, Vietnam, the 120-strong Charlie Company carried out the Vietnam War's most horrific massacre. The US soldiers, who suspected the small village was a hiding place for enemy Vietcong guerrillas who had recently injured and killed some of their comrades, advanced with unbridled ruthlessness:

> Early in the morning the soldiers were landed in the village by helicopter. Many were firing as they spread out, killing both people and animals. There was no sign of the Vietcong battalion and no shot was fired at Charlie Company all day, but they carried on. They burned down every house. They raped women and girls and then killed them. They stabbed some women in the vagina and disembowelled others, or cut off their hands or scalps. Pregnant women had their stomachs slashed open and were left to die. There were gang rapes and killings by shooting or with bayonets. There were mass executions. Dozens of people at a time, including old men, women and children, were machine-gunned in a ditch. In four hours nearly 500 villagers were killed.[1]

When a young GI, Ronald Ridenhour, from the nearby 11th Infantry Brigade learned of what had happened in My Lai, he felt compelled to bring the event to the public's attention. In 1969 he sent a report about it to his congressman and to Richard Nixon, the president of the United States. It was only after several unsuccessful attempts that he managed to make his voice heard, and his account would go on to play a significant part in exposing the horrors of Vietnam to a wider public. This, and other accounts of the savage nature of the war, eventually helped to shake domestic support for the increasingly senseless and unjustified conflict in South-East Asia.

'Whoever invokes humanity wants to cheat,'[2] the legal philosopher Carl Schmitt still felt able to claim in the 1920s, as he saw this 'humanity' as an amorphous mass of inevitably hostile groups and individuals with conflicting interests that were never able to establish true agreement with each other. On the other hand, in 2012, the British philosopher Jonathan Glover gave his moral history of the twentieth century a simple title: *Humanity*.[3] Were we condemned to be forever savage, self-interested and brutish, or were we more than that? Could we be different?

The twentieth century culminated in the most painfully acquired realisation that beyond national, ethnic, linguistic or religious boundaries, it is worth emphasising what all people share: we are all human beings, and we all deserve moral esteem and respect. Kant called this membership in the 'Kingdom of Ends', and the American psychologist Michael E. McCullough writes that the 'kindness of strangers' is the distinguishing feature of modern morality.[4] For McCullough, humans have a natural tendency to reserve respect, compassion and co-operation exclusively for themselves and their loved ones. The twentieth century's moral revolution consisted of getting rid of this spirit of partiality from our morality – or at least trying to. This is the world John Lennon sang about in 'Imagine': a world where all of humanity can fraternise peacefully, and where arbitrary divisions of all kinds are finally overcome.

There is a distinct theme of cooperation that has broadly and consistently run through the history of morality. Cooperation has followed a pattern of growth, enabling ever larger groups of people to come together. In some ways, we see the culmination of this trend in the twentieth century, which finally discovered all of humanity for itself and tried to tear down morally arbitrary boundaries between peoples and 'races' to redraw – or rather *expand* – the circle of moral community. In this *expanding circle* of morality, the moral community's renegotiated boundaries are combined with a new image of humanity, which recognises the individual's social conditioning more than ever and tries to translate this insight into a logic of prevention: above all else, we are products of our social environment, and this determines whether our actions are good or bad.

'What is it in us that lies, whores, steals and murders?' Georg Büchner's title character Danton asked in 1835,[5] and the twentieth century asked the same question again, with unprecedented urgency. Anyone who wants to improve humankind and prevent the next catastrophe must start here. All of this is condensed into the idea of the 'banality of evil'.[6]

Thirdly, there is a growing wave of 'demoralisation' – the recognition that many of the norms that human societies impose on individuals are in fact morally arbitrary, and that many of the supposedly morally significant norms we used to live by – 'premarital sex is wrong', for example – should in fact be treated as morally neutral and relegated to the status of mere convention.

Moral progress?

One possible version of the story of the last few decades goes like this: the twentieth century was a period of moral progress. From here on, our fundamental moral compass shifted, and we felt obliged above all to protect the weak and disenfranchised, who we felt should be given special protection to prevent dominant majorities from infringing upon their rights. Minorities and marginalised groups began to demand the fulfilment of the promise of freedom and equality, whose benefits they had until then been excluded from – as, of course, they still are today. The twentieth century dared to attempt genuine moral progress, which was supposed to grant the privileges of social life beyond just those who already had all the power to start with.

All this may sound like naivety at best – an apology for the status quo – or dangerous ideology at worst – a lullaby for passengers on a sinking ship. Where, we might ask, is this progress to be found today? In autocratic regimes and their fascist flirtation with the idea of a purified ethno-national society? In the rapidly advancing climate change that will either roast us alive, drown us or both? In the global pandemic that divided us politically while claiming millions of lives?

The idea of progress is often ridiculed as being 'Panglossian', and in intellectual circles there is hardly a more damning accusation: many people, I suspect, would rather be revealed as a pervert than a Panglossian, because above all, an intellectual has to be *critical*, and this quality does not pair well with the admission that some things are better today than they once were. In Voltaire's 1759 novel *Candide*, Pangloss is the main character's tutor and, as a faithful follower of Leibniz, is convinced that this world of ours is not only fairly agreeable, but actually the best of all possible worlds. The novel, which sends Candide from one misadventure to another, sets out to satirically refute this out-of-touch hyper-optimism. And for sure, the idea that a better world is not even imaginable is a prime example of the sheer nonsense that the great philosophers have always had a particular talent for producing.

Schopenhauer came closer to the truth when he stated: 'Whoever wants summarily to test the assertion that the pleasure in the world outweighs the pain, or at any rate that the two balance each other, should compare the feelings of an animal that is devouring another with those of that other.'[7] But even a considerable mic drop like this does not prove that the world, as bad it may be, cannot become a *relatively* better place. And the theory of progress says no more – and no less – than precisely that.

A certain scepticism is justified when it comes to believing in 'progress' as an idea that world history is moving towards a goal, and indeed this concept is often dismissed as a metaphysically over-the-top crypto-religion that has simply replaced God with a 'world-spirit'[8] as the puppet master of history. In his *Philosophy of Right*, Hegel argued that the history of mankind was not merely a history of blind coincidences and might makes right, but that it proceeded according to rational principles that guaranteed the historical realisation of an ethical commonwealth. The implications of this worldview are thoroughly ambivalent: if we are all just a short leap away from the end of history, and if the utopia of moral perfection and unlimited happiness is already within reach, then even the greatest sacrifice seems justified if it means we finally – *finally!* – establish this paradise on earth. And it all adds up: if what you stand to gain is eternity, you may as well get your hands dirty, even if the chances are slim. A desire for justice can bring about peace and solidarity; raging thought, however, intoxicated by longing for a perfect society, leads to 'slave camps under the flag of freedom [and] massacres justified by philanthropy or the taste of the superhuman'.[9]

So why fight for justice at all? If the course of history, guided on its inevitable path of progress by laws set in stone, will take care of itself, then our guilty conscience can rest, and we can just sit on our hands, can't we? Why make sacrifices, why make an effort, if the clockwork mechanism of the future has already been wound up and we just have to wait for its realisation? Progress, it seems, permits passivity, and even resignation.

A belief in moral progress seems to stem from a moral cold-heartedness that would rather focus on the winners' gains than consider the losers' losses. There is a question on the awning of a bookshop not far from my home: 'Is the unhappy man allowed to disturb the happiness of the happy man?' The answer, from those who believe in progress, is clearly 'no'. But what priorities do we reveal when we extol the developed world's escape from poverty and war, while millions of children die every year from diarrhoea and malaria and lose their eyesight from river blindness?

Though the inevitability of moral progress is suspect, the possibility of moral progress remains a useful idea. Almost all societies are inherently conservative and wary of innovation; they stick to a traditional way of life, practice or norm even if it is clearly harmful. It was in the interests, for example, of the Ijaw people of Nigeria to promote their population growth through childbirth. Due to beliefs about the taboo or unluckiness surrounding twin births, however, the Ijaw routinely killed twins when they were born, simply because it was customary, until the early twentieth century.[10] Though it is not always as immediately apparent, almost all societies accept enormous costs to maintain complex rituals, crippling superstitions and dysfunctional norms.[11] And despite the disadvantages a society may suffer, there is hardly ever a force strong enough to jolt it out of such a toxic state of inertia.

This is precisely where the idea of moral progress steps in: it now functions like a meme that makes societies receptive to the benefits of social change and technological innovation. 'That's how we've always done it!' is replaced by 'What can we do better?' Tradition is replaced by innovation.

The power of circumstances

What about Ronald Ridenhour? Like many other atrocities, My Lai became emblematic of the disturbingly demonic power of social conformity. It seemed as if it often took only a minor detail to make hitherto respectable people act like murderous gunmen – a lesson already made all too familiar to us by the

Holocaust. Particularly famous from this time is the story told by the American historian Christopher Browning about the Hamburg Reserve Police Battalion 101, which had received the order to 'cleanse' the Polish village of Józefów of the Jews living there in the summer of 1940. When Major Wilhelm Trapp, sometimes affectionately called 'Papa Trapp' by his subordinates, informed his 500 men of the grim mission one morning, he made them an unusual offer: anyone who did not feel able to take part in shooting the 1,500 people should come forward and could step out, without having to expect any consequences. Only about a dozen accepted the offer.[12]

The straitjacket of conformity became one of the dominant themes of twentieth-century moral psychology as the world's most renowned sociologists and psychologists began to study its curious inescapability in more detail. The aim was to understand the conditions that could move apparently harmless citizens to the most extreme forms of violence and cruelty, and how much obedience and submission to authority, esprit de corps and conformism contributed to these conditions.

Most people are familiar with what is known as the Milgram experiment from 1961: study participants could be persuaded without much effort to inflict (supposedly) severe electric shocks on other participants, under the pretext of participating in a study on people's ability to learn.[13] The findings showed that the majority chose the highest shock level, and no one refused outright to heed the increasingly urgent appeals of the scientists present. With just one exception. When the American psychologist David Rosenhan attempted to reproduce Stanley Milgram's results a few years after the original experiment, at Princeton University, there was one dissenter: a young man named Ronald Ridenhour, who refused to give anyone even the slightest shock. For decades, it was celebrated by social psychologists as a curious coincidence that the same person was involved in both the most influential experiment and the most famous massacre committed by Americans in the twentieth century. In both cases, he was the only person who managed to do the right thing against all odds – not least because the purpose of the Milgram experiment had been to illustrate the precise phenomenon of passively sympathising with movements that had led to disaster in My Lai.

It is now known that Ronald Ridenhour never went to Princeton. Or at least not *that* Ronald Ridenhour: they were actually two different people with the same melodiously alliterative name, who had both been tested for their steadfastness in 1968, just a few months apart but far away from each other, in those two separate places. Only a few years ago, the social psychologist Gordon Bear managed to clear up the confusion that had been reported in textbooks and lecture materials for decades; he found out that both had been fighting with the Green Berets in Vietnam around the same time and happened to know each other (and even a third person with the same name) personally.

This confusion, forgivable in itself, teaches us two lessons: studies such as the Milgram experiment and historical events such as My Lai show, first, that our moral values – and even more so our moral actions – are much more greatly influenced by the power of external circumstances than by a person's inner personality. We are – mostly, at any rate – products of external forces, which is why any programme of moral reform has to start with these forces. Second, this insight is extremely counterintuitive. We tend to attribute a person's actions to their individual character, which we consider to be largely stable across different situations.[14] This tendency is so great that even social psychologists, who should have been warned against making this error by their own studies, could not resist the tempting idea that the two Ridenhours must have been one and the same person: after all, hadn't they shown courage when it mattered, both times? Wasn't it obvious that this Ronald Ridenhour was simply an unusually steadfast and anti-authoritarian character who had been twice handed the opportunity to shine by fate?

The banality of evil

When Hannah Arendt flew to Israel in 1961 to prepare a report for the *New Yorker* on Adolf Eichmann, who was due to be tried in the Jerusalem District Court, the intellectual world was eagerly awaiting a portrait of a satanic villain. Instead, they got a maudlin image of an administrative employee who had organised the most grotesque crime of modern times with a fastidious, pen-pushing small-mindedness. Arendt coined one of the most impressive and apt phrases in moral philosophy: the banality of evil.[15]

With the banality of evil, Arendt contradicts both the Christian idea of original sin and also much of philosophical tradition. Even Kant was of the opinion that man was made of such 'crooked wood' that 'nothing entirely straight'[16] could be made of him; in fact, he went so far as to say that man is 'radical evil' as he is naturally inclined to violate the duties required by moral law.[17]

An important difference between radical and banal evil is that the former follows a logic of self-control: our depravity and vice, the idea goes, can only be overcome with self-control, discipline and willpower. In the twentieth century, in contrast, it increasingly dawned on us that it is seldom possible to rein in and overcome the deficiencies of human nature and that they can only be circumvented and contained. The focus shifted away from a call to the individual to pull themselves together and prac- tise virtue, and towards a call for society to set up its structures, practices and institutions so external situational pressure, with its toxic effect to which no human being is immune, could not arise in the first place. It is usually only luck that can prevent us from becoming collaborators of evil under this pressure, so what it boils down to is not allowing the opportunity for col- laboration to come about from the outset.

In social psychology, the paradigm of 'situationism' became established from the late 1960s onwards.[18] It seems there is no such thing as robust, consistent character traits across situations: no matter how hard you look, you will not be able to find them. No one is brave, shy or stingy per se; no one is either good or evil, decent or degenerate. Our personalities are much more fragmentary, and much more bound to concrete situations than our idea of the 'self' might incline us to believe. We might be penny-pinching when we are with friends at a flea market, but generous at dinner with strangers. For fifty years or so, social psychology has been working to show that it is external, situational factors like this that have by far the greatest influence on our behaviour. In a well-known study, whether or not a person helped someone else pick up some papers from the floor depended mainly on whether that person had previously found a coin in a telephone booth (that had been intentionally placed there).[19] Countless other experiments demonstrate the power that external circumstances exert on us.

There is something almost comforting about the banality of evil. The world is not split into radically evil and radically good people constantly fighting out the same battle on the stage of history but never winning it outright. It is made up of people, simply people, who, like the rest of nature, are shaped by their circumstances. They have to deal with these circumstances, and they can come to grief as a result of them. That is not to say there are no bad people who do appalling things, but it does mean that we humans are – at least in principle – able to reform, and that there is no mass of diabolical villains 'in our midst' whose intrinsic depravity the rest of society somehow has to simply deal with.

But though comforting in one way, it is precisely this banality that is, in some lights, incredibly disturbing: 'And with the element of *self-inflicted regression*, what we experienced in the twentieth century is revealed as the intrinsic break with civilisation: far from a "relapse into barbarism", it is the entirely new, henceforth *ever present* possibility of the moral disintegration of an entire nation that had considered itself "civilised" by the standards of the time.'[20] The Holocaust and the gulag, the Khmer Rouge's killing fields in Cambodia and the Rwandan Tutsi genocide, the Srebrenica massacre and the events in Abu Ghraib proved once and for all that we humans should never be underestimated, that the instincts that make us capable of hatred and violence are never completely dormant, and that even a 'wholly enlightened'[21] society is always on the verge of moral implosion.

A fundamental moral transformation in the twentieth century consisted of trying to create socio-political conditions to contain, moderate and channel our destructive tendencies as much as possible, so the childhood dream of a humanity made up of brothers and sisters dwelling under the wings of peace might one day actually become reality.

We know our starting point: around the middle of the century, we exceeded our wildest fears with apocalyptic diligence. We made it our business to *take precautions* and build institutional dams to resist the cruel temptation of misanthropy. Even though these kinds of measures have not always been completely successful, there was perhaps the first serious, comprehensive, deliberate and sustained attempt to put an institutional halt to the most destructive forces of our psychology from this point on. For it to succeed, we had to face up to these destructive tendencies to gain an understanding of how that moral collapse could have come about in the first place.

Laws of blood

It is the autumn of 1943. SS-Obersturmbannführer Konrad Morgen, a lawyer and judge responsible for combating corruption in the German Reich's concentration camp system, holds a package in his hand. It is noticeably heavy. A medical assistant has addressed the parcel to his wife. It contains three lumps of gold, one of which, 'perhaps the size of two fists', weighs several kilograms and is high carat.

It is dental gold, and illegal gold shipments like this are

confiscated by Morgen's customs investigators as a currency subject to inspection. He knows that dental gold from people who died in labour camps is to be collected and sent to the Reichsbank. But, stunned by the lumps' size, Morgen starts to do some sums:

> My further reflection, however, sent no small shudder down my spine, since a kilogram of gold is 1,000 grams ... And a gold filling is only a few grams. One thousand grams, or several thousand grams, thus represented the death of several thousand people. But not everyone had gold fillings in that impoverished time, only a fraction. And depending on whether one estimated that one twentieth or fiftieth or hundredth had gold in their mouths, one had to multiply the number, and so this confiscated shipment represented as it were twenty or fifty or a hundred thousand bodies ... I could have dealt with the case of this confiscated gold shipment very easily. The pieces of evidence were conclusive. I could have had the perpetrator arrested and accused, and the matter would have been taken care of. But given the reflections that I have briefly delineated for you, I absolutely had to have a look for myself.[22]

So SS-Obersturmbannführer Morgen drives to where the parcel came from: a small village in southern Poland called Oświęcim, a village we know as Auschwitz. He wants to see with his own eyes the place he suspects is 'one of the largest human-extermination facilities that the world had ever seen'. He will spend the following years trying to undermine the mass murder from within, or at least slow it down, under the pretext of fighting corruption – after all, he is a self-proclaimed 'fanatic for justice'. Nonetheless Morgen is not, like Oskar Schindler, a philanthropic hero committing himself exhaustively to the task of trying to save human lives, but a bureaucrat motivated by professional ethics, primarily concerned with preventing the concentration camp employees from personally getting rich and bypassing the tax authorities. Good, like evil, has its own banality.

For a long while afterwards, it seemed clear to everyone that the Holocaust had ultimately done away with the idea of moral progress. The American philosopher Martha Nussbaum wrote: 'We should probably abandon the nineteenth century expectation for a steady progress of humanity toward greater and greater overall moral achievement. The wars of the twentieth century extinguished that teleological expectation, and the twenty-first, so far, gives us no reason to revive it.'[23]

What made the Holocaust such a disturbing breach of civilisation was its monstrous scale; the rational, bureaucratic and particularly sinister nature of its organisation, which led victims into the gas chambers with perfidious deception, and also the fact that it was organised in and by a nation thought, at the time, to be one of the most scientifically and civilisationally advanced: Germany – the self-proclaimed birthplace of the Enlightenment, the cradle of Romanticism, the home of German idealism, Schubert and Rilke.[24]

The banality of evil is difficult to accept and comprehend, but it does not necessarily suggest that the world is on a path of overall moral decay. Murderous criminals who seize power and begin to slaughter a hated minority are not new: they are by and large the historical norm. All societies exercise whatever genocidal madness they come up with, to the extent and with the efficiency they are capable of at the time.

It is the Holocaust's specific and exceptional character, in particular, that seems to support rather than refute the idea of moral progress. If our belief in moral progress was merely a naive illusion, we might have expected a very different reaction to the Holocaust – international indifference and inaction, maybe. Actual reactions to these unimaginable atrocities were indeed inadequate in many respects: too tentative, too late, too lax, too inconsistent, but eventually, an international coalition of forces formed that did everything in its power to put an end to the Nazi regime, often at the greatest personal sacrifice.

After all, the Holocaust was an operation kept secret at crucial points. The guillotine executions in central Parisian squares or mass drownings like those in the Loire near Nantes during the French Reign of Terror at the end of the eighteenth century, nicknamed the 'national bathtub', took place in broad daylight before the eyes of an attentive public; Heinrich Himmler, on the other hand, made it unmistakably clear that the planned extermination of the Jews was an 'unwritten and never-to-be-written page of glory' in German history.[25]

The Nazi regime, through a profound understanding of the human psyche and unprecedented sophistication, seemingly managed to convince the majority of Germans of even the most brazen lies through ingeniously manipulative propaganda, with a view to bringing a cunningly poisoned people around to its most murderous plans.

But how does propaganda actually work? In 1940 *The Eternal Jew*, one of the most famous propaganda films, conceived by Joseph Goebbels and directed by Fritz Hippler, depicted the Jewish people as a mass of despicable creatures. Today we cannot help but ask ourselves how anyone could have believed this nonsense. Why did the sheep-like audiences fail to see through what they were being shown? The film is so obviously far-fetched, so outrageously tendentious and biased. How could people be so stupid and gullible to fall for this rubbish?

These questions are due to a misunderstanding about the actual purpose of propaganda. Propaganda does not win anyone over, nor does it try to, and at most, just a few people might be convinced by such a tactic. It is impossible to be won over by *The Eternal Jew*. The film begins by showing poor Polish Jews in their run-down homes, surrounded by dirt and flies. It was supposed to demonstrate that Jews had always been incapable of living civilised lives. The next scene uses various statistics to indicate that a disproportionate number of lawyers, doctors and businessmen in Berlin in the 1920s and 1930s were Jews. This, in turn, was intended to make it clear that Jewish people could not do an honest day's work on the land. Jews are then shown doing the work they are forced to do with a reprehensible lack of joy, while being filmed by the people forcing them to do this work. None of it makes sense.

This is an essential aspect of propaganda, rather than a result of its poor execution. Propaganda does not provide information that is meant to be believed by the people it is addressing. Propaganda mostly provides *signals* of in-group loyalty. It does not tell us what to believe: it tells us what to say. *The Eternal Jew* is too inane and silly, too staged to be convincing. It does not even try to inform its audience, but tells them which messages to adopt, so that other people can assess their loyalty to the cause. To be effective at this, propaganda often *has to* be implausible. Information that is true is believable on its own. But propaganda has to be so patently false and far-fetched, so exaggerated and misleading, that repeating it sends the right signal to other people: the signal that one feels committed to a certain group.[26]

This is an important insight: if we are looking for viable antidotes to the power of propaganda, we need to understand how it works. Propaganda provides the masses with traits that allow them to recognise each other. But beyond this, fighting propagandistic falsehoods with the truth actually reinforces the signal's reliability by implicitly telling people who want to prove themselves faithful precisely what not to say. Propaganda acts as a badge to express which group we belong to.

If the counter-strategy of trumping false information with true information does not seem to work, anti-propagandists like to go one better and try to get their message across even more emphatically and insistently. But sometimes this can backfire, making some people suspicious: why are they going to such lengths to disprove this alleged propaganda? Are we maybe being lied to or brainwashed by these traitors and subverters of military power?

In fact, with the benefit of decades of distance and hindsight, we now know that propaganda mostly convinced the people who were already attracted to the anti-Semitic Nazi agenda. This was true from the outset, but especially so towards the end of the war. An employee of the Schweinfurt security service laconically stated: 'Our propaganda encounters rejection everywhere among the population because it is regarded as wrong and lying.'[27] In particular, the fairy tale of the final victory soon failed to convince anyone, and the Nazi murders camouflaged as 'euthanasia' remained deeply unpopular.

It is often said that in order to achieve their goals, fascist movements use a romanticised vision of the past, discomfort towards sexual transgressions, a desire for law and order, belief in a natural hierarchy of races, peoples or genders, and an anti-intellectualist scepticism towards experts to activate our 'us' and 'them' psychology.[28] Marginalised groups are chosen as scapegoats for all the ills of a degenerate society, so that the upstanding majority might find its way back to the path of virtue. There is a desire for rule-breakers to be punished, a feeling of exuberant nostalgia coupled with pessimism about the future, a move to reject intellectual nerds from newsrooms, government departments and universities in favour of a supposedly incorruptible 'common sense'. And yet, though all these things are typically found in fascist regimes, it is misleading to identify them as specifically fascist. They are, in fact, normal characteristics of the human psyche. And in many cases, this psychological profile has not led to fascists seizing power at all.

Many of these 'normal' psychological traits are indeed disturbing and dangerous. Being biased towards our own group is often problematic and counterproductive; nostalgia and pessimism, sexual moralism and anti-intellectualism are all causes for concern, and these tendencies are best minimised as much as possible. Nonetheless, it is not very helpful to attribute a highly specific style of politics to the way the overwhelming majority of people always think and feel, even if this way is reprehensible. At best, it could be said that fascist movements *tap into* these features of our psyche and exploit them for their own purposes. But then this tapping into and exploitation would be the justification for functioning fascism. All too often, the answer to the question of how totalitarian systems come about is that we humans are, first of all, quite dubious creatures – and I'm not even sure there is a second reason. In fact, Nazi ethics were based on a highly specific colonial and martial logic that made it possible for normal moral values and principles to be neutralised, exploited and perverted.[29]

An appropriate response came disastrously too late. The dynamics of moral progress mentioned earlier – the expansion of the moral circle, the recognition of the banality of evil and the increasing demoralisation of arbitrary norms – began to take shape in Germany about twenty years after the end of the war, because it was only at this point that a generation had grown up that was able to articulate its moral indignation with the self-confidence and reflectiveness it needed. Their fathers and mothers had disappointed and failed them. They had not opposed fascism decisively enough, and this mistake should not be repeated: from then on, every little authoritarian transgression of the state apparatus needed to be interpreted as a subtle indication of recurrent fascism with moral hypersensitivity, and this time the end justified every means: 'fool me once, shame on you, fool me twice, shame on me'.

Odo Marquard, inverting Freud's famous phrase, aptly described this as 'deferred disobedience'.[30] Freud had described deferred obedience as the phenomenon where, after a phase of adolescent rebellion against their own parents, many sons and daughters end up adopting the previous generation's values and attitudes once they have grown up themselves. Fifty years ago, the opposite happened: this time, they took up the fight against fascism in good time, except that tragically fascism was not on the rise, so although some particularly radical students and a few economic and political functionaries were caught up in this fight, it actually failed to help anyone else.

The moral impetus of the left-wing student revolt can hardly be overestimated and, despite some crude ideas, many confused ones and some that were superfluous, it was also a great success story. The hypocritical, conventional morality of the post-war years had to fall – and why not? The norms of decency and upstanding citizenship had failed to prevent the ultimate catastrophe. On the contrary, there even seemed to be an inner complicity between the values of glib virtue, trite sociability and hypocritical prudery, as if these had played their part in making the Third Reich's moral perversions possible in the first place, ultimately leading to the almost total rupture of civilisation.

War and peace

Three days after narrowly and fortunately surviving the atomic destruction of Hiroshima, Tsutomu Yamaguchi – wounded, burned, disoriented and deaf in one ear – arrived back in his hometown of Nagasaki at a truly inopportune time. Yamaguchi died in 2010 at the age of ninety-three and is the only person officially recognised by the Japanese government as a *hibakusha* – a survivor of the atomic bombing of Japan in August 1945 – twice over. There are not many people able to campaign for peace with as much credibility as Yamaguchi, who advocated nuclear disarmament, especially in his later years.

All over Germany, ex-servicemen and conscientious objectors, among other people, live in streets with names like Zietenstrasse, Yorckstrasse and Gneisenaustrasse: streets named after hussar generals and field marshals decades or even centuries ago. They bear witness to an obsolete world. The Second World War and its aftermath helped an intuitively plausible view quickly gain enormous popularity: the notion that wars are almost always a bad idea and that people would be better off without them. It is difficult today to understand how new this idea really was back then.

If a machine gun can fire as many shots as a hundred soldiers, wouldn't that mean that fewer people have to die in wars, because the same battle can be fought with fewer personnel? The suggestion that inventing ever more monstrous instruments of death could bring about the demise of wars is almost a touching mistake that has been made over and over again. But neither the invention of the Gatling gun, a forerunner of the machine gun, nor Alfred Nobel's discovery of dynamite could fulfil the hope of the peace-making powers that more effective killing might hold. Only the threat of nuclear annihilation finally led to the paradoxical result of humanity's ultimate weapon bringing the world's hostile nations into a reasonably stable balance of mutual deterrence – a state we now call the Cold War.

It was not just the civilising effect of technical innovations that was able to free the relationship between politics and war from its Clausewitzian pragmatism which maintains that war is only politics by other means. The condemnation of war was also the result of deliberate efforts to contain violent conflicts by reinforcing certain values and norms. When the Kellogg-Briand Pact was signed on 27 August 1928 at the Quai d'Orsay, US secretary of state Frank Kellogg gifted the German foreign minister Gustav Stresemann a gold fountain pen to mark the occasion. The pen bore the inscription *Si vis pacem, para pacem* ('If you want peace, prepare for peace'), reflecting the pact's two extremely short articles, which stipulated that from then on, international conflicts should only be resolved by peaceful means.[31]

The treaty, also known as the Pact of Paris, is now often dismissed as ridiculous naivety. Trying to end wars by making them illegal seems either childish or cynical. How can an agreement help to prevent wars when they are waged precisely at the moment when every agreement has proved ineffective? But this attitude is just as nonsensical as arguing that it is pointless to declare murder and theft illegal because murder and theft continue to happen. This public expression of the will to resolve conflicts peacefully was unheard of at that time: a real paradigm shift in international politics that is hard to appreciate from our twenty-first-century viewpoint. It could not prevent the Second World War, just as no law can prevent its own violation simply by its very existence. Nonetheless, it created a normative basis for the 'Long Peace', the once unthinkable period of decades without war between many nations previously regarded as sworn enemies, such as Germany or France, England or Russia.[32]

This official commitment to peace was the basis for an epochal change; the declining tolerance of violence within and between modern nations is a very new development in human history. For many millennia, the economy around the world had been more or less a zero-sum game. Not much was produced, and looting was in many cases a quick – or even the only – way to economic growth. Only after modern humankind had discovered through cultural evolution that innovation, trade and markets (all of which require a semblance of peace) could create value that could benefit everyone did we come to realise the potential for wealth and prosperity in peaceful international cooperation, rather than in bloody conflict. In *Perpetual Peace*, Kant acknowledged an interconnected economy as one of the most significant incentive structures of international peace;[33] this attempt to take serious steps outlawing acts of war was historically unprecedented.

The downgrading of war from the first step to the last resort of transnational conflict resolution follows a logic of increasing non-violence that has left its mark on almost every area of life. From murder and rape to assault and abuse, modern societies are developing an increasing intolerance of physical violence.[34] All these acts unfortunately still exist, but modern cooperation structures have had a domesticating effect by gradually replacing violent acts and the corresponding warlike ethic of honour and revenge with less ruthless patterns of action. This is why the recent resurgence in violent conflicts (in regions that Westerners can be bothered to care about, such as Europe or the Middle East) is so frustrating and morally disappointing: it resuscitates a way of carrying out international political conflicts that is, or was or should be, normatively obsolete.

The extent to which societies are prone to violent acts as a means of conflict resolution – and how tolerated that violence is – is usually reflective of socio-economic situations. In fact, the effects of different economic arrangements on the frequency and social acceptance of violent action can still be seen today.[35] A stark example can be seen in the contrast between the Northern and Southern states of the US. In the South, there are still the socio-psychological vestiges of a culture of honour: Southerners (on average) react more to insults and provocations. Murder and bar brawling are more common than in the North, and violence in general is more likely to be excused or seen as understandable.

Contrary to what is often assumed, this is not due to the climate (or at least, not directly). Rather than being a simple reflection of hot-headedness, violent behaviour is related to the differing demands of their economies. Historically, in the Northern states, the economy was largely based on arable farming, whereas in the Southern states, it has been based on livestock. This places quite specific demands on the participants' reputation management in each economy. In general, a herd of cattle can be stolen quickly and in one fell swoop, whereas this is not possible with fields and farms (or at least, not so easily). Individual cattle farmers and ranchers, therefore, need to promptly and credibly make it clear that they would be prepared to defend their livelihoods by force. In the Southern states, where this form of economic activity was much more widespread, this left a culture of honour that still continues to this day, only gradually being watered down by surges of modernisation. It is that very modernisation that decreases tolerance to violence, and places a premium on peace.

Silent revolution

What is moral progress, and how does it happen? In the second half of the twentieth century, a process of moral transformation began, with modern societies gradually shifting from conservative to progressive structures. This change consisted of a greater emphasis on *emancipative* values, which aim at liberation from oppression and disadvantage. Traditional values focused on law, faith and order began to be ousted by secular attitudes, and priorities shifted from concern for material security towards individual autonomy, expressive self-fulfilment and political liberalisation. Increasing acceptance of homosexuality, a furthering of gender equality, a growing appreciation of freedom of speech and thought, social independence, nonconformism, education and personal creativity all reflect these developments.[36] Though there is a way to go yet, the shift towards these emancipative values is demonstrably real and likely to continue.

For several decades, technologically and economically developed knowledge-based societies have been placing more emphasis on individual diversity and political emancipation. These trends vary from region to region, but are fundamentally global. Since 1981, the World Values Survey has been measuring how changing value patterns of this kind can be mapped onto different cultural regions. Although countries with economically poorer or politically more repressive regimes such as Romania or Afghanistan still have great differences in their general values from those in more progressive nations such as Norway, the United States, Australia or the Netherlands, the trend – with a few exceptions, which are mainly found in sub-Saharan Africa – always points towards emancipatory values.[37]

The American political scientist Ronald Inglehart has described these developments as a 'silent revolution'.[38] But will it stay that way? There is a concern that these progressive achievements will be eaten up by ageing effects, driven by the pattern that people tend to become more conservative as they grow older, but this concern seems to be unjustified: the desire for liberalisation, emancipation and tolerance does not gradually go into reverse just because everyone takes on conservative attitudes and values with increasing age. Each previous generation, taken individually and up to its last phase, has gradually become more progressive, and each subsequent generation is altogether more progressive than the previous one, even if individuals may become a little more traditional in their old age. Overall, this creates a global trend moving in a progressive direction[39] – it creates 'moral progress'. But that's not the end of the story; we need to understand *why* it is that, once certain levels of prosperity and stability are reached, this trend towards progressive values exists at all.

It's likely that it comes down to the 'marginal utility' of different social values. Many will be familiar with the concept of the marginal utility of wealth, which is, very simply, that $100 is a huge amount of money to a starving student, but almost entirely irrelevant to a millionaire. The 'value' of the money to the individual differs depending on how much money they already have. Under the conditions of political volatility and economic uncertainty, the marginal utility of economic resources is very high, which means the value of economic resources is high – so high that the traditionalist values that provide economic stability are prioritised. Authenticity, autonomy, liberality and self-realisation exist, but they are less urgent than the values that will ensure economic stability. The more prosperous and secure a cultural region becomes over time, the lower the marginal utility of economic resources. This allows room for the marginal utility of emancipatory values to grow and eventually surpass the value of 'law and order' attitudes. Everyone longs for freedom and autonomy – but it is only when these values' relative importance has grown enough for them to be called for with sufficient force that their realisation can no longer be delayed, even by powerful elites interested in maintaining the status quo.

Filthy lucre

Socio-economic changes unleashed modernity's dynamics of progress from the middle of the twentieth century onwards. Only with relative economic security and political stability could the emancipatory values of equality, inclusion and freedom – those values so closely associated with moral progress – assert themselves.

The idea that money does not make you happy is one of those well-known truths that is not true at all. In fact, it is hard not to suspect that this is an opinion accepted mainly by people who do not have to worry about money, and indeed, just as we explored with our example of the marginal utility of wealth, money can mean an awful lot more to those who do not have it. With lofty stucco ceilings over your head, you can afford a disrespectful opinion of filthy lucre; in damp mud huts and on an empty stomach, it is far less clear whether material resources are really as dispensable as they seem to well-fed armchair theorists.

Since the 1970s, there has been a plethora of robust empirical evidence seemingly showing that wealth and well-being are in fact independent of each other. A phenomenon known as the Easterlin paradox, named after the American economist Richard Easterlin, consisted of the discovery that while, within a country, richer people tended to be happier than poorer people, the *populations* of richer nations were not happier overall than the *populations* of poorer ones.[40] There was nothing to suggest that a wealthy Dane (Denmark being one of the richest countries on earth) would be happier than the (relatively) wealthiest inhabitants of South Sudan (the world's poorest country by GDP). Easterlin's findings, perhaps counterintuitively, showed that a person's satisfaction with life did not steadily decrease with declining wealth – nor did it steadily increase with increasing wealth. But how was this possible? Does wealth make you happier, or does it not?

Easterlin accounted for his irritating discovery by explaining that the subjective assessment of our own happiness is significantly influenced by comparative considerations. People see themselves as happy when they are *happier* than the people they are comparing themselves with – and it is the same with unhappiness. The actual levels of wealth made little difference in his studies, at least beyond about US$20,000 per year. And on top of this, more money did not make people any happier.

An annual income of US$20,000 puts someone in the group of the richest people, in a global comparison. So the Easterlin paradox could never show that drastic improvements in prosperity in the poorest regions of the world would not be worthwhile. It is the case, though, that comparative considerations psychologically have a surprisingly big effect on a person's satisfaction with life. We are social beings, after all, and comparison with others has a very real effect on our well-being. Since its publication, though, new data has shown that the Easterlin paradox is not tenable in its original form. There is less of a difference in happiness between $500,000 and $550,000 than between $50,000 and $100,000. However, this is the phenomenon of diminishing marginal utility, which was already common knowledge, and not a paradox. A closer look at the data available shows that there is in fact a strong positive correlation between increasing wealth and increasing happiness.[41]

According to the British-American economist Angus Deaton, every improvement in income by a factor of four leads to a one-point increase in happiness on a scale of one to ten.[42] As the differences between the poorest and richest countries are so extreme, this has a dramatic effect. The average level of happiness in the wealthiest countries is eight, while in the poorest it is around three. Richer people in developed countries are more content, healthier, report a higher quality of life and have better life opportunities – they are, in short, happier.

There are always exceptions. Ebenezer Scrooge is rich, but stingy and bad-tempered; Tiny Tim is poor and sickly, but always cheerful and in a good mood. All the same, money – on average – makes us happy. This means that money is on average *useful* but *not essential* for our own satisfaction with life. There are no rich countries where people don't do pretty well on average, although there are some relatively poor countries – especially in South America – where people report comparatively high levels of satisfaction despite relatively low incomes. It may be true that we can never determine how happy a person is with any certainty using objective measurements; however, there are some good clues as to what it takes to live a good life. No one wants to go hungry, mourn the death of their own children, do hard, gruelling work or be politically persecuted. Anyone who disputes this ought to explain their reasoning.

Greater prosperity in developed countries produces two types of moral progress. On the one hand, it is progress in itself when people are simply better off. You do not have to be a utilitarian to admit that a world with more joy and health is preferable to a world with more suffering and disease. And on the other hand, greater wealth leads to increased awareness of the phenomenon of poverty.[43] As long as everyone is poor, there is no awareness that this is a regrettable but fundamentally avoidable state of affairs worth fighting against. But in modern societies, there are millions of people who study the problem of poverty scientifically and try to minimise it technologically, politically or through philanthropic efforts. The number of people in what is classed as absolute poverty – where they have to survive on just US$2 per day – has fallen in recent decades from 90 per cent (as measured by today's standards) to less than 10 per cent.[44] And even if we dispute how valid this threshold is, the simple fact remains that before the industrial revolution, almost everyone was poor and now not everyone is.[45] Astonishing progress has recently been made in China and India, in particular, and their socio-political impact is now beginning to emerge. In these areas, too, the emancipatory values of freedom and inclusion are slowly beginning to make themselves heard.

Another persistent myth is that life in modern – and especially in developed capitalist – countries always leads to spiritual impoverishment and that these are populated by materially care-free, but inwardly worn down, nihilistic, depressive or anxious people who have exchanged their psychological well-being for shiny toys in a Faustian trade-off.[46] Cultural critics seem to have been completely seduced by the idea that while material progress under capitalism may be undeniable, it must come at the price of a simultaneous increase in psychopathological phenomena such as depression, phobias or a general feeling of vague existential insecurity. In reality, data shows that there is mostly good news to report: the increase in depression diagnoses is almost entirely due to an increase in depression *diagnoses*, rather than an increase in *cases* of depression. Life has always been tough, difficult and gloomy, but in contrast to bygone times, when mental health problems were at best played down, but more often hushed up or stigmatised as a personal defect, the twentieth century saw an increasing sensitivity to the fragility of the human soul and a proliferation of therapies and proposed solutions. Mental illnesses are made visible and treated – this is a positive development, not a negative one.

The expanding circle

A few minutes before the pastor Dr Martin Luther King Jr gives humanity a glimpse into his dreams, a small man at the peak of his career steps up to the podium in front of the Lincoln Memorial. Like most people here on this day, Joachim Prinz wears a little badge on his lapel with a white hand holding a Black one in friendly determination, framed by the words 'March on Washington for Jobs & Freedom, August 28, 1963'.

Prinz speaks into the six microphones with particular authority: as rabbi of the synagogue on Oranienburger Strasse in Berlin, he soon gained a reputation as an inspiring speaker, and in 1937 he eventually had to accept that Jewish life in Germany had become intolerable. His farewell sermon shortly before his departure for the United States was attended by thousands, including the head of the Jewish section, Department II 112, of the Berlin Security Service: Adolf Eichmann. Here in Washington as an American, as a Jew and as a Jewish American, Joachim Prinz reminds us that we could all be neighbours and that silence, indifference and passivity, even more than hatred and bigotry, can empower even the supposedly most civilised nations to extreme actions.

Around fifty years later, in the autumn of 2011, I am sitting in his grandson's office. Jesse Prinz, a philosophy professor at the City University of New York, jokingly refers to it as a phone booth because of its size. But space is precious in Manhattan, especially for the publicly funded City University. We talk about the origins of morality – as a visiting PhD student I actually do more listening – and why compassion and empathy can often be a questionable and even misleading compass. Empathy is quickly exhausted, easily distracted, biased and receptive only to the most vivid impressions.[47] Stalin is supposed to have once said that the death of one person is a tragedy and the death of millions is a statistic, and this seems to be the maxim of our compassion: we care only about a few people, and only about those we know and love. We are indifferent to most people.

But do we have to accept this?

There are a number of proposals as to what constituted the essence of moral progress in the twentieth century or what might be the defining moral transformation of late modernity, but a central theme is a universal dignity that is due and inherent to all human beings and that remains inviolable regardless of religion, colour or origin. In moral philosophy, the story of moral progress is often told as the story of an 'expanding circle'.[48] The idea is that moral status has long been (and still is) reserved for a tiny social elite. Enjoying recognition as a full member of the community, belonging to the group that can expect the full extent of every right and amenity available in a society, has long been the prerogative of individuals of a particular gender, age, ethnicity or religious affiliation and socio-economic status. This is a phenomenon that can be seen in almost all societies over the last few millennia. Depending on the place and era we focus on, the privilege of moral status was reserved for the Athenian citizens, the aristocracy, the chieftains, the mandarins and Brahmins, the capitalist bourgeoisie or the financially independent upper classes. Women and children, workers and peasants, the poor and sick, immigrants and the disenfranchised, minorities and dissidents were at best second-class subjects whose moral status was denied, minimised, violated, forgotten or ignored.

The American philosophers Allen Buchanan and Russell Powell refer to the expanding circle of morality as the 'inclusivist anomaly'.[49] It is inclusivist because from now on more and more previously excluded people would gain access to the coveted world of moral recognition, and it is an anomaly because an endeavour of this kind is a great rarity in human history – moral status has always been the privilege of the few.

With the moral revolutions that mark the dawn of modernity, the restrictions on access to this circle of moral status are slowly being weakened and it is being extended – admittedly only gradually and with a frustrating lack of speed – to larger and larger groups. Morally arbitrary boundaries between genders, races or classes and the resulting forms of exclusion, discrimination, exploitation, oppression and marginalisation are now being dismantled. Every human being, regardless of their accidental traits, should in principle be recognised as a fully fledged moral subject. Racism, sexism or classism are now seen as morally unjustified forms of discrimination. More recently, even belonging to the correct biological – namely human – species has been called speciesism: another ugly word for an ugly thing. What matters when it comes to qualifying as a bearer of moral status is whether we are capable of thinking and suffering. Reserving this status for just one species turns out to be a pretty obvious prejudice. *Animal Liberation* by the Australian philosopher Peter Singer was published on this subject in 1975, and this was followed by a manifesto on universal rights for all animals and sentient beings in 1979, initiated by what was known as the Oxford Group, also called the Oxford Vegetarians.

Although this dynamic of inclusion contradicts our basic moral instincts, which are actually directed primarily towards our neighbours, it is nonetheless enshrined in various key twentieth-century legal documents, not least in the wake of the Second World War. Article 109 of the Weimar Constitution in Germany codified the abolition of the nobility in 1919, along with the legal equality of men and women, and the Basic Law of the Federal Republic of Germany (1949) and the new Japanese Constitution (1947), as well as the Universal Declaration of Human Rights (1948), share a central theme: the indiscriminate recognition of the dignity and inviolability of every individual.

The notion of an expanding circle of morality originally came from the Irish historian William Lecky, who first coined this term in his *History of European Morals* in 1869. But the precise structure of this circle remains controversial. Some people are of the opinion that the moral circle comprises several concentric circles, which for each individual are essentially determined by relationships of personal – and this means above all genetic – kinship. According to this model, the subject in question would be in the centre of the circle: every man for himself. Then come parents, siblings and children, then grandparents and half-siblings and so on, until we finally reach the circle of people the individual is not genetically related to, but who belong to their own 'in-group', in other words friends and acquaintances.

Outside this sphere are strangers and other members of the human species, followed by other mammalian species, sentient beings in general, and finally the entire living world. This way of drawing the circle of morality is roughly inspired by Hamilton's rule: our willingness to cooperate declines with decreasing kinship.

Psychologically, there seem to be individual differences in where someone might be on the 'moral expansiveness scale'.[50] This also seems to have a political dimension: politically more 'conservative' people draw the circle of moral status tighter by emphasising moral loyalty to their own community, while political liberals identify more strongly with humanity as a whole.[51] While there are various forces at work, determining where you sit in someone else's moral circle (and vice versa), everyone *has* a circle; they simply draw their lines in different ways.

In 1971, John Rawls's *A Theory of Justice* was published, and declared the idea of this type of expansive impartiality to be the central architectural principle of fair social institutions.[52] In doing so, he reinvented political philosophy after decades of theoretical fatigue, delineating how a just society must be structured. Key to a 'just society' was the concept of the 'veil of ignorance': just social institutions must be the ones that people would choose if they did not know what their place was in a society set up in this way. Theoretically, this veil of ignorance would ensure that differences of religion, ethnicity, gender and social class have no influence on what basic freedoms people are entitled to and what life opportunities they can access. Social inequalities in income or status are justified if, and only if, they work out primarily to the advantage of the worst off in a society – for example, if incentives such as higher incomes encourage particularly talented people to become doctors. After all, everyone benefits from the existence of competent doctors.

However, as we are obviously unable to go back to the drawing board and design an existing society from scratch, active steps must sometimes be taken to bring the deficient institutions

and ownership structures bequeathed to us by previous generations as close as possible to this ideal of impartiality. In many
cases, this has led to the introduction of affirmative action programmes committed to the idea of positive discrimination in
favour of marginalised groups. John F. Kennedy's Executive
Order 10925 declared government discrimination on the basis
of race, creed or national origin unlawful in 1961. According to
the tenor of this law, there must sometimes be active attempts
to correct the under-representation of certain groups in certain
professions, for example through blind recruitment procedures
or explicit quotas. The American philosopher Elizabeth Anderson sees this as a shift to the 'imperative of integration': modern
societies must make an effort to overcome inherited forms of
social segregation and disadvantage through active inclusion
measures, once and for all.[53]

The expanding circle of morality was already coming into
play with the discovery of WEIRDness. Hundreds of years ago,
when cultural evolution began to erode the key role of kinship
as a society's construction principle, it discovered the potential
of impersonal prosociality: a society that begins to experiment
with cooperative, altruistic and reciprocally beneficial interactions between strangers eventually finds that it is more of
a hindrance to international trade and a functioning modern
state to view other groups as demonic hordes that must be marginalised, enslaved or slaughtered. Recognising a moral status
inherent in all human beings is, in this way, at least partially
driven by economic interests.

Moral expansion, while important, remains limited: the growing reduction in and tolerance towards violence and murder, for
example, cannot be described as an expansion of moral status
to new members. Women's emancipation, often mentioned as
a key example of the expanding circle of morality, is ultimately
due to a different dynamic. Historically, discrimination against
women cannot be attributed primarily to exclusion from the

circle of morality, which would amount to total dehumanisation. Women were never completely denied moral status; their oppression did not follow the model of dehumanisation, but of subordination: the female was indeed a moral subject, but with specific rights and duties based on supposedly specific characteristics – which were often more or less seen as downright deficits. We need to think of the fight against sexist discrimination through the model of role integration – moving towards female chief medical officers and chancellors – rather than the model of more fundamental *social* integration that merges realms formerly segregated by race, for example. As a universally valid notion of moral progress, the expanding circle of moral affiliation does not therefore cover everything.

The extension of moral recognition occupies a particularly prominent position in many narratives of moral progress, because xenophobia, discrimination, exclusion, dehumanisation or genocide are such blatant moral wrongs that any extension of moral status criteria seems welcome. On the other hand, there are many examples of social developments where 'contractions' of the moral circle, in other words the circle becoming smaller, were on the right side of history. The modern dynamics of secularisation belong in this context, as does the abolition of the nobility. For the liberal state, nothing is sacred, and no one is better than anyone else. Ascriptive – independent of performance – differences in status were levelled out, and claiming to be recognised as the only correct way of salvation (as alleged by every religion) was something suspected to be wrong.

Other contractions of the moral circle are yet to come. We may excuse environmental activists or representatives of indigenous peoples for thinking it is a good idea to want to endow inanimate stretches of nature such as New Zealand's Whanganui River with the rights, duties and responsibilities of a legal entity. Nonetheless, we cannot help feeling there could have been a less animistic and pan-psychic solution to the problem of sustainable interaction with the environment.

The moral circle, as Lecky envisioned it, is not without flaws, and is certainly not a catch-all; indeed, it often has uncomfortable implications. On one side of the coin, we must reckon with the view that exploiting, mistreating and degrading animals – speciesism – is in violation of moral expansion; but on the other side of the coin, what of the moral status of some members of the human species? If moral status depends on certain characteristics, such as a being's ability to think, plan or suffer, we are often forced, for reasons of consistency, to classify some individuals at the beginning or end of human life as borderline cases of moral validity. The suggestion that in extreme cases even the euthanasia of certain people can be morally permissible, or even necessary, has repeatedly (not least in Europe) earned ethicists advocating this, such as Peter Singer, the accusation that they are propagating a form of 'racial cleansing' that views disabled lives as fundamentally unworthy. This criticism is, of course, sheer nonsense, as no bioethicist would dream of ruling against anyone's best or explicit interests, but it shows that there are powerful psychological obstacles that can stand in the way of renegotiating the moral circle.

Moral expansion extends to the entire natural world. The fear of homelessness seems to be an anthropological constant, so much so that it's worth considering whether it might actually be part of our nature. It is very clearly not an invention of the twentieth century, nor of Romanticism, even though this movement made an urge to go back to nature, the only place the tormented soul of modern humankind could be reconciled with itself, one of its main themes. We are clearly plagued by the latent fear of losing our homes, of belonging to the displaced and the exiled who must pack their things one morning, never to return. Incidentally, this concern is not entirely unjustified: history is full of examples of societies that brought about their own collapse by draining their environments dry through overfishing, deforestation, excessive hunting, erosion, problems with soil irrigation or fertility beyond their economic viability.[54]

The fear of out-of-control population growth is a particularly perfidious version of our intrinsically reasonable concern
about the sustainable use of the Earth's resources. This fear is
often accused of being implicitly racist – rightly so, because it is
usually noticeably very specific populations from very specific
regions of the world whose downsizing is being called for. For
example, we never get the impression that there are too many
Norwegians. In 1968, Paul R. Ehrlich's *The Population Bomb* was
published: a neo-Malthusian fever dream whose main strength
lay in being wrong in just about every prediction of the supposedly imminent global famine that would inevitably kill
hundreds of millions of people.[55]

In the same year, the Club of Rome was founded, warning
of the 'limits to growth' in a detailed report in 1972 that became
one of the founding documents of modern environmental
movements. In 1971 Greenpeace was formed, along with the
anti-nuclear movement. The fear of an overpopulated Earth,
whose natural resources would soon no longer be sufficient
to accommodate an ever-growing humanity, was presented by
early environmentalists with less apocalyptic irrationalism than
by Ehrlich, but their message was essentially the same: if we do
not take care and go down a radically different path, we will
lurch into disaster. And who wants a world where our grandchildren will one day be desperate and neglected, starved and
freezing, without hope or a future, clothed in stinking rags and
wandering in small scattered groups through a desolate waste-
land, fighting for the last drops of water from a contaminated
puddle?

Demoralisation

Los Angeles, 1940: this time he wants to get it right. To make it
as hard as possible for his producer David O. Selznick (already
known as overbearing, and emboldened by his success with
Gone with the Wind the previous year) to meddle with his

artistic vision too drastically, Mr Hitchcock cuts his latest film *Rebecca* 'in the camera'.[56] In this laborious process, it is not the usual case of shooting an excess of material and then putting it together into a finished film in the cutting room. In in-camera editing, only the scenes that are actually needed for the finished movie are filmed, in the order in which they appear in the final product. As there is no unnecessary footage on film, no backer, however insistent, can sabotage the artist's final version.

With such fanatical faithfulness to the original, it is all the more surprising that Hitchcock had changed a decisive detail from Daphne du Maurier's novel: in the novel, Maxim de Winter confesses to having murdered his drop-dead gorgeous but arrogant and heartless wife. In the film she dies in an accident: Rebecca, seriously ill with cancer and tired of life, provokes her husband until he finally attacks her in an argument; she then falls, fatally injuring her head.

The reason for this deviation is William Harrison Hays, or more precisely, the 'Motion Picture Production Code' in force at the time, which was also informally known by his name, as Hays was president of the Motion Picture Producers and Distributors of America. This cinematic decalogue was intended to guarantee that the viewer would not be troubled by indecencies such as sensual dancing, suggestive movements and excessive kissing. (The curious foible in older films of actors interrupting their kisses every two to three seconds is due to the time constraints for physical intimacy spelled out in the Hays Code.) Romantic relationships between white and Black people as well as cursing and blasphemy were also forbidden. Similarly, sympathising with criminals or even letting them get away with it had to be avoided. And so Rebecca de Winter dies in an accident in the film and not through murder, so that Maxim and his nameless second wife can finally be happy – and so that they may appear on screen. Even twenty years later, the most scandalous scene in Hitchcock's *Psycho* for the audience at the time was not the death of leading lady Janet Leigh surprisingly early on in the film, but the fact that she flushes the toilet on camera to get rid of a few pieces of paper. Such blatant obscenity had never been seen before.

Hitchcock is not the only legendary director to fall victim to Will Hays's zeal. Anyone watching the 1991 restored version of Stanley Kubrick's *Spartacus* today will unwittingly be missing out on hearing the voice of Laurence Olivier in a scene that was cut in 1960. Only the visual material, but not the soundtrack, could be found of the long-lost shot, so Olivier's Crassus had to be dubbed by Anthony Hopkins, who was able to imitate his former acting teacher's style perfectly. In the scandalous sequence, while bathing, Crassus asks his slave Antoninus, played by the young Tony Curtis, whether he prefers 'oysters' or 'snails', and makes it clear that he considers the preference for one or the other to be a matter of taste, not of morality. Nonetheless, even such a discreetly presented defence of ancient homoeroticism could not be let through by Hays's censors. The offensive scene had to be cut to avoid exposing the puritanical moral sensibility of the time to too much, or as it was originally written in black and white in the Hays Code: 'No picture should lower the moral standards of those who see it.'

A lot has changed since then. The question of which moral principles should be observed by filmmakers and creative artists is still being negotiated. The first 'Screw you!' – or alternatively 'Goddamn you!' – to be heard in mainstream cinemas came from Elizabeth Taylor's mouth in 1966 in *Who's Afraid of Virginia Woolf?* – but initially only in the version intended for the British market. Nowadays, the outlook could hardly be more different: while the proponents of the Hays Code were primarily concerned with depicting the conventional morals of the white, puritanical majority in society, whose exalted concern about the alleged decay of law, order and sexual decency should be catered for cinematically, the moral priorities of the present day are directed at dismantling unjustified privileges, which continue to be increasingly weakened by progressive standards of inclusion and representation. Films wishing to qualify for an Academy Award for best picture from 2024 onwards must therefore ensure that an appropriate number of members of an ethnic, social or sexual minority are represented on screen or involved in production.[57]

Moral norms are part of our cultural heritage. But heritage can be tricky, and we are entitled to reject something we inherit entirely or partially if we feel that it will do more harm than good to our future.

One of the most significant dimensions of moral progress is the *demoralisation* of traditional moral norms that have become obsolete, such as the increased acceptance of premarital sex, which used to be very much stigmatised.[58] This can be down to several reasons: maybe the problem that these norms were once supposed to solve has now disappeared; maybe they have been recognised as ineffective – maybe even as harmful. In all these instances, it can be a good thing to examine and, if necessary, revise the reservoir of moral norms that we were born into and have accepted as a given.

When the demoralisation of a norm is complete, we find we are living in a different world. We have to find out from a book that it was once considered offensive and almost unbearably vulgar to show a toilet in a film. We can no longer *see* it, and we are merely amused by the moral hysteria of imagining the sight of basic aspects of personal hygiene to be the harbinger of moral decline.

In the mid-twentieth century, the dynamics of demoralisation intensified. Norms have repeatedly lost their moral character throughout history; from this point on, this kind of ethical neutralisation, in which supposedly moral norms come to be seen as mere conventions, became reflexive and was pursued vehemently and intently. We start to see social movements fighting to remove the taboo status from certain behaviour, so that people who want to behave in this way can do so undisturbed, as long as they do not harm anyone else. Demoralisation of 'morality' means liberalisation of society.

It often took great personal sacrifice to demand and fight for these developments, of course. Oscar Wilde was thrown into prison for gross indecency at the end of the nineteenth century when he proclaimed the 'love that dare not speak its name' to be something noble and spiritual that needed no apology. Since the riots that began in 1969 at the Stonewall Inn on New York's Christopher Street, the demoralisation of homosexuality has been a unique success story, especially in Western societies. Nowadays, we can no longer even be sure if the pope is still homophobic.

The rejection and punishment of same-sex love, disavowed as 'sodomy', can draw on a millennia-old tradition almost all over the world. It is therefore all the more astonishing how quickly non-heteronormative lifestyles have been socially accepted. Considerable progress has been made here, but it has not yet been replicated when it comes to other manifest-ations of discrimination, such as racism. This is probably due to the comparatively favourable socio-psychological conditions resulting from homosexuality's 'horizontal distribution'.[59] Unlike skin colour, which as the basis of the social construc-tion of supposed 'races' is publicly visible at all times and is 'vertically' distributed with its strong genetic component so that it can serve as a characteristic of segregation or apartheid, homosexuality is scattered indiscriminately throughout society. When more and more queer people come out, the majority of society recognises that there are homosexual people every-where, among friends and relatives, rich and poor, right and left. It is statistically simply impossible not to know and appre-ciate any gay or lesbian people. This paved the way for their full acceptance, which has not yet been completely achieved, but one day will become reality.

Sex before marriage is now considered morally neutral for the most part, and is only raised as a problem when it contributes to the spread of sexually transmitted diseases and unwanted pregnancies. The stigmatisation of premarital intercourse had a certain justification for a long time: before there were reliable contraceptive methods and modern social safety nets that could guarantee the basic care of illegitimate children and their unfortunate mothers outside matrimonial relationships, the deterrence created by a wanton reputation was a repressive but sometimes useful means of social control. This mainly affected women, while the fathers, who were of course 50 per cent involved, were usually met with a shrug of the shoulders.

The increasing demoralisation of sex work also belongs in this context. Morality does not stop at natural desires and appetites: it can condemn entire generations of people to have to endure a straitjacket of silly norms. 'The present generation has little idea of the vast extent of prostitution in Europe before the world wars. While today prostitutes are seen in big cities as seldom as horses in the streets, at the time the pavements were so crowded with women of easy virtue that it was harder to avoid them than to find them.'[60] In *The World of Yesterday*, Stefan Zweig describes with sober irony the unintended side effects that can occur when the 'snag of morality'[61] is used to ignore, repress and ban human sexuality.

Even as a schoolboy, Zweig saw what he would later see confirmed by Freud, that natural urges cannot simply be suppressed; they ultimately always get their way. As if we could fight hunger and disease by hiding the existence of food and viruses from people, the nineteenth century attempted to moralise away, or at least deny, the sexuality of women in particular. The result was that, according to Zweig, almost every young man was terrorised by the constant fear of contracting syphilis from one of the 'itinerant prostitutes', a disease so humiliating, arduous and hard to treat that the diagnosis made many sufferers immediately reach for the revolver. And as for the 'street-walkers' themselves, they almost always suffered more from the toxic situation that brought them not only poverty, disease and exploitation, but also irreparable social exclusion.

At the turn of the twentieth century, European society inflicted this wound on itself by banishing harmless human inclinations and desires to *chambres séparées* with its hysterically over-strict morality. The confusion of sexist prudery with virtue and decency could cause psychosocial havoc for decades. Zweig reports with touching sympathy on the freedom and normality with which the young men and women of the next generation were allowed to redefine the relationship between the sexes – even if the reader already knows that the moral generosity and liberality of the 1920s would soon be a thing of the past.

Adam Smith was of the opinion that it was not appropriate to be paid for singing in public: he compared this to a kind of 'publick prostitution'[62] – bad news for an already struggling music industry. Western philosophy also has a long tradition of disapproving of moneylending for a fee, which was dismissed by Aristotle and Thomas Aquinas as 'usury'. When insurance companies began offering the first life policies, angry protests erupted at the commodification of a human life. In the US, the debate around the moral status of abortion is far from over. In almost all other developed nations, by contrast, abortions have become largely a medical problem.

Other antiquated morals, such as defending a man's personal honour, have also disappeared. The last fatal duel of an American leading politician (probably) took place in 1804.[63] Alexander Hamilton, whose son had already died in a duel in the same place, had left Manhattan in the morning and crossed the Hudson River to Weehawken, New Jersey, to meet Aaron Burr – his long-time enemy, who had challenged him that day – so the two men could grant each other satisfaction. Hamilton, accompanied by his second, Nathaniel Pendleton, had probably planned to spare his opponent. His shot narrowly missed Burr and broke a tree's branch behind him; Burr's infinitely less lenient response hit Hamilton's lower abdomen, shattering several ribs and organs. He succumbed to his injuries the next day.

Duels, although still reasonably popular among gentlemen back then to restore honour and reputation, had been illegal for some time, and Burr was charged with murder soon after, though the case never went to trial. Nonetheless, the two men had apparently felt that their years of dispute, both political and personal, left them no alternative. Moral 'decency' demanded that in cases like this, a man's life must be surrendered to chance and to his enemy's skill with the pistol.

But how do superfluous norms get reproduced in the first place? There can be various reasons why dysfunctional norms do not simply disappear on their own. The Australian philosopher Kim Sterelny uses a term from American military jargon to describe this kind of situation: SNAFU – 'situation normal, all fucked up'.[64] In many cases, long-established norms and taboos survive simply because society is in a state of 'pluralistic ignorance'.[65] Many families in sub-Saharan Africa would prefer not to mutilate their daughters' genitals, but mistakenly believe they are the only ones who feel this way. Once this situation is rectified through education, the norm can erode. Or it might be a customary 'first mover' problem: no one wants to be the first to deviate from a norm that is usually followed. Or while a norm may primarily be harmful or pointless, its perpetuation plays into the hands of powerful elites and vested interests.[66]

Demoralisation, in other words the moral neutralisation of certain actions, is a natural consequence of life in modern societies. The cultural conservative obsession with the present decline in values is, strictly speaking, justified: moral norms and values are being dismantled, and are eroding and disappearing. But this is mainly good news, and here is where the cultural conservative concern is unjustified: the demoralisation of values always equates to a liberalisation of society and an emancipation from restrictions that have become troublesome. This is inevitable because their socio-cultural evolution generates new forms of cooperation. Developed societies are diverse societies simply because of the number of their members, and an established pluralism, which offers the possibility of a multitude of 'experiments in living', by necessity undermines the authority of traditional norms because it demonstrates in practical terms how many of these norms are ultimately optional.

In many cases, the complementary challenge is not only demoralising the wrong things, but also *moralising* the right things. Moralisation is first and foremost a psychological phenomenon.[67] It is not that people modify their moral judgement of a behaviour and now judge a certain action more strictly or leniently, for example, but that an action is perceived as a morally relevant matter for the first time. This is sometimes done to reduce individually harmful behaviour (smoking, for example), or sometimes for direct moral reasons (such as meat consumption).

Moralisation has always existed. What is new to us now is the conscious effort to moralise the right things. The term 'flight shame', for example, is an attempt to strip air travel of its nature of being a given or a status symbol, and to mark it as destructive consumer behaviour, destroying the planet for the sake of individual convenience.

Moral progress happens when bad, harmful, superfluous or unjustified norms and values are neutralised. This is the essence of demoralisation processes. But the opposite is just as important: progress may also consist in the fact that conduct that was once wrongly considered morally neutral begins to appear harmful, offensive, unjust, discriminatory or problematic for the first time. What have we overlooked for too long? And how can we ultimately make it visible without simply hating ourselves and each other?

7

Nonpolitical Reflections

The fire next time

The year 1965 marked the hundredth anniversary of the end of the American Civil War and the abolition of slavery. It was meant to be a celebration of '100 years of freedom', but faced with these festivities, the American author, intellectual and civil rights activist James Baldwin wrote: 'The country is celebrating one hundred years of freedom one hundred years too soon.'[1]

It is hard not to agree with him. Emmett Till's bloated, lifeless body had only been buried ten years earlier; prior to his funeral, his mother had his body laid out in an open coffin to expose and condemn the lynching of her son; Stormé DeLarverie scuffling with a police officer who had abused her in front of the Stonewall Inn in Manhattan on 28 June 1969 was still in the future. Baldwin feared that after the floodgates of the civil rights movement had opened, if the demand for 'liberty and justice for all', the last words of the Pledge of Allegiance, was not soon implemented satisfactorily, everything would end up in flames. And in other parts of the world, too, this 'good news' heralding the alleged end of oppression could well have been announced prematurely and perceived as cynical and tone-deaf.

Since then, more than fifty years have passed with modern societies repeating their promise of liberty and equality for all: no one was to be disadvantaged on the basis of arbitrary differences of origin or skin colour, and no one was to be discriminated against, excluded or disenfranchised because of their gender or religion. These societies were supposed to become inclusive through and through, welcoming everyone, offering everyone equal opportunities and happiness, liberating everyone from servitude and emancipating them from oppression, overcoming the horrors of war and genocide. But whether we have managed to deliver on these moral promises remains an open question.

The hope that the gradual abolition of legal forms of discrimination, segregation and marginalisation and a heightened awareness of the fundamental equality and dignity of all human beings, combined with a liberal social order, would eventually lead to actual social, political and material equality for all still has not come true. The generation of people growing up now feels rightly frustrated, and they show their solidarity in their impatience. They seek a new approach that no longer sees these coveted goals solely in terms of freedom and equal opportunities, with no one being judged, as Martin Luther King once put it, by the colour of their skin, but only by the content of their character.[2]

Instead, this disenfranchised generation is looking for a solution elsewhere: with a particular emphasis on collective identities and group affiliations seeking to voice their claims, demands and disappointments, once and for all.

We have enshrined a firm commitment to socio-economic equality in our social contract, but also an equally firm commitment to individual freedom. Whether either can be truly realised remains to be seen, but more importantly, this second commitment ensures we will never be able to completely fulfil the first one. Western culture is liberal and pluralistic, and therefore has to provide the individual with unusually powerful rights of defence against the majority and against the state's institutions. It may be tempting to believe that equality and freedom go hand in hand, but this liberalism, embedded in the modern age's moral and political infrastructure, makes it impossible to implement our commitment to equality through rigorous state intervention. Racism and social injustice are actually not that hard to fix if you're willing to compromise on individual freedom: all you would need to do is impose legislation on everyone, decreeing who they must be friends with, where they can live and who they should love, and redistributing all wealth completely.

As this kind of ultra-radical interference with private autonomy and property is unreasonable in modern societies that appreciate the importance of individual freedom, we must make do with rebuilding the ship of modernity on the high seas, without ever being able to return to dry dock, so to speak. Our society was not created on the drawing board and so, for better or worse, it has to take on the legacy and burdens of the past: rife with plundering and discrimination, segregation and stratification; fraught with bloodbaths, lynchings and gas chambers; marked by hatred, chaos and instability.

This legacy, sadly, comes hand in hand with structures of disadvantage, marginalisation and inequality, which are extremely hard to remedy. There may be no entirely harmonious solution to this basic conflict. The moral crisis we are in now is a reaction to this tension. No one can say for sure if and how we will resolve and ultimately survive it.

A modern moral crisis

'Things fall apart; the centre cannot hold,' writes W. B. Yeats in his poem 'The Second Coming'. And indeed, only people who have had their head in the clouds might be blissfully unaware of the cultural upheavals of recent years. Others with their feet on the ground, though, cannot help but notice that something new is happening: morality seems to be boiling over. Our moral vocabulary has become mangled, combining a more relentless adherence to our judgements with less forgiveness from those who judge. We have a term for it: the 'culture wars'. In their trenches we see arch-enemies armed to the teeth with indignation and resentment fighting over how our present day should be interpreted, how our past should be understood and how our future should be shaped.

In current discourse, this crisis has intensified in the debate over the now fraught term 'wokeness'. In the second half of the twentieth century, attempts were made to build an inclusive society that would not deprive its members of benefits and privileges on the basis of morally arbitrary traits such as race, gender or socio-economic background.

Even today, this ideal is still accepted and considered sensible almost everywhere. At the same time, in recent decades frustration has grown about the *implementation* of this ideal being so long in coming. Since the abolition of the Jim Crow laws in the mid-1960s, Black and white populations in the United States have been politically and socially equal – formally, that is. Nonetheless, white Americans are still significantly wealthier than the Black population. A similar story plays out in Europe: in Germany, for example, people with a migration background are only half as wealthy as the average person.[3] On average, women earn 18 per cent less than men, and socio-economic mobility is stagnating.[4]

These socio-political inequalities are increasingly perceived as unacceptable. But how have these problems persisted when racist prejudices and sexist chauvinism have, objectively, decreased dramatically and are largely socially ostracised relative to, say, a century ago?[5] It has become increasingly clear, particularly in more recent decades, that social injustice, rather than primarily being preserved by the prejudices, aversions and discriminatory actions of individual people, is kept alive by overarching social structures that are deeply woven into the fabric of society.

To eliminate these systemic forms of disadvantage and marginalisation, they must first be made visible. 'Stay woke' quickly became a slogan: stay alert to the mechanisms of oppression and discrimination so fundamental that they often go unnoticed.

Some see wokeness as the only remaining means of achieving a just society by making everyone, and particularly disadvantaged minorities, aware of the reality of their marginalisation, so it can be overcome once and for all with one final show of strength. Others consider wokeness to be the end of Western civilisation, labelling it as hypersensitive, indignant rhetoric that is trying to undermine the foundations of a free society with bans on thought and speech.

Everything that characterises the moral matrix of late modernity is rolled into one in the phenomenon that is wokeness: the call for justice and freedom; the question of the meaning of identity and group membership; the problem of distribution of power, property and privilege; the battle over our society's symbolic infrastructure; the limits of what can be said. I hesitate even to use the word 'wokeness', which is now usually used ironically or even pejoratively, and very rarely without cynicism.

Originally this term, which was first coined decades ago in the African American community and found its way into the mainstream, was a call to all members of marginalised groups and their allies to remain attentive to the often invisible or generally accepted reality of racist, sexist or ableist discrimination. In social and traditional media, the term gained prominence a few years ago, especially after the murder of Michael Brown by police officer Darren Wilson in Ferguson, Missouri, in August 2014.[6] Conversely, critics use the term to mock the moral outrage of disadvantaged groups as a hysterical show of anxiety more concerned with the hypocritical, superficial display of their own righteousness than with genuine justice.

The cultural moment we are in is the result of a combination of mechanisms and factors that have shaped our norms and values throughout human history. Which demands, claims and worries are justified, and which are not? How can the moral grammar of these opposing approaches be resolved? Which elements of the history of good and evil will be pieced together again?

Waking up

The time of reckoning would probably have come earlier if the intellectual world had not needed to turn its attention to global terrorism and the crisis-prone volatility of the financial markets after the 9/11 attacks in 2001 and the financial crisis in 2008. Even without these events, a similar development would probably have been inevitable at some point: the internet's disruptive forces would sooner or later have put racist and sexist discrimination problems firmly on the agenda. Such are the long-term effects of the 'silent revolution': as societies become more economically prosperous and politically stable, people's support for 'emancipative' values such as liberty and equality, tolerance, diversity and self-expression increases.[7] Wealthier regions with (more or less) well-functioning political institutions inevitably bring about progressive moral shifts.

In the blogosphere of the 2000s, there was a huge focus, initially, on the divisive effects of religion.[8] With the sober authority of people who were always already in possession of the truth, and armed with nothing but keyboards, those who had quickly identified the internet as their new home soon began to assure themselves of their superior, clear-headed rationality by declaring the most foolish dogmas of religious worldviews to be intellectually unsatisfactory, especially those of the American evangelicals. They spent their days inventing pseudo-religions such as the Flying Spaghetti Monster to parody traditional religions' most bizarre narratives and, when that did not work, playing the schoolmaster by pointing out to practising Christians or Muslims why the Immaculate Conception could scarcely have happened as they had imagined. It should come as no surprise that this strategy wasn't effective.

Female participants in this discourse soon realised that the attempts at flirting on online forums from nerds who rarely saw the light of day were usually pretty clumsy. When they responded with disinterest or rejection, the truce was over, and the atmosphere often descended into open misogyny. This made female intellectuals more sensitive to the toxically abusive world women have to navigate on a daily basis.

But at some point, it became apparent that discrimination is actually *intersectional*: disadvantage accumulates, overlaps and intensifies, and although women have their cross to bear, their plights often pale in comparison to the forms of marginalisation that Black, lesbian, disabled and poor women have to endure. Social injustice problems beyond feminism increasingly became the focus of attention. New social movements such as Black Lives Matter, motivated by cases of police brutality and abuse being reported with horribly tiresome regularity, began to direct their social critique to the overshadowing hardships of people of colour.

The woke movement began in the US and, as a Western hegemon, North America once again took up the role of the West's cultural beacon and its vanguard of crisis, as a place where the ruptures and upheavals that make up the current social and intellectual landscape surfaced with the most ferocious urgency and under the pressure of a particularly malignant hysteria.

Wokeness is described by its detractors as the ultimate beacon signifying the final demise of the golden era of freedom and rule of law. In reality, efforts to track down and eliminate the symbolic skeletons in our cultural closet, our language and our thoughts are nothing new, but actually only the spectre of political correctness that was already haunting modern societies and providing a livelihood for journalists and hacks.

Both the problem and the objective of political correctness are here to stay: the more developed modern societies are, the harder it becomes to change them, and the more unwieldy and unmanageable they become. As long as this remains the case – and there is some evidence that it will be for quite some time – social injustices will become increasingly difficult to remedy via political institutions and means. But there seems to be enough wealth at hand to eliminate them with the snap of a finger, so what on earth is going on here? Who are the shady characters who have an interest in sabotaging social progress so unscrupulously? And what is preventing the silent majority from grabbing their pitchforks and heading towards the castle?

The feeling of powerlessness that comes from not being able to achieve fair conditions right away eventually made it impossible to resist the allure of changing things that *could* be reformed with relative immediacy and ease. For urban elites, this means changes to *the way they talk* – which is far easier to alter, unlike recalcitrant institutions, ingrained habits and an inert infrastructure.

Language, as many of us know from cultural studies, shapes thought, and if no one tries to overthrow the blatant injustices surrounding us, it stands to reason that we must be being held captive by noxious ideological thought patterns. It is up to us to 'show the fly the way out of the fly-bottle', as Wittgenstein put it.[9] On top of this, we also have the alluring, numbing, comforting narcotics of the culture industry's opium dens, hypnotically binding the majority to their passivity.[10] So from this point on, society's symbolic superstructure becomes the battleground for a culture war, predominantly within educated circles.[11] When you insist that language is everything, it is not much of a step to dispute whether or not birds' names are racist, as if questions of ornithological nomenclature were actually a matter of life and death.[12]

This shift in focus to linguistic and symbolic issues, rather than systemic and institutional change, has been accelerated by the fact that social injustices are often identified first in academic milieus keen on innovation, where nothing holds more prestige than having a new social pathology named after you.[13] By virtue of their profession, academics find it easy to introduce and use bizarre neologisms, which are then imposed on other people under the guise of moral concern, even though it might be harder for them to adopt new jargon: most people do not spend all their time hanging around in the corridors of NYU just so they can keep up with the latest moral vocabulary.

This inevitably leads to polarisation between people who are increasingly vocal in their calls for compliance with the new language rules and people who feel more and more patronised and judged as a result. Meanwhile, the next generation is already solving the problem, at least in part, by absorbing the cultural elite's language norms as its moral mother tongue. But for this generation, the phenomenon will repeat itself in the following cycle. Political correctness or wokeness is both an irreplaceable driver of moral progress and (for many) ineradicably annoying. There is no entirely conciliatory – or, most importantly, definitive – solution in sight.

This fervent call for social justice is particularly attractive to disaffected elites, who embrace the socially destabilising effects of progressive jargon as a welcome outlet for expressing their own disappointments in life. Sometimes in a society, from ancient Rome via Qing dynasty China to Western societies in the early twenty-first century, structural or demographic conditions can lead to 'elite overproduction'.[14] An entire cohort of highly educated people intellectually armed to the hilt and overwhelmed by high parental expectations enters adulthood with high hopes and brilliant university degrees, only to find that the light at the end of the tunnel is actually an oncoming train rather than a bursting treasure chest. The brutal rivalry in the hamster wheel of having to prove themselves is never-ending, as everyone else is just as well educated, and the implicit assurance that illustrious university degrees seamlessly convert into six-figure salaries turns out to be a gross exaggeration. The number of good, high-prestige jobs is limited, and the majority inevitably come away empty-handed.

At some point, this created the impression for these highly educated – and often highly privileged – elites that something is fundamentally wrong with society. But 'despite the conditions being ideal, I haven't managed to be as successful as I'd hoped, so I'm consumed by envy and resentment' is not really the best political slogan to evoke solidarity and sympathy. And so it is better to claim to be the advocate of the downtrodden, and to mouth subversive slogans, demanding a complete reorganisation of society on other people's behalf – and of course *never* on one's own. If, as a collateral gain, they can outmanoeuvre a competitor for that coveted position in the editorial office or law firm because they had not added their preferred pronouns to their social media bio in time – even better.

Among wealthy white people in particular, this situation is leading to a kind of 'psychodrama', with those who beat themselves up about the existing social injustices, those who would rather pay less attention to the injustices and carry on their lives unchallenged and a small group of Black intellectuals who side with either one narrative or the other all ending up pitted against each other.[15] Meanwhile, the actual, material situation for the socially disadvantaged is not changing one iota.

From a conservative point of view, these phenomena are dismissed as symptoms of typically liberal arrogance which must be condemned as evidence of the left's latent totalitarian moralistic compulsion to control people. While this is an ingenious PR strategy, it is completely out of touch with reality. The conservative mainstream has always had its own forms of political correctness, from the US 'support our troops' to the British remembrance poppy and the German obsession with not having speed limits on the autobahn. The difference is that these forms of identity politics converge with the establishment's interests and ideologies and are therefore perceived as normal, healthy and a matter of course. 'Political correctness', in other words, is being touted as a threat to free speech precisely because its interests do *not* align with those of the establishment.

The term 'identity politics' was first coined in 1977 by the Combahee River Collective, an organisation of Black, socialist and feminist social justice activists.[16] But identity politics in the name of groups that are marginalised, disenfranchised and deprived is invariably portrayed (by the right) as iconoclastic incitement that needs to be nipped in the bud before anarchic left-wingers start to meddle in other people's affairs, expropriate the masses and remind the common man on the street not to beat his wife. It's a slippery slope! 'Communism means everything is chopped to bits,' as Kurt Tucholsky once put it, has long been one of the bourgeoisie's most persistent moral panics.[17]

Opponents to wokeness make the (widespread) mistake of extrapolating existing trends to infinity. The effects the woke project, in its current form, will have for our society are almost always confused with the question of the effects it *would have* if it were pursued indefinitely and fully implemented. Regardless of whether or not this would be a good thing, it is simply not going to happen. Wokeness will remain, but only in a weaker, tamer form; it will eventually become endemic, changing its shape in the process.

The endgame will look something like this: first, wokeness will be watered down and absorbed by capitalism and meritocracy – just as the student revolts of the late 1960s once called for the end of the capitalist system, only to eventually become its slightly more alternative accomplices, so wokeness will find its way into boardrooms, publishing houses, film studios and parliamentary backrooms, where it will survive but also become neutralised and stripped of its most radical manifestations. As a rule, the elite always find a way to incorporate flourishing social movements and adapt them to their own interests – just look at the trend of greenwashing.[18] The West's downfall, both feared and longed for, will therefore fail to materialise. Instead, we will get more women in positions of leadership and more leading roles for Asian and trans people, for example. These will be good, and long-overdue, developments.[19]

Second, wokeness is an important export of Western culture.[20] The effects of political correctness will, to a large extent, be beneficial on this front too. At the end of the day, it is not that important which radical ideas are represented in the theory seminars at Yale, Cambridge or Humboldt University. But if the woke movement can contribute to Belgium's reckoning with its colonial past and can reinforce women's rights in Arab countries, it will have at least partially fulfilled its purpose.

Stay woke

Why is wokeness hated so much? The passionate rejection that the phenomenon has experienced from the outset from large parts of society stems, it seems, from a combination of two factors. The first is the moralistic furore used to promote it. Most of society does not perceive itself as racist – often wrongly, of course – and reacts very poorly to the accusation that it is marked with this flaw through complicity with racist structures, like an original sin. Racism, the suggestion goes, remains impossible to eradicate or can only be remedied, if at all, through constant penitence, soul-searching and flagellation. This, of course, is not too appealing a prospect.

The other factor is the suspicion already mentioned above: the idea that the politically correct agenda is ultimately an elite project from smart alecks and goody-two-shoes who keep coming up with new linguistic landmines to signal that they belong to the moral avant-garde, which always knows itself on the right side of history, and who behave insincerely and self-righteously when they are fighting for political Pyrrhic victories with cheap hashtags, even though it is ultimately only about individual status gains. Nobody wants to be judged by (alleged) hypocrites.

The twentieth century sought to expand the circle of morality by neutralising the dangers of group thinking through a logic of institutional prevention and by demoralising unjustified taboos. To complete this dynamic, hidden unjust structures should now be *moralised* so they can become visible and be removed.

The basic paradox of wokeness, and many inclusive moral movements, is that the norms and values on which they are based are inextricably linked to the socio-economic context they seek to criticise, reject or overcome. Protecting minorities, calling for social justice and demanding equality, anti-discrimination and anti-racism are ideals that are especially prominent in WEIRD societies. Discrimination, exploitation, subjugation, genocide and inequality are *the default*, both historically and in the present, global sense (beyond simple, prehistoric tribal societies). The paradox of wokeness is that in its most extreme manifestations, spurred on by moral hypersensitisation, it could begin to reject the one major form of society that has ever made an imperfect, but at least serious, attempt to overcome the moral deficits it rightly sees as such. At its fringes, wokeness becomes an autoimmune disorder: a desire for moral improvement, which is intrinsically worth striving for, begins to question the foundations that allowed this desire to arise in the first place.

People who flatly reject wokeness and political correctness make the complementary mistake. The basic paradox of anti-wokeness is that it sees Western civilisation's enemies as being those who insist on the full and complete implementation of the very values and norms that make up that civilisation. There is no doubt that the moral goals of inclusive movements are good and right. Everyone agrees that in a modern society, ethnicity, skin colour, sexual orientation, physical health or social background should not affect a person's fate. The only cause for disagreement is on the means by which these objectives are to be achieved. There is an enormous, as yet unrealised, potential for reconciliation among reasonable people.

Supporters of wokeness underestimate the fact that their school of thought, like any other social movement in the name of socio-political progress, is not immune to strategic problems: woke vocabulary, once it has taken hold, can be adopted by problematic actors and become vulnerable to free-riders who fabricate a facade of moral sensitivity to disguise objectively harmful behaviour. Terms such as 'pinkwashing' or 'greenwashing' make it clear that we should not be fooled when global oil companies try to compensate for their devastating environmental record by ensuring 50 per cent of their board members are queer (pinkwashing), posting #TimesUp and getting a few trees planted here and there (greenwashing).[21] The social elite, as we have already seen, almost always finds a way to exploit new movements for its own purposes, and radical chic has been around since the composer Leonard Bernstein held a fundraiser for the Black Panthers in his fourteen-room penthouse at the top of 895 Park Avenue.[22]

Inclusion has its own dialectic. Every institution, every new discourse and every innovative social practice always creates new niches for people who send the right moral signals but in reality pursue anything but noble goals. Emancipatory movements generate their own counterforces in this way when the inclusive vocabulary of equality and identity is co-opted by de facto anti-inclusive movements. Sexually frustrated incels – 'involuntary celibates' – or men's rights activists use the language of redistribution and marginalisation when they try to claim an enforceable right to sexual affection because of the allegedly unjust discrimination against shy or unattractive people. People with disabilities should not be discriminated against; but what about awkward young men? Who is prepared to listen to their worries and cater to their needs? Who will go to bed with them, despite their bad breath and dull personalities?

The fact that there is a mismatch between the amount of sex young men would like to have and the amount they actually have is about as trivial as it gets. But with the spread of social media, this fact developed unexpected social impact. The vast majority of boys have always had to survive extended dry spells before finding a partner to fulfil their physical needs to a lesser or greater extent. But every man had to deal with it somehow, on his own. With the dawn of the internet, the situation changed dramatically. Suddenly, sexually frustrated teenagers, armed with the ability to come together on forums to complain about their suffering, realised they were not alone – 'There are millions of us! We are a new oppressed minority that nobody cares about!' They began to sense a conspiracy, with a few sexually active men – known as Chads – monopolising the few sexually desirable women, the Stacys. It seemed to them that most men were betas condemned to permanent sexlessness. The psychological core of right-wing conservatism has always been the resentment of the sexually frustrated, and so the solution seemed clear to them: those women had to be taught the blessings of the good old patriarchy again.

The alt-right movement, which was founded in around 2010 by Richard Spencer with a view to reinstating 'white supremacy' under the label 'Alternative Right', was not slow to ask why a special solidarity among Black people and a special emphasis on Black cultural identity should be something to strive for, but why something similar for the ethnonational identity of white Americans of European descent should somehow be inappropriate. There seemed to be, according to him, a double standard: the African American community is allowed to celebrate its particular values and idiosyncrasies; why not 'us', too? These are tricky strategies that mobilise racist or sexist resentment under the guise of equality, and Spencer took both metaphorical and literal beatings for them.[23]

Which aspects of the right-wing backlash were really meant seriously, and which were simply provocation, where the ends eventually justified almost every means?[24] In the case of many adolescents, what's left to rebel against when your former hippie parents don't have a problem with drugs and premarital sex? Not infrequently, this next step has consisted of swastikas, crude misogyny and confessions of murder fantasies. Much of it was only ever meant ironically, or more precisely meta-ironically: the irony being to leave it unclear what was really meant ironically and what was not. Unfortunately, some people who had been in on the joke forgot that you have to be careful who you pretend to be, because at some point you become who you pretend to be.

Many, once they'd shed their ironic pose, became real Nazis or real misogynists (and often both).

Almost every social grouping, both right- and left-wing, has to struggle with the problem of extremism inflation, particularly as those few extremists end up dominating discourse. A group's ideology inevitably ends up being dominated by the people who represent the most extreme version of that ideology, and beyond a certain point, this extreme version eventually becomes the new normal. Anyone who wants to join the group or move up within it must be able to demonstrate a particular loyalty to the cause, and that usually means escalating this radicalisation loop even more. From there, it is only a small step to proclaiming that Kim Jong Un can teleport or that the 'Führer' is infallible. Vanishingly few actually believe this nonsense, or indeed that anyone else believes it. But ideological extremism becomes a costly signal, as it is designed to build trust within groups by burning bridges with common sense – and with others – and further consolidating the group's bonds.

This phenomenon of expressing ideological extremism to signal one's belonging to a group can be found across the political spectrum. Some people may deny the existence of climate change, others question whether vaccinations work, while others again might believe that a cabal of Jews controls the world economy. And every social movement will always need to grapple with the quacks, charlatans, fools and disturbed characters it attracts.

Every society has its unjustly disadvantaged and unjustly advantaged. Reducing these social injustices remains one of the modern age's key battles. As soon as this is attempted, there will always be cases where it is exploited. When members of marginalised groups receive particular support or attention, other people are quick to recognise the incentives to exaggerate or invent their own victim status for personal gain. In extreme cases, this can result in a sort of social Munchausen syndrome:[25]

Rachel Dolezal, aka Nkechi Amare Diallo, a white, blue-eyed woman of Central European descent from Montana, pretended to be an African American activist for years; Jessica Krug, a white Jewish woman from Kansas, fought under the name of 'Jess La Bombalera' against the gentrification of East Harlem or, as she called it using the slang of the heavily represented Hispanic population there, 'el Barrio'. Cases like this are extremely rare. But they are likely to undermine confidence in the woke movement's inclusive goals. Most people who speak of their oppression are, of course, not liars, cheats or mentally unstable individuals. But every new social practice creates new incentive structures and new niches, and these niches are sometimes abused.

Incentive structures like these also explain why our moral vocabulary is subject to semantic shifts that gradually reduce its accuracy. Terms such as 'violence', 'trauma' and 'abuse' have enormous impact, and yet their meaning has been increasingly diluted over time. A person who claims to have been traumatised or a victim of violence makes a powerful moral accusation and demands to be listened to and have their violation taken seriously. No matter how unconscious it may be, the temptation to profit from the alarming power of these words is great, particularly in fringe cases. In psychology, this is referred to as 'concept creep': a creeping conceptual shift.[26] Some who want to come across as particularly sensitive and morally uncompromising, for example, are quick to claim that the rape scenes in Ovid's *Metamorphoses* triggered their trauma. This tendency to wallow in our own vulnerability is not exactly a positive development, when we know that trauma ought to be overcome and processed rather than cultivated and amplified.[27]

Stretching moral categories' semantic boundaries carries an illiberal potential that rightly makes critics of wokeness nervous – and ought to be recognised by its advocates.[28] Liberal societies are characterised by the fact that there is a presumption of freedom: what is not forbidden is permissible, bans must be justifiable with good reasons, and an individual's freedom may only be restricted to protect third parties.[29] Violent acts are therefore forbidden (except in cases of self-defence), but offensive *statements* (with a few exceptions) are not, because while mere words can be hurtful, they do not cause anyone real harm. The result of this is a strict norm of freedom of speech. However, the moment the semantic boundaries of concepts such as 'harm' are softened to the extent that making certain verbal utterances is considered 'violence', far-reaching restrictions on freedom of speech can be justified. It is wrong and hurtful to deny that trans women are 'real' women. But it is dangerous to believe that this claim, in and of itself, inflicts the kind of *violence* on anyone that crosses the boundaries of free speech.

Concept creep is exacerbated by a phenomenon known as 'prevalence-induced concept change': the more rarely something occurs, the more often we see it.[30] 'Aggression' was, until recently, reserved for obvious physical or verbal threats and attacks; the more peaceable, domesticated and cooperative a society becomes, the more the objective frequency of 'genuine' aggression decreases, leading us to apply the label 'aggression' to milder and milder instances. In a classic case of 'the boy who cried wolf', we should therefore take care in using terms with serious moral weight excessively, because people who use these concepts' power too often will take away their power completely at some point.

An ambivalent dynamic emerges: on the one hand, our moral standards are *supposed to* become stricter, our tolerance to hurtful behaviour *ought to be* lower: if anything, increasing sensitivity to moral wrongs is moral progress, and accusing others of being too unforgiving about bad behaviour has an air of paradox – because what are we supposed to do? Become more relaxed about rape and murder?

On the other hand, an excessively generous and lax use of morally charged terms can deprive them of their clout, which in turn invites accusations that those who wield them are emotionally immature 'snowflakes' who ought to pull them-selves together instead of feeling constantly attacked and 'melting' at the slightest touch.

It is difficult to define the limits of what can and cannot be said. Of course, it would be nice if discrimination could be abolished by placing discriminatory phrases on the socio-cultural index and banishing them from polite society. As mentioned previously, in this way a lot of the language around homosexuality has changed; while simply being homophobic is not illegal, using homophobic slurs is, by and large, socially unacceptable. Unfortunately, this only works when the attitudes that give these phrases their discriminatory meaning and emotional force also change. In many cases, when a problematic term is replaced by a new one that initially seems unproblematic – such as 'foreigner' being replaced by 'person with a migration background' – the new phrase often quickly adopts the same pejorative connotation as the old one it was replacing. Proposals for linguistic reform often remain trapped in a simply cosmetic 'euphemism treadmill'.[31]

Many words have intrinsically offensive, exclusionary or dehumanising semantics. Ulrike Meinhof, a founding member of the terrorist Red Army Faction in Germany, once made it clear that she regarded police officers as 'pigs' rather than 'human beings', quickly followed by the comment 'And so of course shooting is an option.' Certain terms have an irretrievably pejorative core. In my childhood, the German word 'Neger' was still common to refer to Black people. It is good this is no longer the case, and attempts to rehabilitate the word by looking at the history of language, pointing out that 'niger' only ever meant 'black', have never been convincing. 'Idiotes' once meant 'private person', and yet most people who like to indulge in racial slurs would probably disapprove of being called an 'idiot' in an allegedly value-neutral way. The etymology of a word does not determine its current meaning.

It is clearly progress that there is no longer one separate

word for people with a darker complexion – with the possible exception of well-meaning new creations such as BIPoC (Black, Indigenous and People of Color), which pursue progressive goals from the outset. But what about cases where an insulting, discriminatory or dehumanising word is merely said? Do young rap fans have to mumble over the lyrics of their favourite songs? How are we meant to relate to *Gone with the Wind* or *Django Unchained*, where talk of 'Negroes' is abundant?

Philosophers like to distinguish between a word's 'use' and its 'mention'. 'Saturn' has six letters; but Saturn has none because it is made of hydrogen, not letters. In the first case, the word is mentioned – we are talking *about* the word – in the second it is used – we are saying things *with* it. This does not cause us any problems when we talk about Saturn, but when it comes to our fellow human beings, things can quickly look different. Is it problematic just to mention discriminatory words without actually using them? Does the distinction between using and mentioning sometimes break down?

As a symbolic species, humans have the ability to imbue parts of the world with meaning. Sometimes this meaning is negative, and some negative meanings become so strong that they become taboos. Taboos are the profane cousins of the sacred; although they need no divine disapproval, they convey the same semantics of untouchability. In the context of the US, people almost exclusively say 'the N-word' now, a so-called 'circumlocution' for a purportedly unsayable word. When the *New York Times* recently published an essay in which a (Black) linguist from Columbia University discussed the historical origins of that taboo, it was forced to accompany this essay with an extra article explaining why they had decided to print the unfortunate word without censoring it.[32]

But taboos like this can have unintended consequences. Instead of neutralising an expression's hurtful effect, they can give it new power and recharge its emotional force. We all know it makes a huge difference whether someone uses a racial slur pejoratively, or whether we employ the slur itself in order to criticise someone else for using it. This is usually morally harmless, while actually using the word is morally wrong.[33] But what else can we do? The sentence 'You shouldn't use the "N-word"' is incorrect, after all, because it is the actual word, rather than the circumlocution, that should be avoided.

The current debate about racial slurs is a particularly clear example of the ambivalent strategy of wokeness to promote social justice through linguistic interventions. Overcoming the exclusion built into the implicitness of dehumanising concepts is a commendable and often effective project. But how should we behave when a prominent white person like the American singer/songwriter John Mayer, in an infamous 2010 interview, offsets his musical closeness to the African American community by remarking that someone who has never been denied a table in a restaurant can never really have a 'n***** pass' – in other words, the privilege granted exceptionally to a white person to use a word otherwise reserved only for the Black community?[34]

Social taboos like these are particularly useful to illustrate how the moral conflicts of modernity have moved to largely symbolic terrain. In a now famous clip that has been watched almost a million times, the Black American intellectual Ta-Nehisi Coates points out that not all words 'belong to everyone'.[35] There is a contextual difference, Coates argues, between his wife referring to him as 'honey' and a random woman on the street doing the same. This is, of course, correct. But when it comes to mentioning, but not using, racial slurs, this argument backfires, since it is obviously unproblematic to say 'Ta-Nehisi Coates's wife refers to him as "honey"', rather than saying something like 'the H-word', because the word 'honey' is merely *mentioned*, and not actually *used* in its affectionate sense.

That an all-out taboo on saying certain racial slurs out loud is more due to magical thinking than moral principle can be seen in cases where slurs are used *without* being mentioned.

The comedian Anthony Jeselnik once joked about Mike Tyson by saying that it was hard to describe the boxer in a way that hadn't already been the title of a Richard Pryor album (you are invited to look them up) – and no one in the audience batted an eye. Likewise, it would be much more morally wrong to say to a Black person 'If I were Calvin Candie [of the 2012 film Django Unchained], I'd know what to call you' than to merely mention the slur in a journalistic context. Yet the latter could easily get you fired, while the former would mostly cause confusion.

The closest thing to a collapse of the use/mention distinction I can think of in the German context I am most familiar with is the considerable reluctance everyone – well, almost everyone, I guess – feels when it comes to physically performing the Hitler salute, even in perfectly innocent academic contexts. But in Germany, making the Hitler salute *and meaning it* is an actual felony, punishable by up to three years in prison. At the same time, there are clear legal exceptions to this rule, such as when the salute is shown in a play, or in a scientific context. These exceptions make sense and everyone understands why and when they apply.

Slurs have a 'ballistic' quality so that even mentioning them should be done only with unusual care and diligence.[36] But this ballisticness both under- and over-generalises: the fact that the taboo is subtly different when it comes to other slurs demonstrates this. We can, for example, use the circumlocution 'C-word', to refer to the derogatory term for Chinese people, yet many would associate 'C-word' with another, different – yet still offensive – term. There is no such confusion surrounding the 'N-word', which somehow suggests that discrimination and abuse towards those groups somehow matter less. In this way, taboos can undermine their inclusive purpose by becoming needlessly divisive. Also, some words that merely sound a little similar to a slur, such as the quaint 'niggardly' (which means 'ungenerous'),[37] can acquire a problematic aura even though they have nothing at all to do with the offensive expression they remind people of. Words like this are perfectly fine, and people objecting to their use need to get over it.

It may well be that in many cases, even mentioning a racial slur pragmatically expresses an objectionable attitude of indifference towards affected groups.[38] Perhaps this is true, but the comparably small moral severity of such an indifferent attitude doesn't really explain why people ought to lose their jobs over it. Also, this explanation of the wrongness of mentioning a slur rather than only the recommended circumlocution only works as an explanation once a circumlocution is available in the first place: mentioning the full slur only starts signalling those problematic attitudes once the censored version of the word has become common parlance, so why not get rid of the placeholder instead?

The dynamic, again, is that intellectuals and activists, often (though not always) for no good reason whatsoever, start introducing new linguistic constraints (such as a taboo on mentioning slurs or turning previously inoffensive words into offensive ones) to signal that their concern for equality and justice is greater than everyone else's. At a certain point, continuing to use the expression becomes a sign of actual bigotry, because only actual bigots are still comfortable using it.[39]

Exercising empathy and sensitivity when we talk is often good, but social taboos are often morally dubious, politically imprudent and silly. Everyone understands the difference between a swastika printed in a history book and a swastika painted on the front door of a synagogue. Progressive social movements with commendable goals should make it as easy as possible for people to join them. Any movement that requests that, for people to join, they have to pretend not to understand an obvious distinction everyone in fact understands perfectly well, creates a tremendous recruiting problem for itself.

But life, as Dr Ian Malcolm once observed in *Jurassic Park*, finds a way, and as it happens, the younger generation already distinguishes between the clearly racist 'hard R' and the casual, often playful dropping of the consonant altogether. Marginalised communities do not consist of passive victims, but of autonomous and creative individuals who can reappropriate derogatory words and strip them of their pejorative connotations, such as the 'crip community', a phrase used by people with disabilities ironically and self-assuredly to claim the term 'cripple' for themselves.

Many of the concerns at the top of the woke to-do list are plausible and important: discrimination against women and immigrants, people with disabilities or in poverty is scandalous and unacceptable. Modern societies must continue to work towards making these problems a thing of the past. Yet at the same time, the moral priorities of social justice activists are sometimes surprising. The current *Diagnostic and Statistical Manual of Mental Disorders* (DSM-5) estimates the prevalence of gender dysphoria – an incongruity between a person's gender identity and their physically manifested sex – at 0.014 per cent of the population (it is worth mentioning that in some places, a diagnosis of gender dysphoria is required in order to access gender affirming care) but, whatever the precise number is, it is certainly very low. It should go without saying that every trans person ought to be able to live freely and without discrimination. However, this does not alter the fact that as a pure numbers game, trans identity is relatively rare.

The moral panic from the opposing side is even more difficult to understand. Gender dysphoria is a rare but very real phenomenon, and simply insisting that biological realities dictate who is a woman and who is a man will not help an understanding of this phenomenon or the advancement of appropriate treatment of trans people in society. It can help to make an analogy with the legal and social status of adoptive parents: adoptive parents are the real parents of their adopted children, and it would be hurtful, disrespectful and simply unnecessary to stress at every possible opportunity that they are not biologically the 'genuine' parents.[40] There may be contexts when referring to them in this way is justified, for example when it comes to medical interventions such as organ donation or diagnosing hereditary diseases. But repeatedly suspecting that a horde of sexually abusive trans women are just waiting to find helpless victims in women's changing rooms under the guise of their new identity is ridiculous and transphobic.

And there is one thing we should never forget: the most popular and effective tool in the right-wing conservative toolbox has always been the fanning of people's fears of the new and unknown through clever scaremongering about sexually deviant villains to gain support for their regressive policies.

The fact that the progressive project's moral priorities are sometimes difficult to understand is not a problem specific to the woke movement. It is true of all political movements and parties. Half a million people die of heart disease and cancer every year in the US, and 50,000 of kidney disease, yet no party, newspaper or group of activists is talking about it with the urgency we might expect, given these astonishing figures.[41] This is due to a general pathology in political discourse. Parties and social movements do not focus on the issues that are important as a whole, but on the issues that win over undecided voters and make their opponents look bad. 'Wedge issues', as these are known, are almost always, if not insignificant, comparatively unimportant in the grand scheme of things.[42] The fact that kidney failure is a major problem is not controversial enough, so it is impossible to gain an advantage over political opponents with this issue. This also contributes to the shift of political discourse towards the symbolic and cultural. Eventually, it becomes the dominant political theme *du jour* if Miguel de Cervantes is replaced by critical race theory on the curriculum of Manhattan's private Dalton School, even though it does not make the slightest difference to the everyday lives of the overwhelming majority.[43]

To racism and back again

Classic liberalism always had faith that time would heal all wounds. Once we have granted equal rights to everyone and procedures are established to treat everyone fairly and equally, our desire for justice will take care of itself. But as many activists rightly point out, sometimes it is not that simple: people who merely impose neutral procedures, equal rights and individual freedoms on existing social inequalities will not be able to get rid of them just like that. Radical injustice is self-perpetuating, even in the face of radical freedom.

So why not abandon the illusion of neutrality altogether? At some point, it seemed more promising to emphasise collective group identities so these groups' grievances could directly be amplified. White people were to be reminded of their inescapably white identity and the 'white privileges' associated with it. People of colour were called upon to show solidarity with their brothers and sisters, ultimately to consider themselves a 'tribe' to be able to dismantle racist structures and to exchange their own suffering for political capital.[44] It may seem somewhat ironic that in woke circles, where it is widely and correctly accepted that 'race' is a social construction with no scientific basis, this same social construction is emphasised and highlighted particularly intensely.[45] While emphasising a shared experience can be useful in relating to others, this overemphasis on 'racial' categories, which are recognised as obsolete, makes many people nervous, especially as it has a more sinister flipside. Reinforcing an 'us/them' dichotomy may well fuel the kind of inequality that activists want to eradicate. Who would ever think it was a good idea to constantly remind white people that they are white, for example? Is it really meant to sound progressive and beneficial for white people to be expected to show solidarity under the banner of their *whiteness*, even if it is to collectively apologise and vow to improve?[46]

The seemingly paradoxical tendency to insist on 'racially' loaded categories to combat racism is reminiscent of comedian

George Carlin's view that 'fighting for peace is like screwing for virginity'. Unfortunately, this tendency is deeply embedded in the woke movement: if being woke, for the victims of marginalisation, means remaining alert to the reality of their own discrimination, then their beneficiaries and perpetrators must recognise their own group privileges and, in doing so, constantly view themselves as accomplices of 'white supremacy'.

Social privilege, like injustice and disadvantage, is intersectional. This insight is forgotten by those who consider the term 'white privilege' to be misleading, and the most common argument leveraged against it is that there are also white people with a low socio-economic status. While this is true, of course, it proves absolutely nothing, as privileges only apply *ceteris paribus*: other things being equal. But other things often aren't equal, and the existence of white privilege does not mean that every white person is better off than any non-white person, of course. What it does mean is that in the case of two people who are otherwise comparable, the white person, because of his or her privilege, plays the game of life at a slightly easier level.[47]

Recently, a separate genre of cultural criticism has become established that throws light on the unwillingness with which white people react to the problem of racism.[48] Activists and experts such as Robin DiAngelo offer seminars on how white people can overcome their 'white fragility' by being less sensitive to the idea of benefiting from existing structures of 'white supremacy'. This, too, is an ambivalent matter, to say the least: once equipped with this vocabulary, it becomes difficult to distinguish between legitimate objections to accusations of racism and an unwillingness to acknowledge modern societies' problematic legacy. Anyone who denies having racist prejudices quickly falls into a 'Kafka trap' where rejecting an accusation becomes an indication that the accusation is justified. Many people are unhappy to be called accomplices of injustice and react defensively to it, and it might be beneficial to be more open to self-criticism here. But not every instance of someone denying being the beneficiary of racist structures in a specific case is a symptom of white oversensitivity.

As we saw in the previous chapter, with the emergence of WEIRD societies, the idea prevailed that political communities should no longer be seen as a network of traditional hierarchies and immutable kinship relations, but instead as a social contract that all members of a community could enter into as free and equal signatories. But given the reality of persistent racist, sexist and ableist discrimination, this idea seems vapid and insincere. What if women or Black people were never included in this 'contract'? What if our social contract has always been a 'racial contract' with white men agreeing to terms allowing them to profit from the suffering and exploitation of non-white non-men?[49]

Critical race theory attempts to make these ideological patterns visible: since the abolition of slavery and official segregation, racial discrimination might have lost some of its brutality; in a sense, however, it has only changed its form, becoming more subtle, more unofficial, more toxic.[50] At one time, the kleptocratic conspiracy of white Europeans betrayed itself in the slave overseers cracking whips in the cotton fields of Georgia, coordinated lynchings in Mississippi and separate water fountains in Alabama. But the aftermath of this deep-rooted racism lived on in the bitter hearts of nostalgic revisionists and the bylaws of discriminatory housing policies.

For a long time, the US policy of 'redlining', for example, ensured that African American homebuyers could acquire residential property – the most fundamental form of private wealth and one of the key routes to social security – only under unfavourable conditions and in socially weaker areas. The war on drugs, in combination with the US legal system's other structural pathologies, led to an incarceration rate that is unparalleled worldwide, from which Black men in particular suffer.[51]

As a result, many groups were only ever able to play against marked cards. It is from these structural disadvantages that the claim arises that contemporary society still owes something to the people marginalised in this way today: reparations, or some form of compensation for the injustices inherited from the past.[52] The youngest generation, only inheriting a system riddled with structural disadvantages and devoid of any feelings of guilt about them, in return asks why it should pay for something that it never wanted and that it did not cause. At some point, this creates the feeling of being disadvantaged and unjustly condemned on all sides. The fact that systemic racism is so deeply woven into our society makes it particularly morally complicated. When racism is all-encompassing, it is impossible to avoid it and remain on the sidelines. This quickly creates an oversimplification of the situation: either you are anti-racist and actively fight discriminatory structures, or you do not, in which case you are racist. Simply being non-racist is no longer an option.[53]

The hostility always shown by the majority in society towards minorities, disadvantaged groups and alternative lifestyles eventually migrated from the official social mainstream, in which racist slurs, sexist bigotry and ableist exclusion were once socially acceptable, into the collective unconscious. Our prejudices did not disappear but became implicit, and from then on, they revealed themselves in individuals' automatic, intuitive reactions and judgements, which subjectively were scarcely detectable any more.

Since the late 1990s, therefore, the popularity of psychological tests intended to make these unconscious attitudes visible has grown. The best known is the Harvard Implicit Association Test (IAT), developed by Mahzarin Banaji and Anthony Greenwald.[54] This test, which anyone can do online at home even today,[55] was designed to show that negative attitudes can be present even if we do not notice them or even if we consciously reject them. It is based on the notion that discriminatory attitudes exist in the implicit associations we create between social groups and objects or facts with negative connotations. The test measures the relative reaction times needed to associate positive or negative concepts with images of white or Black people, fat or thin people or people with or without hijabs. It can be uncomfortable and disturbing to find that we are slightly more likely to associate images of firearms or rats with the faces of Black people.

Nonetheless, the scientific credibility of tests of this kind has been increasingly questioned, especially in recent years, as they are neither particularly *valid* nor particularly *reliable*.[56] The Harvard IAT primarily measures reaction times, and it is far from clear that these are identical to real *prejudices*; also, the results obtained often vary drastically when the test is repeated. Unlike a tape measure, which always produces essentially the same measurement results, the Implicit Association Test's results can change completely within minutes, hours or days. And ultimately, its predictive power is extremely poor: a certain IAT result says almost nothing about how discriminatory a person's behaviour is in real life.

It is likely that implicit bias is real: for instance, employers are more likely to respond to the same job application when it bears a distinctively white rather than stereotypically Black name.[57] But how to rectify this situation at scale remains a very complicated matter.

Emphasising racist structures often contradicts the measures and solutions that are suggested to remedy the problem: there is an insistence that criticism of racist and sexist practices is independent of what is going on in people's hearts and minds, because it is actually systemic factors that reproduce the marginalisation of minorities. Nonetheless, the therapies and proposals for reform we see are often aimed at individuals' psychological attitudes and habits, asking them to think more carefully, act more reflectively, admit their complicity or 'check' their privileges. Criticism of racism ought to take its own diagnoses and explanations more seriously, go a step further and identify structural solutions to structural problems, even if it might seemingly exculpate the people who profit from these structures.

To be able to critique society progressively and ambitiously, we have to reconcile two things that pull in opposite directions: on the one hand, it is important to retain the necessary vigilance and potential for outrage that any social critique needs if it is to be perceived as so compelling, convincing and acute that it can inspire action and win over new followers. On the other hand, if it wants to be true to the facts, it ought to admit that considerable progress has already been made, mitigating the evils of racial or sexist discrimination and cruelty. As these two things are difficult to reconcile emotionally – one is alarming, the other appeasing – progressive discourse has descended into the theory that injustice is still there: it is just harder to recognise. Slavery and segregation are in full sight and tangible, whereas racist insults can be heard and felt. But what if, after slavery and racial segregation are abolished, immigrants and their children have become citizens of their new country and have graduated from school here and hold political offices? How do we make the remaining structures of (dis)advantage visible?

The identitarian focus on racism and sexism as the fundamental problems of modern societies leads to the accusation from more traditionally minded leftists that it overlooks the real problems. In reality, according to their theory, modern society's *real* problems are ultimately about the *material* disadvantages that some groups suffer from: woke identity politics adopts the same racial and ethnic categories it promised to transcend, forgetting that exploitation and injustice are a matter of socio-economic *classes*. We get the impression that the ruling elite would like nothing more than intellectuals and social critics quarrelling over questions of identity politics, while leaving the entire system of capitalist exploitation that has made the ruling elite what it is untouched. Neoliberals have been surprisingly accepting of the logic of egalitarian representation: filling their boardrooms with women and people of colour proportionally in exchange for the system continuing to run smoothly.

Vocabulary test

It was Leonard Cohen who once said that there is a crack in everything, since that's how the light gets in. We have reached the point where these cracks need to be exposed, and this is where the woke agenda's strength truly lies: in the creative energies that are used to fine-tune our moral compasses and wake the fabric of society from its dogmatic slumber.

This often requires new words, because we are a symbolic species that feels at home in the medium of meaning: nothing is considered real if it does not have its own name.[58] These new words are often rejected because they inevitably seem artificial and forced. This impulse to reject the new is understandable, but it needs to be overcome: so often it may seem silly, but who knows which of the new suggestions will prove viable and sustainable? And who would doubt the fact that quite a few changes can quickly become second nature to us, and end up being beneficial in the long run?

It is not hard to poke fun at the seemingly trivial differences in the proposals for gender-neutral or otherwise more inclusive language competing with each other. Should it be 'chairperson' or 'chair'? 'Workforce' or 'human resources', instead of 'manpower'? Are people homeless, houseless, unhoused or housing-deprived? These debates are, to a large extent, conducted at a pitiful level; but a dispute is not considered won if one has refuted the most simple-minded representatives of the opposing side. Here both sides owe a concession to the rest of society: the reformers a greater understanding of the tentativeness, negotiability and (sometimes) ugliness of their suggestions; the conservatives a greater willingness to see the righteous core in those endeavours, rather than sulking and pretending they have never had to learn a new word.

Which solution turns out to be the most viable cannot be predicted based on past experience, but instead depends on the free play of forces that pluralistic societies allow, not by deciding their members' way of life by order of a superior authority but through experimental competition. I myself have a weakness for the hermetic poetry of idiosyncratic neologisms that open up a part of the world that I had not noticed before, that I had overlooked, or perhaps was not even aware of. And who wants to come out as a philistine who rejects a new word just because it doesn't fit neatly into their own little world between the open-plan office and the bowling club?

Many people are familiar with the proverbial glass ceiling: the final step on the career ladder to the positions of true power and influence that many women can see, but which seems to be cut off from them by an invisible yet impenetrable obstacle. But who, apart from a small group of people who spend a great deal of time online, has heard of the 'cotton ceiling', which describes the difficulties experienced by trans women who are attracted to cis lesbians? Some of the latter group do not accept the former as real and complete women – or at least only pretend to do so (sexual attraction being an unwieldy creature). And so what started out as a promising flirt often ends at the barrier of the other person's cotton underwear, where many a progressive-minded person has had to learn that desire does not always readily align with one's political convictions. But there is a wealth of experience in that term: an abundance of pain that makes disappointed hopes, shame and sadness tangible even for people who will never share this experience. It would be vulgar and stupid not to understand this.

W. E. B. Du Bois, one of the twentieth century's most significant Black intellectuals and the first African American to earn a doctorate from Harvard, once spoke of the 'psychological wages of whiteness', meaning that even the poorest and most uneducated whites could always console themselves that at least they were not Black.[59] The privilege that subjectively comes with this is a 'habitus', an attitude towards the world and other people, a voice that constantly whispers in your ear that you are OK, that you have a right to be here, or anywhere, and that you have nothing to be ashamed of. It seems obvious to me that privileges like this exist. I myself feel it on every more or less carefree day of my life, when once again I'm not spending my time being accosted or harassed. People who deny these privileges exist are reminiscent of the naive obtuseness of the fish who, when asked how the water was, replied: 'What the hell is water?'[60]

Exaggerated resistance to appeals to use more inclusive language does not stand up to a reversal test.[61] This test was developed by the Oxford philosophers Nick Bostrom and Toby Ord and consists of the following reasoning: if you reject a certain parameter x changing in one direction, you should ask yourself whether a corresponding change in the *opposite* direction would be a better idea. If you do not agree with that, you have to be able to explain why we might be at a local optimum with regard to x.

For example, many people are sceptical about the possibility of increasing our cognitive abilities, such as intelligence, chemically or genetically. But why? Should we all make ourselves a little more stupid chemically or genetically instead? If this does not seem right, it raises the question of why we might have reached the optimal level of intelligence at this point in time, just by chance. Or are we maybe just clinging to the status quo, simply because it is the status quo?

Admittedly, efforts to reform language are sometimes clumsy and often seem alienating. But why should we assume that our language, developed over the course of centuries, is sufficient for the moral requirements we are supposed to be imposing on ourselves now? Who would seriously claim that the corrections we forced on our vocabulary in the past were not justified? Who wants to continue using slurs to describe people with both physical and mental disabilities? But if you do not want to reverse this progress, you must be able to explain why here is where it should stop. Why should the current level of moral improvements to language be the end of the story, the optimum that cannot tolerate any further improvements? This smacks of conservative partiality in favour of the status quo.

Linguistic innovations can make us perceive the world in novel ways. The feminist author Rebecca Solnit, in her fascinating essay *Men Explain Things to Me*, describes a curious situation at a party in a villa in Aspen, where a man smugly lectured her on the contents of a book she had written herself.[62] As soon as you are familiar with the term 'mansplaining', you start seeing it everywhere. Mansplaining is just one manifestation of a more general phenomenon that the English philosopher Miranda Fricker has called *epistemic injustices*, which are inflicted specifically on a person in their role as someone knowledgeable.[63]

People suffer from *hermeneutic* injustice when they are deprived of the conceptual means to adequately understand a particular experience. A secretary who has never heard of 'sexual harassment' may not consider her superior's advances to be an assault in legal terms, but instead an inevitable commonplace event that must be accepted with gritted teeth and patience. If she could understand her experience better, she might be able to classify it more competently and feel entitled to complain.

A *testimonial* injustice consists of not being adequately considered as a *source* of knowledge – as an informant or witness maybe, or an authority or expert. Young female professors are often perceived as doctoral students and doctoral candidates as undergraduate students; rape victims are distrusted as hysterical *femmes fatales*; foreign colleagues are interrupted, ignored or silenced. Mansplaining consists of a kind of epistemic hubris, in which a man's status as a masculine authority is placed above the feminine, inferior authority of demonstrable female experts in an act of informational hubris.

The testimonial injustices that befall women may only be a symptom of an even deeper pathology: the two-faced monster of patriarchy and misogyny. According to the Australian social philosopher Kate Manne in her influential book *Down Girl*, misogyny is the executive power to sexism's legislature.[64] Sexism is the ideology that legitimises the subordination and oppression of women in patriarchy in favour of male hegemony; misogyny is not a feeling of hatred for women, but a social structure: the arm enforcing the ideology of sexism that puts rebellious women in their place with carefully calibrated social sanctions. Men, on the other hand, Manne claims, enjoy 'himpathy', an exaggerated compassion for (powerful) men, simply because they are (powerful) men.

Recently, a whole range of new terms of this kind has become established, from 'dog whistles' and 'gaslighting' to 'microaggression' and 'cultural appropriation', which are intended to draw attention, with culturally critical finesse, to the minor and major injustices and injuries faced by all those who do not meet the normative expectations of white, wealthy, able-bodied, heterosexual men.

Some of them have become part of the general lexicon. 'Dog whistles' convey hidden messages: just as the ultra-high tones of dog whistles are perceived only by dogs, certain connotations can only be passed on to an initiated section of the audience. At first glance, it can sound politically correct to refer to social problems in 'socially disadvantaged hotspots'. Many listeners, however, will understand which areas are being alluded to here, and will know that there are very few Edwards and Charlottes romping in their playgrounds. Demagogues can use this to reach their fawning admirers without having to shed the appearance of the socially acceptable mainstream.

Gaslighting refers to a subtle technique whereby someone can convince another person through manipulative signals that they are irrational, hysterical, unsound or even mentally disturbed. In the 1940 film *Gaslight* (refilmed in 1944), a man tries to make his wife believe she is losing her mind. He hides her jewellery so she cannot find it, even though she was sure she had put it in a certain drawer, and he moves furniture around, claiming she moved it and then forgot she had done it. She imagines the flickering of the gas lights and the footsteps she hears in the attic to be symptoms of her neurasthenic fantasy; in reality, her husband is searching the attic at night for jewels that he once hid there after a murder and robbery. He is trying to stop his wife trusting her instincts with the flickering and noises, to prevent her from suspecting anything. Political capital can also be made from this technique, for example if representatives of social movements can be persuaded that they are merely exaggerating, or that they are seeing problems where there are none, behaving like oversensitive wimps who need to do their 'homework' or have lost their grip on reality.

Microaggressions are components of everyday interactions that may seem minor, but can have a disproportionately hurtful effect on recipients.[65] The classic example is the question of a person's 'true' origins: it is hard to grow up as an ethnic Indian in Britain, as a person of Korean descent in the US or as the daughter of Iranian refugees in Germany without being implicitly reminded hundreds of times that you are perceived as different in some way. Microaggressions are asymmetrical: they can be perceived by the 'perpetrator' as completely harmless and even friendly, but can trigger feelings of exclusion in the 'victim' with a cumulative effect. This reinforces the impression on both sides that they are being treated unfairly. At the same time the new vocabulary's progressive potential reveals itself: microaggressions are inherently self-concealing because of their internal logic – with no words that make the phenomenon palpable, sender and receiver remain trapped in a stalemate of mutual misunderstanding.

The term cultural appropriation is used to describe cases where rituals, artefacts, forms of expression or fashions that are culturally significant for a specific group are permanently or temporarily adopted or used by another group. Again, there is often no bad faith involved, but if the case in question is adopted in an offensive or flippant manner, it may be perceived as disrespectful or derogatory – especially if the act of appropriation is carried out by members of a group that shares a history of discrimination and oppression with the culturally 'expropriated'. Jamaican dreadlocks and Canadian Cree ritual feathers, Bavarian dirndls and Japanese *shiromuku* kimonos are all perceived as symbols loaded with profound significance and emotional force, and really should not be used as fancy dress costumes. The idea is that not everyone is entitled to use these symbols.

A new vocabulary creates new problems. Some conceptual innovations sound plausible at first, but turn out to be toxic and counterproductive; some are legitimate, but may lead to strategic exploitation; others are simply used excessively, robbing them of their critical potential. However, it is only by trying them out for size that we can work out which are effective and which are not.

It seems obvious that cultural appropriation – the theft of cultural property by an oppressive power – is inadmissible. It is reminiscent of colonial invaders literally stealing religious artefacts, wrenching columns and statues from their original context to display in museums and collections of the wealthy. At the same time, cultures are not rigid monoliths, but thrive on exchange, imitation, mutual inspiration and good-natured, creative conglomeration. The notion that there should be insurmountable barriers between cultures that cannot be crossed is regressive and achieves the opposite of what it meant to achieve: a gap becomes calcified between ethnic social groups where solidarity, understanding, familiarisation and togetherness should flourish. Like all the other terms in the new socio-critical vocabulary, this one also ought to be used moderately and contribute to improving coexistence in plural societies, instead of creating new divisions and then reinforcing them.

It is clear that epistemic injustices should be reduced. But how? The most obvious solution to the problem of minorities and victims of discrimination not being listened to, and of their reports from within marginalisation not being believed, seems to be simply listening to them and believing them from here on in. Unfortunately, this cannot work: to be able to believe the oppressed, we first need to be able to identify them as oppressed, and this cannot be done simply by believing people who claim to be oppressed. Independent criteria are essential if we are to avoid falling for the pseudo-worries of white heterosexual men who feel discriminated against.[66] The idea that there are forms of knowledge to which some people have privileged access as a result of belonging to a certain (marginalised) social group is the central concept behind 'standpoint epistemology'.[67] But a request to believe the disadvantaged more or less unquestioningly is easily exploited by parties merely fabricating or exaggerating their own oppression.

Mansplaining or gaslighting are terms with great cultural virality. They capture a phenomenon that is familiar to most people and that can quickly and succinctly be visualised. In no time, these terms are on everyone's lips, and are increasingly applied to behaviour that is only vaguely reminiscent of their original meaning. This leads to a 'critical shift', which is related to the phenomenon of 'concept creep' I mentioned earlier: these terms' potential to diagnose social ills is gradually being eroded by extending them to ever more innocuous or irrelevant cases.[68] At some point, any untrue claim starts being referred to as gaslighting, and every time a male person corrects a female person, it is considered mansplaining. When all you have is a hammer, everything looks like a nail: how do we take a term seriously if this is all we have?[69] When do we listen to the boy who cries wolf?

Wokeness is here to stay. For we cannot do without it: in a modern society committed to the ideals of freedom, equality and human dignity, but which has only implemented them imperfectly so far, there will, and must, always be a social movement that reports on what inequality and disadvantage feel like with the authenticity of those affected, and that takes their authority and formulates demands to help us all get along better. These demands should not be trusted blindly, but they should be listened to.

Truth: an obituary

In war, they say, the first victim is always truth. Yet we are not at war. All the same, the entrenched fronts in the moral discourse of modernity are reminiscent of the irreconcilability of nations taking up arms, unable to see a future without the enemy being destroyed, crushed and definitively humiliated. The martial logic of this discourse is damaging our democratic modus vivendi. Moral progress is bound up with truth (and vice versa).

Have we lost shared, common truths for good? It seems that we live in isolated universes governed by different rules and populated by contradicting facts. This perception is coming to a head in a phenomenon that has been discussed for several years under the banner of 'fake news': falsehoods, lies, balderdash or propaganda masquerading as serious news.

The phenomenon is not entirely new. Even a cultural icon like the German novelist Theodor Fontane, who seemingly belonged to an era that we like to believe was simpler and calmer, during his time as press correspondent in London for the Prussian government provided his readers back home in the 1850s with embellished reports, invented eyewitnesses and dramatised details, pretending to have been personally present at this or that apartment fire in Hampstead, even though he only knew about it from *The Times* delivered to him in Berlin.[70] There was an incentive structure around even back then, with competition for money, influence and recognition motivating a broad-minded relationship with the truth. And it still exists today.

Fake news is not caused by a deficit but by an *abundance* of information that overwhelms the limited information process-ing skills of even the most sophisticated citizens. This leads to disorientation – and a desire to escape it. Fake news serves this need by presenting supposed truths combining seemingly clear facts with seemingly unambiguous enemy stereotypes. But why are viral hoaxes a problem?

An obvious assumption is that people who believe utter nonsense will eventually do bad things. On 4 December 2016, twenty-eight-year-old Edgar Maddison Welch, armed with an assault rifle, raided the Comet Ping Pong pizzeria in Washing-ton, DC, because, misled by misinformation on the internet, he suspected it was the headquarters of an international child pornography ring orchestrated by the Clintons. Welch quickly realised the dark cellar where this conspiracy was allegedly organised did not exist. He was eventually arrested before the situation could escalate further.

But though it might seem at first glance that conspiracies create culprits, the causal order is usually the reverse: people (as a rule) do not commit horrific atrocities because they believe absurd falsehoods; they believe absurd falsehoods because they want to commit atrocities.[71] People are more susceptible to mis-information, such as the claim that Barack Obama is a Muslim, when they are already inclined to dislike him. No minds are changed: a desire for violence comes first, motivating the adoption of beliefs that justify those acts of violence. Disinfor-mation is not at the root of the problem, but lies downstream from personal brutalisation and social anomie.

Fake news is particularly treacherous because we can scarcely do anything about it as individuals. Studies show that we believe it even when we know it is fake, simply because we have heard it, and its traces can be much more long-lasting than we'd like to think.[72] Unfortunately, the potential for political intervention to limit the spread and effects of fake news is also limited. More 'regulation' is often called for as a remedy for the spread of systematic misinformation. But is there anyone who would not hesitate to entrust national governments with administering the truth? Many of us are already familiar with the idea of a 'Ministry of Truth' from George Orwell's *1984*. Once it is given the authority, all that needs to happen is for it to fall into the wrong hands – elected by flesh-and-blood people who are not immune to fake news themselves. Would you trust the man who stamps your passport to draw the line between knowledge and misconception?

Perhaps explaining the current explosion of fake news can give us some pointers. The *postmodern* diagnosis assumed that we had completely lost access to the truth because in modern societies there are absolutely no universal criteria available for distinguishing between true and false. Truths and falsehoods were replaced by mutually incompatible paradigms, world-views and ideologies that it is now no longer possible to decide between. But this is not the case: in fact, it is clear to everyone that there are objective, trustworthy truths and that there are reliable methods for discovering these truths; it is simply very difficult to find out what these truths are – and this has always been the case. In the past, it was social taboos, propaganda or religious delusion that obscured the truth. Today it is pseudo-information shared almost limitlessly by private individuals in social media. But it is important not to lose perspective: every society throughout history has had its own niches where state-of-the-art balderdash and deception, lies and untruths could flourish.

The *political* diagnosis is also incorrect: the idea was that a global rightward shift towards a resurgent reactionary anti-democratic authoritarianism creates a new need for mis-information that can brand progressive developments and their representatives as hostile agents and that can launch anti-liberal power takeovers. But fake news is not a specifically right-wing problem, as even on the left of the political spectrum outra-geous nonsense is often believed. Media and academia have traditionally tended to be left-wing and liberal, which is why there is a greater sensitivity to disinformation from the right-wing camp. However, this view misses the phenomenon's key.

The *psychological* diagnosis for the plethora of fake news does not come up to scratch either: psychologists like the Canadian Gordon Pennycook examine our susceptibility to 'pseudo-profound bullshit' and the psychological mechanisms that mean we fall for all sorts of absurdities.[73] There is nothing wrong with these studies; many people would benefit from cultivating a little more 'bullshit resistance'[74] to avoid going through life as gullible fools who could be taken in by any politically opportune tricksters. But the idea that the spread of fake news can be attributed to individual deficits in critical thinking and rational cognition cannot explain the rise in fake news, simply because the ability to think critically cannot have changed that rapidly or indeed that dramatically in large parts of society over the last five years.

Even the diagnosis that there are informational echo chambers isolated from one another, which allow us to consume and share balderdash among like-minded people, does not stand up to closer scrutiny: echo chambers are another myth.[75] In fact, we are confronted with *more* information and we have a *better* understanding of what other people around us believe. As a result, however, we also have a better understanding of which beliefs belong to 'our' group and which belong to the 'others' and are therefore to be avoided. We are better at aligning our opinions with our own community's opinions within the group, precisely because we have a better understanding of what other people around us believe. Polarisation occurs through identity-based self-sorting and group-oriented calibration of beliefs, not through social segregation. Given the failure of the above diagnoses to explain the phenomenon of fake news, we must conclude that there are structural reasons behind the sharp rise over the past few years.

In some cases, specific individuals are responsible for spreading falsehoods propagating distrust and uncertainty in return for money.[76] This may sound like a conspiracy theory, but it is underestimated how often small groups of scientists who gather in privately funded think tanks, foundations and professional associations deliberately provide the public with misinformation – often as epistemic mercenaries hired by industries to undermine scientific consensus. The physicists Fred Seitz and Fred Singer had helped to build the atomic bomb during the Second World War; between 1979 and 1985 they led a project for the R. J. Reynolds Tobacco Company whose stated aim was to obtain pseudoscientific data capable of casting doubt on the adverse health effects of smoking. William Nierenberg and Robert Jastrow, two other physicists who had worked for the US space programme, produced a report in 1989 in which they questioned the causal link between fossil fuel consumption and global climate change, claiming that acid rain was not caused by man-made pollution, but by volcanic eruptions.

To be successful, this strategy, which has been used time and again over the course of the past few decades, does not need to convince the majority of citizens or decision-makers of these falsehoods. It is enough for the scientific state of affairs to be perceived as controversial and open-ended so it weakens the political will needed to tackle certain pressing problems.

To understand the spread of disinformation, we have to remember our cultural nature. As we are endowed with little innate knowledge, we humans rely on learning almost all of our information and almost every skill from other people. To optimise these social learning processes, we have developed various filters and methods to decide who we should learn from.[77] We rely on a plethora of clues that mark an information source as trustworthy. In the present day, this includes academic degrees as well as shared values.[78] Only in the rarest cases can we form our own judgements about what the study situation and the scientific data available might reveal. We have to decide who to believe because we, as thoroughly social animals, depend on cultural transfer and adoption of knowledge.

To be able to make decisions on whom and what to trust, we rely on what is called 'second-order evidence'. *First-order* evidence is evidence of what the facts are: thermometers indicate how warm or cold it is, for example. In almost every case, however, we lack the expertise to evaluate this first-order evidence. There is literally not one person who individually has the physical, biological, geological, economic, psychological, legal and sociological knowledge needed to comprehensively examine the viability of even the simplest political proposals for solutions. We depend on an epistemic division of labour.

Second-order evidence is evidence of how to evaluate first-order evidence. This is almost always done by identifying other people whose assessment we can agree with. But this choice – who we can trust and who we should believe – cannot itself be made on epistemic grounds: laymen – as we all are, in almost every subject – cannot check for themselves who the real experts are. It is therefore often shared values and belonging to the same social group that make us believe in some people and not in others. The susceptibility to fake news is explained by this kind of network of trust.

This problem runs deep. Culturally, there is no alternative except networks of trust regulating the flow and transmission of information. We cannot help but acquire almost all our knowledge from other people, and we cannot help but be guided in this process by rough rules of thumb about who we should and should not believe, who is a reliable expert and who is a politically biased charlatan. The notion that some people are simply too stupid or irrational to distinguish true from false is inaccurate and self-righteous – because of course, only other people are irrational and deluded. In reality, we are all mere consumers of cumulative cultural capital that holds us hostage in informational captivity. The processes that lead some people to adopt fake news are, counterintuitive though it sounds, completely rational – the same mechanisms are at work that we have used to acquire any other form of knowledge. It is not individual deficits but a damaged environment of knowledge transmission that enables widespread disinformation – epistemic pollution, so to speak.

The internet can exacerbate this problem. The business model of social media such as Facebook or TikTok is, in principle, not immune to fake news: as these providers are largely financed by advertising revenue, there are structural mechanisms that promote the spread of falsehoods. Spectacular hoaxes attract more attention, generate more 'likes' and are shared more often than family photos of the latest new citizen of the world, whose crumpled face only a parent could love. Social media's financial incentive structure guarantees the dissemination of pseudo-information.

The internet undermines our social herd immunity to nonsense. Everyone has all sorts of opinions, attitudes and beliefs that are confused, stupid, contradictory or simply wrong. Until recently, these opinions faltered under scrutiny from our immediate social circle of friends and family, who would quickly let us know when we had started spouting nonsense again. But the internet allows us to skip that first common-sense filter and get together directly with other people who believe the same rubbish. This is how local epidemics of untruth come about.[79]

Anyone who considers fake news to be a problem therefore has a key argument against many forms of (right or left) identity politics that see social groups as elementary political building blocks: we should place as little emphasis on political group affiliations and identities as possible, because they undermine our ability to process information. Almost all our knowledge is acquired from others. For this to happen, we have to trust these others. But if mutual social trust is undermined by perceived or real polarisation and constant reminders of our own and others' political loyalties and disloyalties, we lose the ability to acquire knowledge from others.

As a result, even reputable sources – such as virologists or climate researchers – are perceived by many people as unreliable as soon as their political and moral 'identity' is emphasised, because the processes of measuring trust and acquiring social knowledge, which function well in themselves, are disrupted politically. The flipside of this corruption dynamic is that some people simultaneously become excessively susceptible to utter nonsense and blatant misinformation such as conspiracy theories, simply because they are spread by people who belong to their own moral or political group. So we are starting in the wrong place if we try to understand the phenomenon individualistically, for example by seeing someone as having an individual shortcoming, being largely gullible and prone to bullshit because of intellectual inferiority. Fake news is a thoroughly social phenomenon in which the flow of information, sharing of knowledge, trust and attachment to values and group identities blend in toxic ways.

A certain amount of stoicism is advisable. The 'activist fallacy' goes like this: 'We have to do *something*; this is *something*; therefore, we have to do *this*.' But not every problem has a good solution, and many have none at all. Whatever happens, a significant minority of people believes crazy stuff, and nothing can be done about it. Modern societies have to live with this fact and make their media and political institutions resilient to it – in other words, implement structural changes. There are still people who claim that AIDS does not exist, that the Holocaust never happened, that Kennedy was assassinated by the CIA, that the footage of the moon landing was shot at Paramount Studios, and that the Catholic Church systematically covers up child abuse. Or is some of this perhaps true, after all?

No platform!

If there are people and organisations who spread falsehoods, whether with honest motives or malicious intent, there seems to be one simple solution: we have to take the microphone away from these people, remove them from the stage, and preferably not invite them and give them an aura of credibility in the first place.

The practice of not offering the representatives of certain opinions and theories a public forum for them to defend their crude, offensive or untrue positions is called 'no-platforming'. But sometimes it is too late for that: a prominent person already has an audience, and the no-platforming ship has already sailed. If this is this case, the disgraced person will have to be removed from their position of influence and visibility – or maybe just from their workplace – as a result. Sanctions like this, where people are deprived of their jobs, prestige or audience, are known as 'cancellations', and the assumption that we currently live in a time when the possibility of these sanctions creates a subtle but permanent threat intended to exclude controversial opinions from public discourse, prompting a substantial number of people to exercise self-censorship, is reduced to the term 'cancel culture'.

The concept of cancel culture is politically tendentious. It is hard to overlook the fact that it is predominantly used by opponents of this approach, who see an over-zealous discourse police at work, wanting to impose their puritanical moral standards on society with righteous fury, but in reality creating an unhealthy climate of self-censorship and moralistic denunciation and crippling our freedom of thought and speech.[80] Its proponents, on the other hand, insist that what critics pejoratively describe as cancel culture is in fact an 'accountability culture', a long-overdue culture of responsibility. For far too long, old white men's sexist slogans and the expression of racial prejudice have had no consequences. Now it is finally being made clear that there is no longer any place for this in our society, and certainly no applause for it.

The Justine Sacco case is the earliest cancellation I can remember.[81] She lost her job as senior director of corporate communications at InterActiveCorp in 2013 after tweeting that she was flying to Africa and hoped she wouldn't get AIDS, before adding with sarcastic relief, 'Just kidding. I'm white!' It has never been conclusively clarified whether she was fired for moral reasons or for the performative proof of her professional incompetence as head of communications.

But the phenomenon is no newer than political correctness or fake news. In 1988, the president of West Germany's Bundestag, Philipp Jenninger, had to resign because he had shown too much understanding for the 'fascination with Hitler' and his policies during a speech to the Bundestag on the fiftieth anniversary of Kristallnacht; Peter Singer has repeatedly been ostracised, shouted down, vilified and slandered in Germany for taking positions on the ethics of life and death that many are unable to distinguish from Nazi eugenics.

We should not confuse 'true' cancellations with other, harsher sanctions. It is sometimes suggested that Bill Cosby and Harvey Weinstein were 'cancelled', whereas in reality, they did not disappear from the public eye for a few months as a result of careless statements, but were convicted of serious crimes and imprisoned for years. Louis C. K.'s career as a stand-up comedian had to cope with an extended break after several female comedians reported that C. K. had been masturbating on the phone, in hotel rooms or comedy club dressing rooms in front of them.

The term 'Me Too' was introduced back in 2006 by activist Tarana Burke and was intended to give the ubiquity of sexual harassment a catchy phrase; it became a global movement with a corresponding hashtag when actress Alyssa Milano used her public platform to popularise #MeToo. A social reappraisal of the problem of sexual harassment by men – as they are invariably the perpetrators – was urgently needed, as was an agreement on destigmatising victims and socially renegotiating the norms in interaction between women and men.[82] At the time, a female friend told me how commonplace it was just a few years ago for the prettiest young colleagues to be assigned to entertain the more important corporate guests at their Oktoberfest tables. This is true patriarchy, and although many men may find it regrettable that even chivalrous flirtation has been eliminated from their dance-floor repertoire, a world in which every woman needs an arsenal of techniques up her sleeve to get rid of an unwelcome hand on her knee with the sensitivity, paradoxically, expected of her, must sooner or later become a thing of the past.

But even #MeToo was not immune to the strategic forces that can throw any social movement off balance. There is always a reactionary backlash against progressive movements; it is fuelled when legitimate criticism of sexual harassment is eventually extended to increasingly ambivalent or even harmless cases at some point. Sexual attraction and communication cannot be arbitrarily standardised. Was the US comedian Aziz Ansari just another name on the list of male sex offenders who at some point believed that having enough power and wealth meant they could get away with anything? Or did he and his acquaintance just have a bad date?[83]

The proposed solutions have also often been based on a misdiagnosis of the problem. When women report sexual harassment or rape, they are all too often not believed. 'Believe women', as the slogan was originally worded, is sound advice. But the invocation to 'believe *all* women' that gained notoriety put many people off. The latter version is a combination of anti-feminists constructing a patently absurd straw man to undermine a movement and a minority of over-zealous activists in that movement actually embracing the straw man. Clearly women sometimes lie, too, and as with all other offenders, male sex offenders also deserve to be presumed innocent until proven guilty. Again, the whole focus on whom to believe and when gets the situation's strategic logic wrong: the problem was never that the women who described unpleasant or traumatising experiences with influential film producers were not believed. *Everyone* in Hollywood knew the rumours surrounding Harvey Weinstein were true; powerful men are protected less by sexist distrust of their victims than by the structure of collective action that makes it extremely risky to be the first person to claim to be a victim. Will other victims come forward too? Or will I ruin my career without having made a difference? This misdiagnosis of the problem leads people to suspect the influence of ominous forces, such as the aforementioned 'himpathy', to explain what is going on, when in reality we have powerful people (who are often male) behaving badly and a large number of people being trapped in a first-mover problem.

Donald McNeil Jr was a respected veteran journalist at the *New York Times* who had just earned widespread recognition for his coverage of the COVID-19 pandemic; he lost his job after it came to light that when he had been talking to a group of high school students on a trip to Peru in 2019 he said the 'N-word' – admittedly in a question to a pupil as to whether it was justifiable to rap along with the word if it appeared in a song.[84] James Damore was fired by Google for violating their code of conduct: in a memo titled 'Google's Ideological Echo Chamber'.[85] Damore had questioned the legitimacy of Google's diversity and inclusion programme by pointing to empirical studies showing that women are under-represented in the tech sector, among other things, because female individuals are, on average, more interested in people than objects, and therefore become psychotherapists rather than software engineers. Meanwhile, there are websites that curate entire lists of cancellations.[86] But what good do no-platforming and cancellations actually do?

As a strategy of epistemic environmental cleansing, no-platforming tends towards latent paternalism. Responsible citizens do not need a pre-filtered diet of information. They can form their opinions autonomously and think for themselves about what they see; they do not accept what they hear uncritically, and do not have to be protected from problematic statements or theories. The truth prevails, and wrong is seen as wrong. But no-platforming does not need to be paternalistic or violate rational thinkers' autonomy by infantilising them and pretending they cannot judge the truth in the light of the evidence available. In some cases, though, can it be justified to deny a person and the opinions they represent a platform?[87]

The concept of second-order evidence once again plays an important part here: offering someone a public audience is not an epistemically or morally neutral act, especially when that public audience is surrounded by prestigious signals, for example when someone is invited to speak at a famous university. Invitations like these generate second-order evidence that the first-order evidence provided by the guest – the content of what the speaker says – may be taken seriously and should be heard. Getting a platform transmits credibility. Depriving someone of this platform deprives someone of this credibility, and in some cases it may be justified. But when, exactly?

No-platforming has nothing to do with a constitutional right to freedom of speech and opinion. Since no one has a *right* to speak at the Mansion House or from the lectern at MIT, no one who has been deprived of this opportunity or was never granted it has had their rights violated. Denying someone a platform is also not incompatible with academic freedom, because universities and other educational and research institutions have the positive freedom – and the duty – to decide which theories and arguments they believe meet disciplinary standards according to their expert judgement.[88] The vast majority of people do not meet these standards.

There are clearly views and opinions that do not deserve a platform. Historians cannot be expected to repeatedly go over the question of whether the Holocaust really took place or whether it could be an invention of the Zionist world conspiracy to help the Jews gain their own state once and for all. Likewise, reputable biologists no longer have to provide a platform for biblical creationists. What is worth noting here, though, is that these debates have already taken place and have been unequivocally decided. As long as no new data, arguments or evidence come to light, there is no need for these zombie debates to be revived. Other views, on the other hand, are genuinely controversial, and may even be harmful, but they still have to remain debatable. There are no general rules and principles here that could indicate when a theory, argument or person deserves a platform or not. This has to be decided on a case-by-case basis.

No-platforming is not the same as 'deplatforming'. No-platforming means not inviting a person in the first place, whereas deplatforming is retrospectively depriving someone of a platform. The latter is riskier because it can generate another kind of second-order evidence, namely that a person's views are somehow dangerous and unpopular, original and renegade, cool, forbidden and inconvenient, and that the people calling for their platform to be withdrawn are either fearful cowards or patronising gatekeepers. Many people love the charisma of a rebel, so deplatforming can often have undesirable side effects, even increasing a person's credibility among certain segments of the audience – usually those segments where it is least desirable.

As far as no-platforming is concerned, something important but consistently underestimated to bear in mind is that it is out of our hands whether a person gets a platform or not. We can decide not to give someone a platform. What we cannot do is make sure *no one else* gives them one. We do not have a choice between platforming and no-platforming. In reality, we do have the choice between a world in which someone problematic gets a platform populated by fawning, uncritical admirers, or a platform populated by fawning, uncritical admirers *and us*, the people who will – we hope, at any rate – ask critical questions and dare to point out the obvious about the emperor's new clothes, in full view. Either we manoeuvre a controversial, bigoted, hateful or untrue point of view into a safe environment of yes-men on obscure internet forums and fraternities where it can gain followers, undisturbed by critical questions, or we expose this point of view to real resistance and let it founder under the uncoercive coercion of the better argument.

The only choice we have is when people already have a platform. And in these cases, no-platforming is unjustified because it creates the misleading impression that no one has a serious answer to the controversial opinion and that conspiratorial silence is the only thing we have to counter that opinion. It is an illusion to believe that no-platforming is an option. The only option we have is influencing whether someone enjoys an undisturbed platform or a platform where the undecided section of the audience that might still be convinced has the opportunity to be shown the gaps in an argument.

And if we were able to deprive someone of all publicity at the click of a finger, should we? Maybe, but this is not how it is. As a general rule of thumb with this decision, the following applies: if in doubt, go for the platform, as the epistemic, moral and/or political gains that potentially arise from the intellectual exchange of ideas in the free marketplace are so great and the reasons against narrowing the discourse corridor so strong that it is almost always worthwhile to debate an opinion freely and expose it to the critical gaze of the public. It is more catastrophic to have tabooed an idea that in hindsight turned out to be worth taking seriously than to have tabooed an idea that in hindsight turned out to be nonsense. There is no need to be afraid of the truth: bad ideas and immoral opinions embarrass themselves.

Virtue signals

Cancel culture and no-platforming are negative sanctions that are intended to socially enforce the observance or adoption of new, more demanding moral standards. Complementing this, morally motivated parties can try to send positive signals that they themselves support these standards, expect them to be accepted and are prepared to reprimand their violation.

In current discourse, publicly displaying our own moral concerns is often referred to as 'virtue signalling'. This was also initially a value-neutral term describing the fact that some people send out 'virtue signals' to express their solidarity with certain moral or political ideas; more recently, the image of the moral self-promoter has increasingly fallen into disrepute, because more and more often we have come to suspect cynical and hypocritical motives behind the all-too-public presentation of people's own moral sensitivities, seeking to profit from the high-minded tone of moral concern without really wanting to engage sincerely with the cause that is supposedly so important.

Many cases of virtue signalling are nothing more than 'moral grandstanding', a kind of moral sensationalism.[89] The problem is that emphatically sending conspicuous virtue signals establishes a practice that can easily degenerate and soon begins to diminish the quality of moral discourse as a whole: moral sensationalism often creates an unsympathetic dynamic of collective intimidation (piling on), increasingly harsh escalation (ramping up) and condemnation of moral offences that are not really moral offences (trumping up). Moral discourse becomes a performative competition to outbid each other. The underlying evil is that the self-promoter is not primarily concerned with doing and saying what is morally right, but with improving their own position within, and belonging to, a certain social group. This ends up degrading morality to merely a loyalty signal.

But virtue signalling does not always consist of a cynical act of self-expression. Articulating our moral values and concerns publicly can build trust, and if those values are presented positively and confidently, it can contribute to convincing other people of these values and help them act in accordance with them.[90] It can also play a part in overcoming harmful or outdated moral norms kept alive by reciprocal behavioural expectations and 'pluralistic ignorance'.[91] We often do things because we believe the rest of society expects us to, but sometimes the rest of society does these same things for the identical reason. Publicly proclaiming a new moral standpoint can undermine these collective traps of ignorance. Flight shaming, for example, can serve this goal if – ideally prestigious – people publicly commit to giving up their flights.

We should distrust people who offer simple solutions. If you suspect disingenuous pseudo-indignation behind every utterance of moral judgement, you may become deaf to cases where a person or group articulates legitimate grievances. And if you uncritically accept every social media post from someone signalling moral outrage, you are forgetting that one of the oldest tricks in the evolution book is disguising our own selfish interests with high-minded moral vocabulary.

Against the grain

At the same time, a movement has developed over recent years promoting social justice activists' moral goals – the fundamental equality of all sentient beings, a commitment to the weak, marginalised, disenfranchised and oppressed, a desire for a moral transformation of modern societies – pursued with completely different means and methods: *effective altruism*.

Whereas the woke programme is expressive, symbolic and follows collectivistic thinking, effective altruism is radically anti-symbolic and individualistic: the basic idea is that our altruistic motivations should also be based on the principle of cost–benefit calculation. People who want to do good are usually guided by what is directly in front of them, but the ethical 'marginal utility' of £1,000 donated to their local preschool in Notting Hill and used to renovate a climbing frame is negligible – the quality of life for the children who benefit from this investment changes only very, very marginally. But if the money was used to purchase malaria nets or fund a deworming campaign in a Central African country, the same amount could literally save several lives. Or so the movement claims.[92]

Effective altruism is a movement that goes back to Peter Singer's hard-nosed utilitarianism and is now being elaborated upon, especially at the University of Oxford. Philosophers such as William MacAskill call for *doing good better*.[93] This is basically consistent end-to-end thinking around the inclusivity dynamic mentioned in the previous chapter: the fate of relatives, friends, acquaintances or fellow citizens is no more important than that of any other person. The well-being of those less fortunate than ourselves is morally much more significant, because 'we' are already so rich and content that our lives will hardly improve from spending another hundred quid on ourselves. Effective altruism implies that we must do much, much more to combat, or at least alleviate, global poverty and disease. This might include a vegetarian lifestyle that avoids any further support of the horrors of the meat industry, and some dramatic restrictions in our lifestyle, because the consumption of most luxury goods is not conducive to improving the well-being of humanity as effectively as possible. And the concept of luxury goods is interpreted extremely broadly in this context: even a new winter coat or a visit to the cinema is included – in fact anything that does not stand up to a moral cost–benefit calculation.

The average person works 80,000 hours in their lifetime. Non-profit organisations such as 80,000 Hours offer a service that advises individuals on how to align their career choices with the principles of effective altruism.[94] Managing a hedge fund on Wall Street does not sound like the most ethical of careers at first glance. But what if I decided to finance microloans in Sri Lanka with the millions I have earned from it, so poor people might be able to buy a bike or fruit stall? Websites such as Give-Well or The Life You Can Save provide information on which charities stand up to particularly thorough scrutiny of how much 'bang for your buck' they can pledge.[95]

Effective altruism is a radical break with our moral gut feelings because its ultra-cerebral recommendations have little intuitive resonance. This is no coincidence, as this movement's rationalist attitude is met with great scepticism from the outset by our feelings. Human compassion is often a bad adviser: it is short-sighted, biased, exhaustible and easily distracted.[96] It is not enough to have our hearts in the right place, if those hearts' impulses are not filtered through the mercilessly surgical hard-heartedness of economically informed calculations.

Almost everyone will generally accept the basic idea of effective altruism, once they stop to think about it: if we only have to take on small costs to help people in need, we should do it.[97] Only very few people, however, accept the full force of the moral implications of this basic idea. For some people, though, their guilty consciences are weightier, the discreet shame of the bourgeoisie is a heavier burden for them, and the desire to subordinate their own lives to what seems good and right is perceived as acute and unavoidable. As children, they become vegetarians, and later turn vegan; they volunteer in homeless shelters and food banks, spend sabbaticals in workshops for people with disabilities and hospices, or become social workers, activists or *médecins sans frontières* – like, for example, Jeff and Julia Kaufman, who lie in bed one night and cry over the misery in the world.[98] But it doesn't stop there: when their tears have dried, they come up with a plan. Julia will give up 100 per cent of her income, and Jeff 50 per cent. After they have paid for their rent and food, they both have $38 pocket money each. Doing the right thing is hard: 'Oh duty, why hast thou not the visage of a sweetie or a cutie?' says Ogden Nash.

Toby Ord, one of the main proponents of effective altruism, has taken what is known as the 'giving pledge', the voluntary pledge permanently to renounce a significant part of one's own income and to donate it to charity. It is also possible to make this pledge on the organisation Giving What We Can's website, which was launched by Ord.[99] Are you prepared to do that? Probably not; if you are hesitating, you can always check how rich you are in a global comparison on the 'How Rich Am I?' page.[100] Most people think it is other people who are rich, but a person in the UK with an income of £50,000 after tax is

among the richest people in the world – they are, literally, the
1 per cent. And for anyone worried that the donated money
could seep away and never really reach those for whom it was
intended, there is GiveDirectly: there are no middlemen, and
you can donate your money directly and immediately to those
in need.[101]

Effective altruists warned of the dangers of global pandemics and nuclear wars before it was cool to do so: the economic
growth and technological advances that modern societies have
made possible not only gave us vaccines and the internet, but
also created new, previously unanticipated *anthropogenic* problems – created by humans ourselves – that grew into existential
risks and began to threaten the future for all of humanity.[102]
A variety of effective altruism called 'long-termism' takes a
serious view of these concerns, which are forgotten, ignored
or underestimated by most people, and asks whether we are
adequately prepared for supervolcanoes erupting, the impact
of giant asteroids, the consequences of climate change and the
apocalyptic potential of out-of-control artificial intelligence.[103]
All we wanted was never to go hungry again – but did we bite
off more than we can chew?

Moral absolutism

Social justice movements such as the woke programme or
effective altruism start from radically different moral prem-
ises and arrive at radically different moral conclusions. The key
moral transformation that we have witnessed over the last five
years consists of a tendency where both movements are deeply
united: in a moral absolutism that always views the private as
political, which allows no compromise and knows no escape,
to which everything must subordinate itself in the eternal
struggle of the good (to which we belong) against the evil (to
which the others belong), which makes every waking moment
and every sphere of life, from loving and laughing to eating and

sleeping, subject to the dark and monastic asceticism of a moral demand for purity. But like any monomania, there is something adolescent about the ethical exuberance of our current times; and that means, if nothing else, that it will pass.

Conclusion

The Future of Everything

Man-eater

> But Charles always swam alone. And before he was
> brought back to shore, he was already dead.

Neither residents nor tourists knew what to do. The prevailing scientific opinion was that these animals did not attack humans. But this was the second incident within a short time: a week earlier, Mr Epting Vansant from Philadelphia had bled to death on the manager's desk at the Engleside Hotel in Beach Haven. Charles Bruder, on the other hand, who had recently left Switzerland and found a job as a bellboy at the Essex & Sussex Hotel in Spring Lake, died in the lifeboat; both his legs had been bitten off, one below his knee and one above. The *New York Times* of 7 July 1916 reported that women fled the beach and men in shock had to be escorted to their rooms after seeing Charles's mutilated body.

There were three more attacks on 12 July, and fear gripped the New Jersey coast. Lester Stillwell was only eleven years old; Watson Stanley Fisher had tried to save him and was only twenty-four; only Joseph Dunn survived, so badly injured that he wouldn't be discharged from hospital until two months later. Local fishermen soon began searching for the animal, which they called the 'man-eater' with a blend of hatred and awe. But the incidents only stopped when the German-born lion tamer Michael Schleisser from Harlem killed a great white shark that had almost reached the shores of New York City. Charles

323

Bruder's mother, back at home in Switzerland, learned of her son's fate a short time later, in a letter containing money that the sympathetic hotel guests had collected for her.

For Woodrow Wilson, the president of the United States at that time, the shark attacks of that summer brought only bad news: his share of the vote in the affected coastal regions of New Jersey decreased by 10 per cent in the election that same year, although historians are in agreement that he had nothing to do with the attacks.[1]

Our political positions are often little more than arbitrary. Floods, shark attacks or pandemics influence our political attitudes more than we think. But the greatest influence on them is our values and the way these values determine our identity. The history of morality I have told has been about these values, about the feelings, norms and institutions that shaped our coexistence. It has taken us from the flat landscapes of East Africa, millions of years ago, where small numbers of non-human creatures struggled to survive, to a globally interconnected modern society that exchanges goods, weapons and knowledge like no other living being has ever done before.

What is next? What can we hope for, and what should we fear?

Lessons

The current moral crisis is a crisis of division, or, to put it more precisely, a crisis of apparent division. The contradictory two-pronged promise of freedom and equality that modern societies have pledged to us has never been fulfilled. The resulting frustration and indignation have unleashed the forces of age-old instincts, once again making us divide the world into 'us' and 'them'. If we want to overcome this crisis, we need to understand the mechanisms that have led to this social division. The identity struggle defining our current times is a result of the forces that have always driven the biological, cultural and social evolution of humanity.

Conclusion

The evolution of cooperation explained why our morality is *group-oriented*. Cooperative behaviour could only prevail because, and if, it was limited to a small number of people – 'us' – and withheld from others – 'them'. 'Us' and 'them' emerge because only kinship, reciprocal exchange and cooperative behaviour within our narrowly defined group created the conditions for the benefits of moral behaviour to outweigh its costs.

To be able to further stabilise our group's cohesion and to make us even more capable of cooperation, we began to safeguard the moral norms that ensure social cohesion through sanctions. We acquired the ability to conform to norms, to monitor and punish their violation. Our group-oriented moral psychology became punitive.

The greater need for flexibility resulting from a volatile environment set in motion a process of cultural evolution that made us social learners. We began to construct our own environment, populated by increasingly complex technology and institutions. Our life in the group depended on a cumulative reservoir of skills and information that we acquired from others. Shared values and identity markers created the requisite social trust. Our punitive, group-oriented moral psychology became *identity-oriented*.

Over the course of cultural evolution, large societies of ever-increasing size emerged, generating a surplus income which, legitimised by the first ideologies, was organised hierarchically and distributed unequally. Our social realms split into small ruling elite groups and a majority of exploited and oppressed people. It became *inegalitarian*.

Our aversion to inequality and domination remained. As socio-cultural evolution progressed, a call for individual emancipation, equality and autonomy was resurrected. Social norms and institutions emerged that brought about WEIRD, increasingly individualistically minded people and began to question both the function of kinship relationships as a key organising principle of society and the legitimacy of arbitrarily inherited privileges.

With modern developments, the existing inequalities and moral transgressions of war, genocide, discrimination and exploitation of an enlightened society became increasingly morally unacceptable. The call for freedom and equality for all became more and more urgent and was accelerated by the catastrophic experiences of the twentieth century. As this call could only be implemented frustratingly slowly, moral discourse became overheated and egalitarian demands began to be expressed with a growing urgency. Moral battles were more symbolic, because this meant progress could be made at a speed that satisfied our moral impatience. Social media created the impression of polarised, irreconcilable camps that either fought even more fiercely for social justice or seemingly tried to put a stop to it. Our punitive group psychology came up against our aversion to social inequality, making our moral identities even more visible. The flow of cultural information was disrupted because social trust was granted only to those who supposedly belonged to our own moral camp.

The current moral climate is due to an adverse combination of the self-same factors that have always shaped the history of our morality. We see a conflict between groups whose members are friendly and cooperative among themselves but are outwardly suspicious and hostile, defending their own norms and values with sometimes harsh sanctions and trusting only the people they identify with. These groups have built a world of glaring social inequality over centuries, while expressing individualistic values that condemn these inequalities. The struggle to overcome these injustices by implementing egalitarian values more and more persistently, such as redistributing resources or quota regulations, brought about the hoped-for results only very slowly (and sometimes not at all). The converse move to achieve social justice through a renewed emphasis on collective identities by paying particular, and sometimes exclusive, attention to a person's group identity, such as their ethnicity or sexual orientation, is currently threatening to implode under our noses.

Conclusion

Before the old problems are solved, our morals already have to adapt to new challenges they were not made for. It might even be our last big challenge before we venture beyond this planet – because we want to or because we must. Our morality has always had the function of establishing rules for our coexistence that allow us to cope with acute social cooperation problems in small groups. But the geopolitical problems we are now facing are beyond us. It remains to be seen whether we have the ability to develop values and strategies that are globally and sustainably resilient. How can social cooperation come about on a scale that encompasses all of humanity, and includes generations living far into the future? This is the first time we have faced this task: we do not know if we are capable of doing it, or if we have created a world where we can never feel at home again.

Political division stands in the way of a solution to these problems. But our political beliefs are superficial, and more fleeting than we think. They are dependent on coincidences such as shark attacks, and are, in general, less rational, less stable and less informed than we would like to think. Our politics have more to do with shared group identities than with facts or thoughtful solutions to concrete problems. But this also means that political polarisation runs less deep than we generally believe. We don't disagree – we just hate each other. This division can be overcome if we see that our political loyalties are less robust than we think.

These collective identities ought to be like a flimsy jacket that we can throw off whenever we fancy. But fate turned them into a straitjacket from which it is hard to free ourselves. Our moral values, on the other hand, are much less superficial and much less ephemeral than we think: in fact, they are extremely stable, and they are shared universally. In reality, it is simply not true that, at the most fundamental level, different cultures have different values. There is an underestimated potential for reconciliation that is hard for us to see and that is worth returning to: between the extremes of 'being on time is white supremacy' and 'we must revitalise Western Christianity's cultural hegemony', there is a silent majority of reasonable people. Collective identities suggest to us that we are enemies, even though we could be friends and neighbours who support (or at least ignore) one another. But political divisions can be overcome if we appeal to the moral values and norms we share, to be able to face the future of everything.

Fragile ideologies

Political beliefs are unstable. They are easy to manipulate: if participants in an experiment can be tricked into believing they have claimed the opposite of what they actually claimed, they can be prepared to justify a political opinion that was not theirs at all.[2]

The Swedish psychologist Thomas Strandberg and his colleagues from Lund University asked study participants to indicate how far they agreed with various statements with political content on a scale of one to nine, on a page on a clipboard: for example, 'Israel's violent actions in the conflict with Hamas are morally justified, despite the civilian casualties on the Palestinian side,' or 'It is morally reprehensible to harbour immigrants when they have been declared illegal by the Swedish government and they should return to their homeland.' To move on to a second set of statements, the test subjects had to flip over the top page; unbeknown to the study participants, when they turned this page back again, it brought with it a hidden section with the content of the statements reversed, so that if they had agreed with Swedish immigration policy, for example, it showed a disagreement (and vice versa). When asked about their choices, a majority of the participants were, without hesitation, prepared to justify the stance they had rejected in the first round, but now apparently felt positive about.

A second study conducted by Strandberg and his colleagues

Conclusion

during the US presidential debates in 2016 showed how easily seemingly extreme political positions can be depolarised.[3] The participants in the study, mostly randomly selected people walking in various public parks in Manhattan, were invited to judge the two candidates, Hillary Clinton and Donald Trump, with a form of slider system, according to several personality traits – charisma, courage, passion, experience or trustworthiness. The scientists secretly recorded their test subjects' assessments and returned them shortly afterwards, albeit in a much more moderate form. Again, only a small minority discovered the manipulated answers; the majority had no difficulty in providing plausible-sounding justifications for the falsified answers. One participant, who had shifted the slider to 94 per cent 'experienced' for Clinton, justified his apparently more neutral 59 per cent answer as follows: 'I think they're both experienced in their field. Trump is a really successful businessman. And then, Hillary has had a lot of years [of] practice in office. So I . . . feel like they both are really experienced.'

Our political irrationality does not stop at any one issue. How should we deal with climate change? What is the right stance on stem cell research, same-sex marriage, the minimum wage or immigration policy? Should the death penalty be reintroduced? Most political issues concerning moral issues have little to do with each other in terms of content: they are 'rationally orthogonal' – in other words, logically independent of each other; the correct answer to any of these questions has no bearing on what the correct answer to any of the others might be. Nonetheless, in most cases, we can deduce someone's opinion on an issue from the opinions they have on any other subject. People who consider climate change to be a serious problem requiring immediate drastic action are also likely to have a liberal attitude towards same-sex marriage. People who advocate the death penalty are probably not pro-immigration. But why is this the case, if we can actually combine these viewpoints freely?[4]

How likely is it that one side of the political spectrum will reliably take the right stance on a range of logically independent issues, while the other side will reliably take the wrong one? And what makes us so sure that we are on the 'right' side? If we just base our political beliefs on what 'our' group believes, we form our opinions in a way that can hardly be rationally justified. This does not mean it is always irrational to adopt beliefs from others we trust: the absorption of knowledge from others is, as we have repeatedly seen, worthwhile and inevitable. The problem, conversely, is that an informational environment that is ideologically pre-sorted corrupts the rational transmission of knowledge.

The American economist Bryan Caplan therefore proposes an *ideological* Turing test:[5] can you articulate your opponent's political opinions and proposals in such a way that *your opponents* would accept them? If you cannot – and there is much to suggest that most people would have a hard time passing this test – you have probably fallen victim to your own ideological biases. Your political beliefs are so intertwined with your identity and values that you can only view political opinions that differ from your own as a symptom of stupidity or malice.[6]

For example, why are many people sceptical about a more aggressive climate policy? Because, deceived by lies, disinformation and capitalist growth ideology, they would rather see the value of their stock portfolio rise than worry about the future of humanity. Or why do many people think that wealth should be redistributed more radically? Because, being work-shy, resentful and economically clueless, they begrudge other people their success. These explanations might even occasionally be true. But it is unlikely that climate sceptics and advocates of redistribution would justify their own opinions in this way. As a starting point for a productive debate, these descriptions of a political opponent's motives are inappropriate. Would you pass the test?

The lies that bind

When it comes to political issues, we become ideological partisans with behaviour more reminiscent of fanatical hooligans cheering on their team than autonomous citizens using their rational skills to find reasonable solutions to concrete problems.[7]

The Anglo-Ghanaian philosopher Kwame Anthony Appiah describes our social identities as the 'lies that bind'.[8] We see ourselves as Germans or Japanese, Catholics or Hindus, Europeans or Africans, white, Black or Brown, upper class or working class, heterosexual, lesbian or queer – but however real these identities may be, they are only social constructions; from space you cannot see any national borders, and our DNA says nothing about whether we are 'old money' or 'new'.

Our political affiliations seem to depend on which ideological positions we accept. But that is not the case. It is actually the other way around: the substantive positions we accept are determined by which political identity we feel we belong to. Social existence determines ideological consciousness. For decades in the US, the Democratic Party has been a proponent of expanding social safety nets and providing more generous funding for various policies aimed at social justice and socio-economic equality for the disadvantaged. Republicans tend to be more sceptical of welfare-state intervention, arguing instead for reducing government deficits, stressing the importance of individual freedom and responsibility, and warning of the problematic incentive structures that can result from well-intentioned redistributive measures. But if we describe a strictly streamlined package of measures to self-declared Democrat supporters and claim that it is proposed by their own party, they are in favour of it without any hesitation; and if we present Republicans with an unusually generous package and assign it to the conservative camp – contradicting their party's supposed ideological core in terms of content – they will also support that. Our assessment of a political candidate's moral qualities also depends enormously on identity-related factors: the same act is classified as a harmless faux pas if attributed to a member of our own political camp, and as an inexcusable moral error if it comes from the enemy camp.[9] As far as our political convictions are concerned, it is almost always party over policy.[10]

Most people are what is known in political science jargon as *ideologically innocent*.[11] They find it difficult to understand or even articulate political positions. They are incapable of participating in a discussion of political principles, behave in a confused or indifferent way at the suggestion of abstract concepts such as 'liberalism' or 'socialism', and have no opinion at all on virtually every concrete issue on the political agenda, from tax rates to school policy or healthcare, even when these issues concern them. Distracted by everyday demands, they are too busy doing their shopping and checking the children's homework to seriously and thoroughly address the ideological options advocated by the various party platforms. Which party we feel we belong to is almost exclusively a question of social identities. 'From each according to his abilities, to each according to his needs.' When asked, half of all Americans say that this sentence is in the Constitution of the United States; in fact, it comes from Marx's *Critique of the Gotha Programme*.[12]

Political issues are complex. Adopting an informed position on even the simpler topics requires a wealth of expertise that even exceeds the competence of experts who have dedicated their entire lives to a single scientific field. Who can really claim to be even remotely competent in assessing the macroeconomic details of European monetary policy *and* the agricultural industry's subsidy needs *and* the educational situation for socially disadvantaged families *and* the advantages and disadvantages of competing health insurance systems *and* the requirements of a fair housing policy *and* the diplomatic relations between our country and Israel and Palestine *and* appropriate defence budgeting *and* museum, theatre and public park funding requirements? It is breath-taking how flippantly we – *all of us* – form our political opinions on complex issues like this, and how confidently we articulate them and condemn people with different opinions as inhuman bigots.

Political participation is a classic problem of collective action, a prisoner's dilemma where the individually rational alternative course of action is collectively devastating.[13] Voting, demonstrating and posting on social media all give us that nice warm feeling inside of being politically active, and they mean we can reap the status gains that come with loyalty signals to our political in-group. But the cost of *my* individual irrationality and ignorance is close to zero, as my single voice makes no difference anyway. As this *applies to everyone*, we *all* consume more political irrationality than is good for our community. The Austrian economist Joseph Schumpeter summed up this phenomenon eighty years ago: 'The typical citizen drops down to a lower level of mental performance as soon as he enters the political field. He argues and analyzes in a way which he would readily recognize as infantile within the sphere of his real interests. He becomes primitive again.'[14]

The myth of polarisation

Not that long ago, scholars and intellectuals in Western democracies considered the opposite problem to be more urgent: 'our political landscape is *not polarised enough*' was a complaint often voiced in the post-war period, because a democratic polity can only survive if it offers its citizens genuine alternatives.[15] Unfortunately, it seemed, political reality confirmed the 'median voter theorem', according to which trying to win elections must ultimately lead to an equilibrium of ideological homogeneity, because each party is most likely to win votes by moving slightly more towards the preferences of the 'average' voter.

Wishing for more polarisation seems poignant to us today: in the world we live in now, half of all parents would refuse to let their children marry a partner from the 'other' political camp; in the 1960s, this would have been a tiny minority.[16] This segregation of political identities is also reflected in people's lifestyles, cultural preferences and, above all, where they choose to live.[17] Over recent decades, cities, districts and neighbourhoods have increasingly become segregated, ensuring that cultural milieus and political affiliations gained more of a social profile, until we reached a point where places like Shoreditch, Kreuzberg or the East Village consist only of indistinguishable nonconformists.

But political polarisation is, to a large extent, a superficial phenomenon among particularly visible minorities.[18] What is known as the '1 per cent rule' states that only 1 per cent of all website users actively participate and add new content; the remaining 99 per cent are just 'lurkers' hanging around passively. The composition of that 1 per cent is not ideologically neutral: it is, of course, the people with the most extreme political viewpoints who are most motivated to publicly flaunt their opinions and suggestions. With the remaining 99 per cent keeping quiet, with far less extreme attitudes, it creates the impression that just about everyone on social media is an ideological fanatic, when in fact the overwhelming majority accepts moderate viewpoints and believes that hostile ideological camps should be more willing to compromise.[19] As a result, we are getting worse and worse at passing the ideological Turing test because we attribute far more extreme and radical political viewpoints to our political 'enemies' than they actually adhere to.[20]

Polarisation does not consist of political groupings clinging to certain beliefs and gradually representing increasingly extreme versions of these beliefs, but of a cumulative *sorting* into opposing political factions.[21] Whereas fifty years ago liberal and conservative, more left-wing and right-wing viewpoints could be found in every party, in recent decades there has been an ever-accelerating reorientation of political groups and ideological attitudes. It has more to do with segregation than with radicalisation. From a partisan perspective, this problem is particularly acute in the United States, where the political system, because of its 'winner takes all' principle, is almost guaranteed to lead to a two-party field (this tendency is called 'Duverger's law'). But we have also witnessed very similar developments towards a re-ideologisation of the political establishment in Europe.

After all, political polarisation has to a large extent no ideological dimension at all, but is a purely affective phenomenon. As I said before: we don't disagree, we just hate each other.[22] This growing hostility between political camps is evident in all kinds of data, from surveys to implicit assessment methods, and in visible behavioural differences in economic games.[23] Our aversion to ideologically opposed groups is even more significantly pronounced than any racist prejudices: when study participants are asked to grant candidates a (fictitious) scholarship, there are hardly any differences in favour of white or Black candidates; but 80 per cent of all Democrats or Republicans prefer a candidate from their own political camp, even if their academic qualifications are worse. Forms of political polarisation like this are closely related to intra-group moral self-representation: radicalisation arises from a competition to outbid each other, where increasingly extreme political positions are pitted against each other for gains in social prestige.[24]

Political polarisation, even if it is primarily affective rather than ideological, can amplify the devastating effect of ideological echo chambers. If you are in an epistemic bubble, you do not come into contact with other people and opinions: you are disinformed by isolation.[25] But the inhabitants of an epistemic echo chamber are even worse off: they have learned to *actively distrust* viewpoints that deviate from the group consensus. This distinction is important because bubbles and chambers call for different therapies. A bubble can be burst by infiltrating it with new, previously unknown information through education; but in an echo chamber, being confronted with unfamiliar and different perspectives is ineffective and can reinforce people's epistemic isolation in the chamber, because hearing dissenting opinions from individuals they already distrust can further confirm their own opinions.

The logic of cooperation means we want to be identified as trustworthy group members. Our thinking is 'tribal': made for tribalism.[26] Within our groups, it is important to send loyalty signals that can be perceived by other tribe members and understood as a sign of reliability. This function may primarily be fulfilled by beliefs that can have the effect of constituting an identity – not by being accepted by just anybody, but remaining group-specific. Scepticism about and rejection of the effectiveness of vaccinations or the reality of man-made climate change are predestined to play this identity-forming role.

The results are fatal if they provoke a reaction from opposing groups that leads to a dynamic of escalating extremism. Many social pathologies are, in reality, simply collective action problems and must be understood as such when it comes to combating them. Climate change is the classic example: the warming of the Earth's atmosphere due to CO_2 emissions is a prisoner's dilemma because it is rational for everyone individually to consume energy; the disadvantages of this consumption can be almost entirely externalised, because there is no one person who owns the environment and who would ask me to foot the bill for its damage, to reduce my environmentally harmful behaviour to an ecologically acceptable level.

The problem is that it is extremely counterintuitive to view the world in this way. This is inevitable as collective action problems are self-concealing: 5 million years of biological, cultural and social evolution have shaped our minds in such a way that we automatically take the cooperative option for granted and do not see that the strategic equilibrium favours the non-cooperative option. When experts first identified alarming patterns in the global climate's fluctuations a few decades ago, they began to warn of humanity facing a very serious problem that would have catastrophic consequences: even people who are sceptical of the most alarmist predictions do not deny that global warming will have a host of very serious consequences, ranging from catastrophic losses in the global economy to increasing natural disasters and extreme weather events and on to famine, a dramatic loss of biodiversity and coastal residents becoming displaced.[27]

There was an obvious hope that, faced with this threat and the impossibility of addressing these problems at a national level, humanity would come together to resolutely confront this first truly global anthropogenic crisis. When this reaction failed to materialise, environmental activists began to intervene, but because they misunderstood the nature of the problem, they began to issue warnings about the risks of global warming ever more vehemently. If people did not come together to solve the problem, it was obviously because they were not afraid enough. So they had to scare them more and more until they would finally pull themselves together and take action. When this did not happen, the activists began to suspect the influence of sinister interests. It was clearly more important to unscrupulous capitalists to make the last profits from their businesses than to leave their children and grandchildren a habitable planet. This led to greater and greater panic, cruder and cruder exaggerations of the situation and more and more extreme proposals that became less and less acceptable to the masses: 'We have to reduce the world's population to a billion people within twenty years and all live off the produce from our back gardens from now on, otherwise we'll be threatened with the apocalypse' is not a particularly acceptable proposal. The reaction in the opposing political camp was to ignore the inherently serious predictions of concerned climate scientists. The result is that we have a number of politically influential, anti-science climate sceptics and a number of politically influential, anti-science end-time prophets who either deny the existence of the problem or propose counterproductive measures because both sides have fundamentally misunderstood the scenario's logic.

Political polarisation can be overcome if its origins are known. Our political beliefs are unstable, superficial, irrational and uninformed; polarisation is a largely emotional phenomenon: we distrust other people if we cannot identify with them; we begin to hate them if they do not belong to 'us', when in reality there are more things that we share with each other than that divide us.

Today I'm trying out my new sword (on an unsuspecting walker)

The Etoro and the Kaluli disagree on what it means to grow up:

> In the tropical forests of New Guinea, the Etoro believe that for a boy to achieve manhood he must ingest the semen of his elders. This is accomplished through ritualized rites of passage that require young male initiates to fellate a senior member. In contrast, the nearby Kaluli maintain that male initiation is only properly done by ritually delivering the semen through the initiate's anus, *not* his mouth. The Etoro revile these Kaluli practices, finding them disgusting.[28]

The phenomenon of moral diversity has long haunted the canon of the West. Two and a half thousand years ago, the Greek historian Herodotus told this story in his *Histories*:

> During Darius' reign, he invited some Greeks who were present to a conference, and asked them how much money it would take for them to be prepared to eat the corpses of their fathers; they replied that they would not do that for any amount of money. Next, Darius summoned some members of the Indian tribe known as Callatiae, who eat their parents, and asked them in the presence of the Greeks, with an interpreter present so that they could understand what was being said, how much money it would take for

338

Conclusion

them to be willing to cremate their fathers' corpses; they cried out in horror and told him not to say such appalling things. So these practices have become enshrined as customs just as they are, and I think Pindar was right to have said in his poem that custom is king of all.[29]

Michel de Montaigne, in his famous essay *Of Cannibals*, used a similar observation to denounce the hypocritical self-righteousness of sixteenth-century French society.[30] But is this still true today? Does custom really reign supreme?

The fact that we humans share universal moral values with one another can be supported not only by hand-picked anecdotes, but also proven by rigorous social science methods.[31] For decades, the World Values Survey has repeatedly confirmed that there are fundamental values that are considered binding by all people in all cultures. Personal safety and freedom, care and tolerance, happiness, autonomy and self-fulfilment are considered important in every culture all over the world. The different priorities given to these values are mainly due to socio-economic differences and not radically divergent morals.[32]

The Human Relations Area Files are an ethnographic collection that archives thousands of documents from every cultural region of the world. Using strict criteria, Oliver Curry and his colleagues selected 3,460 passages from 603 sources from this collection, originating from sixty different societies – large and small, simple and complex, traditional and economically developed – from every continent and from different centuries, and examined them for moral content. They instructed staff who were unaware of the study hypothesis to pick out the content independently of each other, and then another independent person was asked to code it to determine whether the selected behavioural patterns were described as *good* or *bad*. The intercultural agreement on values such as helpfulness, cooperation, respect, fairness, bravery or ownership equated to 99.9 per cent.[33] But is it not clear that there are radical moral differences

339

of opinion and that other people in different places and at different times had fundamentally different values from us? Do we not see, when we look at other cultures and epochs, a bizarre panorama of cannibalism, slavery, human sacrifice, gladiator fights, witch hunts, foot binding, female genital mutilation, genocide and infanticide?

Moral differences between human societies must be balanced against intercultural similarities. There are few cultures that deviate more from modern Western societies than ancient China. But even the moral differences we find between these cultures, separated by thousands of years and miles, are marginal. Confucius recommended self-control, virtue, respect for friends and parents, compassion for the weak, the significance of promises and the importance of justice.[34] The phrasing is antiquated and alien, and the ethical priorities do not correspond exactly to ours, but the notion that this is a moral culture that conflicts radically with ours and whose values are incompatible with ours is harmful and wrong, and is often misused by oppressive regimes to delegitimise external criticism.

Despite all the acceptance, back then, of practices that we now (rightly) consider abominable and immoral, we should not underestimate the degree of intracultural difference of opinion that already existed at that time. It is inaccurate to say that a few centuries ago slavery was considered morally unproblematic. The arrival of a slave ship in the port of Lagos was described by Gomes Eannes de Azurara, a fifteenth-century Portuguese royal chronicler, as follows:

> But what human heart, no matter how hard, would not be stabbed by pious feelings when gazing upon such a company of people? For some had their heads held low and their faces bathed in tears, as they looked upon one another. Others were moaning most bitterly, gazing toward heaven, fixing their eyes upon it, as if they were asking for help from the father of nature. Others struck their faces with the palms

of their hands, throwing themselves prostrate on the ground; others performed their lamentation in the form of a chant ... But to increase their suffering even more, those responsible for dividing them up arrived on the scene and began to separate one from another, in order to make an equal division of fifths; from which arose the need to separate children from their parents, wives from their husbands, and brothers from their brothers.[35]

In this passage we can search in vain for an indifferent shrug of the shoulders from someone trapped in a culture that considered slavery natural, good and right. Instead, we hear healthy human compassion that sees the horrors of slavery for what they are. Whenever *we* reject an action, practice or behaviour as immoral when we come across it in a seemingly alien historical or socio-cultural context, there were also people *there at that time* who would have shared our opinions and considered it equally shameful and reprehensible. And it is astonishing that when we claim that at that time the enslavement of people was considered permissible, we almost always fail to mention what *the enslaved people themselves* would have thought of it. But the titillating horror that comes from exoticising the past is so tempting that it makes us ignore the similarities and exaggerate the differences.

We should not take the wrong side. In medieval Japan, we sometimes hear, it was considered morally acceptable to try out a new sword on an unsuspecting walker.[36] This practice, called *tsujigiri*, involved a samurai testing how sharp his newly acquired *katana* was by taking a man by surprise and slicing into him from shoulder to hip with one blow. But *who* thought this reckless inhumanity was morally acceptable? At most, the samurai themselves, and even then only a few of them; but what about those unsuspecting walkers who were murdered? What about their families, their friends, their fellow citizens? It is doubtful that anyone other than those who indulged in it could have considered *tsujigiri* morally unobjectionable or honourable. (In fact, it is now considered controversial how widespread this code of conduct was, and even whether it existed at all. It could have been the excesses of individual murderous people, who were considered cruel and criminal even back then and were punished accordingly.)[37] In many cases where a foreign or past practice such as human sacrifice, genital mutilation or slavery is cited as evidence of fundamental conflicts of value, the situation is similar: most of the time, we let what an entire culture supposedly thought was good and right be dictated to us by the whims of a small social elite, whose cruel and egotistical aberrations we consider authoritative for that culture as a whole.

There have always been privileged social groups that justified their unscrupulous behaviour with sophisticated ideologies, presenting it as having no alternative and being unavoidable, trivialising its consequences or dehumanising its victims. If we accept their point of view, we are not tolerating cultural diversity, but instead once again siding with the powerful, letting them decide retrospectively what their culture's values were, and silencing the weak and vulnerable for a second time.

Calm after the storm?

The moral values that unite us run deeper than we believe, and the political divides that separate us run less deep than we think.

With increasing prosperity and longer-lasting peace, our priorities shifted. Material comfort and socio-political stability set in motion a liberalising dynamic towards emancipatory values.[38] The boundaries of the moral community were extended to more and more members, new freedoms were granted, arbitrary norms were put up for debate. Problematic traditions and discriminatory practices were moralised and, if necessary, put forward for abolition. Modern societies were increasingly able to afford to take the concerns of marginalised groups a little more seriously.

But many of the anticipated improvements took a long time to come, or failed to materialise. Recognising that racism, sexism and other forms of exclusion and disadvantage are wrong and should be overcome did not always lead to their swift elimination, for modern societies are recalcitrant monstrosities that cannot easily be reshaped just to satisfy the egalitarian ideals of a moral vanguard, no matter how praiseworthy, noble and justified they may be.

Out of desperate urgency, the focus increasingly shifted to symbolic and linguistic territory, because the ethereal world of words and images is easier and faster to change than the intractable, immobile realm of traditions and institutions. As the old ideals of freedom, individuality and equal opportunities had not delivered, at some point these were also declared suspect. If, in a society of free and equal people, the oppression of certain groups is not eventually eradicated by itself, it may be because it is precisely those ideals that show us the wrong way. The *values* of freedom and equality did not provide for the *reality* of freedom and equality, and therefore, for modernity to finally win this battle with itself, they must be replaced by their opposites: if the powerful core of society simply does not want to stop discriminating on the basis of race, culture or gender, then – as if in an act of defiantly bold reappropriation of the identities that had previously been forced upon people – those identities must finally be given their due.

An informational environment shattered by social media and partisan propaganda meant we could retreat into epistemic isolation, where our affectively charged socio-political identities only heard things that confirmed their own views. Without any real differences of opinion, we sorted ourselves into seemingly hostile camps we can no longer find our way out of, although there is actually a way.

What more can I say? I think that's enough. We have seen

familiar things in a new light and new things we had no idea about. A broken land with a thousand hairy beings, a bacchanalian revel in which not a single member isn't drunk, united in blood and sweat and lust; spindly fingers searching in the dust for the first knowledge; teachers and pupils, stick figures on limestone, sesame oil lamps made of stone in the markets of Babylon; we cooked together and alone, saw salvation and sacrifice, the full alphabet of bones, roots and earthen pots, ships swallowing stolen people, playing children tormenting a shiny beetle; the starry sky above and the moral law within us; we went over there, beyond the village, down to the river, took the last train to the coast, where moss grows on the stones, so moist, cool and green; we saw bound feet, dismembered bodies on stakes, stones inscribed with laws and stones without, naked people, corpses and kings with big hats, robbers and policemen, signed treaties and promises that were first broken, then made, the weeping of millions, unconsoled, unavenged, unremembered and gone forever, like tears in rain.

It's been a long story. Will we, now that it's over, still feel the same way about ourselves? Maybe one day this very big feast of feverish discord and hatred will come to an end. And maybe – who knows? – a feast of calm and community will once again take its place, unleashed and conquered by reason.

Notes

Introduction

1   Nietzsche, 2013 (1887), p. 65.
2   Wittgenstein, 1972, § 141.

1. 5,000,000 Years

1   Wood, 2019, p. 65 ff.
2   Wood, 2019, p. 65 ff.; Dunbar, 2016, p. 8 ff.
3   Pattison, 2020; see also Leakey & Leakey, 2020.
4   Wood, 2019, p. 71.
5   Pievani & Zeitoun, 2020.
6   Dunbar, 2016, p. 84.
7   Newsom & Richerson, 2021.
8   Freud, 2004 (1930).
9   Tomasello, 2016.
10 Dunbar, 1992.
11 Dunbar, 1996, p. 77.
12 Pinker, 2011, p. 31 ff.
13 Bowles, 2009.
14 Turchin, 2016.
15 Kant, 2000 (1790), pp. 312–13.
16 Dennett, 1995, p. 48 ff.
17 Mukherjee, 2010.
18 Nietzsche, 1990 (1886), p. 102, § 146.
19 Stanovich, 2004.
20 Dennett, 1995.
21 Greene, 2013, p. 12.
22 Hrdy, 2009, p. 1 ff.
23 Hardin, 1968.
24 Veblen, 2007 (1899).
25 Schelling, 1980 (1960).
26 Simler & Hanson, 2018, p. 28.

27 Fehr & Gächter, 2000.

28 Luhmann, 1996.

29 Bowles & Gintis, 2011.

30 Bloom, 2013, p. 26.

31 de Waal, 2006.

32 Brosnan & de Waal, 2003.

33 Nietzsche, 2013 (1887).

34 Wittgenstein, 1972, § 141.

35 Dawkins, 2016 (1976).

36 Stanovich, 2004.

37 Hamilton, 1964.

38 Trivers, 1971.

39 Axelrod, 2006 (1984).

40 Sinnott-Armstrong, 2006, p. 40 ff.

41 Pagel, 2013.

42 Simler & Hanson, 2018.

43 Zahavi, 1975.

44 Wilson, 1975; Smith, 1964.

45 Darwin, 1871, pp. 159–60.

46 Sober & Wilson, 1998.

47 Richerson et al., 2016; Steven Pinker, 'The false allure of group
     selection', *Edge*, 2012, https://www.edge.org/conversation/
     steven_pinker-the-false-allure-of-group-selection.

48 Haidt, 2012.

49 Henrich & Muthukrishna, 2021.

2. 500,000 Years

1   Lyons, 2003.

2   Pinker, 2011, p. 149.

3   David von Drehle, 'The death penalty is in the death throes',
     Washington Post, 5 February 2021, https://www.washingtonpost.
     com/opinions/the-death-penalty-is-in-the-death-throes/2021/02/
     05/e332c23e-67cb-11eb-8c64-9595888caa15_story.html.

4   Wrangham, 2019, p. 163.

5   Dunbar, 2016, p. 11.

6   Nietzsche, 2013 (1887), p. 70.

7   Nietzsche, 2013 (1887), pp. 70–1.

8   Nietzsche, 2013 (1887), p. 44.

9   Nietzsche, 2013 (1887), p. 52.

10 Foucault, 1977, p. 3.

11 Foucault, 1977, p. 3.
12 Hare & Woods, 2020; Hare, 2017.
13 Wrangham, 2019, p. 24 ff.
14 Hare & Woods, 2020, p. 20 ff.
15 Dugatkin & Trut, 2017.
16 Wilkins, Wrangham & Fitch, 2014.
17 Damasio, 1994.
18 Lee, 2013, p. 129.
19 Dunbar, 2016, p. 156.
20 Cochrane, 2019.
21 Boyd & Richerson, 1992.
22 Bowles & Gintis, 2011, p. 24 ff.
23 Fehr & Gächter, 2002.
24 Greene, 2008, p. 50 ff.
25 Aharoni & Fridlund, 2012.
26 Baron & Ritov, 1993.
27 Aharoni & Fridlund, 2012.
28 Lorenz, 2009.
29 Fodor, 1983.
30 Cosmides & Tooby, 2013.
31 Dunbar, 1996.
32 Hume, 2007 (1739–40), p. 375.
33 Kant, 2015 (1788), p. 122.
34 Kant, 1996 (1797), p. 212.
35 Henrich, 2016, p. 188.
36 Roth, 2014, p. 19.
37 Kitcher, 2011, p. 140.
38 https://ourworldindata.org/homicides.
39 Roth, 2014, p. 11; Lyons, 2003, p. 71 ff.
40 Henrich, 2020, p. 400.
41 Henrich, 2020, p. 311.
42 Herrmann, Thöni & Gächter, 2008; Henrich, 2020, p. 216 ff.
43 Henrich, 2020, p. 401 ff.
44 Kant, 1996 (1797), p. 106.
45 Hegel, 1991 (1820), § 100.
46 Leeson, 2017.
47 Kadri, 2006.
48 Wrangham, 2019, p. 143.
49 https://warorcar.blogspot.com/2008/09/panda-stealth-bomber.
    html.

50 Surprenant & Brennan, 2020.
51 Roth, 2014, p. 11.
52 Levy, 2015.
53 Kleiman, 2009.
54 Ransmayr, 2020, p. 69 ff.
55 Bataille, 1989 (1961), pp. 206–7.
56 Petersen et al., 2012.

3. 50,000 Years
1   Sykes, 2020.
2   Suzman, 2021, p. 134 ff.
3   Hare & Woods, 2020, p. 33.
4   Dunbar, 2016, p. 15.
5   Marean, 2015.
6   Sterelny, 2010.
7   Wild, 2008.
8   Harari, 2011.
9   Kant, 2006 (1798), p. 226.
10 Schofield et al., 2018.
11 Aplin, 2019.
12 Henrich, 2016.
13 Herder, 1827 (1782).
14 Nietzsche, 1990 (1886), § 62.
15 Scheler, 2009 (1928).
16 Plessner, 2019 (1928).
17 Gehlen, 1988 (1940).
18 Henrich, 2016, p. 2.
19 https://www.youtube.com/watch?v=BWKfJQpZtaM.
20 Wrangham, 2009.
21 Wrangham, 2009, Chapter 2.
22 Sterelny, 2012.
23 Dawkins, 1982.
24 Sterelny, 2007a.
25 Henrich, 2016, p. 57.
26 Laland, 2017, p. 215 ff.
27 Heath, 2014, p. 84; see also Ed Regis, 'No one can explain why planes stay in the air', *Scientific American*, 1 February 2020, https://www. scientificamerican.com/article/no-one-can-explain-whyplanes-stay-in-the-air.
28 Elsen, Cizer & Snellings, 2013.

29 Nick Baumann, 'Did America forget how to make the H-bomb?',
    Mother Jones, 1 May 2009, https://www.motherjones.com/politics/
    2009/05/fogbank-america-forgot-how-make-nuclear-bombs.

30 Dawkins, 2016 (1976).

31 Sperber, 1996.

32 Boyd & Richerson, 2006, p. 5.

33 Boyd & Richerson, 2006, p. 237.

34 Sterelny, 2017.

35 Heyes, 2018.

36 Fodor, 1983.

37 Nagell, Olguin & Tomasello, 1993.

38 Henrich, 2016, p. 28.

39 Henrich, 2016, p. 97 ff.

40 Christakis, 2019, p. 372.

41 Wilson & Keil, 1998.

42 Henrich, 2016, p. 104 ff.

43 Leeson, 2017, p. 101 ff.

44 Freud, 1981 (1917).

45 Schopenhauer, 1974 (1859), p. 3.

46 Nietzsche, 2010 (1873), pp. 17–18.

47 Kelly & Hoburg, 2017.

48 Kant, 2009 (1784).

49 Levy & Alfano, 2020.

50 Burke, 2014 (1790), p. 173.

51 Christakis, 2019, p. 59 ff.

52 Richerson, 2013.

4. 5,000 Years

1   Maisels, 1999, p. 25 ff.

2   Wengrow, 2010.

3   Jaspers, 2021 (1949).

4   de Waal, 1998.

5   Renfrew, 2008.

6   Widerquist & McCall, 2015.

7   A recent paper (Anderson et al., 2023) tries to challenge this
    division, but ultimately unsuccessfully. It is true that in a number
    of societies women do participate in hunting, but there remain
    considerable sex differences in frequency and type of game.

8   Manvir Singh, 'Beyond the !Kung', *Aeon*, 8 February 2021, https://

aeon.co/essays/not-all-early-human-societies-were-small-scale-egalitarian-bands.

9   Diamond, 1987; see also Diamond, 1998 and 2005.

10   Hobbes, 1962 (1651), p. 100.

11   Rousseau, 1984 (1755).

12   Clark, 2007; Sahlins, 2017.

13   Boehm, 1999.

14   Lee, 1979, p. 264.

15   Lee, 1979, p. 246.

16   Marx, 1970 (1844), p. 131.

17   Scott, 2017.

18   Turchin, 2016.

19   Morris, 2015.

20   Diamond, 2005.

21   Diamond, 2005, p. 79 ff.; DiNapoli, Rieth, Lipo & Hunt, 2020.

22   Tainter, 1988.

23   Turchin, 2016, p. 131 ff.

24   Flannery & Marcus, 2012.

25   Singh & Glowacki, 2022.

26   Graeber & Wengrow, 2021.

27   Graeber & Wengrow, 2021, p. 96.

28   Fukuyama, 1992.

29   Kramer, 1963, p. 336 ff.

30   Norenzayan, 2013.

31   Whitehouse et al., 2019.

32   Henrich, 2020, p. 123 ff.

33   Shariff & Norenzayan, 2007.

34   Cohen, 2009; Brennan, 2014.

35   Norton & Ariely, 2011.

36   Boyer & Petersen, 2018.

37   Starmans, Sheskin & Bloom, 2017.

38   Parfit, 1997.

39   Frankfurt, 1987.

40   Nozick, 1974.

41   Leiter, 2019.

42   Husi, 2017.

43   Sterelny, 2021, Chapter 4.

44   Scheidel, 2017.

45   Gottfried, 1983, p. 45.

46   Diemer et al., 2013.

47 Piketty, 2014.
48 Kuznets, 1955.
49 Piketty, 2014.
50 https://www.oxfam.org.uk/media/press-releases/worlds-22-richest-men-have-more-wealth-than-all-the-women-in-africa.
51 Clark, 2014.
52 Bourdieu, 2010 (1979).
53 O'Connor, 2019.
54 Wilkinson & Pickett, 2010.
55 Case & Deaton, 2020.
56 Smith 1976 (1776), Book 5, Chapter II.
57 Freiman, 2017, Chapter 6.
58 McCullough, 2020, Chapter 7.
59 Markovits, 2020; Sandel, 2020.
60 Sandel, 2020, p. 33.
61 Sandel, 2020, p. 90.

5. 500 Years
1   Tönnies, 2010 (1887).
2   Durkheim, 1984 (1893).
3   Weber, 2014 (1919).
4   Henrich, 2020, p. 192.
5   Henrich, Heine & Norenzayan, 2010.
6   Henrich, 2020, p. 44.
7   Henrich, 2020, p. 44.
8   Asch, 1956.
9   Henrich, 2020, p. 216 ff.
10 Henrich, 2020, p. 24.
11 Henrich, 2020, p. 33.
12 Barrett et al., 2016.
13 Henrich, 2020, p. 53.
14 Henrich, 2020, p. 410.
15 Henrich, 2020, p. 491 ff.
16 Henrich, 2020, p. 162 ff.
17 Henrich, 2020, p. 197.
18 Henrich, 2020, p. 192.
19 Henrich, 2020, p. 236.
20 Henrich, 2020, p. 416.
21 Weber, 2014 (1919).
22 Aristotle, *Physics*, Book II (B).

23   *Physiologus*, 2009.
24   McCullough, 2020, p. 193 ff.
25   Kehlmann, 2020, pp. 18–19.
26   Schneewind, 1998.
27   Hume, 2007 (1739–40), Book III, Part I, Section I.
28   Kant, 2012 (1785), p. 49.
29   Homer, 2014, p. 206.
30   McCloskey, 2006.
31   Elias, 1978, p. 68 ff.
32   Malthus, 1970 (1798).
33   Pomeranz, 2001; Deaton, 2013.
34   https://ourworldindata.org/economic-growth.
35   Diamond, 1998.
36   Tolstoy, 2016 (1878).
37   Brecht, 1976, p. 241.
38   Brennan, 2020.
39   Baptist, 2014; Levy, 2012; Beckert, 2014; Hannah-Jones et al., 2021.
40   Livingstone Smith, 2011, p. 76.
41   Hochschild, 1998.
42   Acemoglu & Robinson, 2012.
43   Henrich, 2016, p. 220 ff.
44   Henrich, 2020, p. 477.

6. 50 Years

1   Glover, 2012, p. 58.
2   Schmitt, 1996 (1932), Section 6.
3   Glover, 2012.
4   McCullough, 2020.
5   Büchner, 1998 (1835), p. 37.
6   Arendt, 2006 (1963).
7   Schopenhauer, 1988 (1851), § 149.
8   Hegel, 1995 (1840), p. 447.
9   Camus, 2000 (1951), p. 12.
10   Edgerton, 1992.
11   Sterelny, 2007b.
12   Browning, 2001 (1992).
13   Milgram, 1963.
14   See Malle, 2006.
15   Arendt, 2006 (1963).
16   Kant, 2009 (1784b), p. 16.

17   Kant, 1998 (1793/4).
18   Doris, 2002; Doris & Murphy, 2007.
19   Isen & Levin, 1972.
20   Habermas, 2022, p. 174 (translation by Jo Heinrich).
21   Adorno & Horkheimer, 1972 (1947), p. 39.
22   Pauer-Studer & Velleman, 2015, p. 1 ff.
23   Nussbaum, 2007, p. 939.
24   Pleasants, 2016.
25   Speech by Heinrich Himmler, 4 October 1943, https://www.
     yadvashem.org/odot_pdf/Microsoft%20Word%20-%204029.pdf.
26   Mercier, 2020, p. 129 ff.
27   Kershaw, 1983, p. 199.
28   Stanley, 2020.
29   Chapoutot, 2018.
30   Marquard, 1989.
31   Hathaway & Shapiro, 2017.
32   Pinker, 2011, p. 189 ff.
33   Kant, 2003 (1795/6).
34   Pinker, 2011.
35   Nisbett & Cohen, 1996.
36   Welzel, 2013, p. 71.
37   Welzel, 2013, pp. 107, 143.
38   Inglehart, 1977; Inglehart, 2018.
39   Pinker, 2018, p. 226 ff.
40   Easterlin, 1974.
41   Stevenson & Wolfers, 2008.
42   Deaton, 2013.
43   Martin Ravaillon, 'Awareness of poverty over three centuries',
     14 February 2011, https://cepr.org/voxeu/columns/awareness-poverty-
     over-three-centuries?fbclid=IwAR0d8_eC586C1GZ5dhUhPHbdq
     XNYFgMbRpD5FqkyoOl3Hmonvsn_4wQReaA.
44   https://ourworldindata.org/extreme-poverty-in-brief.
45   Hickel, 2016.
46   Dornes, 2016; Schröder, 2018, p. 100 ff.
47   Prinz, 2011.
48   Singer, 2011.
49   Buchanan & Powell, 2018, p. 153 ff.
50   Crimston et al., 2018.
51   Waytz et al., 2019.
52   Rawls, 1971.

53 Anderson, 2010.

54 Diamond, 2005.

55 Ehrlich, 1968.

56 Spoto, 1988, p. 218.

57 Josh Rottenberg, 'New Oscars standards say best picture contenders must be inclusive to compete', *Los Angeles Times*, 8 September 2020, https://www.latimes.com/entertainment-arts/movies/story/2020-09-08/academy-oscars-inclusion-standards-best-picture.

58 Buchanan & Powell, 2018, pp. 239–73.

59 Kumar, Kodipady & Young, 2020.

60 Zweig, 2009 (1942), p. 104.

61 Zweig, 2009 (1942), p. 105.

62 Quoted in Nussbaum, 1998.

63 Appiah, 2011.

64 Sterelny, 2007b.

65 Bicchieri, 2005; Bicchieri, 2016.

66 Buchanan & Powell, 2018.

67 Rhee, Schein & Bastian, 2019.

7. 5 Years

1 Baldwin, 1963, p. 21.

2 King, 1986, pp. 217–21.

3 https://www.armuts-und-reichtumsbericht.de/SharedDocs/Downloads/Service/Studien/analyse-verteilung-einkommen-vermoegen.pdf?__blob=publicationFile&v=3.

4 https://www.destatis.de/EN/Themes/Labour/Labour-Market/Quality-Employment/Dimension1/1_5_GenderPayGap.html.

5 Pinker, 2018, p. 216.

6 Aja Romano, 'A history of wokeness', *Vox*, 9 October 2020, https://www.vox.com/culture/21437879/stay-woke-wokeness-history-origin-evolution-controversy.

7 Inglehart, 2018.

8 'The rise and fall of online culture wars', https://astralcodexten.substack.com/p/the-rise-and-fall-of-online-culture.

9 Wittgenstein, 1958, p. 103.

10 Adorno & Horkheimer, 1972 (1947), p. 198.

11 Frank, 2004.

12 'The racist legacy many birds carry', *Washington Post*, 2021, https://www.washingtonpost.com/climate-environment/interactive/2021/bird-names-racism-audubon.

Notes

13 Al-Gharbi, forthcoming.
14 Turchin, 2013.
15 Bright, forthcoming.
16 Táíwò, 2022, p. 6 ff.
17 Tucholsky, 2017 (1928).
18 Táíwò, 2022.
19 David Brooks, 'This is how wokeness ends', *New York Times*, 13 May 2021, https://www.nytimes.com/2021/05/13/opinion/this-is-how-wokeness-ends.html?searchResultPosition=3.
20 Tyler Cowen, 'Why wokeism will rule the world', Bloomberg, 19 September 2021, https://www.bloomberg.com/opinion/articles/2021-09-19/woke-movement-is-global-and-america-should-be-mostly-proud.
21 Ramaswamy, 2021; https://spectrejournal.com/whats-new-about-woke-racial-capitalism-and-what-isnt/.
22 Tom Wolfe, 'Radical chic: That party at Lenny's', *New York* magazine, 8 June 1970, https://nymag.com/news/features/46170.
23 https://www.youtube.com/watch?v=aFho8JEKDYk.
24 Nagle, 2017.
25 Helen Lewis, 'The identity hoaxers', *Atlantic*, 16 March 2021, https://www.theatlantic.com/international/archive/2021/03/krug-carrillo-dolezal-social-munchausen-syndrome/618289.
26 Haslam, 2016.
27 Haidt & Lukianoff, 2018.
28 Joseph Heath, 'Woke tactics are as important as woke beliefs', *The Line*, 23 June 2021, https://theline.substack.com/p/joseph-heath-woke-tactics-are-as.
29 Mill, 2012 (1859).
30 Levari et al., 2018.
31 Steven Pinker, 'The game of the name', *New York Times*, 5 April 1994, https://stevenpinker.com/files/pinker/files/1994_04_03_newyorktimes.pdf.
32 John McWhorter, 'How the N-word became unsayable', *New York Times*, 30 April 2021, https://www.nytimes.com/2021/04/30/opinion/john-mcwhorter-n-word-unsayable.html; 'Why *Times* opinion decided to publish this slur', *New York Times*, 30 April 2021, https://www.nytimes.com/2021/04/30/opinion/times-opinion-mcwhorter-essay.html; Conor Friedersdorf, 'The educators who decided that context doesn't matter', *Atlantic*, 7 February 2022,

https://www.theatlantic.com/ideas/archive/2022/02/
logical-end-language-policing/621500.

33 https://3quarksdaily.com/3quarksdaily/2021/05/do-mention-it.
html.

34 John Mayer, interviewed in *Playboy*, March 2010.

35 https://www.youtube.com/watch?v=QO15S3WC9pg.

36 Stillman, 2021.

37 Steven Pinker, 'Racist language, real and imagined', *New York Times*,
2 February 1999, https://www.nytimes.com/1999/02/02/opinion/
racist-language-real-and-imagined.html.

38 Bolinger, 2017.

39 https://www.astralcodexten.com/p/
give-up-seventy-percent-of-the-way.

40 Chappell, 2021.

41 CDC, 'Leading causes of death', https://www.cdc.gov/nchs/fastats/
leading-causes-of-death.htm.

42 Heath, 2021a.

43 Lysandra Ohrstrom, 'Inside the antiracism tug-of-war at an elite
NYC private school', *Vanity Fair*, 15 April 2021, https://www.
vanityfair.com/news/2021/04/
inside-the-antiracism-tug-of-war-at-an-elite-nyc-private-school.

44 Ta-Nehisi Coates, 'Gathering the tribe', *Atlantic*, 17 May 2011,
https://www.theatlantic.com/national/archive/2011/05/gathering-
the-tribe/239060.

45 McWhorter, 2021.

46 DiAngelo, 2018.

47 https://whatever.scalzi.com/2012/05/15/straight-white-male-the-
lowest-difficulty-setting-there-is.

48 DiAngelo, 2018; Okun, 2010.

49 Mills, 1997.

50 Delgado, 1995.

51 Alexander, 2012; Pfaff, 2017.

52 Ta-Nehisi Coates, 'The case for reparations', *Atlantic*, June 2014,
https://www.theatlantic.com/magazine/archive/2014/06/the-case-
for-reparations/361631.

53 Kendi, 2019.

54 Singal, 2021, Chapter 6.

55 https://implicit.harvard.edu/implicit/takeatest.html.

56 Machery, 2022.

57 Kline, Rose & Walters, 2022.

Notes

58 Maitra, 2018.

59 Du Bois, 1998 (1935).

60 David Foster Wallace, 'This is water', 2005, https://fs.blog/david-foster-wallace-this-is-water.

61 Bostrom & Ord, 2006.

62 Solnit, 2014.

63 Fricker, 2007.

64 Manne, 2018.

65 Rini, 2021.

66 'What does identitarian deference require?', https://mattbruenig.com/2013/02/26/what-does-identitarian-deference-require.

67 Toole, 2021.

68 Freddie deBoer, 'When good political arguments go bad: On "critique drift"', *In These Times*, 11 March 2015, https://inthesetimes.com/article/nyu-grad-students-win-contract.

69 Maslow, 1966, pp. 15–16.

70 McGillen, 2023.

71 Mercier, 2020, p. 202 ff.

72 Levy, 2017.

73 Pennycook et al., 2015.

74 Hübl, 2018; Hübl, 2019. Translation by Jo Heinrich.

75 Dubois & Blank, 2018.

76 Oreskes & Conway, 2010.

77 Boyd & Richerson, 2006.

78 Levy, 2022.

79 O'Connor & Weatherall, 2019.

80 Anne Applebaum, 'The new puritans', *Atlantic*, October 2021, https://www.theatlantic.com/magazine/archive/2021/10/new-puritans-mob-justice-canceled/619818.

81 Ronson, 2015.

82 Ronan Farrow, 'From aggressive overtures to sexual assault: Harvey Weinstein's accusers tell their stories', *New Yorker*, 10 October 2017, https://www.newyorker.com/news/news-desk/from-aggressive-overtures-to-sexual-assault-harvey-weinsteins-accusers-tell-their-stories.

83 Katie Way, 'I went on a date with Aziz Ansari. It turned into the worst night of my life', *Babe*, 13 January 2018, https://babe.net/2018/01/13/aziz-ansari-28355.

84 Donald G. McNeil Jr, 'NY Times Peru N-word, part one: Introduction', *Medium*, 1 March 2021, https://donaldgmcneiljr1954.

medium.com/nytimes-peru-n-word-part-one-introduction-57eb6a3e0d95.

85 https://s3.documentcloud.org/documents/3914586/Googles-Ideological-Echo-Chamber.pdf.

86 https://www.canceledpeople.com/cancelations.

87 Levy, 2019.

88 Simpson & Srinivasan, 2018.

89 Tosi & Warmke, 2016.

90 Levy, 2021.

91 Bicchieri, 2016.

92 Coyne, 2013.

93 MacAskill, 2015.

94 https://80000hours.org.

95 https://www.givewell.org; https://www.thelifeyoucansave.org.

96 Prinz, 2011.

97 Singer, 1972.

98 MacFarquhar, 2015, p. 71 ff.

99 https://www.givingwhatwecan.org.

100 https://howrichami.givingwhatwecan.org/how-rich-am-i.

101 https://www.givedirectly.org.

102 Ord, 2020.

103 MacAskill, 2022.

Conclusion

1   Achen & Bartels, 2016, Chapter 5.

2   Hall, Johansson & Strandberg, 2012.

3   Strandberg et al., 2020.

4   Joshi, 2020.

5   Bryan Caplan, 'The ideological Turing test', *Econlog*, 20 June 2011, https://www.econlib.org/archives/2011/06/the_ideological.html.

6   Parker et al., 2021.

7   Brennan, 2016, Chapter 1.

8   Appiah, 2019.

9   Walter & Redlawsk, 2019.

10 Cohen, 2003.

11 Kinder & Kalmoe, 2017.

12 Brennan, 2016, p. 29; Freiman, 2021, p. 12.

13 Caplan, 2007.

14 Schumpeter, 2008 (1942), p. 262.

15 Klein, 2020, Chapter 1.

Notes

16 Bail, 2021.

17 Bishop, 2009; Murray, 2012.

18 Fiorina, Abrams & Pope, 2005.

19 Mercier, 2020, p. 211.

20 Bail, 2021, p. 75; DellaPosta, 2020; Sauer, 2015.

21 Levendusky, 2009.

22 Mason, 2018a; Mason, 2018b; Iyengar & Westwood, 2015.

23 Iyengar et al., 2019.

24 Grubbs et al., 2020.

25 Nguyen, 2020.

26 Funkhouser, 2022.

27 Heath, 2021b; Nordhaus, 2013; Brennan & van der Vossen, 2018, Chapter 11; Pinker, 2018, Chapter 10; see also Wallace-Wells, 2019 and, as contrast, Lomborg, 2021 and Shellenberger, 2020.

28 Henrich, Heine & Norenzayan, 2010, p. 1.

29 Herodotus, 2008, pp. 185–6.

30 de Montaigne, 1958 (1580), pp. 150–8.

31 Schwartz et al., 2012.

32 https://www.worldvaluessurvey.org/wvs.jsp.

33 Curry, Mullins & Whitehouse, 2019; see also Sauer, 2019.

34 Eric Schwitzgebel, 'Why I deny (strong versions of) descriptive cultural moral relativism', *New Apps*, 19 February 2015, https://www.newappsblog.com/2015/02/why-i-deny-strong-versions-of-descriptive-cultural-moral-relativism.html.

35 Drescher, 2009, p. 60; see also Philippe Lemoine, 'What a Portuguese chronicler may teach us about moral relativism', *Nec Pluribus Impar*, 31 January 2017, https://necpluribusimpar.net/portuguese-chronicler-may-teach-us-moral-relativism.

36 Midgley, 2005.

37 Jordan Sand, 'Tsujigiri: Mary Midgley's misleading essay, "Trying out one's new sword"', https://www.academia.edu/40029018/Tsujigiri_Mary_Midgley_s_Misleading_Essay_Trying_Out_One_s_New_Sword.

38 Welzel, 2013.

Bibliography

Acemoglu, D. & Robinson, J. A. (2012). *Why Nations Fail: The Origins of Power, Prosperity, and Poverty.* London: Profile.

Achen, C. H. & Bartels, L. M. (2016). *Democracy for Realists: Why Elections Do Not Produce Responsive Government.* Princeton, NJ: Princeton University Press.

Adorno, T. W. & Horkheimer, M. (1972 [1947]). *Dialectic of Enlightenment,* tr. J. Cumming. New York: Seabury.

Aharoni, E. & Fridlund, A. J. (2012). Punishment without reason: Isolating retribution in lay punishment of criminal offenders. *Psychology, Public Policy, and Law,* 18(4), 599–625.

Alexander, M. (2012). *The New Jim Crow: Mass Incarceration in the Age of Colorblindness.* New York: New Press.

Al-Gharbi, M. (forthcoming). *We Have Never Been Woke: Social Justice Discourse, Inequality and the Rise of a New Elite.* Princeton, NJ: Princeton University Press.

Anderson, A., Chilczuk, S., Nelson, K., Ruther, R. & Wall-Scheffler, C. (2023). The myth of man the hunter: Women's contribution to the hunt across ethnographic contexts. *PLoS One,* 18(6), e0287101.

Anderson, E. (2010). *The Imperative of Integration.* Princeton, NJ: Princeton University Press.

Aplin, L. M. (2019). Culture and cultural evolution in birds: A review of the evidence. *Animal Behaviour,* 147, 179–87.

Appiah, K. A. (2011). *The Honor Code: How Moral Revolutions Happen.* New York: W. W. Norton.

Appiah, K. A. (2019). *The Lies That Bind: Rethinking Identity.* London: Profile.

Arendt, H. (2006 [1963]). *Eichmann in Jerusalem: A Report on the Banality of Evil.* London: Penguin.

Asch, S. (1956). Studies of independence and conformity: A minority of

Bibliography

one against a unanimous majority. *Psychological Monographs*, 70(9), 1–70.

Axelrod, R. (2006 [1984]). *The Evolution of Cooperation*. Cambridge, MA: Basic Books.

Bail, C. (2021). *Breaking the Social Media Prism: How to Make Our Platforms Less Polarizing*. Princeton, NJ: Princeton University Press.

Baldwin, J. (1963). *The Fire Next Time*. London: Michael Joseph.

Baptist, E. E. (2014). *The Half Has Never Been Told: Slavery and the Making of American Capitalism*. New York: Basic Books.

Baron, J. & Ritov, I. (1993). Intuitions about penalties and compensation in the context of tort law. *Journal of Risk and Uncertainty*, 7(1), 17–33.

Barrett, H. C., Bolyanatz, A., Crittenden, A. N., Fessler, D. M., Fitzpatrick, S., Gurven, M. . . . & Laurence, S. (2016). Small-scale societies exhibit fundamental variation in the role of intentions in moral judgment. *Proceedings of the National Academy of Sciences*, 113(17), 4688–93.

Bataille, G. (1989 [1961]). *The Tears of Eros*, tr. P. Connor. San Francisco, CA: City Lights.

Beckert, S. (2014). *Empire of Cotton: A Global History*. New York: Knopf.

Bicchieri, C. (2005). *The Grammar of Society: The Nature and Dynamics of Social Norms*. Cambridge: Cambridge University Press.

Bicchieri, C. (2016). *Norms in the Wild: How to Diagnose, Measure, and Change Social Norms*. Oxford: Oxford University Press.

Bishop, B. (2009). *The Big Sort: Why the Clustering of Like-Minded America is Tearing Us Apart*. Boston: Mariner.

Bloom, P. (2013). *Just Babies: The Origins of Good and Evil*. London: Bodley Head.

Boehm, C. (1999). *Hierarchy in the Forest: The Evolution of Egalitarian Behavior*. Cambridge, MA: Harvard University Press.

Bolinger, R. J. (2017). The pragmatics of slurs. *Noûs*, 51(3), 439–62.

Bostrom, N. & Ord, T. (2006). The reversal test: Eliminating status quo bias in applied ethics. *Ethics*, 116(4), 656–79.

Bourdieu, P. (2010 [1979]). *Distinction: A Social Critique of the Judgement of Taste*, tr. R. Nice. London: Routledge.

Bowles, S. (2009). Did warfare among ancestral hunter-gatherers affect the evolution of human social behaviors? *Science*, 324(5932), 1293–8.

Bowles, S. & Gintis, H. (2011). *A Cooperative Species: Human Reciprocity and Its Evolution*. Princeton, NJ: Princeton University Press.

Boyd, R. & Richerson, P. J. (1992). Punishment allows the evolution of

Bibliography

cooperation (or anything else) in sizable groups. *Ethology and Sociobiology*, 13(3), 171–95.

Boyd, R. & Richerson, P. J. (2006). *Not by Genes Alone: How Culture Transformed Human Evolution.* Chicago: University of Chicago Press.

Boyer, P. & Petersen, M. B. (2018). Folk-economic beliefs: An evolutionary cognitive model. *Behavioral and Brain Sciences*, 41, 1–51.

Brecht, B. (1976). *Poems, Part Two 1929–1938*, ed. J. Willet & R. Manheim. London: Eyre Methuen.

Brennan, J. (2014). *Why Not Capitalism?* London: Routledge.

Brennan, J. (2016). *Against Democracy.* Princeton, NJ: Princeton University Press.

Brennan, J. (2020). *Why It's OK to Want to Be Rich.* New York: Routledge.

Brennan, J. & van der Vossen, B. (2018). *In Defense of Openness: Why Global Freedom Is the Humane Solution to Global Poverty.* New York: Oxford University Press.

Bright, L. K. (forthcoming). White psychodrama. *Journal of Political Philosophy.*

Brosnan, S. F. & de Waal, F. (2003). Monkeys reject unequal pay. *Nature*, 425(6955), 297–9.

Browning, C. R. (2001 [1992]). *Ordinary Men: Police Battalion 101 and the Final Solution in Poland.* London: Penguin.

Buchanan, A. & Powell, R. (2018). *The Evolution of Moral Progress: A Biocultural Theory.* New York: Oxford University Press.

Büchner, G. (1998 [1835]). *Danton's Death, Leonce and Lena, Woyzeck*, tr. V. Price. Oxford: Oxford University Press.

Burke, E. (2014 [1790]). *Reflections on the Revolution in France.* In: Burke, E. (2014). *Revolutionary Writings.* Cambridge: Cambridge University Press, 1–251.

Camus, A. (2000 [1951]). *The Rebel*, tr. Anthony Bower. London: Penguin.

Caplan, B. (2007). *The Myth of the Rational Voter: Why Democracies Choose Bad Policies.* Princeton, NJ: Princeton University Press.

Case, A. & Deaton, A. (2020). *Deaths of Despair and the Future of Capitalism.* Princeton, NJ: Princeton University Press.

Chapoutot, J. (2018). *The Law of Blood: Thinking and Acting Like a Nazi.* Cambridge, MA: Belknap Press.

Chappell, S. G. (2021). Transgender and adoption: An analogy. *Think*, 20 (59), 25–30.

Christakis, N. (2019). *Blueprint: The Evolutionary Origins of a Good Society.* New York: Little, Brown Spark.

Bibliography

Clark, G. (2007). *A Farewell to Alms: A Brief Economic History of the World*. Princeton, NJ: Princeton University Press.

Clark, G. (2014). *The Son Also Rises: Surnames and the History of Social Mobility*. Princeton, NJ: Princeton University Press.

Cochrane, L. (2019). *Miracle in the Cave: The 12 Lost Boys, Their Coach, and the Heroes Who Rescued Them*. New York: HarperCollins.

Cohen, G. L. (2003). Party over policy: The dominating impact of group influence on political beliefs. *Journal of Personality and Social Psychology*, 85(5), 808–22.

Cohen, G. A. (2009). *Why Not Socialism?* Princeton, NJ: Princeton University Press.

Cosmides, L. & Tooby, J. (2013). Evolutionary psychology: New perspectives on cognition and motivation. *Annual Review of Psychology*, 64, 201–29.

Coyne, C. J. (2013). *Doing Bad by Doing Good: Why Humanitarian Action Fails*. Stanford, CA: Stanford University Press.

Crenshaw, K. (1989). Demarginalizing the intersection of race and sex: A Black feminist critique of antidiscrimination doctrine, feminist theory, and antiracist politics. *University of Chicago Legal Forum*, 1989 (1), 139–67.

Crimston, D., Hornsey, M. J., Bain, P. G. & Bastian, B. (2018). Toward a psychology of moral expansiveness. *Current Directions in Psychological Science*, 27(1), 14–19.

Curry, O. S., Mullins, D. A. & Whitehouse, H. (2019). Is it good to cooperate? Testing the theory of morality-as-cooperation in 60 societies. *Current Anthropology*, 60(1), 47–69.

Damasio, A. (1994). *Descartes' Error: Emotion, Reason, and the Human Brain*. London: Penguin.

Darwin, C. (1871). *The Descent of Man*. New York: Appleton.

Dawkins, R. (1982). *The Extended Phenotype: The Long Reach of the Gene*. Oxford: Oxford University Press.

Dawkins, R. (2016 [1976]). *The Selfish Gene*. Oxford: Oxford University Press.

Deaton, A. (2013). *The Great Escape: Health, Wealth, and the Origins of Inequality*. Princeton, NJ: Princeton University Press.

DellaPosta, D. (2020). Pluralistic collapse: The 'oil spill' model of mass opinion polarization. *American Sociological Review*, 85(3), 507–36.

Delgado, R. (ed.) (1995). *Critical Race Theory: The Cutting Edge*. Philadelphia, PA: Temple University Press.

Bibliography

Dennett, D. (1995). *Darwin's Dangerous Idea: Evolution and the Meanings of Life*. London: Penguin.

de Waal, F. (1998). *Chimpanzee Politics: Power and Sex Among Apes*. Baltimore, MD: Johns Hopkins University Press.

de Waal, F. (2006). *Primates and Philosophers: How Morality Evolved*. Princeton, NJ: Princeton University Press.

Diamond, J. (1987). The worst mistake in human history. *Discover*, 8(5), 64–6.

Diamond, J. (1997). *Guns, Germs, and Steel: A Short History of Everybody for the Last 13,000 Years*. New York: Random House.

Diamond, J. (2005). *Collapse: How Societies Choose to Fail or Succeed*. London: Penguin.

DiAngelo, R. (2018). *White Fragility: Why It's So Hard for White People to Talk about Racism*. Boston: Beacon Press.

Diemer, M. A., Mistry, R. S., Wadsworth, M. E., López, I. & Reimers, F. (2013). Best practices in conceptualizing and measuring social class in psychological research. *Analyses of Social Issues and Public Policy*, 13(1), 77–113.

DiNapoli, R. J., Rieth, T. M., Lipo, C. P. & Hunt, T. L. (2020). A model-based approach to the tempo of 'collapse': The case of Rapa Nui (Easter Island). *Journal of Archaeological Science*, 116: 105094.

Doris, J. M. (2002). *Lack of Character: Personality and Moral Behavior*. Cambridge: Cambridge University Press.

Doris, J. M. & Murphy, D. (2007). From My Lai to Abu Ghraib: The moral psychology of atrocity. *Midwest Studies in Philosophy*, 31 (1), 25–55.

Dornes, M. (2016). *Macht der Kapitalismus depressiv? Über seelische Gesundheit und Krankheit in modernen Gesellschaften*. Frankfurt am Main: Fischer.

Drescher, S. (2009). *Abolition: A History of Slavery and Antislavery*. Cambridge: Cambridge University Press.

Dubois, E. & Blank, G. (2018). The echo chamber is overstated: The moderating effect of political interest and diverse media. *Information, Communication & Society*, 21(5), 729–45.

Du Bois, W. E. B. (1998 [1935]). *Black Reconstruction in America*. New York: Free Press.

Dugatkin, L. A. & Trut, L. (2017). *How to Tame a Fox (and Build a Dog): Visionary Scientists and a Siberian Tale of Jump-Started Evolution*. Chicago: University of Chicago Press.

Bibliography

Dunbar, R. (1992). Neocortex size as a constraint on group size in primates. *Journal of Human Evolution*, 22(6), 469–93.

Dunbar, R. (1996). *Grooming, Gossip, and the Evolution of Language*. London: Faber & Faber.

Dunbar, R. (2016). *Human Evolution*. New York: Oxford University Press.

Durkheim, E. (1984 [1893]). *The Division of Labour in Society*, tr. W. D. Halls. London: Palgrave Macmillan.

Easterlin, R. A. (1974). Does economic growth improve the human lot? Some empirical evidence. In: *Nations and Households in Economic Growth: Essays in Honor of Moses Abramowitz*, ed. P. A. David and M. W. Reder. New York: Academic Press.

Edgerton, R. B. (1992). *Sick Societies: Challenging the Myth of Primitive Harmony*. New York: Free Press.

Ehrlich, P. (1968). *The Population Bomb*. New York: Ballantine.

Elias, N. (1978). *The Civilizing Process*, tr. E. Jephcott. New York: Urizen.

Elsen, J., Cizer, O. & Snellings, R. (2013). Lessons from a lost technology: The secrets of Roman concrete. *American Mineralogist*, 98(11–12), 1917–18.

Fehr, E. & Gächter, S. (2000). Cooperation and punishment in public goods experiments. *American Economic Review*, 90(4), 980–94.

Fehr, E. & Gächter, S. (2002). Altruistic punishment in humans. *Nature*, 415(6868), 137–40.

Fiorina, M. P., Abrams, S. J. & Pope, J. C. (2005). *Culture War? The Myth of a Polarized America*. New York: Pearson Longman.

Flannery, K. & Marcus, J. (2012). *The Creation of Inequality: How Our Prehistoric Ancestors Set the Stage for Monarchy, Slavery, and Empire*. Cambridge, MA: Harvard University Press.

Fodor, J. (1983). *The Modularity of Mind*. Cambridge, MA: MIT Press.

Foucault, M. (1977). *Discipline and Punish*, tr. A. Sheridan. New York: Pantheon.

Frank, T. (2004). *What's the Matter with Kansas? How Conservatives Won the Heart of America*. New York: Owl Books.

Frankfurt, H. (1987). Equality as a moral ideal. *Ethics*, 98(1), 21–43.

Freiman, C. (2017). *Unequivocal Justice*. London: Routledge.

Freiman, C. (2021). *Why It's OK to Ignore Politics*. New York: Routledge.

Freud, S. (1981 [1917]). *A Difficulty in the Path of Psycho-Analysis*, tr. J. Strachey. In: *The Standard Edition of the Complete Psychological Works of Sigmund Freud* (Vol. 17): *An Infantile Neurosis and Other Works*. London: Hogarth Press.

Bibliography

Freud, S. (2004 [1930]). *Civilization and Its Discontents*, tr. D. McLintock. London: Penguin.

Fricker, M. (2007). *Epistemic Injustice: Power and the Ethics of Knowing.* Oxford: Oxford University Press.

Fukuyama, F. (1992). *The End of History and the Last Man.* New York: Free Press.

Funkhouser, E. (2022). A tribal mind: Beliefs that signal group identity or commitment. *Mind & Language*, 37(3), 444–64.

Gehlen, A. (1988 [1940]). *Man: His Nature and Place in the World*, tr. Clare McMillan and Karl Pillemer. New York: Columbia University Press.

Glover, J. (2012). *Humanity: A Moral History of the 20th Century.* New Haven, CT: Yale University Press.

Gottfried, R. S. (1983). *The Black Death: Natural and Human Disaster in Medieval Europe.* London: Robert Hale.

Graeber, D. & Wengrow, D. (2021). *The Dawn of Everything: A New History of Humanity.* New York: Farrar, Straus & Giroux.

Greene, J. D. (2008). *The Secret Joke of Kant's Soul.* In: *Moral Psychology* (Vol. 3): *The Neuroscience of Morality: Emotion, Brain Disorders, and Development*, ed. W. Sinnott-Armstrong. Cambridge, MA: MIT Press.

Greene, J. (2013). *Moral Tribes: Emotion, Reason, and the Gap between Us and Them.* New York: Penguin Press.

Grubbs, J. B., Warmke, B., Tosi, J. & James, A. S. (2020). Moral grandstanding and political polarization: A multi-study consideration. *Journal of Research in Personality*, 88, 104009.

Habermas, J. (2022). *Auch eine Geschichte der Philosophie* (Vol. 1): *Die okzidentale Konstellation von Glauben und Wissen.* Frankfurt am Main: Suhrkamp.

Haidt, J. (2012). *The Righteous Mind: Why Good People Are Divided by Religion and Politics.* London: Allen Lane.

Haidt, J. & Lukianoff, G. (2018). *The Coddling of the American Mind: How Good Intentions and Bad Ideas Are Setting Up a Generation for Failure.* New York: Penguin Press.

Hall, L., Johansson, P. & Strandberg, T. (2012). Lifting the veil of morality: Choice blindness and attitude reversals on a self-transforming survey. *PLoS One*, 7(9), e45457.

Hamilton, W. (1964). The genetical evolution of social behaviour. I. *Journal of Theoretical Biology*, 7(1), 1–16.

Hannah-Jones, N., Roper, C., Silverman, I. & Silverstein, J. (2021). *The 1619 Project: A New Origin Story.* New York: Oneworld.

Bibliography

Harari, Y. N. (2011). *Sapiens: A Brief History of Humankind*. London: Vintage.

Hardin, G. (1968). The tragedy of the commons. *Science*, 162(3859), 1243–8.

Hare, B. (2017). Survival of the friendliest: Homo sapiens evolved via selection for prosociality. *Annual Review of Psychology*, 68(1), 155–86.

Hare, B. & Woods, V. (2020). *Survival of the Friendliest: Understanding our Origins and Rediscovering our Common Humanity*. New York: Random House.

Haslam, N. (2016). Concept creep: Psychology's expanding concepts of harm and pathology. *Psychological Inquiry*, 27(1), 1–17.

Hathaway, O. & Shapiro, S. J. (2017). *The Internationalists, and Their Plan to Outlaw War*. London: Penguin.

Heath, J. (2004). Liberalization, modernization, westernization. *Philosophy & Social Criticism*, 30(5–6), 665–90.

Heath, J. (2014). *Enlightenment 2.0: Restoring Sanity to Our Politics, Our Economy, and Our Lives*. Toronto: HarperCollins.

Heath, J. (2021a). Post-deliberative Democracy. *Analyse & Kritik*, 43(2), 285–308.

Heath, J. (2021b). *Philosophical Foundations of Climate Change Policy*. New York: Oxford University Press.

Hegel, G. W. F. (1991 [1820]). *The Philosophy of Right, or Natural Law and Political Science in Outline*, tr. H. B. Nesbit. Cambridge: Cambridge University Press.

Hegel, G. W. F. (1995 [1840]). *Lectures on the Philosophy of History I: Greek Philosophy to Plato*, tr. E. S. Haldane. Lincoln, NE: University of Nebraska Press.

Henrich, J., Heine, S. J. & Norenzayan, A. (2010). The weirdest people in the world? *Behavioral and Brain Sciences*, 33(2–3), 61–83.

Henrich, J. (2016). *The Secret of Our Success: How Culture Is Driving Human Evolution, Domesticating Our Species, and Making Us Smarter*. Princeton, NJ: Princeton University Press.

Henrich, J. (2020). *The WEIRDest People in the World: How the West Became Psychologically Peculiar and Particularly Prosperous*. New York: Farrar, Straus & Giroux.

Henrich, J. & Muthukrishna, M. (2021). The origins and psychology of human cooperation. *Annual Review of Psychology*, 72, 207–40.

Herder, J. G. (1827 [1782]). *Treatise on the Origin of Language*, tr. unknown. London: Longman, Rees, Orm, Brown & Green.

Bibliography

Herodotus (2008). *The Histories*, tr. Robin Waterfield. Oxford: Oxford University Press.

Herrmann, B., Thöni, C. & Gächter, S. (2008). Antisocial punishment across societies. *Science*, 319(5868), 1362–7.

Heyes, C. (2018). *Cognitive Gadgets: The Cultural Evolution of Thinking*. Cambridge, MA: Belknap Press.

Hickel, J. (2016). The true extent of global poverty and hunger: Questioning the good news narrative of the Millennium Development Goals. *Third World Quarterly*, 37(5), 749–67.

Hobbes, T. (1962 [1651]). *Leviathan, or The Matter, Forme and Power of a Commonwealth, Ecclesiastical and Civil State*. New York: Collier.

Hochschild, A. (1998). *King Leopold's Ghost: A Story of Greed, Terror, and Heroism in Colonial Africa*. New York: Mariner.

Homer. (2014). *Homer's Iliad and Odyssey: The Essential Books*, tr. B. B. Powell. New York: Oxford University Press.

Hrdy, S. (2009). *Mothers and Others: The Evolutionary Origins of Mutual Understanding*. Cambridge, MA: Harvard University Press.

Hübl, P. (2018). *Bullshit-Resistenz*. Berlin: Nicolai.

Hübl, P. (2019). *Die aufgeregte Gesellschaft: Wie Emotionen unsere Moral prägen und die Polarisierung verstärken*. Munich: Bertelsmann.

Hume, D. (2007 [1739–40]). *A Treatise of Human Nature: A Critical Edition, Volume 1*. Ed. Norton, D. F. and Norton, M. J. Oxford: Clarendon Press.

Husi, S. (2017). Why we (almost certainly) are not moral equals. *Journal of Ethics*, 21(4), 375–401.

Inglehart, R. (1977). *The Silent Revolution: Changing Values and Political Styles among Western Publics*. Princeton, NJ: Princeton University Press.

Inglehart, R. (2018). *Cultural Evolution: People's Motivations are Changing, and Reshaping the World*. Cambridge: Cambridge University Press.

Isen, A. M. & Levin, P. F. (1972). Effect of feeling good on helping: Cookies and kindness. *Journal of Personality and Social Psychology*, 21(3), 384–8.

Iyengar, S. & Westwood, S. J. (2015). Fear and loathing across party lines: New evidence on group polarization. *American Journal of Political Science*, 59(3), 690–707.

Iyengar, S., Lelkes, Y., Levendusky, M., Malhotra, N. & Westwood, S. J. (2019). The origins and consequences of affective polarization in the United States. *Annual Review of Political Science*, 22(1), 129–46.

Bibliography

Jaspers, K. (2021 [1949]). *The Origin and Goal of History*, tr. Michael
   Bullock. London: Routledge.
Joshi, H. (2020). What are the chances you're right about everything?
   An epistemic challenge for modern partisanship. *Politics, Philosophy
   & Economics*, 19(1), 36–61.
Kadri, S. (2006). *The Trial: A History from Socrates to O. J. Simpson*.
   London: Harper Perennial.
Kant, I. (1996 [1797]). *The Metaphysics of Morals*, tr. M. Gregor.
   Cambridge: Cambridge University Press.
Kant, I. (1998 [1793/94]). *Religion within the Boundaries of Mere Reason*, tr.
   A. Wood. Cambridge: Cambridge University Press.
Kant, I. (2000 [1790]). *Critique of Judgment*, tr. J. H. Bernard. New York:
   Prometheus.
Kant, I. (2003 [1795/1796]). *To Perpetual Peace: A Philosophical Sketch*, tr.
   T. Humphrey. Indianapolis, IN: Hackett.
Kant, I. (2006 [1798]). *Anthropology from a Pragmatic Point of View*, tr. R.
   B. Louden. Cambridge: Cambridge University Press.
Kant, I. (2009 [1784a]). *An Answer to the Question: 'What is
   Enlightenment?'*, tr. H. B. Nisbet. London: Penguin.
Kant, I. (2009 [1784b]). *Idea for a Universal History with a Cosmopolitan
   Aim: A Critical Guide*, tr. A. Wood. Cambridge: Cambridge
   University Press.
Kant, I. (2012 [1785]). *Groundwork of the Metaphysics of Morals*, tr. M.
   Gregor & J. Timmerman. Cambridge: Cambridge University Press.
Kant, I. (2015 [1788]). *Critique of Practical Reason*, tr. M. Gregor.
   Cambridge: Cambridge University Press.
Kehlmann, D. (2020). *Tyll*, tr. R. Benjamin. London: riverrun.
Kelly, D. & Hoburg, P. (2017). A tale of two processes: On Joseph
   Henrich's *The Secret of Our Success*. *Philosophical Psychology*, 30(6),
   832–48.
Kendi, I. X. (2019). *How to Be an Antiracist*. New York: Oneworld.
Kershaw, I. (1983). How effective was Nazi propaganda? In: *Nazi
   Propaganda: The Power and the Limitations*, ed. D. Welch. London:
   Routledge.
Kinder, D. R. & Kalmoe, N. P. (2017). *Neither Liberal Nor Conservative:
   Ideological Innocence in the American Public*. Chicago: University of
   Chicago Press.
King, M. L. (1986). *A Testament of Hope: The Essential Writings and
   Speeches of Martin Luther King, Jr*, ed. J. L. Washington. New York:
   HarperCollins.

Bibliography

Kitcher, P. (2011). *The Ethical Project.* Cambridge, MA: Harvard University Press.

Kleiman, M. (2009). *When Brute Force Fails: How to Have Less Crime and Less Punishment.* Princeton, NJ: Princeton University Press.

Klein, E. (2020). *Why We're Polarized.* London: Profile.

Kline, P., Rose, E. K. & Walters, C. R. (2022). Systemic discrimination among large US employers. *Quarterly Journal of Economics,* 137(4), 1963–2036.

Kramer, S. N. (1963). *The Sumerians: Their History, Culture, and Character.* Chicago: University of Chicago Press.

Kumar, V., Kodipady, A. & Young, L. (2020). A psychological account of the unique decline in anti-gay attitudes (preprint).

Kuznets, S. (1955). Economic growth and income inequality. *American Economic Review,* 45, 1–28.

Laland, K. (2017). *Darwin's Unfinished Symphony: How Culture Made the Human Mind.* Princeton, NJ: Princeton University Press.

Leakey, M. & Leakey, S. (2020). *The Sediments of Time: My Lifelong Search for the Past.* Boston: Houghton Mifflin Harcourt.

Lee, R. B. (1979). *The !Kung San: Men, Women, and Work in a Foraging Society.* Cambridge: Cambridge University Press.

Lee, R. B. (2013). *The Dobe Ju/'hoansi.* Belmont, CA: Wadsworth.

Leeson, P. (2017). *WTF?! An Economic Tour of the Weird.* Stanford, CA: Stanford University Press.

Leiter, B. (2019). The death of god and the death of morality. *The Monist,* 102(3), 386–402.

Levari, D. E., Gilbert, D. T., Wilson, T. D., Sievers, B., Amodio, D. M. & Wheatley, T. (2018). Prevalence-induced concept change in human judgment. *Science,* 360(6396), 1465–7.

Levendusky, M. (2009). *The Partisan Sort: How Liberals Became Democrats and Conservatives Became Republicans.* Chicago: University of Chicago Press.

Levy, J. (2012). *Freaks of Fortune: The Emerging World of Capitalism and Risk in America.* Cambridge, MA: Harvard University Press.

Levy, N. (2015). Less blame, less crime? The practical implications of moral responsibility skepticism. *Journal of Practical Ethics,* 3(2).

Levy, N. (2017). The bad news about fake news. *Social Epistemology Review and Reply Collective,* 6(8), 20–36.

Levy, N. (2019). No-platforming and higher-order evidence, or anti-anti-noplatforming. *Journal of the American Philosophical Association,* 5(4), 487–502.

Bibliography

Levy, N. & Alfano, M. (2020). Knowledge from vice: Deeply social epistemology. *Mind*, 129(515), 887–915.

Levy, N. (2021). Virtue signalling is virtuous. *Synthese*, 198(10), 9545–62.

Levy, N. (2022). *Bad Beliefs: Why They Happen to Good People*. Oxford: Oxford University Press.

Livingstone Smith, D. (2011). *Less Than Human: Why We Demean, Enslave, and Exterminate Others*. New York: St Martin's Press.

Lomborg, B. (2021). *False Alarm: How Climate Change Panic Costs Us Trillions, Hurts the Poor, and Fails to Fix the Planet*. New York: Basic Books.

Lorenz, K. (2009). Kant's doctrine of the a priori in the light of contemporary biology. In: *Philosophy after Darwin: Classic and Contemporary Readings*, 231–47. Princeton, NJ: Princeton University Press.

Luhmann, N. (1996). *Social Systems*, tr. J. Bednarz, Jr. Stanford, CA: Stanford University Press.

Lyons, L. (2003). *The History of Punishment*. London: Amber.

MacAskill, W. (2015). *Doing Good Better: How Effective Altruism Can Help You Help Others, Do Work that Matters, and Make Smarter Choices about Giving Back*. New York: Avery.

MacAskill, W. (2022). *What We Owe the Future: A Million-Year View*. London: Oneworld.

MacFarquhar, L. (2015). *Strangers Drowning: Voyages to the Brink of Moral Extremity*. London: Penguin.

Machery, E. (2022). Anomalies in implicit attitudes research. *Wiley Interdisciplinary Reviews: Cognitive Science*, 13(1), e1569.

Maisels, C. K. (1999). *Early Civilizations of the Old World: The Formative Histories of Egypt, the Levant, Mesopotamia, India and China*. London: Routledge.

Maitra, I. (2018). New words for old wrongs. *Episteme*, 15(3), 345–62.

Malle, B. F. (2006). The actor-observer asymmetry in attribution: A (surprising) meta-analysis. *Psychological Bulletin*, 132(6), 895.

Malthus, T. R. (1970 [1798]). *An Essay on the Principle of Population*. Harmondsworth: Penguin.

Manne, K. (2018). *Down Girl: The Logic of Misogyny*. Oxford: Oxford University Press.

Marean, C. W. (2015). An evolutionary anthropological perspective on modern human origins. *Annual Review of Anthropology*, 44, 533–6.

Markovits, D. (2020). *The Meritocracy Trap*. London: Penguin.

Marquard, O. (1989). *Farewell to Matters of Principle*, tr. R. M. Wallace. New York: Oxford University Press.

Marx, K. (1970 [1844]). *Critique of Hegel's 'Philosophy of Right'*, tr. A. Jolin & J. O'Malley. Cambridge: Cambridge University Press.

Maslow, A. (1966). *The Psychology of Science: A Reconnaissance*. New York: Harper & Row.

Mason, L. (2018a). Ideologues without issues: The polarizing consequences of ideological identities. *Public Opinion Quarterly*, 82(S1), 866–87.

Mason, L. (2018b). *Uncivil Agreement: How Politics Became Our Identity*. Chicago: University of Chicago Press.

McCloskey, D. N. (2006). *The Bourgeois Virtues: Ethics for an Age of Commerce*. Chicago: University of Chicago Press.

McCullough, M. E. (2020). *The Kindness of Strangers: How a Selfish Ape Invented a New Moral Code*. London: Oneworld.

McGillen, P. (2023) 'I was there today': Fake eyewitnessing and journalistic authority from Fontane to Relotius. In: *Journalists and Knowledge Practices: Histories of Observing the Everyday in the Newspaper Age*, ed. H. Ziemer. London: Routledge.

McWhorter, J. (2021). *Woke Racism: How a New Religion Has Betrayed Black America*. New York: Portfolio/Penguin.

Mercier, H. (2020). *Not Born Yesterday: The Science of Who We Trust and What We Believe*. Princeton, NJ: Princeton University Press.

Midgley, M. (2005 [1981]). Trying out one's new sword. In: *Ethics in the Workplace: Selected Readings in Business Ethics*, ed. R. Larmer, 159–65. Belmont, CA: Wadsworth.

Milgram, S. (1963). Behavioral study of obedience. *Journal of Abnormal and Social Psychology*, 67(4), 371.

Mill, J. S. (2012 [1859]). *On Liberty*. Cambridge: Cambridge University Press.

Mills, C. W. (1997). *The Racial Contract*. Ithaca, NY: Cornell University Press.

Montaigne, M. de (1958 [1580]). *The Complete Essays of Montaigne*, tr. D. M. Frame. Stanford, CA: Stanford University Press.

Morris, I. (2015). *Foragers, Farmers, and Fossil Fuels: How Human Values Evolve*. Princeton, NJ: Princeton University Press.

Mukherjee, S. (2010). *The Emperor of All Maladies: A Biography of Cancer*. New York: Simon and Schuster.

Murray, C. (2012). *Coming Apart: The State of White America, 1960–2010*. New York: Crown Forum.

Bibliography

Nagell, K., Olguin, R. S. & Tomasello, M. (1993). Processes of social learning in the tool use of chimpanzees (*Pan troglodytes*) and human children (*Homo sapiens*). *Journal of Comparative Psychology*, 107(2), 174.

Nagle, A. (2017). *Kill All Normies: Online Culture Wars from 4Chan and Tumblr to Trump and the Alt-Right*. Winchester: Zero Books.

Newsom, L. & Richerson, P. (2021). *A Story of Us: A New Look at Human Evolution*. New York: Oxford University Press.

Nguyen, C. T. (2020). Echo chambers and epistemic bubbles. *Episteme*, 17(2), 141–61.

Nietzsche, F. (2010 [1873]). On truth and lies in a nonmoral sense, tr. T. Carman. In: *On Truth and Untruth: Selected Writings*. New York: Harper Perennial.

Nietzsche, F. (2013 [1887]). *On the Genealogy of Morals*, tr. M. A. Scarpitti. London: Penguin.

Nietzsche, F. (1990 [1886]). *Beyond Good and Evil*, tr. R. J. Hollingdale. London: Penguin.

Nisbett, R. E. & Cohen, D. (1996). *Culture of Honor: The Psychology of Violence in the South*. Boulder, CO: Westview Press.

Nordhaus, W. (2013). *The Climate Casino: Risk, Uncertainty, and Economics for a Warming World*. Cambridge: Cambridge University Press.

Norenzayan, A. (2013). *Big Gods: How Religion Transformed Cooperation and Conflict*. Princeton, NJ: Princeton University Press.

Norton, M. I. & Ariely, D. (2011). Building a better America – one wealth quintile at a time. *Perspectives on Psychological Science*, 6(1), 9–12.

Nozick, R. (1974). *Anarchy, State, and Utopia*. New York: Basic Books.

Nussbaum, M. C. (1998). 'Whether from reason or prejudice': Taking money for bodily services. *Journal of Legal Studies*, 27(S2), 693–723.

Nussbaum, M. (2007). On moral progress: A response to Richard Rorty. *University of Chicago Law Review*, 74(3), 939–60.

O'Connor, C. (2019). *The Origins of Unfairness: Social Categories and Cultural Evolution*. Oxford: Oxford University Press.

O'Connor, C. & Weatherall, J. O. (2019). *The Misinformation Age: How False Beliefs Spread*. New Haven, CT: Yale University Press.

Okun, T. (2010). *The Emperor Has No Clothes: Teaching about Race and Racism to People Who Don't Want to Know*. Charlotte, NC: Information Age.

Ord, T. (2020). *The Precipice: Existential Risk and the Future of Humanity*. London: Bloomsbury.

Bibliography

Oreskes, N. & Conway E. M. (2010). *Merchants of Doubt: How a Handful of Scientists Obscured the Truth on Issues from Tobacco Smoke to Global Warming*. New York: Bloomsbury.

Pagel, M. (2013). *Wired for Culture: Origins of the Human Social Mind*. New York: W. W. Norton.

Parfit, D. (1997). Equality and priority. *Ratio*, 10 (3), 202–21.

Parker, V. A., Feinberg, M., Tullett, A. & Wilson, A. E. (2021). The ties that blind: Misperceptions of the opponent fringe and the miscalibration of political contempt (preprint).

Pattison, K. (2020). *Fossil Men: The Quest for the Oldest Skeleton and the Origins of Humankind*. New York: Morrow.

Pauer-Studer, H. & Velleman, D. (2015). *Konrad Morgen: The Conscience of a Nazi Judge*. London: Palgrave Macmillan.

Pennycook, G., Cheyne, J. A., Barr, N., Koehler, D. J. & Fugelsang, J. A. (2015). On the reception and detection of pseudo-profound bullshit. *Judgment and Decision Making*, 10(6), 549–63.

Petersen, M. B., Sell, A., Tooby, J. & Cosmides, L. (2012). To punish or repair? Evolutionary psychology and lay intuitions about modern criminal justice. *Evolution and Human Behavior*, 33(6), 682–95.

Pfaff, J. F. (2017). *Locked In: The True Causes of Mass Incarceration – And How to Achieve Real Reform*. New York: Basic Books.

Physiologus: A Medieval Book of Nature Lore, tr. M. J. Curley (2009). Chicago: University of Chicago Press.

Pievani, T. & Zeitoun, V. (2020). *Homo Sapiens: Der große Atlas der Menschheit*. Darmstadt: WBG.

Piketty, T. (2014). *Capital in the Twenty-First Century*. Cambridge, MA: Belknap Press.

Pinker, S. (2011). *The Better Angels of Our Nature: The Decline of Violence and Its Causes*. London: Allen Lane.

Pinker, S. (2012). The false allure of group selection. https ://www.edge.org/conversation/steven_pinker-the-false-allure-of-group-selection.

Pinker, S. (2018). *Enlightenment Now: The Case for Reason, Science, Humanism, and Progress*. New York: Viking.

Pleasants, N. (2016). The question of the Holocaust's uniqueness: Was it something more than or different from genocide? *Journal of Applied Philosophy*, 33(3), 297–310.

Plessner, H. (2019 [1928]). *Levels of Organic Life and the Human: An Introduction to Philosophical Anthropology*, tr. M. Hyatt. New York: Fordham University Press.

Pomeranz, K. (2001). *The Great Divergence: China, Europe, and the*

Bibliography

Making of the Modern World Economy. Princeton, NJ: Princeton University Press.

Prinz, J. (2011). Against empathy. *Southern Journal of Philosophy*, 49, 214–33.

Ramaswamy, V. (2021). *Woke, Inc.: Inside Corporate America's Social Justice Scam*. New York: Center Street.

Ransmayr, C. (2020). *Cox or The Course of Time*, tr. S. Pare. Calcutta: Seagull.

Rawls, J. (1971). *A Theory of Justice*. Cambridge, MA: Belknap Press.

Renfrew, C. (2008). *Prehistory: The Making of the Human Mind*. London: Phoenix.

Rhee, J. J., Schein, C. & Bastian, B. (2019). The what, how, and why of moralization: A review of current definitions, methods, and evidence in moralization research. *Social and Personality Psychology Compass*, 13(12), Article e12511.

Richerson, P. (2013). Group size determines cultural complexity. *Nature*, 503(7476), 351–2.

Richerson, P., Baldini, R., Bell, A. V., Demps, K., Frost, K., Hillis, V. . . . & Ross, C. (2016). Cultural group selection plays an essential role in explaining human cooperation: A sketch of the evidence. *Behavioral and Brain Sciences*, 39, 1–68.

Rini, R. (2021). *The Ethics of Microaggression*. London: Routledge.

Ronson, J. (2015). *So You've Been Publicly Shamed*. London: Picador.

Roth, M. P. (2014). *An Eye for an Eye: A Global History of Crime and Punishment*. London: Reaktion.

Rousseau, J.-J. (1984 [1755]). *A Discourse on Equality*, tr. M. Cranston. London: Penguin.

Sahlins, M. (2017). *Stone Age Economics*. London: Routledge.

Sandel, M. J. (2020). *The Tyranny of Merit: What's Become of the Common Good?* London: Allen Lane.

Sauer, H. (2015). Can't we all disagree more constructively? Moral foundations, moral reasoning, and political disagreement. *Neuroethics*, 8(2), 153–69.

Sauer, H. (2019). The argument from agreement: How universal values undermine moral realism. *Ratio*, 32(4), 339–52.

Scheidel, W. (2017). *The Great Leveler: Violence and the History of Inequality from the Stone Age to the Twenty-First Century*. Princeton, NJ: Princeton University Press.

Scheler, M. (2009 [1928]). *The Human Place in the Cosmos*, tr. M. S. Frings. Evanston, IL: Northwestern University Press.

Schelling, T. (1980 [1960]). *The Strategy of Conflict*. Cambridge, MA: Harvard University Press.

Schmitt, C. (1996 [1932]). *The Concept of the Political*, tr. George Schwab. Chicago: University of Chicago Press.

Schneewind, J. B. (1998). *The Invention of Autonomy: A History of Modern Moral Philosophy*. Cambridge: Cambridge University Press.

Schofield, D. P., McGrew, W. C., Takahashi, A. et al. (2018), Cumulative culture in nonhumans: Overlooked findings from Japanese monkeys? *Primates*, 59, 113–22.

Schopenhauer, A. (1974 [1859]). *The World as Will and Representation* (Vol. 2), tr. E. F. J. Payne. New York: Dover.

Schopenhauer A. (1988 [1851]). *Parerga and Paralipomena* (Vol. 2), tr. E. F. J. Payne. Oxford: Clarendon Press.

Schröder, M. (2018). *Warum es uns noch nie so gut ging und wir trotzdem ständig von Krisen reden*. Salzburg: Benevento.

Schumpeter, J. (2008 [1942]). *Capitalism, Social and Democracy*. New York: Harper Perennial.

Schwartz, S. H., Cieciuch, J., Vecchione, M., Davidov, E., Fischer, R., Beierlein, C. . . . & Konty, M. (2012). Refining the theory of basic individual values. *Journal of Personality and Social Psychology*, 103(4), 663.

Scott, J. C. (2017). *Against the Grain: A Deep History of the Earliest States*. New Haven, CT: Yale University Press.

Shariff, A. F. & Norenzayan, A. (2007). God is watching you: Priming God concepts increases prosocial behavior in an anonymous economic game. *Psychological Science*, 18(9), 803–9.

Shellenberger, M. (2020). *Apocalypse Never: Why Environmental Alarmism Hurts Us All*. New York: HarperCollins.

Simler, K. & Hanson, R. (2018). *The Elephant in the Brain: Hidden Motives in Everyday Life*. New York: Oxford University Press.

Simpson, R. M. & Srinivasan, A. (2018). No platforming. In: *Academic Freedom*, ed. J. Lackey, 186–209. Oxford: Oxford University Press.

Singal, J. (2021). *The Quick Fix: Why Fad Psychology Can't Cure Our Social Ills*. New York: Farrar, Straus & Giroux.

Singer, P. (1972). Famine, affluence, and morality. *Philosophy and Public Affairs*, 1(3), 229–43.

Singer, P. (1995 [1975]). *Animal Liberation*. London: Pimlico.

Singer, P. (2011). *The Expanding Circle: Ethics, Evolution, and Moral Progress*. Princeton, NJ: Princeton University Press.

Singh, M. & Glowacki, L. (2022). Human social organization during the

Bibliography

Late Pleistocene: Beyond the nomadic-egalitarian model. *Evolution and Human Behavior*, 7(22).

Sinnott-Armstrong, W. (2006). *Moral Skepticisms*. Oxford: Oxford University Press.

Smith, A. (1976 [1776]). *An Inquiry into the Nature and Causes of the Wealth of Nations*. Oxford: Oxford University Press.

Smith, J. (1964). Group selection and kin selection. *Nature*, 201(4924), 1145–7.

Sober, E. & Wilson, D. (1998). *Unto Others: The Evolution and Psychology of Unselfish Behavior*. Cambridge, MA: Harvard University Press.

Solnit, R. (2014). *Men Explain Things to Me*. Chicago: Haymarket Books.

Sperber, D. (1996). *Explaining Culture: A Naturalistic Approach*. Oxford: Blackwell.

Spoto, D. (1988). *The Dark Side of Genius: The Life of Alfred Hitchcock*. London: Muller.

Stanley, J. (2020). *How Fascism Works: The Politics of Us and Them*. New York: Random House.

Stanovich, K. (2004). *The Robot's Rebellion: Finding Meaning in the Age of Darwin*. Chicago: Chicago University Press.

Starmans, C., Sheskin, M. & Bloom, P. (2017). Why people prefer unequal societies. *Nature Human Behaviour*, 1(4), 1–7.

Sterelny, K. (2007a). Social intelligence, human intelligence and niche construction. *Philosophical Transactions of the Royal Society B: Biological Sciences*, 362(1480), 719–30.

Sterelny, K. (2007b). Snafus: An evolutionary perspective. *Biological Theory*, 2(3), 317–28.

Sterelny, K. (2010). Minds: Extended or scaffolded? *Phenomenology and the Cognitive Sciences*, 9(4), 465–81.

Sterelny, K. (2012). *The Evolved Apprentice*. Cambridge, MA: MIT Press.

Sterelny, K. (2017). Cultural evolution in California and Paris. *Studies in History and Philosophy of Science Part C: Studies in History and Philosophy of Biological and Biomedical Sciences*, 62, 42–50.

Sterelny, K. (2021). *The Pleistocene Social Contract: Culture and Cooperation in Human Evolution*. Oxford: Oxford University Press.

Stevenson, B. & Wolfers, J. (2008). Economic growth and subjective well-being: Reassessing the Easterlin paradox. National Bureau of Economic Research.

Stillman, Richard P. (2021). Slurs as ballistic speech. *Synthese*, 199 (3–4), 6827–43.

Strandberg, T., Olson, J. A., Hall, L., Woods, A. & Johansson, P. (2020).

Depolarizing American voters: Democrats and Republicans are equally susceptible to false attitude feedback. *PLoS One*, 15(2), e0226799.

Surprenant, C. & Brennan, J. (2020). *Injustice for All: How Financial Incentives Corrupted and Can Fix the US Criminal Justice System*. New York: Routledge.

Suzman, J. (2021). *Work: A Deep History, from the Stone Age to the Age of Robots*. New York: Penguin Press.

Sykes, R. (2020). *Kindred: Neanderthal Life, Love, Death, and Art*. London: Bloomsbury Sigma.

Tainter, J. A. (1988). *The Collapse of Complex Societies*. Cambridge: Cambridge University Press.

Táíwò, O. O. (2022). *Elite Capture: How the Powerful Took Over Identity Politics (and Everything Else)*. Chicago: Haymarket Books.

Tolstoy, L. (2016 [1878]). *Anna Karenina*, tr. R. Bartlett. Oxford: Oxford University Press.

Tomasello, M. (2016). *A Natural History of Human Morality*. Cambridge, MA: Harvard University Press.

Tönnies, F. (2001 [1887]). *Community and Civil Society*, tr. J. Harris & M. Hollis. Cambridge: Cambridge University Press.

Toole, B. (2021). Recent work in standpoint epistemology. *Analysis*, 81(2), 338–50.

Tosi, J. & Warmke, B. (2016). Moral grandstanding. *Philosophy & Public Affairs*, 44(3), 197–217.

Trivers, R. L. (1971). The evolution of reciprocal altruism. *Quarterly Review of Biology*, 46(1), 35–57.

Tucholsky, K. (2017 [1928]). *The Creed of the Bourgeoisie*, tr. H. Zohn. In: *Germany? Germany! Satirical Writings: The Kurt Tucholsky Reader*, ed. Eva C. Schweizer. New York: Berlinica.

Turchin, P. (2013). Modeling social pressures toward political instability. *Cliodynamics*, 4: 241–280.

Turchin, P. (2016). *Ultrasociety: How 10,000 Years of War Made Humans the Greatest Cooperators on Earth*. Chaplin, CT: Beresta.

Veblen, T. (2007 [1899]). *The Theory of the Leisure Class*. New York: Oxford University Press.

Wallace-Wells, D. (2019). *The Uninhabitable World: Life after Warming*. New York: Tim Duggan.

Walter, A. S. & Redlawsk, D. P. (2019). Voters' partisan responses to politicians' immoral behavior. *Political Psychology*, 40(5), 1075–97.

Waytz, A., Iyer, R., Young, L., Haidt, J. & Graham, J. (2019). Ideological differences in the expanse of the moral circle. *Nature Communications*, 10(1), 1–12.

Weber, M. (2014 [1919]). *Science as a Vocation*, ed. P. Lassman, I. Velody & H. Martins. London: Routledge.

Welzel, C. (2013). *Freedom Rising: Human Empowerment and the Quest for Emancipation*. Cambridge: Cambridge University Press.

Wengrow, D. (2010). *What Makes Civilization?* Oxford: Oxford University Press.

Whitehouse, H., Francois, P., Savage, P. E., Currie, T. E., Feeney, K. C., Cioni, E. . . . & Turchin, P. (2019). Complex societies precede moralizing gods throughout world history. *Nature*, 568(7751), 226–9.

Widerquist, K. & McCall, G. (2015). Myths about the state of nature and the reality of stateless societies. *Analyse & Kritik*, 37(1–2), 233–58.

Wild, M. (2008). *Die anthropologische Differenz: Der Geist der Tiere in der frühen Neuzeit bei Montaigne, Descartes und Hume*. Berlin: de Gruyter.

Wilkins, A. S., Wrangham, R. W. & Fitch, W. T. (2014). The 'domestication syndrome' in mammals: A unified explanation based on neural crest cell behavior and genetics. *Genetics*, 197(3), 795–808.

Wilkinson, R. & Pickett, K. (2010). *The Spirit Level: Why Equality Is Better for Everyone*. London: Penguin.

Wilson, D. S. (1975). A theory of group selection. *Proceedings of the National Academy of Sciences*, 72(1), 143–6.

Wilson, R. A. & Keil, F. (1998). The shadows and shallows of explanation. *Minds and Machines*, 8(1), 137–59.

Wittgenstein, L. (1958). *Philosophical Investigations*, tr. G. E. M. Anscombe. New York: Macmillan.

Wittgenstein, L. (1972). *On Certainty*, tr. D. Paul and G. E. M. Anscombe. New York: Harper & Row.

Wood, B. (2019). *Human Evolution: A Very Short Introduction*. Oxford: Oxford University Press.

Wrangham, R. (2009). *Catching Fire: How Cooking Made Us Human*. New York: Basic Books.

Wrangham, R. (2019). *The Goodness Paradox: How Evolution Made Us Both More and Less Violent*. London: Profile.

Zahavi, A. (1975). Mate selection: A selection for a handicap. *Journal of Theoretical Biology*, 53(1), 205–14.

Zweig, S. (2009 [1942]). *The World of Yesterday*, tr. A. Bell. London: Pushkin Press.

Acknowledgements

I have received a lot of support while writing this book. I am very grateful for that.

Special thanks go to Izzy Everington, my editor at Profile, for her trust and judgement; Jo Heinrich, for her thoughtful translation; Tom Etherington and Steve Coventry-Panton, Robert Davies and Sarah Jane Forder, Georgina Difford, Sarah Kennedy and Ali Nadal, Audrey Kerr, Valentina Zanca and Alison Alexanian and the whole Profile team.

I am grateful to everyone at Piper, my German publisher, especially Felicitas Lovenberg, Anne Stadler, and Anja Melzig; my German editors Charlyne Bieniek, Martin Janik and Steffen Geier for their encouraging and insightful feedback; Michael Gaeb, Andrea Vogel, Eva Semitzidou, Elisabeth Botros and Bettina Wissmann from my agency; Philipp Hübl for crucial impulses; my students and colleagues at Utrecht University; the members of my research project Charlie Blunden, Cecilie Eriksen, Karolina Kudlek and Paul Rehren, for talking things through with me; Volker and Kerstin Flemming who made me do it; my family. And Romina, Clara and Julia for being (in) my life.

I dedicate this book to everyone I learned anything from.

Index

Index

Index

Index

inequality and 141, 155, 158–9,
    160, 165
moral absolutism and 321
moral progress and 224
punishment and 85, 93, 155
soul and 155
testimonial injustices 297–8
utopian society and 130
wokeness and 265, 266, 267,
    269, 270, 271, 272, 275, 276,
    285, 288, 289, 291, 293, 297,
    321, 340

K
Kafka trap 289
Kalani'ōpu'u 152
Kaluli 338
Kant, Immanuel 21, 80, 85–6, 128,
    199, 228
    animal rationabile definition 101
    categorical imperative 3, 205
    'Kingdom of Ends' 221
    Perpetual Peace 239
Kaufman, Jeff and Julia 320
Kellogg-Briand Pact/Pact of Paris
    (1928) 238
Kellogg, Frank 238
Kennedy, John F. 251, 309
King Jr, Martin Luther 246
King William Island 109
kin selection 41–2, 48, 51
kinship ties 4, 84, 130, 147, 188,
    189, 190–99, 211, 218, 249, 250,
    251, 290, 325
Kleefeld, Kurt von 166
Kleine Feldhofer Grotte cave,
    Germany 96
Kowalczewski, Bruno 97
Krug, Jessica 279
!Kung San 66–7, 145–6

Kuznets, Simon 164

L
lactose tolerance 105, 113–14, 195
Laetoli footprints 13
Lagos, Portugal 340–41
Lamarck, Jean-Baptiste de 22
language
    artificially esoteric 48
    cumulative culture and 105
    evolution of 15, 79–80, 98–9,
        101, 105, 144
    'use' and 'mention' 282
    wokeness and 267, 269–86,
        294–300, 312, 313
learning
    capacity 111, 115
    cultural 111–12
    high-fidelity 99–100
    individual 119–20
    social 99, 103, 104, 119–21, 306
Lecky, William: *History of
    European Morals* 249, 253
Lee, Richard Borshay 67
legal documents, key twentieth-
    century 249
Leiden University 179
Lennon, John: 'Imagine' 221
Leopold II of Belgium, King 213
lex talionis (law of retribution) 82
'lies that bind' 331–2
ling chi (Creeping Death) 92–3
Lisbon earthquake (1755) 202–3
Locke, John 155, 199
'Long Peace' 239
long-termism 321
looking-time studies 34
Lorenz, Konrad 77
Luhmann, Niklas 33
Lukeino Formation 10

Index